Colour, Class and Community –
The Natal Indian Congress,
1971–1994

Colour, Class and Community – The Natal Indian Congress, 1971–1994

Ashwin Desai and Goolam Vahed

WITS UNIVERSITY PRESS

Published in South Africa by:
Wits University Press
1 Jan Smuts Avenue
Johannesburg 2001

www.witspress.co.za

First published 2021

http://dx.doi.org.10.18772/12021117151

978-1-77614-715-1 (Paperback)
978-1-77614-716-8 (Hardback)
978-1-77614-717-5 (Web PDF)
978-1-77614-718-2 (EPUB)

Project manager: Elaine Williams
Copyeditor: Lisa Compton
Proofreader: Tessa Botha
Indexer: Margaret Ramsay
Cover design: Hybrid Creative
Typeset in 11.5 point Crimson

Contents

List of Illustrations

Acknowledgements

The impetus for this study was enhanced by conversations with Yunus Carrim and his willingness to share information with us. We would like to say a special thank you to those NIC members who so readily shared their experiences with us in person, via email or telephonically. It is unfortunate that others who could have provided insights have either passed on, were ill or were unavailable to contribute to this study. The names of those whom we interviewed are listed in the Bibliography.

We wish to acknowledge the work of Iain Edwards, whose studies of Natoo Babenia and Mewa Ramgobin are invaluable. Shireen Hassim has likewise made a valuable contribution in compiling Fatima Meer's key writings. Interviews with Congress activists conducted over the years by Julie Frederikse, Gail Gerhart, Jeremy Seekings and Padraig O'Malley are another important historical source that we draw upon.

We would also like to thank staff at the Killie Campbell Library, the Alan Paton Archives at the University of KwaZulu-Natal, the South African History Archives, the William Cullen Library at the University of Witwatersrand, and the Gandhi-Luthuli Documentation Centre at the University of KwaZulu-Natal who provided transcripts of various interviews held in their collections. Thanks also to the many individuals and organisations who supplied photographs. They are acknowledged in the text.

We are grateful for the valuable feedback provided by the anonymous peer reviewers. We would also like to thank Roshan Cader and the team at Wits University Press for their support and professionalism in seeing this study to completion.

Acronyms and Abbreviations

ANC	African National Congress
AWB	Afrikaner Weerstandsbeweging
AZAPO	Azanian People's Organisation
BC	Black Consciousness
BCM	Black Consciousness Movement
BPC	Black People's Convention
CBD	central business district
CHAC	Chatsworth Housing Action Committee
CODESA	Convention for a Democratic South Africa
COSAS	Congress of South African Students
COSATU	Congress of South African Trade Unions
CRC	Coloured Representative Council
DHAC	Durban Housing Action Committee
EFF	Economic Freedom Fighters
HOD	House of Delegates
IFP	Inkatha Freedom Party
LAC	local affairs committee
MDM	Mass Democratic Movement
MF	Minority Front
MK	Umkhonto we Sizwe
MP	member of Parliament
NEC	National Executive Committee
NEUM	Non-European Unity Movement
NGO	non-governmental organisation

NIC	Natal Indian Congress
NIS	National Intelligence Service
NP	National Party
NUSAS	National Union of South African Students
PAC	Pan Africanist Congress
PWC	Phoenix Working Committee
RC	Revolutionary Council
RDP	Reconstruction and Development Programme
REC	Regional Executive Committee
RMC	Release Mandela Committee
SACP	South African Communist Party
SADF	South African Defence Force
SAIC	South African Indian Council
SARS	South African Revenue Service
SASO	South African Students Organisation
SRC	Student Representative Council
TIC	Transvaal Indian Congress
TRC	Truth and Reconciliation Commission
UDF	United Democratic Front
UDW	University of Durban-Westville
UN	United Nations
US	United States

Introduction

The pre-eminent political organisation among Indians in South Africa through the first half of the 20th century was the Natal Indian Congress (NIC), founded by Mohandas K. Gandhi in 1894. In the 1940s a battle for the soul of the NIC was fought between groups dubbed 'moderates' and 'radicals'. The latter group, under the leadership of Dr Monty Naicker, emerged victorious, with Dr Kesaveloo Goonam, a fellow student of Naicker's at Edinburgh University in the 1930s, becoming vice-president of the NIC, the first woman to hold this position. The NIC entered into an alliance with the African National Congress (ANC) in the 1950s. It was a dramatic move for the NIC, which, for the first half of the twentieth century, had shied away from alliances with Africans. In a series of momentous pioneering moves, the NIC joined with the ANC in the 1952 Defiance Campaign, and rallied behind the Freedom Charter adopted in 1955 at the Congress of the People in Kliptown. Through these actions, NIC leaders were pronouncing that the freedom of Indians was inextricably tied to the liberation of the African majority.

From 1960 the state went on the offensive, banning the ANC and the Pan Africanist Congress (PAC). Although the NIC had not been declared illegal in this period, it had through the weight of 'bannings, detentions and imprisonment ... virtually folded up', according to one of its executive members, Thumba Pillay.[1]

Dr Goonam related an incident that vividly illustrates the weakness of the NIC at the time. Emerging from the home of a patient, she encountered a man sitting under a tree:

> He called me and asked: 'You coming from Congress Ma?' I said: 'Yes.' Then he fiddled with the turban he was wearing and took out a note from his pocket. It stated: 'You Venkatsamy, are notified by the City Council to leave your plot number so and so ...' When I finished reading, he said, 'Ma, I've been living in this place for the last fifty years. Where do I go now? I got a smallholding here where I grow ... household vegetables ... Can't Congress do something?' I said I would speak to Congress but I knew nothing could be done.[2]

Venkatsamy was a victim of the 1950 Group Areas Act, which legally sanctioned the drive to divide South African cities into racially delimited zones. Through the 1960s, Durban's City Hall became one of the most zealous implementers of the Act. Legal writs, guns and bulldozers put thousands of Indians on the move away from areas close to the Durban city centre. From places with a vibrant community life, such as Clairwood in the south and Riverside straddling the Umgeni River in the north, Indians were forcibly evicted. Most were summarily and arbitrarily dumped into Chatsworth in the south and, later, Phoenix in the north. Extended families and neighbours of long standing were often forced to go their separate ways. There would be legal battles, protests and individual heroics, but, in Dr Goonam's words, 'nothing could be done' collectively by the NIC to stop the juggernaut of forced relocation.

There were murmurings of the revival of the NIC from the late 1960s. The city of Durban, in which these discussions were taking place, was the site of emergent anti-apartheid organising and debate. Steve Biko and a coterie of university students were propagating the philosophy of Black Consciousness (BC). Biko's movement preached unity of the oppressed and disenfranchised, and sought to galvanise Africans, coloureds and Indians into a single organisation.[3] Workers were also on the march, pounding the streets of Durban in the 1973 strikes and signalling the possibility of collective organisation.[4] Emergent subjectivities reached back into old organisations; others willed new ones into existence. These stirrings, taking place after a period of relative quietism, have come to be seen as the 'Durban Moment'.[5]

The NIC was officially revived in 1971 in an environment of renewed anti-apartheid politics, combined with dislocation and uncertainty as new residents of the bare townships on the city's edge began to rebuild their cultural and sporting organisations. Those who had escaped the eviction dragnet faced the constant spectre of a piece of paper commanding them to leave their home.

But just as the state sought to hem Indians into tight racial corners, so new opportunities were opening. As the 1970s unfolded, the state's 'own (racial) affairs' policy kicked in and the apartheid civil service offered long-term job security. For the first time, Indians were graduating in substantial numbers with professional qualifications from the newly constructed University of Durban-Westville (UDW). Many, taking advantage of relaxed interprovincial movement, found well-paying jobs in the country's economic epicentre on the Highveld. Thousands of teachers, degrees in hand, were able to imagine a stable middle-class life as the schooling system expanded and opportunities for promotion increased.

Moreover, as much as the headlines were grabbed by the debates over the 'I' in the NIC, the newly revived organisation was also propelled by movements on the ground as people in the new 'Group Areas' began to organise and confront the authorities on issues that affected their everyday lives. One of the first examples was the government's banning in 1973 of Indian-owned buses in Chatsworth to force commuters onto trains. This act spurred commuters and bus owners into massive protests. The newly minted NIC leadership responded with solidarity work, giving it an early taste of mass organisation after nearly a decade on the sidelines. The flooding of Tin Town on the Springfield Flats in 1976 brought the NIC to the fore once more. This form of community support gave impetus to the formation of the Phoenix Working Committee (PWC) and the Chatsworth Housing Action Committee (CHAC). These experiments in community organising eventually led to the establishment of the Durban Housing Action Committee (DHAC).

For activists, the challenge was to find ways of organising that both acknowledged and contested existing racial categories imposed by the apartheid state, while prefiguring the non-racialism and progressive eroding of poverty and inequality that was envisaged in the society to come. In the chapters ahead we detail these developments.

The NIC also had to contend with the often hostile and deeply divisive debates that emerged between the adherents of the Black Consciousness Movement (BCM), who argued for a People's Congress, and those who wanted to retain the 'I' in the NIC. While Steve Biko was rebuffed by the NIC, he ironically faced a *black*lash for what some of his comrades saw as too close a relationship with Indians.[6]

NIC activists were far from wilting flowers in defending themselves against those they saw as challenging their dominance of the progressive voice of the Indian community. The problem with the BCM, according to senior NIC figure Paul David, was that it was

> an idea mainly in the head ... The leading lights in the BCM were all students. You compare that to the way the Congress movement grew among students. We were not just students. We were involved every-where at a practical level. And so the idea that this was just a notion was not our weakness. But it was certainly a problem with the BCM. It was debate, debate, debate.[7]

The leftist Non-European Unity Movement (NEUM) was formed in the Cape in 1943 with a membership comprised mainly of intellectuals. This organisation was written off as a talking shop whose members 'would come to meetings and put up this rhetoric', according to NIC executive member Thumba Pillay, who noted 'that is where action ended'.[8] Or, as NIC executive member Jerry Coovadia put it,

> the Unity Movement guys were full of reams of criticism, but it's easy to be like them. They can give you a dissertation on everything, but they will not do a damn thing to make anything happen. They were great theoreticians. They knew everything about say, Lenin. Lenin's second wife was this and [his] third wife was this, but they couldn't translate history into anything meaningful.[9]

In this study, we situate discussion about the 'I' in the NIC in the broader context of the liberation movement and the orientation of the ANC.

Despite the narrative of the 'unbreakable thread of non-racialism',[10] the issue of membership of non-Africans dogged the ANC. The approach from the inauguration of the alliance between the Indian Congresses and the ANC, which envisioned 'equality under African leadership',[11] lent itself to a fog about what non-racialism meant in practice. Activists imprisoned on Robben Island were not immune from the debate. In a purported ANC leadership struggle on the island between Nelson Mandela and Govan Mbeki – a split along so-called nationalist and communist lines – the right of non-Africans to vote in the leadership contest was questioned. Ahmed Kathrada, who was imprisoned on Robben Island at the time, recalled:

> As the debate rose to a crescendo, everything pointed towards an election. The 'communist bloc' realised that in order to have a fight-ing chance, they needed to reduce the number of potential Mandela supporters ... They argued that because the ANC constitution limited membership to Africans, Indian and Coloured comrades would not be allowed to vote.[12]

The ANC opened its membership to non-Africans at the Morogoro Conference of 1969, but they were excluded from standing for elec-tion to the National Executive Committee (NEC). They could, how-ever, be members of the newly created Revolutionary Council (RC): Yusuf Dadoo, an Indian, was its vice-chairman, alongside Reginald (Reg) September, a 'coloured', and the white communist Joe Slovo.[13] But the ANC 'had to tread carefully, always wary of the ideological force of hard-core Africanists among its members (and political rivals)'. It was only at the Kabwe Conference in 1985 that the NEC was thrown open to non-Africans.[14]

This storyline, related to ways of organising, conflicts over African leadership and non-racialism sparked by the NIC's revival, and the challenge of the BCM, runs through this book. Stated baldly, the NIC was an ethnic/racial organisation committed to building a non-racial South Africa. As such it was always haunted by a Janus-faced gaze: it sought to reach out and develop links with Africans while defending the need to orga-nise Indians separately. There were many nuances to this position, compli-cated by the seeming paradox of an ANC which espoused non-racialism while emphasising African leadership. This conundrum was a persistent complexity which the NIC had to negotiate throughout this period.[15]

The NIC's Janus-faced gaze fed into allegations of an Indian 'cabal', accusations which surfaced in the 1980s and continue to live in the present. Some in the NIC leadership came to play roles that straddled the boundaries of the legal and 'illegal', of public and clandestine activity. This is epitomised by the story of Pravin Gordhan, a leading member of the NIC:

> In 1974, a young man who had recently completed a pharmacy degree at Salisbury College, which became the University of Durban-Westville, joined the executive of the NIC as a representative of the youth ... Those who met him at the time were in awe of his intelligence ... Certainly he was a strategist, a thinker and a doer ... Gordhan had a 'triple identity': a place in the ANC underground (and later Communist Party), one in the overtly political but legal NIC, and the third in local community organisation ... Gordhan was later to become a key operative in one of the ANC's most critical operations, Operation Vula, which was set up to re-establish the ANC as the central resistance organisation in the country.[16]

Gordhan's many-sided roles were applauded as much as they fed suspicion, then and now. While we were writing this book, Gordhan, who holds the vital portfolio of minister of public enterprises in President Cyril Ramaphosa's cabinet, was coming under attack from Julius Malema's Economic Freedom Fighters (EFF) party, which alleged that Gordhan was part of a faction (insinuating 'cabal') responsible for the economic exclusion of the EFF's supposed constituency. The EFF has made aspersions that Gordhan, as a member of an Indian 'cabal', isolated and marginalised radical voices in the United Democratic Front (UDF) in the 1980s. Witness Malema in 2018: 'During the UDF times, [Pravin] isolated those he didn't agree with. When the ANC didn't recognise him for the negotiations, he came through an Indian cabal.'[17]

In this book we interrogate how the allegations of 'cabals' emerged and were maintained in various discursive forms. There were several sightings of the cabal in different locations: in the NIC, in which a small leadership group supposedly made key decisions; in the UDF; and in the ANC under-ground, which seeped above ground post-1990. We pursue the different threads of these assertions, which refuse to leave the stage despite the demise of the NIC.

In addition to examining the often acrimonious debate between those committed to the NIC and BCM members, this study explores the peren-nial debate within the NIC of whether or not to participate in organisa-tions created by the government in the 1960s and 1970s. These included the South African Indian Council (SAIC) and the local affairs committees (LACs), which were seen to be making headway among Indians. This debate threatened to tear the NIC apart, but each time splits were averted and the boycott position prevailed. Confronting what has been an under-researched subject, we track the work of the SAIC. We pick through the minutes of its meetings to understand the issues that animated the organisation, and to determine whether and how successful it was in convincing the regime to mitigate the apartheid machine's debilitating effects on Indians.

Our focus is the history of the NIC from its revival in 1971 until 1994, when it effectively ceased functioning. We explore the internal divisions in the NIC, and the organisation's role in the struggle to defeat apartheid through a (cross-)examination of media reports, official documents, min-utes of meetings, explosive and revealing communications between antag-onists, as well as extensive oral interviews. Our aim is to interrogate the debates, divisions and ways of organising that came to characterise the organisation.

In doing so we build on research that we have done over several years on aspects of the history of the NIC published as a series of co- or single-authored journal articles,[18] or as part of monographs and political biographies of Indian activists that we have written.[19] Others too have cov-ered aspects of this history. Surendra Bhana's *Gandhi's Legacy* (1997) and Bhana and Bridglal Pachai's *Documentary History of Indian South Africans* (1984) may be viewed as early precursors to this study. Bhana, however, devotes just one chapter of his slim volume to the period 1971–1994, and in any event his focus is largely on the structures and workings of the NIC.

Arguably the most comprehensive effort to document the history of the post-1960 liberation movement is the project by the South African Democracy Education Trust (SADET), *The Road to Democracy in South*

Africa, which was initiated in 2004 under the presidency of Thabo Mbeki. SADET has thus far published six volumes on the period from 1960 to 1996, with a single chapter on the NIC.[20]

Colour, Class and Community: The Natal Indian Congress, 1971–1994 is the first in-depth study of the revived NIC. This study is able to break new ground through its use of a wide range of oral history sources and other documents.[21] We have drawn on extensive interviews with activists undertaken over a period of several decades, starting from the late 1970s. The strength of these interviews is that they were conducted, sometimes with the same activists, after a time lapse of many years. Julie Frederikse conducted her interviews in the period 1979–1990; Padraig O'Malley's interviews covered the period 1985–2005. The Gandhi-Luthuli Documentation Centre at the University of KwaZulu-Natal's Westville campus initiated a 'Voices of Resistance' project, which resulted in some 50 interviews being conducted during 2002 and 2003. In addition, we ourselves have interviewed many NIC activists over the past 15 years.

These oral history collections were fundamental in contesting and deepening our understanding of key events. Although they provide first-hand perspectives on the strategy and tactics of the NIC, we have used them with what E.P. Thompson called 'attentive disbelief'.[22] That is, we have kept in mind issues of contemporary politics, subjectivity, selective remembering and forgetting, and traumatic experiences that may have impacted on testimony. The oral sources were incredibly insightful, but we also came to them with an awareness that

> memory is not a passive depository of facts, but an active process of creation of meanings. Thus, the specific utility of oral sources for the historian lies, not so much in their ability to preserve the past, as in the very changes wrought by memory. These changes reveal the narrators' effort to make sense of the past and to give a form to their lives and set the interview and the narrative in their historical context. Changes which may have subsequently taken place in the narrators' personal subjective consciousness or in their socio-economic standing, may affect, if not the actual recounting of prior events, at least the valuation and the 'colouring' of the story ... The most precious

information may lie in what the informants *hide*, and in the fact that they do *hide* it, rather than in what they *tell*.[23]

Given the important role played by the NIC in the last decade of the anti-apartheid struggle, and the continuing resonance of the issues it grappled with – especially that lingering chestnut, race – this is an important story to which greater critical attention is long overdue.

As we were writing this book, we often accused each other of being short-sighted or looking too far into the distance. We encouraged ourselves by looking at the ground beneath our feet, and asking hard questions of our own particular historical location in which race was a persistent shadow that threatened to engulf our lives. In post-apartheid South Africa, the shadow of race disappears behind a corner only to reappear with a vengeance. This is not a time to ignore the continuing resonance of race thinking, as much as we are motivated by the quest to subvert it.

In the pages ahead, we interrogate many of the issues that animated the liberation movement, including Black Consciousness and the revival of the NIC in the 1970s; the strategic thinking and energy behind the civic movement that organised around local issues in the townships and identity politics; the (racial) contradictions between African leadership and non-racialism; the different class interests within the Indian community; tensions between internal activists and those in exile; debates about armed struggle and non-violence; arguments over strategic participation in and boycott of government institutions; the heady days of the unbanning of the ANC and the consequent debate about the future of the NIC and the UDF – all amid Shakespearean accusations of cabals and coups.

This is a compelling story of people pulling apart and pulling together, all the while committed to destroying apartheid and dreaming of a new society that would be built out of its ashes. It is apposite that our story begins at a place called Phoenix, where Gandhi established a settlement in 1904, a decade after he had established the NIC.

1 | Repression, Revelation and Resurrection: The Revival of the NIC

B y the early 1960s the NIC, battered by state repression, was no longer a significant force in the anti-apartheid struggle. Ela Gandhi,
great-granddaughter of the Mahatma and who became vice-president of
the revived NIC in 1971, recounted that within South Africa the 1960s were

> really dark years when we felt complete disillusionment ... The ban-
> nings took place in 1963, the arrests took place within three years, and
> there was a deep sort of gloom and unhappiness. There was a lot of
> fear in the community ... because there was this scare of communism
> orchestrated from the government ... fear as they could detain you
> without any reason, they could ban you without any reason. There
> was a lot of gloom until the student movement started.[1]

This 'gloom' came in the aftermath of the heady days of the 1950s. Yet
before this, there had been years of advance. Dr Monty Naicker's emergence as leader in the 1940s took the NIC in a more radical direction, and
in a parallel development in the Transvaal, Dr Yusuf Dadoo, Naicker's contemporary at Edinburgh University, became leader of the Transvaal Indian
Congress (TIC).

In the early 1950s the Indian Congresses began to stitch together a
working relationship with the ANC that saw them engaging jointly in a
series of anti-apartheid campaigns. This relationship was consolidated
with the adoption of the Freedom Charter in 1955. As Ela Gandhi pointed
out, this progress was blunted by the banning of the ANC and the PAC

following the Sharpeville massacre of March 1960. While the NIC was not proscribed, the imprisonment, banning and forced exile of key members resulted in its diminution in the public domain. Support work continued, and NIC founding father Gandhi and leaders of the 1940s, such as Monty Naicker and Kesaveloo Goonam, continued to evoke respect, but there was a lack of visible leadership among Indians. 'Own affairs' institutions set up by the apartheid government began to gain ground. It was only at the end of the decade that the NIC began to stir again, sparked partly by the celebrations in 1969 to mark the centenary of Gandhi's birth.

Congress Alliance of the 1950s

Through the first half of the 20th century, the NIC had taken up a series of issues on behalf of Indians as the noose of segregation tightened. In 1948, the National Party (NP), gung-ho after its unexpected election victory, and smarting from India's belligerent stance against segregation at the United Nations (UN), promised a battery of discriminatory legislation and even raised the spectre of repatriation for Indians.

Through the 1940s the concept of interracial cooperation had sparked discussions within the Indian Congresses. An important factor in this was the election of Walter Sisulu as general secretary of the ANC in December 1947. Elinor Sisulu, his daughter-in-law, recounted:

> Walter had become convinced of the need for Africans and Indians to work more closely together after the Durban riots of 1949 ... He and Ismail Meer toured the riot area in an open loudspeaker van to appeal for calm ... Walter had been horrified to see two oppressed peoples at each other's throats and was convinced that the only way to prevent future such occurrences was through joint action ... through a policy of principled nonracialism.[2]

The form and content of this non-racialism was not spelt out, but there was a sense that it had to be forged in joint struggle. The path which Sisulu set out was not easy to travel, not least because of suspicions from the ANC leadership. Nelson Mandela, who came to epitomise the non-racialism of the ANC, remembered that when Sisulu mooted the idea of a national disobedience campaign in 1951,

> [I] differed from Walter on the question of who should take part ...
> I urged that the campaign should be exclusively African. While I had
> made progress in terms of my opposition to communism, I still feared
> the influence of Indians. In addition, many of our grassroots African
> supporters saw Indians as exploiters of black labour in their role as
> shopkeepers and merchants. Walter vehemently disagreed, suggest-
> ing that Indians, Coloureds and Africans were inextricably bound up
> together.[3]

Voted down at a national conference in December 1951, Mandela 'fully accepted the agreed-upon decision' of cooperating with the Indian Congresses.[4]

The 1952 Defiance Campaign was a non-violent anti-apartheid resistance mobilisation involving organisations representing all racial groups:
the ANC, the South African Indian Congress, the Coloured People's
Congress and the (white) Congress of Democrats. This civil disobedience
campaign was a springboard for deepening working relationships and
non-racial cooperation among movement leaders and volunteers, a grouping that came to be known as the Congress Alliance. Their work culminated in the adoption of the Freedom Charter in 1955, which proclaimed
that 'South Africa belongs to all who live in it'.

The fostering of this multiracial Congress Alliance led to a split and
the formation of the PAC under the leadership of Robert Sobukwe, partly
because of what the PAC saw as the growing influence of non-Africans and
communists in the ANC. One of the first PAC pronouncements on mass
action was a call for the burning of passes which Africans had to carry
in urban areas. There was a brutal response from police at Sharpeville
on 21 March 1960, resulting in 69 deaths.[5] The government used the
Sharpeville demonstration as a pretext to ban the ANC and PAC, and to
arrest over 2 000 activists, who were imprisoned without trial for up to
five months. An editorial in the *Natal Witness* linked government authoritarianism to the announcement by the ruling party in January 1960 that it

wanted to declare South Africa a republic. The greater the perceived internal and external threat, the editorial argued, the more likely it would be that whites would vote for a republic.[6] On 5 October 1960 white South Africans duly voted in favour of the formation of a republic.

Meanwhile, Pietermaritzburg hosted the All-In Africa Conference on 25–26 March 1961 as the Congress Alliance tried to regather momentum. As a prelude, the NIC held its annual conference in the town on 3–5 March. This meeting was opened by Professor Z.K. Matthews, luminary of Fort Hare, a Treason Trialist in 1956 and recently released from six months' imprisonment. His presence was a powerful signal that, despite repression, the NIC was determined to remain in the Congress fold. NIC president Monty Naicker stated in his presidential address: 'We are the smallest racial minority in this country but because we believe in the democratic ideal, the question of other racial groups swamping us never worries us when we discuss the question of the vote.'[7]

The conference was at once a powerful affirmation of the commitment of the NIC to a non-racial South Africa as well as a rejection of the government's attempts to consolidate its policy of separate development. In the future this rejection would sometimes prove hard to sustain. For example, in 1960 the state set up a college for Indians on Salisbury Island in Durban Bay, which was granted university status in 1971. In 1972 this institution was moved to a campus in Westville and named the University of Durban-Westville. The condemnation of a racially exclusive Indian university did not deter Indians, including those of working-class background, from aspiring to send their children to the institution, which, ironically, was to become a hotbed of radical thought and anti-apartheid organising.

Nelson Mandela delivered the keynote address at the All-In Africa Conference, his last public appearance before he went underground to organise mass protests against the declaration of a republic. Amidst a maelstrom of events, the Congress Alliance met in Stanger. After acrimonious debate, agreement was reached that Mandela would establish Umkhonto we Sizwe (MK), the armed wing of the ANC, as an independent organisation, while the ANC remained committed to non-violent resistance.[8] MK's independence allowed the ANC to maintain the moral high ground as a non-violent organisation. The distinction also allowed MK to be a non-racial organisation, as against the ANC's exclusive African membership.[9] Yet, as Sunny Singh, one of the early recruits to MK, pointed out, this did not mean that racial realities were ignored: 'In 1962 I joined an Indian structure of MK. You had to have an all-white unit or an all-Indian unit ... because Africans were not allowed to be in town at night.'[10] The first Indian members of MK came via the Communist Party and trade unions.[11]

The screws of repression continued to tighten as the Nationalist majority in Parliament increased after the whites-only general election of October 1961. The year ended with Albert Luthuli collecting the Nobel Peace Prize in Oslo, Norway, on 10 December, while MK made its presence known to the country by setting off bombs in Johannesburg, Port Elizabeth and Durban on 16 December 1961.

Billy Nair, Natoo Babenia, Ebrahim Ebrahim and Sunny Singh were among the first NIC members to be arrested in Durban and incarcerated on Robben Island. The Congress Alliance was dealt a heavy blow when Mandela was arrested on 5 August 1962.[12] On 11 July 1963 the police raided Liliesleaf Farm, a safe house for ANC activists, and arrested 19 MK members. In what came to be known as the Rivonia Trial, Mandela and Ahmed Kathrada were among those sentenced to life imprisonment on Robben Island.

The 1960s

The state used a combination of bannings, banishments, house arrests, imprisonment and torture to crush resistance. This rendered most of the NIC's leaders ineffective. Some who joined MK were imprisoned on Robben Island. M.P. Naicker, H.A. Naidoo and George Ponnen were part of the flow of working-class leaders and communist stalwarts who went into exile, while leaders such as Monty Naicker and Ismail (I.C.) Meer were removed from political life through banning orders. As Saul Dubow (2014: 131) points out, 'by 1965 the liberation movements in South Africa had been smashed and eviscerated'.[13] This did not mean that there was no political work being done, but it had to be carried out in much more careful and clandestine ways.

State repression was accompanied by an economic boom in South Africa that saw foreign investment double and white immigration increase. The crushing of black resistance generated confidence in South African capitalism and foreign investment flowed into the country. With black workers' wages maintained at a consistently low level, corporate profits rose well above the world average. Apartheid South Africa's gross domestic product jumped 9.3 per cent between 1963 and 1968.[14]

During the 1960s Afrikaner firms became integrated on favourable terms with monopoly capital. The Afrikaner petty bourgeoisie also benefited, from jobs in state departments and from the implementation of a comprehensive system of racial zoning with the objective of 'protecting' white business from Indian traders in particular.[15] As apartheid spread its bounty within the white community, the NP used the economic boom and the muting of anti-apartheid resistance to consolidate separate development. Racially segregated 'Group Areas' were created for Indians and coloureds, and homelands ('Bantustans') for Africans.[16]

In Durban the Group Areas Act started to bite deeply into the highly urbanised Indian community. Protests could not stymie the court summons and bulldozers, and thousands were forcibly removed from areas such as Clairwood, Cato Manor and Riverside. The evictions took place just as a pattern of urban life was consolidating after the slow drift of indentured workers from the plantations. Two huge dormitory townships, Chatsworth in the south in the 1960s and Phoenix in the north in the 1970s, began to take shape as people rebuilt their cultural, sporting and religious organisations. It would take more than a decade for civic and political structures to be re-established in the new segregated townships.[17]

The Group Areas Act limited where traders and professionals could open businesses and practices, and severely curtailed the employment of Indian graduates.[18] Indians managed to gain employment as semi-skilled operatives in the rapidly expanding clothing industry, which proved crucial as agriculture progressively diminished in importance as a source of work. While apartheid eroded some areas of economic life, others were opening up. One of the significant changes was the expansion of secondary education and an increase in degree options at the university.

The profile of Indians as a group changed rapidly in the 1960s in terms of their geographical spread as well as their levels of education and employment patterns. The NIC was revived in a context that differed from that of the 1940s, when the leadership, mainly from the merchant and professional classes, had spoken to a largely working-class audience.

There were important political changes as well. For more than a century since the arrival of the first Indians in Natal in 1860, the official policy of successive white minority regimes in Natal and in a unitary South Africa was to repatriate Indians. The threat of that perpetual sword of Damocles that hung over Indian South Africans began to diminish with Prime Minister H.F. Verwoerd's announcement on 7 December 1960 that his government was willing to consider allowing Indians to develop as South Africans within the apartheid system of separate development. This announcement was followed by the establishment of an Asiatic Affairs Division in February 1961 under minister of the interior Johannes de Klerk, who said that the division would 'serve as a channel through which the rightful needs of the Asiatic community can be brought to the attention of the Government'.[19]

With the Congress Alliance on the back foot, the NP felt confident, not only about recognising Indians as citizens, but also about its power to channel their demands through government institutions designed to deal exclusively with their 'own affairs'.[20] As the policy of separate development was becoming more clearly outlined with regard to Indians, South Africa became a republic on 31 May 1961.

On 2 August 1961, Prime Minister Verwoerd announced that a Department of Indian Affairs (DIA) would be established to oversee the economic and social development of Indians. NIC president Monty Naicker criticised the department as 'a logical development under Apartheid' and called for 'one department, non-racial in character, dealing with all internal problems and avoiding financial wastage'.[21] However, the Indian Congresses, struggling to survive in the tentacles of an increasingly repressive state, failed to mount serious opposition to these government initiatives. W.A. Maree, the first minister of Indian affairs, laid out the objectives of the Nationalists with regard to Indians: '... self-development socially, economically and politically in order that they may be enabled to accept, in conformity with separate development, a steadily increasing say in and eventually such measure of self-government in those matters peculiar to them'.[22]

As part of this effort, the government made plans to launch a National Indian Council consisting of 21 nominated members. It is likely that the name was chosen deliberately so as to share an acronym with the Natal Indian Congress. A meeting with around a hundred 'prominent' Indians was convened in the Indian township of Laudium near Pretoria in December 1963. It was clear that the state would brook no opposition. On the day before the conference, Security Branch officers confiscated pamphlets highlighting the plight of Indians in the Transvaal under the Group Areas Act, which were to have been distributed at the meeting.[23]

The Council came into being on 3 February 1964, and was renamed the South African Indian Council (SAIC) in 1965. Dr M.B. Naidoo, who was a member of the Council, noted that

> for the first time in the history of the Indian people a channel of communication was established. Previously, only with the approval of the Ministers were Indians permitted to interview them when a political crisis arose. They then went virtually hat in hand and suffered the humiliation of being tolerated.[24]

While Naidoo saw the SAIC as an advance, given the lack of any mechanism that had hitherto existed, members of the NIC and TIC feared that it would entrench racial division and push back the gains made through non-racial organising in the 1950s. The NIC's ability to confront the SAIC was severely curtailed by the banning of its leaders. Its impotence was cruelly highlighted by the fact that it could not mobilise in any significant way on behalf of the thousands forcibly relocated under the Group Areas Act. The DIA gradually assumed importance in the lives of Indians. For example, from 1 April 1966 Indian education in Natal fell under its jurisdiction.[25]

The minutes of meetings in the 1960s show that the SAIC took an interest in wide-ranging issues. These included the right of interprovincial movement, low compensation offered for affected properties under the Group Areas Act, improved rail facilities for Indians, and even getting the Indian university to introduce a degree in engineering from 1967.[26] These issues could not be scoffed at, as they spoke to some of the immediate concerns of Indians. Restrictions on interprovincial movement, for example, stymied the ability of Indians to move from Natal to other provinces in search of work, especially to the Transvaal, which was the heartbeat of the South African economy. The number of Indian civil servants began to increase, and they saw their jobs as giving them long-term security. Local affairs committees (LACs) were formed from 1966, and by the early 1970s there were Indian town boards at Verulam and Isipingo. The expansion of courses at the university offered new job prospects. When the Council met in October 1971, minister of Indian affairs F.W. Waring emphasised that the SAIC had to 'acknowledge the fact that the government has a policy of separate development' and be 'prepared to work within the broad frame-work of that policy for the welfare of its people'.[27]

As participation in government-created bodies deepened, plans were afoot to revive the NIC. The growing influence of the SAIC in the immediate, everyday lives of Indians, and how to relate to it, would be one of the key concerns of the NIC.

Centenary of Gandhi's birth

Mahatma Gandhi was a revered figure among Indian South Africans, given his seminal role in taking up the cudgels of resistance against anti-Indian legislation during his South African sojourn, while his subsequent role in India's liberation struggle had made him a global icon. Strong family links to Durban reinforced Gandhi's local resonance.

As the centenary of Gandhi's birth approached (2 October 1969), the contemporary lack of leadership among Indians in Natal was a point hammered home by *Leader* columnist Ranji Nowbath:

> There were leaders at one time but most of them have been cut off from leadership by being banned or otherwise proscribed. When ... Dr Monty Naicker or Dr Yusuf Dadoo or Messrs I.C. Meer or J.N. Singh ... or their organisations called a meeting, they could be assured of packed meetings ... These men did have followers. They were leaders. And then too men like A.M. Moolla and P.R. Pather had substantial followings from a different class of Indian [South Africans]. When they spoke, people listened. Mass meetings were not for them, but closely reasoned arguments put forward carefully and reasonably. They too were leaders. Now, however, the unfortunate fact is that there is no person in the community today who can honestly call himself leader of the Indian people.[28]

The call for reviving the NIC in the context of this leadership vacuum was made by Ela Gandhi and her husband, Mewa Ramgobin, from the historic

Phoenix Settlement, founded by the Mahatma in 1904. Ramgobin was a central figure in the revival of the NIC. His grandparents arrived in Natal among the more than 152 000 indentured workers imported to the colony between 1860 and 1911. His grandfather took up farming in Inanda after completing his indenture, and his father followed in his footsteps. Ramgobin was born in Inanda in 1932. He completed a BA degree at the University of Natal Non-European Section, married Ela Gandhi, a fellow student activist at Natal University, and was running the Mahatma Gandhi Clinic in Phoenix.

Ramgobin's activism led to his banning and house arrest for five years in 1965. He highlighted the centenary of Gandhi's birth as an important moment for him in contemplating the revival of the NIC. The Phoenix Settlement Trust convened a Mahatma Gandhi Centenary Committee under the chairmanship of novelist and former Liberal Party member Alan Paton, a long-time friend of Gandhi's son Manilal, who was a fellow member of the Liberal Party.

Ramgobin found that his base at the Phoenix Settlement made his banning order 'tolerable' because it allowed him to be the de facto organising secretary of the centenary celebrations and to engage with young activists 'who passed through Phoenix Settlement – people like Steve Biko, "Terror" Lekota, Pravin Gordhan, Saths Cooper, Ben Ngubane ... albeit that we belonged to different political schools of thought'.[29] One subsequent initiative arising out of these meetings was the Gandhi Work Camp programme, whose first camp was held in January 1971 at the Phoenix Settlement. The camp focused on practical work and educational programmes, as well as research into the needs of the surrounding community, and attracted many students and activists.[30]

Gandhi's birthday, 2 October 1969, was declared a holiday for Indian schoolchildren. On one level, this was a significant concession by the apartheid government. But coming in the aftermath of the crushing of resistance and given that the occasion fitted in with the idea of 'own affairs', one can see why a holiday was granted.

The day started with a function for children at the Curries Fountain Sports Stadium, which included a rendition of Gandhi's favourite hymns and a display by drum majorettes. Sushila Gandhi, wife of Gandhi's son Manilal, hoisted a white flag to symbolise 'truth and purity'. In the evening there was a meeting for adults, where the speakers included Paton, who was also chairman of the Phoenix Settlement Trust, and A.M. Moolla, a moderate politician and member of the Mahatma Gandhi Trust Board.[31] The invited speakers were an affirmation that Gandhi attracted people from across the political spectrum, but also an indication that the hard political lines that would be drawn in the 1970s were not yet clear-cut. In his speech Paton said that Gandhi

> would have nothing to do with the kind of dealing with evil by which people keep their mouths shut and their noses clean, keep out of politics, and keep politics out of religion by reciting the great religious principles in the temple, mosque, church and synagogue but leave them there when they leave such places, afraid to bring those principles into the streets where they might get dirty and soiled.[32]

Figure 1.1: Gandhi Centenary Commemoration: Mangosuthu Buthelezi (*left*), Sushila Gandhi and Alan Paton. (Courtesy of African News Agency)

In Pietermaritzburg, the Indian Centenary Celebrations Committee pro-duced an elaborate programme at the Lotus Hall that ran from 29 September to 2 October.[33] Well-known NIC leaders of the 1950s, such as Monty Naicker, Chota Motala, I.C. Meer and J.N. Singh, were absent from the celebrations, as they were banned from public gatherings. Despite this, the centenary created an opportunity for NIC stalwarts and new activists to come together for the first time in almost a decade.

Ramgobin's revelation

Mewa Ramgobin had 'tasted the capacity and the successes of mobi-lization' as organising secretary of the Mahatma Gandhi Centenary Celebrations. These lessons combined with a 'revelation' in January 1971, when, shortly after his banning order had expired, Ramgobin went to Cape Town on holiday. He was filming on Table Mountain with his movie camera, which, he recounted, kept 'zooming onto Robben Island'. He felt 'very uncomfortable taking this holiday', and his wife Ela and chil-dren agreed 'that we should go back home'. They returned to Phoenix, and Ramgobin 'called up a few friends and expressed to them the wish that we should now organise ourselves demanding the release of our leaders from Robben Island'. It was an opportune time, as the tenth anniversary of the Republic was approaching.[34]

Within a week, he had established a 'Committee of Clemency' that campaigned for the release of political prisoners, as well as clemency for those who were banned, under house arrest or in exile. Ramgobin was chairperson of the committee; deputy chairpersons included Alan Paton, Archbishop Denis Hurley and Alex Boraine, a clergyman who was pres-ident of the Methodist Church from 1970 to 1972, and would serve as deputy chairperson of the Truth and Reconciliation Commission (TRC) in post-apartheid South Africa. Other committee members included Advocate Louis Skweyiya, Sushila Gandhi, Dr R.S. Rustomjee, Steve Biko and Lawrence Schlemmer. The committee gathered signatures, published pamphlets and organised meetings. While the call for clem-ency fell on apartheid ears conditioned not to hear, the lesson Ramgobin took from the campaign was that 'we had the capacity regardless of the

Figure 1.2: *Left to right*: Mewa Ramgobin, Alan Paton, Norman Middleton (Labour Party leader), Paul Pretorius (Natal University SRC president) and Louis Skweyiya address a Committee of Clemency meeting. (Courtesy of Mewa Ramgobin and Iain Edwards)

depth of repression and the intensity of oppression, to relate to mass mobilization'.[35] His was a high-powered non-racial committee.

Rumours about the possible revival of the NIC drew immediate response. Pat Poovalingam, one-time member of the Liberal Party and a prolific columnist for the *Graphic* newspaper under the pen name Sadiq Allie, was quickly out of the blocks. In a March 1971 article, he agreed on the need 'for a political organisation' but took issue with the revivers' use of the name of the NIC. He accused NIC leaders of the 1950s of engaging 'in the deliberate exploitation of the name of Mahatma Gandhi purely for purpose of personal or political gain'. Excluding 'Honest Monty' from his criticism, he argued that a 'High Command' had taken control of the 'decision-making apparatus' of the NIC, which was 'controlled effectively by a group of persons in Johannesburg who ... took the Congress a long, long way away from the path first set by Mahatma Gandhi'.[36]

Poovalingam was referring to the NIC hitching its wagon to the ANC, to Yusuf Dadoo's links to the Communist Party, and, in particular, to its turn to armed struggle, the antithesis of the NIC's Gandhian passive resistance lineage. For Poovalingam, between the right and the left was the space of the Liberal Party led by Alan Paton and Peter Brown, of which he had been a member. He subsequently entered the institutions that the apartheid government set up to 'represent' the interests of Indians.

Ramgobin was undeterred by criticism and discussed the road forward with former Communist Party member Rowley Arenstein. They concluded that the introduction of government institutions that were gaining a foothold in the community underscored the need to revive the NIC. In June 1971 he met with a few friends at the Phoenix Settlement and an ad hoc committee was formed to take the proposal to 'the community for a mandate'.[37]

Ramgobin, unbanned and working as an insurance salesman, was elected chairperson, while committee members included mainly professionals and union leaders.[38] Ramgobin's document, 'The Case for the Revival of the Natal Indian Congress', was discussed at a meeting at the Bolton Hall in Durban on 25 July 1971, which was attended by former ANC members Florence Mkhize, Ma Bala and Pindi Duma.[39] According to the document:

> We as a people have recognised that South Africa is a multi-racial society. Therefore we reject racial discrimination on any level ... With the rest of black South Africa we must remind ourselves that all these humiliations cannot and must not be allowed to go on indefinitely. We will through our Congress call out to the government that we can still extend the hand of friendship ... but also unhesitatingly remind [it] that a people can be pushed thus far and no further ... And in our attempts to realise these ideals we will be performing our duties to be identified with the vast mass of blacks in southern Africa.[40]

Almost immediately, and in the years ahead, Ramgobin's seamless use of 'multi-racial and black South Africa' would come to be the source of much debate and division, but also an inspiration for those wanting to build a non-racial country.

The process of reviving the NIC involved painstaking groundwork. Dilly Naidoo, who grew up in Port Shepstone on the south coast of Natal and became politicised during his studies at the Natal Medical School in the 1960s, played a pivotal role in the revival of the NIC. He recounted travelling around Natal to meet with and inform the public:

> We used to organise meetings in Newcastle, Ladysmith, Stanger, Port
> Shepstone and so on. There was Omar Badsha and myself, Mewa
> [Ramgobin], [George] Sewpersadh, Jerry [Coovadia], Farouk [Meer],
> and others. Inevitably we had to work, so we'll have our meetings in
> the evenings [and] on the way back we put the lights on [in the car]
> and the guys are dictating, writing the press statements, tell[ing] them
> what a big number of people we had and that kind of thing, just to get
> things across.[41]

Jerry Coovadia, who completed his medical degree at the Grant Medical School in Bombay in the 1960s and became a professor at the Natal Medical School and a vice-president of the NIC, emphasised the energy and stamina involved:

> We worked really hard, every day and every night. The intensity of
> this single-minded pursuit of political freedom, for example, diverted
> me from my nascent career as a serious medical researcher, but made
> me a different person, far better equipped to understand the wider
> contexts of health and medicine and society, such as poverty and
> unemployment. I have never regretted those 'missing' years.[42]

Fanning out across the province paid dividends: within a month, 29 NIC branches were established throughout Natal.

The NIC was officially relaunched at a convention at the Phoenix Settlement on 2 October 1971. The moment and place of rebirth bristled with symbolism. The deliberately chosen date was the birthday of Gandhi, who had founded both the NIC and the settlement,[43] and the conference was opened by Nokukhanya Luthuli, widow of former ANC president Albert Luthuli.[44]

Ramgobin was not present, as he had been slapped with another five-year banning order and placed under house arrest just two weeks before the convention. He responded by undertaking a 14-day fast in Gandhian tradition, which drew much publicity and support.[45] The conference went ahead with George Sewpersadh elected as president, and when he was banned in 1973, M.J. Naidoo was appointed president in his place. Sewpersadh returned as president when his banning order expired in 1978.[46] Sewpersadh's life as a lawyer was rendered incredibly difficult because of the banning order. His willingness to take over the presidency was a courageous move that scoffed at the government's attempt at intimidation through repression. It was this kind of sacrifice that was to garner respect even as the NIC struggled to embed itself in the community.

Sewpersadh was a reluctant leader. Fellow NIC member Thumba Pillay, Sewpersadh's classmate at Sastri College and Natal University, said that Sewpersadh 'was by nature a private person and did not enjoy the high-profile position he held. His commitment and sincerity to the cause was never in doubt and he enjoyed popular support.'[47] According to Yunus Carrim, Sewpersadh 'was a unifying figure. He was a Gandhian. He was the reluctant politician. He was driven more by moral imperatives. He wasn't a saint but he was a wonderful man, very straightforward.'[48] Jerry Coovadia added: 'George was a decent man, moreover well-read. Because he did not speak so well publicly, people didn't give him the recognition that was his due.'[49] Sewpersadh was admired by many within the NIC, and even by those who did not support the Congress, because of his courage and the simple way he lived his life.

Banning leaders and organisations that challenged apartheid was the modus operandi of the state. Ramgobin, who set in motion the wheels to revive the NIC, would not – at least in public – be part of the debates that animated the organisation in the first decade, ranging from participation in government bodies to the organisation's ethnic label. In all, Ramgobin was banned for 17 years. By the time he completed his last banning order in July 1983, the anti-apartheid movement was operating in a different terrain. As a latecomer to the executive and with a sense that he was predestined to lead, he drew antipathy and even scorn from some in the NIC.

One of the earliest criticisms of the NIC was its racial tag. Attorney Ahmed Bhoola, a stalwart of the NIC in the 1950s, and Mandela's friend and fellow student at the University of the Witwatersrand, was critical of reviving an 'Indian' political body. He warned in August 1971, before the NIC was officially launched:

> In present day South Africa and in the larger context of Africa, resurgent, free Africa, to the North of us and in the context of the United Nations, the NIC [revival] is an anachronism ... By labelling themselves Indian, they have denied themselves the right to speak for one and all.[50]

This is an issue examined in the next chapter, as we explore the persistent debate about the 'I' in the NIC.

2 | Black Consciousness and the Challenge to the 'I' in the NIC

From its beginnings in the 1960s, the emergent Black Consciousness Movement (BCM) attracted many young Indian university students. Steve Biko, who was the inspiration and driving force behind Black Consciousness (BC), was born in the Eastern Cape and began to study medicine at the University of Natal in 1966. He was frustrated by what he regarded as the paternalistic attitude of the white liberal National Union of South African Students (NUSAS) towards 'blacks', which in his expanded definition included Indians and coloureds. He argued that fundamental to the struggle for freedom was the mental liberation of black people, whom he called upon to shun white paternalism and to be in control of their own organisations and destiny.

With its genealogy in the ideas of Anton Lembede in the 1940s and Robert Sobukwe in the 1950s,[1] BC meant more than merely crossing apartheid boundaries. Biko wrote in December 1971 that 'by describing yourself as Black ... you have committed yourself to fight against all forces that seek to use your blackness as a stamp that marks you out as a subservient human being'. He clarified that

> the term black is not necessarily all-inclusive; i.e. the fact we are all *not white* does not mean that we are all *black* ... Any black man who calls a white man 'Baas', any man who serves in the police force or Security Branch is *ipso facto* a non-white. Black people – real black people – are those who can manage to hold their heads high in defiance rather than willingly surrender their souls to the white man.[2]

In the aftermath of the crushing of the liberation movements by a deter-minedly repressive apartheid state, BC preaching was an eclectic mix of ideas that held great attraction for the young in particular.

Among the students of Indian ancestry who joined Biko were Asha Rambally, Sam Moodley, Saths Cooper and Strini Moodley. Cooper matriculated from Sastri College in 1967, and proceeded to the University College for Indians on Salisbury Island. He was a member of the South African Students Organisation (SASO), which was formed after Biko led the walkout from NUSAS in 1968. Cooper explained that his generation refused to accept 'white as a point of reference and describe everything else in the negative ... Black Consciousness was a way of identifying subjectively with the conditions we found ourselves in objectively.' Young activists aimed to 'rise above any narrow ethnic or tribal defini-tion because the apartheid State was busy increasing the Bantustans in our country'.[3] As their ideas evolved and confidence grew, these activ-ists opposed the creation of structures designed exclusively for Indians, coloureds and African groups.

Strini Moodley, whose father was a trade unionist and a member of the South African Communist Party (SACP), also matriculated from Sastri College and attended the Indian university college. He was expelled in 1967, ostensibly for 'causing a riot'. Moodley explained what lay behind the BC impetus:

> We felt that Black people can't sit and watch what is happening in this country when they are the victims. Black Consciousness was based on the philosophy that Black people had to first of all redefine them-selves: that you are a Black person, that you are proud of being Black, that your blackness is a weapon for restoring humanity to the world.[4]

In rejecting apartheid-created institutions, Biko warned in June 1971 that he feared that blacks would soon passively accept that they could only enjoy 'political rights in our "own" areas'. Pointing to the Indian experi-ence, he said:

> Witness the new swing amongst leaders of the Indian community in Durban (I must admit I say this with pain in my heart). Ever since

Figures 2.1 and 2.2: Saths Cooper (*left*) and Strini Moodley (*right*), key members of the Black Consciousness Movement, were imprisoned on Robben Island. (Cooper: Courtesy of Gandhi-Luthuli Documentation Centre. Moodley: Courtesy of African News Agency)

word was let loose that the Indian Council will at some near future be elected, a number of intelligent people are thinking of reviving the Indian Congress and letting it form some kind of opposition within the system. This is dangerous retrogressive thinking which should be given no breathing space.[5]

It is true that the revival of the NIC was in part a response to the government's upscaling of Indian representation in apartheid structures. However, in its formative stage the NIC appeared more an attempt to provide a counter-voice, aiming to work not from within the system but from without. Biko's argument might have been a deliberate provocation to influence what was clearly going to be a contested issue, stimulated also by the attraction of some anti-apartheid coloured politicians in government-created bodies.

Mewa Ramgobin later recalled that Biko and academic-activist Rick Turner were present at the July 1971 meeting in Bolton Hall, Durban, where 'we got a unanimous mandate from the community to revive the Congress'. This is not strictly accurate. BCM members, as stated unequivocally by Biko, protested at the revival of the NIC on the grounds that it would reinforce ethnic and racial divisions. In advocating for a single organisation of the oppressed (Indian, coloured and African), they struck at the heart of the NIC's attempt to cast itself as fighting for non-racialism. Strini Moodley was of the view that 'all of these ethnic organisations were terrified of us, primarily because we didn't bring Indians, Africans and Coloureds together, we brought "Black" people together. The failure to embrace this concept was a lost opportunity because white South Africa was afraid of Black unity.'[6]

Biko himself faced opposition for including coloureds and Indians as part of the rubric 'black'. Mamphele Ramphele, Biko's comrade and partner, recounted that the debate about the role of Indians in the BCM was played out with both humour and malice:

> Aubrey Mokoape used to engage Steve in serious all-night discussions ... Aubrey argued from his Africanist perspective against the inclusion of 'Coloureds' and 'Indians' in the Black Consciousness Movement ... He would argue that Indians should be reminded that there was a ship leaving Durban harbour every Thursday for India which they should be encouraged to make use of ... The rise of Idi Amin as the leader of Uganda and his expulsion of Asians simply fuelled the fires of hatred and mistrust. Strini Moodley, the SASO Director of Publications at the time, devoted an entire address to warn Indian students that they would face the same fate unless they dedicated themselves to the struggle for liberation and justice for all.[7]

While Moodley advocated the catch-all 'black', his need to cajole Indians to join the struggle for liberation through the spectre of Idi Amin was also a recognition of their different location in South Africa's racial hierarchy. More often than not, the approach was the unequivocal assertion of 'blackness' without taking cognisance of different histories and hierarchical positions. Simply using the word 'so-called' before 'Indian', as BC activists were wont to do, could not wash away the history that came with that ethnic label and its impact on everyday life.

Jerry Coovadia and some others in the NIC were dismissive of BC ideology. According to Coovadia, BC was

> a totally false perception of the roots of the freedom struggle in South Africa, based on borrowed language from the US, foreign to the conviction that paths to democracy must include all 'racial' groups or else the end product could not be fully non-racial or democratic, and would be the antithesis of all the great socialist and 'liberal human rights' philosophies into which we had been attracted.[8]

It was a strange stand-off. Moodley rejected racial and ethnic exclusivity, but wanted to build a movement that excluded whites. For his part, Coovadia criticised the exclusion of whites but appeared comfortable with being part of an ethnic organisation, albeit for strategic reasons. One wonders also about the sneer of 'borrowed language', given that the Congress movement, as Coovadia himself attests, was infused with a myriad of influences, including Marxism and liberal human rights philosophies. Is there ever a pure home-grown language of resistance?

Ramgobin acknowledged the positive dimension of BC but also pointed to its limitations in a 1986 interview: 'The BC movement was a psychological reassertion of a personality that was being trampled all over all the time ... but does it become an end in itself?'[9] In an interview three years later, he was much more scathing of Black Consciousness, recounting an incident where he told young BC activists, including Biko:

> Ultimately these guys are a bunch of PAC [Pan Africanist Congress] guys, because this is the very argument used by PAC in 1958, 1959. PAC people broke away from the ANC and immobilized in some ways the cohesive opposition to apartheid ... Barney Pityana and Steve Biko ... said, 'Look, please stop dividing my rank and file.' Now at that stage (please publish this when I am dead) I said to Biko that I will fight you with the same intensity as I fight the Nats today. I want you to remember this. That is one ideological warfare.[10]

Ramgobin further argued that when the NIC was revived, 'we did not hesitate for a single moment to say that we are reviving a historical tradition, a legacy left to us by preceding generations, and that we were not going to say that our struggle began with the revival of the NIC'. In contrast, the 'proponents of the BC movement, I believe, arrogated to themselves the role of creators of a new resistance movement. This is historically incorrect ... It disregarded the existence of both the ANC and the PAC.'[11]

While Ramgobin was pointing to one of the dangers of a psychological assertion that could 'become an end in itself', would not the 'I' in the NIC reinforce ethnic ways of thinking? In addressing this question, academics Mala Singh and Shahid Vawda argue that '[t]he NIC did not provide a clear response to the critique of BC directed to the revival of an ethnically based political organization'. The danger, for them, was that 'discourses which jumble together intra-community concerns and trans-community commitments may produce the effect that the "Indian" as an ethnically constituted political subject remains intact'.[12]

NIC activists argued that this critique did not take cognisance of the long history of racial divides imposed by successive white minority governments. It was difficult to mobilise Indians and coloureds over the pass laws, or Africans around the local affairs committees (LACs) formed for Indians and coloureds. Racial segregation also influenced the consciousness of the different racial groups. To expect Indians to simply adopt the identity 'black' and join organisations dominated by Africans was not feasible, as Pravin Gordhan argued in 1986:

The man in the street didn't identify himself as a black, he was an Indian person. He didn't identify himself with some kind of nebulous national culture, he had what he considers to be his Indian culture or Coloured culture or whatever. [And] if one was interested in organising people to effectively participate in changes, then one had to relate to people on the basis of the reality in which they lived and actually perceived themselves. And that has always been a strong guiding factor in our [NIC] work. For those like the BC people who really don't have a great commitment to organising people, relating to people on a day-to-day level is not really very important.[13]

One of the ironies of Gordhan's position was the neglect of the cultural impulses of Indians. There was a sense from the mainly younger professional leadership of the 1980s that to talk of 'Indian culture' was to enter an area of conservatism, of 'imagined traditions', to draw on Terence Ranger's evocative phrase.[14] They saw themselves as part of those with a deracinated, 'modern' outlook, whether of a Marxist or liberal lineage.

A similar critique could be made of the BCM. It never quite defined what the cultural assemblage that came with being Indian would mean with the assertion of 'black' identity. Would Indians have to subsume their particular histories and ways of being into an African identity, however that was defined? Biko himself struggled with the notion of some 'pure' African past that could be rescued and the idea that something new would emerge in the cauldron of the struggle. Those of Indian origin in the BCM did not deal with this issue in any substantial way. Nevertheless, the move by the BCM to confront apartheid categories and imagine new identities had a profound effect on the language and ways of organising anti-apartheid resistance.

At the ANC's 1969 Morogoro Conference in Tanzania, the organisation's 'Strategy and Tactics' document acknowledged that Indians and coloureds too suffered 'varying forms of national humiliation, discrimination and oppression' and that unity of the oppressed groups 'was fundamental to the advance of our liberation struggle'. But 'the primary role of the most oppressed African mass' in leading the struggle was non-negotiable. 'A mechanical parity between the various national groups' would result in 'inequality at the expense of the majority' and give the ANC's opponents further opportunity to accuse it of being 'dominated by minority groups'. The ANC argued, however, that 'this has never been so and will never be so'.[15] Non-Africans could be part of the Revolutionary Council but not the ANC's National Executive Committee.

The ANC was wary both of the Africanist lobby within its ranks and of the PAC charge that it was under the thumb of Indians and communists. The Africanist impulse in the ANC manifested itself in many ways. Zarina Maharaj, for example, reflected that her husband, Mac Maharaj, a senior ANC figure, was seen by some in the organisation as

an 'unapologetic' Indian, one who did not know his place in the struggle ... As a member of an ethnic minority that had in apartheid South

Africa been afforded more privileges than the African majority, he was regarded by some as neither contrite nor deferential ... Obviously some comrades thought Mac [Maharaj] was mistaken to believe that being equally in the struggle, he was equal in the struggle.[16]

Inside the country there were ongoing debates about ways of organising, whether it be multinationally, non-racially, along BC lines, or by defending the independent organisations of the working class.

Paul David, as a Natal university student and an NIC member from his teenage years, and later as NIC secretary, was intimately involved in the organisational debates of the 1960s. He recounted that students in the 'Non-European' section of the University of Natal wanted to form a non-racial branch of the ANC on campus in 1959, and he accompanied a delegation to seek Albert Luthuli's permission. Following an 'amazing meeting', Luthuli advised them that 'it's not possible to have a non-racial branch on campus, but he says informally all the Congress-inclined people can get together, have discussions. For all intents and purposes, he said, you are a branch.' Against this background, David discounted the BC arguments:

I said it's a practical problem, you know, are we now going to take it upon ourselves to go and work among African people? Will they accept us? Do we know the language? I said there are practical diffi-culties and we have history and it's a good history. And I said, we're a non-racial organisation and what makes it non-racial is our approach to our work. Maybe not our membership, but the way we work, I mean, we are not communalists and racists. The ANC accepts us for what we are.[17]

NIC president George Sewpersadh, while not directly replying to the BC critique, argued in 1972 that the revival of the NIC filled a need among Indians for a voice. Not only did the Nationalists ban most leaders, but the establishment of government structures meant that Indians had to 'contend with the humiliation of having their representatives chosen by the very Government that had always shown them scant, if any, respect'. Sewpersadh saw the revival of the NIC as 'practical and realistic'. Apartheid had separated South Africans according to race, and an 'organisation representing all the races ... is unlikely to get massive support from the different races'. The NIC, Sewpersadh said, viewed its task as convincing

> Indians that their problems cannot be divorced from the problems of other oppressed races. Constant co-operation with people of other races will no doubt pave the way for the creation of a democratic organization consisting of human beings and not a particular racial group.[18]

Ramgobin also argued that organising among Indians was a practical necessity. His view was in line with the Congress Alliance's notion of 'four nations', which viewed South Africa as being made up of distinct African, coloured, white and Indian groupings, or 'nations':

> If I were to take the typical definition of a nation, not one of the groupings would constitute a nation, but I'm prepared to live with the contradiction because the ideals enshrined therefrom are higher than the whimsical, non-community-based aspirations ... Whilst we're working towards a non-racial democratic society, we do recognise the concept of national groups.[19]

M.D. Naidoo was an NIC and SACP stalwart who had gone to the UN in 1946 to present the case of Indian South Africans and was later incarcerated on Robben Island. He offered a defence of the NIC with characteristic sophistication. Naidoo dismissed the notion that a separate organisation was necessarily racist:

> The content of racism is racial discrimination where one group which exercises power uses that power to gain advantages and to exploit other race groups ... If people of a particular kind get together because they find it more convenient to mobilise themselves, but the objectives for which they are working are identical with a similar group of a different kind – that's not racism. We needed an Indian organisation to reach [out] not only to the politically articulate, but [to] the people who were politically less developed, even the conservative elements. You had to find an organization which, on the basis

of tradition, on the basis of history, would be meaningful to them, and the NIC fulfilled that role ... [And] it's not much use for an Indian who can barely speak the language to go out to the rural areas and talk to Africans who'd see him in terms of the prejudices that the apartheid regime has promoted.[20]

Naidoo contended that apartheid's divide-and-rule ideology was not just an imposition from above. It also had impulses from below that fed into the idea of 'people of a particular kind' – and this 'kind' was racially circumscribed. Like Ramgobin, Naidoo did not articulate at what point or how Indians and Africans would join together in a common political organisation. This issue would become urgent as the geography of apartheid consolidated and the NP speeded up 'own affairs' departments for Indians.

Dhaya Pillay was an NIC activist in the 1970s, involved in key political trials in the 1980s, and appointed a judge in the post-apartheid period. She insisted that the organisation welcomed members of all race groups:

The NIC was a political home at a time when a broad-based, non-racial mass democratic movement didn't exist. The NIC was used strategically, in the sense that its main line of activity was to organise Indian communities politically, because the Indian community identified politically with Mahatma Gandhi. And one had to approach people on issues that they could identify with in order to get them listening to you and to act in an organised way and collectively thereafter. But if you look at the activists within the NIC, they were involved in every other non-racial structure that existed. So if you want to be critical of form, then that's your choice, but you ignore the substance of what the NIC was if you don't look beyond the 'I' in the NIC.[21]

Pillay points to the NIC's strengths, but these very strengths can be seen as weaknesses. While the leadership was involved in broader non-racial movements, this rarely included the rank and file that the NIC supposedly spoke for. These upper-level connections led to allegations that NIC leaders achieved their influence in the broad-based UDF, not through the support of the Indian masses, but through the resources they brought into play and their networks with the ANC in exile. Some professionals within the NIC, for example, ran legal practices that looked after the interests of detainees and were a conduit for funds that came from many sources. While legitimate, this leverage would lead to accusations of control by Indians that came to be encapsulated by the word 'cabal', an issue we turn to later.

Jerry Coovadia recounted that when the mandate was given to launch the NIC, discussions were held with BC members at seminars, conferences and community meetings, where 'differences became even more pronounced'. These debates, he said, consolidated the NIC perspective that the foundations of a new society should 'give substance to the Freedom Charter and the beliefs and aims of the socialist/communist left in the ANC'.[22]

While some NIC members, like Coovadia, were open to socialism and communism, others were less inclined towards this position, and these divisions became more acute as exile politics and its machinations reached into the NIC. As Paul David attested, 'the communists in the NIC were very few and were accused of weakening the organisation. So we had to be very tactful of how we recruited.'[23] This need to be clandestine would come back to haunt some in the NIC as the notion of a cabal reared its head. For David, however, it was the BCM's anathema against socialism that rankled. He argued that Biko 'was a very strong proponent of the free market and capitalist system. And we debated this *ad nauseum* for months and months. He just wouldn't agree to any kind of socialist programme.'[24] It was probably disconcerting to David and Coovadia, given the close bond between the SACP and the Soviet Union, that Biko, writing in the early 1970s, saw them both as imperialist, leading to the sneer of 'capitalist':

> In being so critical of the economic self-interest in the Third World on the part of American capitalism, I at the same time have no illusions about Russia. Russia is as imperialistic ... but Russians have a less dirty name: in the eyes of the Third World they have a cleaner slate ... Their policy *seems* to be acceptable to revolutionary groups. Here we are probably faced with the greatest problem in the Third World today. We are divided because some of us think that Russian

imperialism can be accepted as purely an interim phase while others, like myself, doubt whether Russia is really interested in the liberation of the black people.[25]

The Black People's Convention (BPC) was formed in April 1971 to find ways to forge unity among black organisations. A second meeting, where speakers included Chief Mangosuthu Buthelezi and Biko, was held in Pietermaritzburg in mid-August 1971, and a third in Lenasia on 23 January 1972. Jerry Coovadia and George Sewpersadh attended the Lenasia meeting, but Sewpersadh made it clear that they were there merely as 'observers', as they advocated non-racialism.[26]

Although they opposed ethnic organisation, Saths Cooper and Strini Moodley initially participated in the NIC, which, they said, had agreed to 'investigate' the possibility of becoming non-racial.[27] BC adherents such as Cooper, Moodley and Ashwin Trikamjee were active in the powerful NIC Durban Central branch. At the (re)launch of the NIC on 2 October 1971, the Durban Central branch submitted a memorandum to change the organisation's name to the People's Congress. In a close decision, the NIC's provincial congress voted 32–30 to retain the name.[28]

The Durban Central branch then organised a symposium on Black Consciousness held on 12 December 1971 at the Bolton Hall in Durban. Speakers included Strini Moodley, Daphne Masekela, Temba Sono, Fatima Meer, D.K. Singh, Jerry Coovadia, Paul David, Ashwin Trikamjee, and the poet Adam Small. Social worker Daphne Masekela told the symposium that Black Consciousness 'sprouts from the depth and heart of the Black people, who, with their peculiar problems, a peculiar cultural heritage, a unique history of oppression and sufferings are solving their own problems and difficulties in the midst of White racism'. D.K. Singh was unconvinced and rejected Black Consciousness as, in his view, 'racial exclusiveness led to racial hatred'. By all accounts, the meeting was a stormy one, with NIC delegates from Clairwood and Isipingo, led by Durag Behari, walking out as they were not allowed to address the meeting.[29] *The Graphic* reported on 24 December 1971 that following the symposium, the full executive of the NIC passed a resolution (with Saths Cooper abstaining) 'that any dogma or group which propagates racialism of any kind is unacceptable in Congress. ...

This meeting directs all members of Congress not to identify Congress in any way whatsoever with any philosophy or creed of racial exclusiveness.' R. Ramesar, NIC Organising Secretary, said that the executive and branch members 'severely criticised the officials of the Durban Central branch for associating Congress with Black exclusiveness and for expounding beliefs that are foreign to Congress'.[30] One correspondent to the *Graphic*, writing under the pseudonym 'Interested-Disinterested-Interested', commented on the irony that the NIC, by rejecting 'racial exclusiveness', was in fact 'passing a death-blow to themselves'. They were refusing to drop the word Indian 'which has immense racial connotations in this country ... How can they reconcile their policy with their recent boo-hoo?'[31]

The NIC was officially reconstituted at a two-day inaugural conference in Durban on 28–29 April 1972,[32] which was attended by representatives from 31 branches.

The banning of eight BC members, including Saths Cooper, Strini Moodley and Steve Biko, in March 1973 saw the war of words between BCM and NIC adherents subsiding.[33] However, the issue of the 'I' in the NIC did not disappear. A.S. Chetty and R. Paparam of Pietermaritzburg proposed at the July 1973 NIC provincial conference that the organisation change its name to the South African People's Conference. Their motion read that a 'purely Indian body, political in character, and operating outside the system of apartheid, is an anachronism'.[34]

This proposal led to a variety of responses. The lawyer-activist Rabi Bugwandeen, in his unique and idiosyncratic style, asked: 'What right have Indians to take a unilateral decision to become non-racial? Without first consulting other race groups, how can we presume to foist Indian leadership on the other races?' Jerry Coovadia described non-racialism as 'a brilliant idea' but one that would get Congress 'nowhere if it lost the support of Indians'. Chetty and Paparam withdrew the motion after a two-hour debate, with the 45 members 'bitterly divided'.[35] Instead, a subcommittee comprising A.S. Chetty, Ela Gandhi, R. Paparam, Mannie Jacobs, A.H. Randeree, D. Beharie, Bala Mudaly and M.J. Naidoo was appointed to investigate the issue.[36] Six branches from Chatsworth were represented at the meeting, the first time that any delegates from the township had attended a provincial conference.[37]

There was a concession at the NIC's September 1974 conference when a resolution was passed that 'with the changing events in Africa [the NIC] could no longer remain an Indian-only organisation'.[38] This 'effectively broke a longstanding tradition of exclusiveness on the part of the NIC in their membership'.[39] NIC president M.J. Naidoo told the annual *Black Review* that he hoped to facilitate cooperation with the BPC, although he was personally uneasy with BPC's closing its doors to whites, even democratic ones who were sincere in opposing apartheid.[40] The decision to open the NIC's membership while retaining its name sounds contradictory, but it should be remembered that the ANC was banned and there was no organisation that spoke for the Congress tradition of the 1950s. The NIC justified its existence in part on the basis that it was keeping the ideals of the Freedom Charter alive.

Unlocking the NIC's ethnic/racial door was a concession to the impact of the BCM, but there were unintended consequences. African comrades who were seen as close to the NIC, such as Archie Gumede, were open to criticism that they were being manipulated by the organisation. Initially the NIC did not seek to organise or solicit African membership in everyday politics. It kept within a tradition that saw the country as divided into national groups that would organise under their own ethnic/racial banners, but would come together in an alliance that would be led by the ANC and committed to majority rule. It was in this sense that M.J. Naidoo could defend the NIC as non-racial: not because of its name or membership, but by its commitment to a non-racial South Africa.

The NIC continually felt obliged to justify the retention of 'Indian' in its name. At its annual conference in November 1978, white, coloured and African speakers addressed the gathering. Among them were Helen Joseph, who had spearheaded the 1956 anti-pass-law women's march to the Union Buildings, and the Reverend Ernest Baartman, a Methodist preacher and early BC proponent. Jerry Coovadia 'spoke at length on the name of the Congress'. He supported the inclusion of 'Indian' not because the Congress served Indians only, but for 'historical and practical reasons'. The Congress was a link between the past and the future, filling the gap in black politics caused by deaths, exile and bannings.[41] According to Ela Gandhi, the thinking of NIC activists was that 'the link that the NIC had both to

Gandhiji [the Mahatma] and to the Congress Alliance and the Freedom Charter should not be lost by changing the name'.[42]

Pat Poovalingam, former member of the Liberal Party and who participated in government-created structures in the 1980s, described the 1970s as a decade when the NIC

> forgot its high principles and earned the derision of the community by its silly shilly-shallying at being a non-racial body whereas it remained a purely Indian political organisation. One understood the problem. The NIC leaders really believe in non-racialism. But they know that if the NIC becomes a non-racial body it will quickly become non-est [extinct], for its main reason for existence would disappear. For let us face it, the NIC officials know, as everyone else knows, that it was as a purely racial political organisation designed to serve purely Indian interests in Natal that Mahatma Gandhi formed the NIC. But times have changed and there is no real defence by people who refuse to have any truck with any racial compartmentalisation, to maintain racial compartmentalisation in political organisations ... But to carry this out honestly and genuinely to its logical conclusion would mean that the claim to be M.K. Gandhi's heir may be lost ... If they in fact cease to be an Indian organisation they will lose even the few supporters they have ... So we find the sad spectacle of an organisation which has the capacity of providing dynamic leadership of the Indian community hobbled by its own inconsistencies and contradictions.[43]

While Poovalingam's criticisms bit hard, this was a difficult time in South African politics. Tactics and strategies were debated in an environment of repression and amid attempts to regroup anti-apartheid forces. The Labour Party, a political party established by coloureds, had resolved to take the fight against apartheid into the chambers of the Coloured Representative Council (CRC). Mangosuthu Buthelezi, while refusing to accept an independent Bantustan for Zulus, served within those confines. The NIC attempted to negotiate this difficult period with a degree of consistency so that it could mobilise against government structures while also claiming to continue the aspirations of the Freedom Charter.

Through the 1970s the NIC attempted to keep alive the ideals of the banned ANC, to provide support for those returning after long years on Robben Island, and to facilitate the building of links between internal activists and those in exile and the 'underground'. It was on the level of everyday organising, however, that the newly revived NIC would face its greatest challenge.

While the NIC soldiered on despite the changing terrain of organising, the BCM faced the full might of apartheid repression. Saths Cooper and Strini Moodley were among SASO/BPC members arrested in October 1974 for organising a pro-Mozambique 'Viva Frelimo' rally in Durban. They were charged with terrorism and, after a trial lasting two years, were incarcerated on Robben Island in 1976. Others, such as Sam Moodley and Asha Ramabali, were banned. The main organisations of the BCM were also banned. Steve Biko was murdered while in police custody in September 1977.

In reflecting on the 'I' in the NIC, Paul David was keen to underscore the point that NIC activists did not confine their work to the Indian community. He illustrated by way of example that during the 1973 strikes in Durban the NIC

> raised a great deal of money for striking workers and provided them with support services and legal help. It was a very practical way of saying that the NIC was not just Indian in name, because for the first time we had to work closely in practice with African people. The other occasions were all political campaigns and not in a day-to-day struggle for food and things like that. So it revolutionised some of the people in the NIC. And they realised that we can't just bandy this argument that we're only Indian in name. We [had] to be nonracial in practice, with an Indian tag.[44]

Critics would argue that this non-racialism went only so far and that the majority of Indians were not exposed to a non-racial environment. This is an issue we return to in the chapters that follow.

Through this period the NP continued to punt the SAIC as the only way for Indians to defend and advance their position in the country. One of the central tasks of the NIC was to formulate a response to the Nationalist government's determination to recognise and work only with this government-created body. The NIC was caught in a tangle of repression while attempting to build a mass base that would confront the strictures of apartheid. But as the SAIC gained power and influence, controversy raged within NIC ranks over participation in government-created structures. We examine this debate in the next chapter.

3 | Between Principle and Pragmatism: Debates over the SAIC, 1971–1978

Through the 1960s South Africa gained global notoriety for its repression of anti-apartheid organisations and activists. Repression, however, was only one aspect of the state response. The other was to create organs of 'representation' for the oppressed within the confines of the apartheid project. Granting citizenship to Indian South Africans was accompanied by the setting up of institutions to deal with matters 'affecting them'.

Since its beginnings in the mid-1960s, the SAIC had garnered increasing power over what was termed 'own affairs' by the early 1970s. As the SAIC clamoured for more jurisdiction over the everyday life of Indians, the NIC had to find ways to respond. It could not simply call for people to boycott 'own affairs' offices, for example, because these dealt with pensions and grants and the identity documents needed to negotiate daily life. The power of the state was used to channel people's lives into racially bounded institutions and, over time, to 'normalise' these practices.

Participation in the SAIC was an issue that rallied both proponents and opponents within the NIC. This debate over participation persisted through the 1970s and 1980s, and created divides within the broader extra-parliamentary forces, turned comrade against comrade inside the NIC, and reached into the upper echelons of the ANC in exile.

Three positions emerged: boycott, participation and what came to be known as rejectionist participation. Even before the NIC was officially constituted, attorney Ahmed Bhoola, NIC stalwart of the 1950s, expressed a fear that the NIC would spend more time 'fighting the so-called Indian Council than the real power behind that Council'. He warned against participation:

> You know the old saying: 'If you can't beat them, join them.' They [NIC members] must remember that the SAIC is a State-paid body appointed to do the government's job. It has no power to change the course of government policy ... Let no one in the revived Congress go searching for a MANDATE on this score.[1]

The position of Steve Biko and the BCM was that Bantustans served only to 'contain' the aspirations of black people, restrict what government critics could say, support apartheid tribalisation and maintain the mental subjugation of black people.[2] Saths Cooper argued that the BC position was not simply one of non-collaboration but anti-collaboration, which placed emphasis 'on self-determination and self-activity'. This, in his view, explained the creation of 'alternative education, alternative ways of running community events, alternative accountability mechanisms'.[3]

The Non-European Unity Movement (NEUM), established in 1943 by young Cape intellectual activists, stuck to the principle of non-collaboration and referred to those who participated as 'quislings'.[4] The NEUM position was intransigent on non-collaboration and brooked no debate on the issue.

The ANC, in contrast, had over the decades shied away from a reflexive boycott position. In a 1958 article, 'Our Struggle Needs Many Tactics', Mandela argued that 'the boycott is in no way a matter of principle but a tactical weapon whose application should ... be related to the concrete conditions prevailing at the given time'. He believed that the democratic movement should make use of all available avenues to 'reach the masses of the people and rally them behind us'.[5]

He made a similar point some decades later. Writing from Robben Island in the immediate aftermath of the 1976 Soweto rebellion, Mandela took issue with organisations like the NEUM and BCM which, he asserted, did not distinguish 'between principle and practice', inserting an 'inflexible line' between 'collaboration and non-collaboration'. Without using the words, he offered a defence of rejectionist participation when he argued against the NEUM position that labelled as mere 'collaborators' those who sought 'to capture' institutions of separate development 'and use them to reach the people and to prevent the people from using them as originally planned or who kill and paralyse them in the process'.[6] Ahmed Kathrada made a similar argument:

> The history of the freedom struggles is full of examples where similar institutions were used to good effect. The activities of the Bolsheviks in the Tsarist Duma and the capture of state governments by the All India Congress are but two outstanding instances ... The utilisation of these institutions by the freedom movement is not a matter of principle but a tactic.[7]

Walter Sisulu, serving a life sentence with Mandela and Kathrada, argued that the boycott position had failed and that, with the coming of 'independence', simply ignoring this

> would play into the hands of the enemy. We have an alternative to offer the people in these areas. We shall be able to offer it if we accept the reality of the political 'independence' of those Bantustans and set out to ... expose the contradictions that make their 'independence' unreal ... One of the greatest mistakes is to see in every man and woman who works within these apartheid institutions an enemy of the revolution.[8]

Govan Mbeki, an ANC and SACP stalwart, saw the continuing attempt by the NP to create divisions 'between the different racial groups in the country' as feeding into different class interests. He observed in the 1970s:

> The capitalist and middle class among the Indians and Coloureds ... are filling positions in the respective councils provided for under apartheid policies ... Amongst the Africans the government has relied mainly on its servants – the chiefs – in the Bantustans and on merchants in the urban councils.[9]

Mbeki was concerned that if Africans were

> forced to accept the citizenship of one or other of the Bantustans, then the liberation forces must accept the fact that the Coloured and Indian racial groups will be open to intensified wooing and promises by white supremacists ... The liberation forces must face the fact that certain sections of the minority black groups fear a rampant African nationalism.[10]

The ANC's 'Strategy and Tactics' document of 1969 noted that the Nationalists were attempting to 'feed on the insecurity and dependency which is often part of the thinking of minority oppressed groups'. The Nationalists strived to make Indians and coloureds believe that the coming to power of the ANC would mean that 'White domination will be replaced by Black domination'. To prevent the apartheid regime from 'recruit[ing] substantial numbers' of Indians and Coloureds 'to actively collaborate with it', the document argued that the latter should be made to see themselves as 'an integral part of the liberation movement and not as mere auxiliaries'.[11]

Taken together, these perspectives indicate how the ANC was seeking to understand the changing terrain and to respond creatively to the possibility that both coloureds and Indians would be dragooned into the camp of the 'enemy'. The ANC also recognised how class fracturing could create the conditions for division and co-optation.

Meanwhile, within the NIC ranks, the debate about participation began in earnest in 1972, a year after the government made provision for the election of five members to the SAIC. There were some murmurings within the NIC about using the SAIC as an instrument to raise the civic consciousness of communities. The NIC's two-day conference in late April 1972 was opened by Sonny Leon of the Coloured Labour Party, which had decided on participating in state bodies as a way to delegitimise them. According to Leon, 'We must elect men to the dummy councils who will oppose any attempt by the "yes" men, who would, if there was no opposition on these dummy bodies, sell the people. We must expose and embarrass these institutions.'[12]

Despite Leon's passionate plea, the NIC rejected the SAIC. According to Ben Khoapa, one of the leading figures in the BCM, 'this closed a long chapter of speculation that the NIC had been revived amongst other things to be able to participate in an eventual election of the SAIC'.[13] However, a year later, at the July 1973 NIC conference, some members again argued that it would be 'prudent' to follow the example of Mangosuthu Buthelezi, who rejected the homelands policy but used government structures in KwaZulu to further the agenda of Zulus. Once again this argument failed to win the day.[14]

There was a change in SAIC membership in 1974. Previously made up of government appointees, the SAIC now had 15 members appointed by the government and 15 selected by Indian LACs, which had been introduced in 1963 to give Indians some power to run local affairs. Effectively 111 people participated in the nomination out of a population of 600 000.[15] In rejecting the SAIC, the NIC stated that the 'opportunists' or 'confused, well-meaning individuals' who served on it were to blame for perpetuating the 'inequality and subjection' of Indians. Since members were elected by members of town boards and LACs who themselves were not elected, the SAIC was nothing more than a 'dummy organisation'.[16]

At the NIC's September 1974 conference in Durban, held shortly before the SAIC meeting, acting president M.J. Naidoo reaffirmed the boycott position in his opening address but did not completely rule out participation. He argued that since members were being banned for 'demanding the rights that are due to the people and they spoke their minds freely', the NIC should consider participation 'because of the protection that attaches to the parliamentary privilege afforded to these statutory bodies'. The NIC should consider using the SAIC as a 'protected platform ... to reach the people on the one hand, and to make the Government hear its demands on the other hand'. Naidoo insisted that Congress policy had not changed, only 'the method of reaching its goal'.[17]

The position on collaboration and non-collaboration set out by Mandela, Sisulu and Kathrada found an echo in Naidoo's address and in the NIC's debates over participation. Ironically, that position would also be used by those who participated in such institutions and were labelled 'sell-outs' by the NIC. Mahmoud (Mamoo) Rajab, who was later involved in the Tricameral Parliament, argued: 'To us the ANC has never stood against participation. If you read Nelson Mandela's book *No Easy Walk to Freedom*, it devotes a chapter to participation and he said very clearly there that if

Figure 3.1: M.J. Naidoo was at the centre of debates about participation in government structures. (Courtesy of Gandhi-Luthuli Documentation Centre)

there is a possibility of any reactionary unit taking over any institution, participation in fact is mandatory.'[18]

Both Mangosuthu Buthelezi, chief minister of the KwaZulu Bantustan, and Frederik van Zyl Slabbert, who sat in Parliament as a member of the (white) Progressive Party, addressed the 1974 NIC conference. This suggested that while lines were hardening at one level, the NIC was prepared to listen to those working within the system. Buthelezi advised that the 'structures of separate development should be used up until they burst at the seams'. Calling those who participated in government structures 'sell-outs was understandable from a doctrinaire point of view', he said, but it achieved little in the way of tangible progress for ordinary people. The time had come to stop 'spending all energies and time showing to what extent one's hands have been "kept clean" by not doing anything to advance the cause of our people because one cannot operate in the muck of separate development tactics'.[19]

While the approach to government-created bodies was still up for debate, a strong boycottist pulse ran through the NIC. In his annual report to the 1974 conference, NIC general secretary R. Ramesar called for the boycott of separate-development institutions which had been 'created by the Government for its own salvation and not for the benefit of the Black People'. Addressing the same conference, Fatima Meer, sociologist at the University of Natal, said that the SAIC could not be compared to Leon's Coloured Representative Council. Leon had commanded a majority in an election and 'speaks in the manner he does because he feels the strength of the Coloured people. On whose strength will the 30 members of the SAIC speak? They cannot lean on the strength of the Indian people.'[20] NIC vice-president D.K. Singh added that since the conference had resolved that the NIC should open membership to all race groups, participation in racially exclusive organisations was 'indefensible'. The house decided by 22 votes to 12 to boycott the SAIC.[21]

Jerry Coovadia recounted that the question of participation was robustly debated in public and private:

> The impact of this conference and others like it, with a similar range of good, bad and so-so speakers, pales into insignificance compared to the internal debates which were intense. Many, many debates took place among the leadership of the NIC. We argued every conceivable point of view. In addition, there was an incredible programme of public participation through the length and breadth of the province. I was never involved as a speaker in so many political meetings than at that time.[22]

The constant recurrence of the debate led one newspaper to describe the NIC in 1975 as being in 'a state of suspended animation ... Some members of the NIC are now seriously of the view that the NIC should be dissolved. From a practical point of view this is not likely to make a difference to the political set-up of the community.'[23] While this was a strong indictment, it reflected the genuine difficulties that the NIC was experiencing in rebuilding support. Bannings, imprisonment, exile and forced relocations had

Figure 3.2: *Left to right*: J.N. Reddy and A.M. Moolla, pictured here with Prime Minister John Vorster and minister of Indian affairs Chris Heunis. (Courtesy of 1860 Heritage Centre)

created a leadership vacuum, and a new generation was seeking to win the trust of the masses while trying to clarify their political understanding and strategies on the hoof. The first meeting of the newly constituted SAIC was held from 26 to 28 November 1974. J.N. Reddy, managing director of the Indian-owned New Republic Bank and who had working-class roots, was appointed as the Council's executive chairperson. The session was opened by Prime Minister B.J. Vorster.

In the course of putting his own NP policy in the best possible light, and ignoring the oppression and misery it had inflicted, Vorster appeared extraordinarily sympathetic to the circumstances of the Indian population.

Because there had been no official channel of communication with the Government in the 1950s and early 1960s, the community had been forced to adopt less favourable methods to bring their aspirations, their special needs and yes, their frustrations and their complaints to the attention of authority. During this period the lack of a means of communication must have left the community with the idea that the Indians of South Africa were a forgotten people, that they lived in South Africa but were not part of South Africa and this led to misunderstanding. The establishment of the Department of Indian Affairs in 1961, however, saw an end to this era of uncertainty.[24]

The ironies were obvious. The Nationalists had created the uncertainty Vorster describes with their threat of repatriation. Their intransigent attitude towards Indian lobbying for mitigation of the worst of apartheid's policies had seen the NIC gravitate towards extra-parliamentary resistance, while also creating the conditions for India to attack South Africa in international forums. Vorster was keen to airbrush the historical antipathy of the whites towards Indians and to focus on the achievements of the SAIC:

> The fruits of co-operation and dialogue through means of the SAIC are many and varied. To mention but a few, there is an easing of travelling restrictions; the repeal of the Asiatic Registration laws in the Transvaal; the extension of education certificates which entitle holders to live in other provinces for an indefinite period; the participation in local affairs through membership of Local Affairs Committees and other such bodies; military training and ever-increasing opportunities to progress in the various branches of the public service and other professions.[25]

It was undoubtedly true that, as Vorster pointed out, careers were opening up for Indians in the public service, while children of working-class parents were increasingly seizing the opportunity to obtain jobs which allowed them long-term security. With graduates in engineering and accountancy on the rise, and teachers obtaining degrees in large numbers, new economic avenues were available. Vorster hoped that these developments would cut off attempts by extra-parliamentary forces in the community to coalesce with other disenfranchised groups, and instead attract them to work through institutional channels provided by the Nationalist government.

Adopting a carrot and stick approach, Vorster warned that 'the policy of confrontation so often propagated by certain organisations ... results in a lack of sympathetic understanding on the part of the authority which in turn leads to frustration on the part of the community. It is in fact a road that leads nowhere – a cul de sac.'[26] J.N. Reddy assured the prime minister that Indians were fully supportive of the government: 'The fact that our men are joining the Defence Forces ... is testimony to our loyalty and sincerity.'[27]

The 1974 Council saw the arrival of younger, more assertive members, such as Baldeo Dookie, Amichand Rajbansi and S. Abram-Mayet. Rajbansi had been on the political scene for some time and, despite many knock-downs, would display a remarkable ability to reinvent himself. He was born in Clairwood, from where his family was forced to relocate to Chatsworth under the Group Areas Act. He studied history and psychology at the University College for Indians in Durban, and was a sports referee and administrator before serving in the LAC. As early as 1972, when the NIC was first debating participation, he told a reporter:

> Although I do not accept apartheid, I would prefer to co-operate with the State and to talk frankly with the Government. Acceptance of the SAIC is the only way that this can be done. We are prepared to cooperate with the Government but we will only do so on a basis of absolute equality. There will be no more of this master-servant business. Our aim is direct representation in Parliament ... This will take time but we will work with this in mind.[28]

It was this kind of fighting talk, even when it lacked substance in actual dealings with the government, that made Rajbansi a formidable foe for the NIC.

True to their promise, the new members of the SAIC immediately swung into action when Abram-Mayet proposed a motion, seconded by Rajbansi, that all Group Areas legislation should be repealed. The SAIC also focused on issues of school accommodation, the need for trading and industrial sites, and greater access to economic and sub-economic housing.[29]

The quest to broaden opportunities for university education also occupied the SAIC's attention. At its fifth meeting, in 1976, the SAIC asked for a branch of the University of Durban-Westville (UDW) to be opened in the Transvaal, and for permits to be issued to Indians so that they could be admitted to 'white' universities for the courses that were not offered by UDW.[30] Clearly the SAIC was responding to the growing numbers of Indians finishing high school and their desire for tertiary education. While some legitimately argued that separate education meant accepting the basic tenets of apartheid, there were few alternatives on offer. The NIC challenge to the formation of a separate Indian university had been mounted in the early 1960s but had run out of steam. UDW, which had gained university status in 1971 and moved to the Westville campus in 1972, became a major avenue through which Indian children of working-class parents could gain entry into the professional class. It is one of the ironies of Nationalist policy that this institution became a centre of anti-apartheid dissent and the site of new NIC recruits.

Early in 1975, reacting to growing alienation from the community, SAIC members proposed 'a timetable for full elections, delegation of executive functions leading to full control over some services, legislative powers and the subsequent raising of the executive committee to the status of a cabinet'.[31] Vorster proposed an Inter-Cabinet Council (ICC) in 1976. A consultative body, the ICC was to comprise members of the SAIC, the Coloured Representative Council and white ministers. Dr M.B. Naidoo, a member of the SAIC, made an impassioned case for participation in the ICC:

> Indian politics just now calls for pragmatism, for involvement in new deals and an eagerness to accept every concession aimed at upgrading the Indian community by raising their standards of living and advancing and fulfilling their educational aspirations. When the time arrives for a common society in South Africa, the Indian will have equipped himself for his rightful role. It is important that we do not put the clock back for ideological reasons.[32]

The SAIC decided by 21 votes to 4 to give the ICC a year's trial. Rajbansi, who voted against participation, resigned from the executive committee but remained a member of the Council.[33] It was these gymnastics in which he was seemingly prepared to take a principled stance while remaining within the system that gave Rajbansi a longer shelf life and greater popularity than many others who simply accepted what the NP had to offer.

Given these developments within the SAIC, participation in government-created bodies remained a source of tension within the NIC. In June 1975 the NIC convened an emergency meeting mediated by veteran NIC activist Advocate Hassan Mall, who later chaired the amnesty committee of the TRC. The aim of the meeting was to arrive at a clear position on the SAIC issue 'once and for all'. After lengthy debate, it was agreed that the NIC was to have nothing to do with the SAIC and to ostracise those who stood for elections.[34]

Prior to the NIC's next provincial conference in March 1976, General Secretary Ramesar insisted that delegates would not 'waste any time discussing its position vis-à-vis the LACs and SAIC'.[35] Yet, the headline of the *Leader* report on the conference, 'NIC – In Search of Direction', captured the organisation's ongoing dilemma.[36] It was not by chance that two of the speakers at the conference were the Reverend Allan Hendrickse of the Coloured Labour Party and Hector Ngokazi of the Democratic Party in the Transkei, both of whom embraced government structures. Other speakers included ardent anti-apartheid activists such as Winnie Mandela and the Reverend Beyers Naudé. As one newspaper article explained, the NIC was caught between principle and pragmatism: 'be pragmatic, work within the system, proclaim principles, but lay them aside and get involved in the day-to-day problems of the community' or 'nail principles to the mast, then withdraw like a tortoise into its shell, and let those who do not carry the community have a free platform'.[37]

In opening the conference, M.J. Naidoo expressed concern that 'leaders generated by the government are growing in stature' while black leaders 'of high principles are stagnating in prolonged inactivity and will soon fade away'. Naidoo said that the proponents of participation feared that 'in the absence of democratic voices in these institutions the field is left open to those who may be properly classed as stooges and profiteers, who, relishing their new found status ... constantly espouse the Government's cause, even justifying the artificial division of the people created by the Government'.[38]

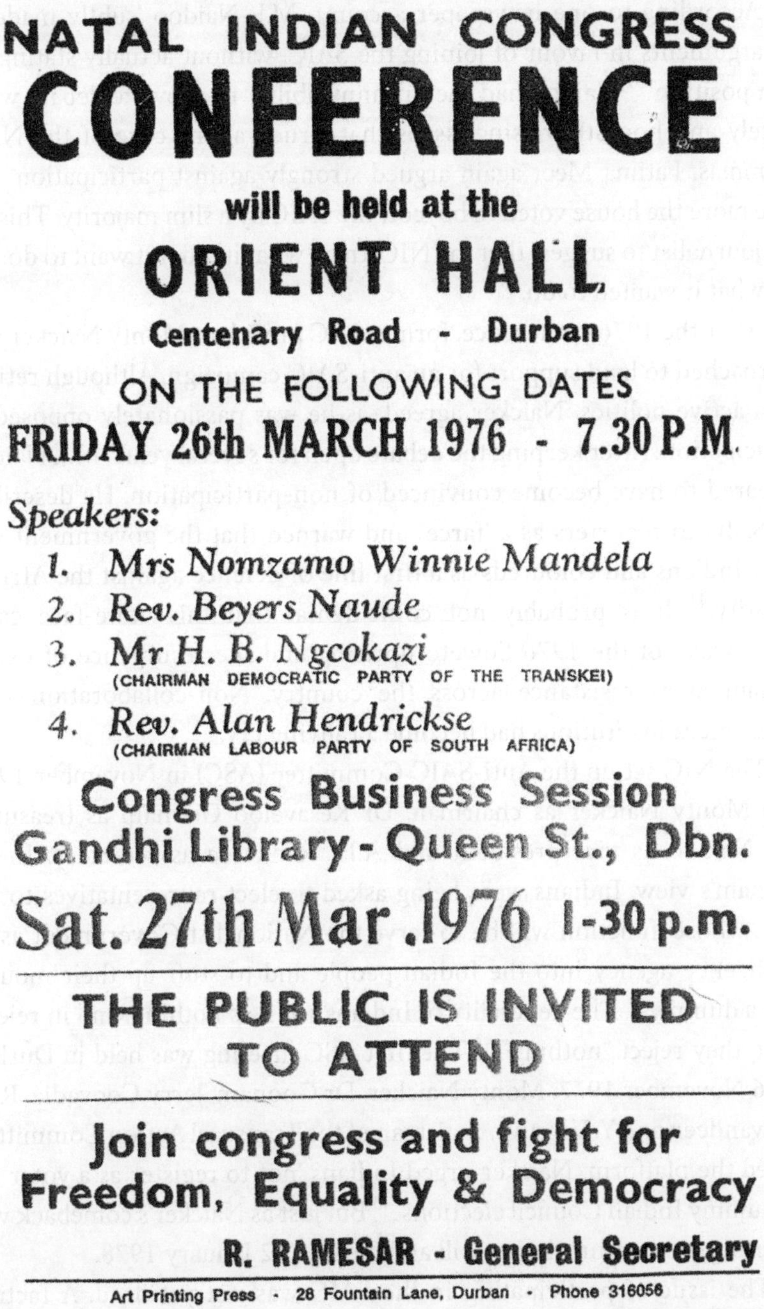

NATAL INDIAN CONGRESS
CONFERENCE
will be held at the
ORIENT HALL,
Centenary Road - Durban

ON THE FOLLOWING DATES
FRIDAY 26th MARCH 1976 - 7.30 P.M.

Speakers:
1. Mrs Nomzamo Winnie Mandela
2. Rev. Beyers Naude
3. Mr H. B. Ngcokazi
   (CHAIRMAN DEMOCRATIC PARTY OF THE TRANSKEI)
4. Rev. Alan Hendrickse
   (CHAIRMAN LABOUR PARTY OF SOUTH AFRICA)

Congress Business Session
Gandhi Library - Queen St., Dbn.

Sat. 27th Mar. 1976 1-30 p.m.

THE PUBLIC IS INVITED
TO ATTEND

Join congress and fight for
Freedom, Equality & Democracy

R. RAMESAR - General Secretary

Art Printing Press · 28 Fountain Lane, Durban · Phone 316056

Figure 3.3: Pamphlet advertising the NIC conference, 1976. (Courtesy of Gandhi-Luthuli Documentation Centre)

According to one newspaper account, M.J. Naidoo 'subtly made all the arguments in favour of joining the SAIC, without actually stating his own position'.[39] Naidoo had the uncanny ability to provoke debate while acutely and honestly raising issues that struck at the core of the NIC's dilemmas. Fatima Meer again argued strongly against participation, and once more the house voted to boycott the SAIC by a slim majority. This led one journalist to suggest that the NIC knew what it did not want to do, but not what it wanted to do.[40]

After the 1976 conference, former NIC president Monty Naicker was approached to lend support for an anti-SAIC campaign. Although retired from active politics, Naicker agreed, as he was passionately opposed to participation. After keeping the debate open for several years, M.J. Naidoo appeared to have become convinced of non-participation. He described the SAIC to reporters as a 'farce', and warned that the government was using Indians and coloureds as a first line of defence against the African majority.[41] It is probably not coincidental that this volte-face came in the wake of the 1976 Soweto uprising and the resurgence of extra-parliamentary resistance across the country. Non-collaboration with government institutions had become a rallying cry.

The NIC set up the Anti-SAIC Committee (ASC) in November 1977, with Monty Naicker as chairman, Dr Kesaveloo Goonam as treasurer, M.J. Naidoo as vice-president and A.H. Randeree as secretary. In Dr Goonam's view, Indians were being asked to elect representatives to the SAIC whose 'function will be to serve the Nationalist Government as an intelligence agency into the Indian people and to stuff up their mouths with a dummy ... The generality of Indians see it as nothing, and in reject-ing it, they reject "nothing".'[42] The first ASC meeting was held in Durban on 26 November 1977. Monty Naicker, Dr Goonam, Jerry Coovadia, Rabi Bugwandeen and Y. Variawa, chairman of the Transvaal Action Committee, shared the platform. Naicker urged Indians 'not to register as a voter for the dummy Indian Council elections'.[43] But just as Naicker's comeback was gathering momentum, he took ill and died on 12 January 1978.

The issue of participating in the SAIC was not yet dead. A faction (unnamed) in favour of participation prepared two memorandums. M.J. Naidoo, as NIC vice-president, prepared counter-arguments. Responding to Kathrada's argument, quoted earlier, that the Bolsheviks

Figure 3.4: Monty Naicker (*seated*) and Kesaveloo Goonam (*centre*), who were both educated at Edinburgh in the 1930s and led the NIC in the 1940s, were recruited by the NIC to spearhead the anti-SAIC campaign. (Courtesy of African News Agency)

had participated in the Russian Duma when the tsar still held power, and to the fact that the ANC had been involved in the Native Representative Council (NRC), Naidoo asserted that one could not always draw conclusions from 'historical decisions which in their context and in their time might well have been correct'.[44] He warned that there was also the relationship with Africans to consider:

> If we should capitulate now, we cannot hope to retain their [African] sympathy nor can we escape the suspicion that we have joined the White laager out of fear of the African 'hordes' and in opposition to African aspirations for the doubtful privilege of sitting in an Indian 'Parliament'. The feeling could gain currency that the present struggle between the racist oppressor and the Black oppressed majority will be turned into one between the laager (consisting of White,

Indian and Coloured) and the African oppressed. It would also provide ready ammunition for the racially inclined towards inciting, aiding and abetting Indo-African hostility as in 1949. In such a situation we would be the arbiters of our own misfortune. Never in the history of any oppressed people have they courted mass suicide in such naked fashion. No reasonable man will come to any other conclusion, taking into account that the Indian is presently receiving navy training and is promised army and air force training, than that he walked voluntarily into the White man's racist laager.[45]

It was a powerful warning of the resulting dangers if the NP succeeded in its attempt to cut Indians and coloureds off from Africans by giving them a junior role in the running of the apartheid machine. For Naidoo, the option of participation was now closed.

As the 1970s came to an end, organisations linked to the BCM had been banned, many young activists had fled the country, and the Nationalists appeared to have regained a semblance of control after the rebellions sparked by the 1976 Soweto uprising. Resistance was stymied but not crushed. Soon forces would regroup, and in 1980 students would once more take to the streets. At the same time the question of participation refused to leave the stage.

We will return to the thread of tactics and strategy within the broad anti-apartheid forces as they confronted government attempts to co-opt and divide. But first we explore the growth of civics which sought to address the everyday issues confronting black South Africans in urban areas.

4 | Changing Geographies and New Terrains of Struggle

Important changes in terms of class and geographical location took place within the Indian community in Durban in the 1970s. Increased access to secondary and tertiary education facilitated the emergence of a significant middle class as the UDW churned out graduates in accountancy, engineering, pharmacy, teaching and law. Many of the new professionals came from the working class and were often the very first in their family to go to university.

The city's map was also redrawn, as bulldozers uprooted homes and dumped Indians on the outer edges of the city. The NIC's political base in its old stamping grounds of the Durban CBD, Clairwood and Cato Manor was increasingly eroded as the working and lower-middle classes took up residence in Chatsworth and Phoenix, while the middle and upper classes populated areas as far afield as Reservoir Hills and Isipingo Beach. Faced with these dramatic changes in places of residence, younger members of the NIC, in seeking to move beyond workshops and peace camps, turned their focus to these new areas to the north and south of the city. In these areas thousands of people were adjusting to new conditions and struggling to rebuild their cultural and sporting organisations.

It was the long trek to work, which dominated the lives of newly minted Chatsworthians, that presented the NIC with an initial entry point.

Chatsworth bus ban of 1972

Many of the new residents of Chatsworth, 25 kilometres south of Durban, were forcibly relocated from areas close to the city. Overnight they faced the daily prospect of travelling long distances to their places of work. Chatsworth had just one arterial road, private cars were a luxury and single-lane roads were congested. For commuters to the CBD, transport times and costs doubled.

Indian bus owners moved their operations into Chatsworth as Group Areas enforcement began to erode the old Indian areas. However, in a typical apartheid-era diktat, in 1972 the Durban City Council decided to ban buses from operating between Durban and Chatsworth. The aim was to force residents to use the newly developed rail system, which they had resisted because it was difficult to access and more expensive.

Various Indian political organisations took up the issue. A.M. Rajab, executive chairman of the SAIC, described the ban as 'shocking, most unreasonable and outrageous', and promised to take up the issue with the minister of Indian affairs, Senator Owen Horwood.[1] Protests that were to continue for nearly two years commenced in August 1972, attracting support from bus workers and owners, civic and political bodies, and residents.

On 14 September 1972, the LAC appointed a six-person committee to seek temporary certificates for bus operators so that they could beat the end-of-September deadline, when bus licences were to expire. The committee resolved to join forces with the SAIC and seek an urgent interview with the minister of Indian affairs to address the crisis.[2]

The recently revived NIC also expressed its opposition to the ban. George Sewpersadh, NIC president, described the bus ban as 'inhumane and cruel'. It confirmed that 'to the whites of this country, the needs, feelings and desires of the Black people are of no consequence whatsoever'. He stated that 'the time has come for Indians of all classes and from every part of the country to unite and oppose every assault on our dignity'.[3]

Bus owners organised a mass protest on 22 September 1972. Illustrating the continued importance of the clothing and textile industries as a source of employment for Indians, especially for women, Harriet Bolton, secretary of the Garment Workers' Union, was among the speakers.[4] The protest meeting attracted a large crowd, with Sewpersadh giddily estimating that there were over 10 000 people present.[5]

After a rowdy start, NIC member D.K. Singh was elected chairman of the meeting. Jerry Coovadia, NIC executive member, reminded the crowd that the people of Alexandra in Johannesburg, Gelvandale in Port

Elizabeth, and Hammarsdale outside Durban had walked to work for the sake of principle, and that the people of Chatsworth could do likewise.[6]

These leading voices of the NIC – Singh an attorney and Coovadia a medical doctor – were incongruent with the mainly working-class people who relied on buses to get to work. As noted by Yunus Carrim, an NIC official in the 1980s and a minister in the post-apartheid ANC government, these professionals from central Durban were no longer 'rooted in a base because of Group Areas relocation. You can talk about the business community and the professional community in the city centre, but the real strength now lay in Phoenix and Chatsworth.'[7]

Moderate leaders at the meeting were criticised. J.N. Reddy, who lived in Chatsworth, was booed off the stage because he was an SAIC member. One Chatsworth resident, E. Christopher, wrote to the Natal-based *Post* newspaper to say that the crowd's reaction to Reddy was in 'no uncertain terms' an outright rejection of him as a civic leader. He also warned LAC members that if they did not act in accordance with the wishes of the people, they would not be re-elected.[8] While warning LAC members not to betray the people, Christopher's intervention also hinted at supporting those who were closely aligned with the wishes of the people. Although suspicions abounded, there was no outright rejection of the LAC and SAIC. Rather, the situation reflected the NIC's ongoing dilemma of participation versus boycott through the 1970s.

The NIC, determined not to be muscled out by supporters of the SAIC, arranged a mass meeting on 22 October 1972, the day before the issue was to be heard by the National Transport Commission. R. Ramesar, NIC secretary, told reporters that the NIC viewed the ban on Chatsworth buses with 'grave concern' and that 'other forms of action' would be taken if the ban was not lifted.[9] The SAIC hit back. When addressing the town council on 24 October in the presence of bus owners, A.M. Rajab warned that 'certain organisations' were already 'fishing in the troubled waters of the Chatsworth bus dispute' and trying to incite the people to take 'irresponsible action'. While not mentioning the NIC by name, he accused it of using slogans such as 'Boycott trains' and 'Down with the SAIC'. Rajab pleaded with the authorities to allow the buses to continue operating or else risk public opinion turning against the SAIC.[10] If the NIC faced the paradox of carrying an ethnic tag while pronouncing that it

NATAL INDIAN CONGRESS

A PUBLIC MEETING

of THE RESIDENTS of UNIT 9

to be held at

The Big Tent

ADJOINING ROAD 911 - HOUSE 24

on

Saturday, 16th December, 1972

AT 3.00 P.M.

To Form the Moorton Branch of the Natal Indian Congress

Prominent Speakers from Head Quarters
will address the meeting

Join Congress — The Voice of the People

R. RAMESAR (Provincial Organiser)

Printed by GANASEN PRESS, 19a Short Street, Durban.

Figure 4.1: Pamphlet advertising meeting to form an NIC branch in Chatsworth, 1972. (Courtesy of Gandhi-Luthuli Documentation Centre)

was committed to non-racialism, the SAIC faced the conundrum that it could knock on the door of the Nationalist government, but the knock fell mostly on deaf ears.

Following another mass meeting in Chatsworth in mid-October, bus owners organised a petition bearing the names of 70 000 Chatsworth residents in support of the bus service. The petition was handed to J. Driessen, chairman of the National Transport Commission, at a hearing on 23 October.[11] In February 1973 the NIC distributed 10 000 handbills which referred to the ban as an 'inhuman act' and urged Chatsworth residents to walk to work rather than take the train.[12] While the protests were ongoing, bus owners took the matter to court. They were vindicated when, in September 1973, Justice Henning of the Natal Supreme Court upheld their appeal to be allowed to continue operating.[13]

Tin Town, 1976

As the NIC began to find its way around the changed socio-spatial structure of the city, UDW-educated activists began to make their presence felt beyond their alma mater. These activists included Pravin Gordhan, Yunus Mohamed and Yousuf Vawda.

The experience of law student Yousuf Vawda was typical of young activists of this period. Vawda found the UDW climate 'very repressive' because most of the 'lecturers were handpicked by the Broederbond', but it was also 'a melting point for ideas'. Students protested against dress codes, rules about hairstyle and other restrictions that made the university as 'rigid as the school system'. Vawda was inspired by Steve Biko and Rick Turner, but it was Zak Yacoob, Pravin Gordhan, Yunus Mohamed and others who 'provided the campus leadership in that period'. It was at university that politics 'came alive in a focused way' for Vawda, who had initially been attracted to BC because it was 'strident and forthright'. He came to feel that '[BC] didn't really look at issues of class. It tended to put everybody in racial categories and one needed to go beyond that.'[14]

It appears ironical that student activists argued that BC was restrictive, in both its lack of emphasis on class and its exclusion of whites, while they became increasingly involved in a racially exclusive organisation that blurred class divisions. It would be easy to write this off as hypocrisy.

Figure 4.2: Advocate Zak Yacoob (*centre*), pictured here with lawyers and activists Phyllis Naidoo and Ebrahim Goga, was one of the younger, university-educated professionals who joined the NIC in the 1970s. (Courtesy of African News Agency)

But in the pages ahead we unpack the very real challenge of mobilising people on the day-to-day issues that affected them, in the context of the racially compartmentalised environments in which they lived.

Vawda read the Freedom Charter for the first time at university, and came to realise through his discussions with other activists that the problems at the university were 'linked to something bigger. There was a repressive government which made it possible for repression to continue at campus level, and if you really wanted significant change in your life as a student, you needed to look beyond the campus.' The 1973 workers' strikes in Durban and the burgeoning trade union movement drew many students into community and worker organisations. Under the auspices of the South African Council of Higher Education (SACHED), Vawda taught English to adult workers at the Roman Catholic Emmanuel Cathedral in Cathedral Road, and volunteered to provide tuition for high school pupils in the predominantly coloured area of Sydenham.[15]

The floods of 1976 provided activists with an opportunity to get involved in community issues. As the Group Areas Act denied Indians living spaces close to the city centre, many took refuge in shack settlements like Tin Town in Springfield, where 781 families were living in 482 shacks. The area was flooded in March 1976, and the Durban City Council established a Flood Relief Fund. The fund was managed by a committee whose members included the NIC-aligned Fatima Meer and D.K. Singh, as well as system politicians Amichand Rajbansi and J.N. Reddy. The disaster provided a rare moment when those on opposing sides of the political spectrum worked together.[16]

Tin Town shack dwellers could not return to their homes, and the Durban City Council agreed as a priority to build sub-economic houses for them in the new Phoenix township north of Durban. While this was playing out, the Tin Town residents were housed at the Asherville Sports

Figure 4.3: The flood-prone Tin Town, which started as a temporary shelter in 1971, persisted until 1976. (Courtesy of Gandhi-Luthuli Documentation Centre)

Ground. Students at UDW and the Springfield College of Education helped to erect 'Tent Town', raise funds, organise kindergarten classes, distribute clothing and supervise meals.[17]

Paul David recounted that the floods in Tin Town provided an important lesson to activists:

> There were a lot of debates about organisation. We knew that the motive force for change was the people in action, but we didn't know how best to organise. Pravin and [Yunus Mohamed's] experience in the Springfield flood disaster taught us that by working around issues that affected people in their daily lives – you know, they don't relate to a political argument about change, but they will support you if they trust you. At that time, literature from the Philippines, Maglaya's book,[18] was really a manual for activists and we read that. It was introduced to me as the theory of what we are doing. We had it photocopied, as the book was banned. We met and talked and we said, isn't this the way forward? Eventually we will call upon people to resist the government and the only way to convince them that what we're doing is right is if they trust us, and they'll trust us if we show that what we're doing is not for us, not for our ego, not for our profile, but for them.[19]

Figure 4.4: Removal of the last tent at Tin Town. Most residents were moved to the new township of Phoenix. (Courtesy of Gandhi-Luthuli Documentation Centre)

According to Coovadia, Pravin Gordhan was pivotal in NIC strategising in this period:

> [Gordhan] was absolutely critical. He taught us to think in broad, strategic terms. Fundamental to the experiences he shared with us was community organisation, which has lasted up to today. It applies in medicine, in all these primary health-care facilities, all depend on community organisation. To me, it became a model for progressive medicine. Nobody else expressed that idea as vividly as he did. He convinced most of us that that was the way to go because, remember, we were mostly middle-class intellectuals, lawyers and doctors, but he was, despite his pharmacy training, really rooted in the struggle on the ground ... based on the day-to-day problems of communities who were poor and living in those new Indian townships.[20]

Everyday issues of survival and adjustment to new conditions far outside the city centre occupied the life of working- and lower-middle-class Indians. Younger members of the NIC cottoned on to this and devised ways to address issues of rents and services as building blocks for a political movement. In this entry into the community, they involved themselves initially as individuals rather than as members of the NIC.

Gordhan was born in Durban in 1949. He matriculated at Sastri College, completed a degree in pharmacy at UDW in 1973, and found work at a state hospital, King Edward VIII, in Sydney Road. He was drawn to activism during his university years, but the challenge for him was to do political work without being shut down by the state:

> From '74 to '81 [my activism] ranged from joining the NIC as an executive member, learning the limits of open legal work yet keeping the Congress flag alive ... Around '75/76 a group of us became involved in community organising. In that part of the world began the concept of house meetings, street-level organising and community-based struggles, and we experimented with what it meant to work on what we called communistic issues but with a political flavour, having on the right hand the political book and on the left hand the community book, sometimes keeping them separate, sometimes

cautiously linking them so that the police wouldn't very quickly identify the political nature of community mobilising and endanger it in that way.[21]

In another interview, Gordhan recounted that he and other activists were initially forced to work in secrecy:

> Civic mobilising happened at a time when many of us were on the NIC executive, but the people that we worked with on the ground didn't know that. Sometimes we had to ensure that the NIC executive didn't know what was going on on the other side, because you didn't want to implicate community-based people and community-based leadership in political activities.[22]

This need for secrecy probably saved Gordhan and his colleagues from terms of detention and may have laid the foundations for the underground work that lay ahead. However, it also fostered suspicion among some long-standing members of the NIC. They regarded the tight groupings and secrecy as a way to exercise control within the NIC through undemocratic practices.

Yunus Mohamed, a contemporary of Gordhan and Vawda at UDW who trained as a lawyer, argued on the other hand that their community activism

> gave a platform to the NIC executive fellows. A number of them, like M.J. Naidoo and so on, actually had the ability to come in and address people at those meetings. They were now interacting with working-class, poorer people within the community and not simply getting a fresh statement issued on those kind of issues.[23]

This perspective at once acknowledged the leadership of long-established NIC members such as M.J. Naidoo while also providing a critique: unlike 'us', they were not organising working-class people but issuing statements. Evidence of a generational divide surfaced as this group of activists used their energy to ignite community politics around bread-and-butter issues. It would lead to accusations that these activists were eschewing accountability to the NIC leadership and acting in concert to support some and marginalise others in the NIC.

The birth of civics

The birth of civic movements in Indian townships was part of a national phenomenon. As Daryl Glaser points out:

> Civics began their life in the late 1970s as local associations campaigning for improved living conditions in black townships and opposing municipal authorities foisted on townships by the white minority state. From the outset they have organised residents around both local material issues and broader political goals ... Civic membership has historically tended to be an informal affair, with civic leaders communicating to their rank-and-file through open general meetings.[24]

Phoenix Working Committee

Activists initially focused on housing in Phoenix because the new township, as described by Vawda, consisted of 'blockhouses which were hardly comfortable or even good from a health standard, and it became important to focus on how to go about getting the best possible housing that we could get under the circumstances'.[25] These activists had initially formed a committee to help Tin Town residents 'negotiate a better deal and a good transition from the old to the new'. They now joined up with similar committees formed by residents who had arrived in Phoenix from various parts of Durban. This grouping coalesced into the Phoenix Working Committee (PWC).

Conditions were challenging for the first residents of Phoenix. For example, Dhaya Rambaran, former chairperson of the PWC, recounted in a 2003 brochure commemorating the 25th anniversary of the founding of the organisation:

> When my family and I arrived into the Westham area of Phoenix, there were very few families in the area, there were gravel roads, no

Figure 4.5: Led by Mrs J. Maharaj (*centre*), members of the Phoenix Working Committee and the Phoenix Rent Action Committee march in protest against rental increases, January 1981. (Courtesy of African News Agency)

street lighting; in short, the entire place that we were to call our home was under-developed. At night we often had to grope our way home; going to work in the morning, especially if it rained, meant that we went to work with double soles. Transport was worse, buses had to drop passengers off in Redfern, and residents from Westham did the long trek every morning and evening to and from Redfern and Westham. Life was difficult.[26]

One newspaper reported that 'at least ten people from each area are put on the eviction list every week ... If there is a slight increase in wages (by 5 percent) the rent goes up by 20 percent.'[27] Residents were also subject to water and electricity disconnections because of their inability to pay. A 1982 survey revealed that around half of the residents of the township were living below the poverty line.[28]

Most of the units into which Phoenix was divided formed residents' associations, and in January 1978 association representatives formed the PWC with Roy Sukuram as chairperson. PWC official Sharm Maharaj recounted the role of NIC members from around 1978:

I heard the first time about some people who were having meetings about facilities in Phoenix. I said I rather go and see what is it they are offering and when we went there, I was just so interested about the kind of language that was spoken, the kind of demands which were being made. I saw a thousand people saying, 'Yes, I also want that.' It was George Sewpersadh, it was Pravin Gordhan, it was Yousuf Vawda, those sorts of people. They were on the stage and said a whole lot of slogans, but the kind of things they told us were not meant to incite us, they were connecting with us.[29]

Others involved in the PWC, however, believe that the role of Phoenix residents in forming the committee has been underplayed. According to Sukuram, its first chairman, 'if you look at the website [of the PWC], you will find that the PWC was literally started, run, taught, brained by middle-class people, you know, the Vawdas, the Gordhans, the Coovadias, the Patels ... but that was not so.'[30] Sukuram was born in Cato Manor. His father worked in the Indian Market in Warwick Avenue, where Sukuram helped out on weekends. He attended Sastri College and the Springfield College of Education. He became a member of the Student Representative Council (SRC) and was attracted to the BCM, but was expelled for his political activism. Sukuram's family were among the earliest residents of Phoenix. He described the PWC as an organic movement growing out of Phoenix:

The NIC was a middle-class organisation with essentially vested interests in the middle class. From the time of Gandhi and even latter-day NIC, I think the working class is more an arrow in the bow ... a tool to be used for vested self-interest. If I can recall the words I said to one of them, 'We are not some sick pariahs who are here looking for your leadership or handouts. We are more than capable of leading ourselves.'[31]

While there are differing opinions about the relative influence of an organic township leadership or outside NIC members, it is agreed that the PWC became a major player in mobilising Phoenix residents on issues central to their daily lives.

Aside from day-to-day struggles over rent and service delivery, the key issue facing the township was the Durban City Council's intention to grant autonomy to Phoenix in 1977/78. Chatsworth had been offered autonomy in 1976, but it was rejected.[32] As Sukuram recounted, legislation had been

> promulgated for the excision of Phoenix from the City of Durban. They wanted Phoenix to become a town on its own. We played a major role in galvanising the community against that. The NIC, NGOs, church groups, other communities really bloomed into an incredible mass movement. To cut a long story short, the city council had to reverse the decision at the end of the day. That was changing history. It would have become like Isipingo or Verulam. That was a major, major, major victory.[33]

Ela Gandhi asserted that the quick involvement of activists was crucial, as autonomy would have had negative consequences for the residents of Phoenix:

> The activists quickly prepared a newsletter telling people the drawbacks of accepting autonomy. The people then mounted a campaign against autonomy ... This protest happened because the community was educated about what would happen if they accepted autonomy. If you have autonomy in Phoenix you have to buy bulk electricity from Durban. When you do this, the price of electricity is going to be higher than in Durban ... In addition, this was another racially based government body and it would alienate the various race groups if such options were accepted.[34]

Sukuram believes that the community leaders and residents of Phoenix were radicalised by the experience, and won victories in terms of amenities and making the township a 'no-go' area for those in government structures. This was probably true when the SAIC elections took place in 1981, but as the decade wore on, support for those in government structures grew.

Chatsworth Housing Action Committee

In Chatsworth, the likes of Roy Padayachie, Ray 'Shoots' Naidoo, Devan Pillay, Charm Govender, Hashiem Bham and Maggie Govender began to emerge as influential local organisers from the late 1970s. They were involved in residents' associations, youth organisations and trade unions, and later in the NIC and the underground structures of the ANC. One of the key NIC figures in Chatsworth was Radhakrishna 'Roy' Padayachie, who was the minister of public service and administration at the time of his death in 2012. Padayachie went to school in Chatsworth, and completed a BSc degree at UDW and an MSc at the University of London. He joined the NIC in the late 1970s and became an executive member. With NIC activists Patsy Pillay and Charm Govender, he started the Chatsworth Early Learning Centre, and became a highly influential leader in the civics movement.

According to Charm Govender, young activists engaged in 'pamphlet distribution, spraying graffiti, painting banners and calling meetings'. They worked within the NIC, 'but the NIC then did not have a formal system of membership because of the repressive conditions, so we used to create ad hoc organisations as we went along'.[35] Education, poor-quality housing, evictions due to the inability of residents to pay rents, and workers' rights were key issues around which people were organised. Residents formed housing associations to take up their struggles in most units of Chatsworth: Montford, Bayview, Mobeni, Silverglen, Kharwastan, Umhlatuzana, Moorton, Crossmoor, Westcliff and Croftdene.

Following a hiatus of several years after the bus-ban mobilisation, the NIC became active in the township again from about 1979. In November of that year, D.K. Singh addressed a meeting of the Croftdene Ratepayers' Association, and was mandated by the thousand people who attended to take up the high price of sub-economic housing with the minister of community development.[36] Some of the residents' associations came together to coordinate their struggles through the Chatsworth Housing Action Committee (CHAC), formed to oppose a 15 per cent rental increase which was to take effect in January 1980. 'Outside' members of CHAC included George Sewpersadh and Farouk Meer of the NIC, and D.K. Singh, Yunus Suliman and Krish Govender, subsequently of the National Association of Democratic Lawyers. Joseph Hoover, CHAC chairman, noted that the Durban City Council stood to make a profit of R16 million from housing sales. He considered it deplorable that this profit was to be ploughed into the coffers of the National Housing Fund, the body responsible for building houses in townships: 'There is no logic in taking from the poor to give to the poor. It is the duty of the state to provide housing to the poor.'[37]

Engagement with the people of Chatsworth on central community issues had significant political outcomes. Charm Govender noted that the formation of CHAC 'helped us to win inroads into civic organisations that were democratic but not very active. So, we got them to become active within their respective communities.'[38] According to Maggie Govender, CHAC 'took up a whole range of community issues, ranging from the sale of houses, rent struggles, discriminatory rates'. CHAC also had a political element to it, in that its slogan was '"Houses, Security and Comfort" ... straight out of the Freedom Charter'. She recounted that the struggles of communities in Chatsworth's sub-economic areas led to 'an increase in their political understanding of what was going on ... Ordinary women who were at home would get onto a public platform and talk, and they commanded tremendous support. It was a good period to build grass-roots leadership.'[39]

Durban Housing Action Committee

The founding of civics spurred mobilisation around everyday issues, but these structures remained rooted within their own localities and fought the Durban City Council individually. Although there was cooperation between the various civics and their leaders, there was no broad integrative leadership or organisation within which they could unite. Cognisant of the situation, the NIC convened a meeting on 29 March 1980 at the Kajee Hall in Durban to discuss rent increases and high rates. This resulted in 30 housing committees – including those from Phoenix, Newlands East, Merebank, Chatsworth, Cato Manor, Asherville and Sydenham Heights – joining forces to form the Durban Housing Action Committee (DHAC). D.K. Singh was elected chairman, with Virgil Bonhomme and Pravin Gordhan as joint secretaries. By April 1980 organisations throughout the wider Durban region, including Merebank Ratepayers' Association, Tongaat Civic Association, Greenwood Park Ratepayers' Association and the PWC, along with UDW students, had pledged their support for the DHAC.[40]

In the face of a 15 per cent increase in rents, the DHAC succeeded in forcing the City Council to issue a moratorium on rental increases from

May 1980 to February 1981; grant land subsidies in Newlands East; and agree to investigate the entire housing scheme.[41] This was portrayed as a great victory by civics in widely distributed pamphlets. Rent boycotts, protest marches and mass meetings were hallmarks of the DHAC's opposition to the Durban City Council and LACs, as they drew thousands to their meetings. The DHAC's close ties with the NIC linked the housing struggles with the broader anti-apartheid struggle. In Pietermaritzburg, activists such as Chota Motala, A.S. Chetty, M.D. Moodley and Vasu Chetty organised the Pietermaritzburg Combined Residents and Ratepayers' Association, which took up similar issues in the capital. One of the features of these community struggles was that women were actively involved and often led public marches. They formed the Durban Women's Committee and led a march to City Hall on 10 December 1980.[42]

Indian and coloured communities tried to bridge racial divides as they organised against apartheid's socio-economic policies. According to Gordhan, these activities were important in building non-racialism:

> Pre-1980, the relationship between the Coloured and Indian communities was nil, politically speaking. The City Council increased rents in the townships and the NIC took the lead and called community organisations, and the DHAC was launched. Now, it is through ... struggling together on community issues that at one level an identification developed between Indian and Coloured people. In the day-to-day responses, Newlands East, a Coloured area, would now see Phoenix as allies in battles with the City Council or vice versa.[43]

Khetso Gordhan, a student activist from 1980, recounted the difficulty of cross-race organising:

> In places like KwaMashu, it was only African people, only African activists ... In Indian areas, it would have been Indian activists, or Coloured activists in Newlands East. Newlands East activists didn't know KwaMashu activists who were right next door. In the Coloured areas, we formed something called the United Committee of Concern, and that was a very conscious decision [after] a very long, bitter debate about whether we needed a Coloured-specific organisation

that represents Coloured political aspirations in Durban. And the NIC had its own tradition of organising in Indian areas, where the civics were a lot more established than in the African areas.[44]

Building links with African communities proved difficult. The Inkatha Freedom Party had a network of patronage and influence that made joint organising difficult. There were language barriers and often different priorities as much as there was suspicion and fear. Pravin Gordhan explained:

> When we have mass rallies or mass events people from all communities come together. But it is a limited process ... The factory floor is certainly an easier site of cooperation and joint action than the communities. We have to cross Group Areas barriers in order to actually get people to combine with each other. Also, there are very different realities that people have to work with. The authorities that levy rentals in an African township are very different to an authority that levies rentals in an Indian and Coloured township and that makes joint action very difficult. Whereas the boss in a factory is a common boss.[45]

And yet, as Gordhan pointed out, even trade union leaders found it difficult to organise Indians and coloureds jointly with African workers in the same unions.

> After many years of effort, some unions have made a breakthrough, but we can by no means say that the majority of the Indian working class in the Durban area is in fact organised into the same unions as the African worker or Coloured workers.[46]

A Joint Rent Action Committee (JORAC) was set up in some African areas, but as Jeremy Seekings has observed:

> The Charterist movement [the ANC, NIC, UDF and all those who subscribed to the Freedom Charter] in Natal had a dual divided character, divided in large part along racial lines. DHAC brought together civic groups in coloured and Indian areas, whilst JORAC linked civic

groups in African areas ... By and large there was a significant gap between the different sides of the Charterist movement.[47]

Activists of the time reflect that the different racial communities were affected by different laws and problems, which posed serious challenges for building interracial unity. This did not mean, however, that networks were not developing underground.

The revived NIC was 'not a mass-based organisation in the 1970s', as Jerry Coovadia emphasised in a 1988 interview. It consisted of leaders and a small number of activists. The NIC's annual meetings of delegates drew around 80–90 members and public meetings attracted a few hundred people, except when there was a major issue such as the death of activist Ahmed Timol. Notwithstanding these shortcomings, involvement in issues of concern to the working classes in the townships enabled the NIC to draw on broader layers of support.[48]

In listening carefully to the voices of people like Pravin Gordhan, one gets the sense that the turn to the masses was also predicated on a Leninist form of organising: a vanguard with a heightened political consciousness that would ensure that struggles were, in Lenin's words, 'politically directed'. Who got selected to do the directing and how this related to the workings of the NIC – in other words, who was in and who was out – was an issue that would be raised within the NIC and later the Mass Democratic Movement (MDM) of the 1980s.

5 | Class(rooms) of Dissent: Education Boycotts and Democratic Trade Unions, 1976–1985

The decade from the mid-1970s to the mid-1980s was a crucial period for the NIC in the broader struggle against apartheid. The impetus from students and workers would see the organisation tap into networks that consolidated into what would become known as the Mass Democratic Movement (MDM), and an anti-apartheid struggle that was rapidly becoming a global phenomenon.

On 16 June 1976 student protests broke out in Soweto and then spread rapidly across the country. Since the repression of the liberation movements in the early 1960s, the Soweto uprising was the most sustained confrontation with the apartheid state. As Fatima Meer wrote at the time:

> Soweto's children strained against their educational system, police reaction shocked the world. Soweto burnt. A spate of bannings and detentions muzzled local black protests – and South Africa's Western Allies reeled in embarrassment and shock at Nationalist excesses. Something had to be done.[1]

Mewa Ramgobin later reflected that '1976 was the catalytic point in lots of people's lives. There is an affirmation in us that even though we were banned at that stage, that you cannot keep a people down.'[2]

Students at UDW sprang into action in solidarity. On 19 August, Yunus Carrim and fellow student leaders Lloyd Padayachee and Rashid Meer (son of anti-apartheid activists Fatima and I.C. Meer) were detained without trial for organising demonstrations against the killing of students in Soweto. The NIC formed a parents' committee to support the students, which included Fatima Meer (until her arrest), Hassan Mall and Chota Motala.[3]

State repression

The Soweto revolt led to a brutal crackdown in which the state resorted to detention without trial on a massive scale. Fatima Meer was arrested at the end of August 1976, days after the arrest of her son Rashid. She had formed the Institute for Black Research (IBR), which cut across political divides, especially between the BCM and the Charterists. She worked closely with the South African Students Organisation (SASO), as well as with Winnie Mandela, with whom she had formed the Black Women's Federation. She was held in detention at the Johannesburg Fort Prison until December 1976, and chronicled her 113 days in incarceration in her book *Prison Diary*.[4] The artworks she produced in prison are now housed at the Constitutional Hill heritage site (formerly the Old Fort Prison Complex). Winnie Mandela was a fellow inmate.

Many prisoners died in detention during this period. Among them was Dr Hoosen Mia Haffajee of Pietermaritzburg, an intern at King George V Hospital in Durban. He was arrested under the Terrorism Act on 2 August 1977 and taken to the Brighton Beach Police Station in south Durban. There he was interrogated, and placed in a police cell shortly after midnight. He was found dead the following morning. An inquest into Haffajee's death in March 1978, presided over by magistrate T.L. Blunden, produced the usual apartheid-era cover-up. Despite 62 injuries (to the skull, ribs and loins) found on Haffajee's body, all caused by the application of 'blunt force', state pathologist Professor I. Gordon concluded that death was caused by hanging, and that the injuries were a result of Haffajee's 'resistance' to arrest. The NIC's Dr Chota Motala, Dr W. Cooper and Ismail Mahomed represented the Haffajee family and challenged the findings, but to no avail. An angry Dr Motala recorded in his notebook: 'We provided detailed evidence to the inquest that there were numerous injuries on Dr Haffajee's body which remained unexplained. Needless to say, as with the [Steve] Biko hearing, no one was found to blame by the inquest.'[5]

Steve Biko was subjected to sustained violence after his arrest in Port Elizabeth on 19 August 1977. He died after Drs Ivor Lang and Benjamin Tucker authorised his transfer to Pretoria despite his extensive injuries. Biko was transported semi-comatose, naked and handcuffed on the floor of a motor vehicle, and died on 12 September 1977. Magistrate Marthinus Prins ruled in early December 1977 that no one was criminally responsible for Biko's death. The white-controlled South African Medical and Dental Council (SAMDC), the national regulatory body of doctors and dentists, resolved not to take action against the doctors for what was a clear case of negligence. This decision was supported by the Medical Association of South Africa (MASA), which cleared the doctors of negligence in 1980.

SAMDC and MASA's collusion with the apartheid regime angered black doctors, and 52 health-care professionals established the National Medical and Dental Association (NAMDA) on 5 December 1982. One of the founding members was the NIC's Jerry Coovadia, a professor at the University of Natal Medical School. According to Coovadia, NAMDA 'opposed apartheid medicine in all its ugly forms, from the killing of Biko to the type of health services to the plans for the future health service'. The doctors who had treated Biko were eventually brought to book as a result of the perseverance of Professor Philip Tobias of Wits University, Yusuf Variawa of the Transvaal Indian Congress and several other doctors, who obtained a Pretoria Supreme Court ruling to force the SAMDC to reopen the case in 1983. At a hearing in May 1985, eight years after Biko's death, the SAMDC found Lang and Tucker guilty of improper conduct. Tucker was struck off the roll (but was later reinstated); Lang was suspended for three months.[6]

The state's brutal repression in response to the Soweto uprising suppressed resistance in the short term although protests continued intermittently. Large numbers of pupils were expelled or dropped out of school, while others fled across South Africa's borders and joined the liberation movement in exile. Many believed that the collapse of the apartheid regime was imminent and embraced the slogan 'Liberation before Education'. The schooling of a generation of students was curtailed or severely disrupted. These boycotts set the tone for the next decade, in which protests spread to all sectors of society.

Mewa Ramgobin was of the view that this exodus of young people into exile was critical in bolstering support for the ANC:

> Black Consciousness had fulfilled its short-term goals. I think it would be not unkind to maintain that the BC movement had neither a long-term objective nor a strategic approach [to achieve that] ... Having set an objective, having defined a strategic approach, it must logically lead to mobilisation and for that mobilisation to be channelled into some kind of an organisation. All of these components for political work, the BC Movement, at that historical moment, lacked. And the available channels in terms of the accumulated experience historically were offered abroad by the ANC. And I think it would be a fair historical assessment to also say that it precipitated the creation of internal cells of the ANC, which could coordinate and correlate activities from abroad.[7]

Student protests, 1980

The year 1980 was to prove decisive for the NIC. In April, student protest at textbook shortages started in the Western Cape. It soon spiralled into anger at the huge disparities between black and white education, including the poor quality of teachers, the high cost of books and uniforms, and the shocking state of school buildings, ranging from run-down to dilapidated. Protests spread nationwide, involving thousands of students at schools and universities, including Indian students in Natal. The consequent closure of educational institutions drew parents and NIC leaders into the boycott. In turn, students got involved in community struggles.[8]

As protests intensified countrywide, the police responded with brutal force that brought back memories of 1976. Alf Karrim, a UDW student leader in 1980 and a future NIC member, reflected on the significance of these protests:

> The first time I got involved in politics was in 1979 at the University of Durban-Westville. I was studying for a B.A. Law. During that year we formed the SRC. For the previous ten years, there was a resolution which said that we should not form an SRC because it would

give credibility to a racist administration. But it also said that the only form of SRC that could be formed was a totally democratic one controlled by students, and we had taken that resolution forward to the student body. We felt that what was needed on campus was organisation, and we had a very idealistic view – we'll form this SRC, unite the students, and attack the administration.

What really changed for my age group was the 1980 boycott. The very committee that formed the SRC co-ordinated a boycott which ran over three or four months and was the best demonstration of student unity up to this point on that campus. We had clashes with the authority – with the SADF [South African Defence Force] – lots of students being beaten up. It was a very powerful boycott. There were many incidences ... they [army and police] had come in and told students: 'You must leave now – leave the campus because we're going to close it.' We refused to and they beat people up. I remember one of my very close friends lost a baby in that incident, and there were over a hundred people seriously hurt – I mean fairly seriously hurt, *sjambok* [whip] lashes and things like that.

Lots of students were detained as well, and all students in the Indian community, whether at university or at any school, had actually come out on boycott, which was a very powerful demonstration of the kind of attitude of the younger generation of Indian people. We were clearly saying at that point that what we wanted firstly was a democratic society. Secondly, we wanted an educational system that was democratic and included all people under one system, and that that was only possible in a democratic society itself. I think that was our first real political experience that sort of reshaped our consciousness.[9]

Pregs Govender, also a student leader at UDW, recounted that on the day of the SADF attack (June 18), many women students were

singing defiantly in the square between the library and the cafeteria. The security forces announced their countdown before attacking with dogs and batons. We scattered. A few of us ran in the direction of the engineering faculty buildings, picked up some of the sticks and metal pipes lying around, and ran directly at the men in uniform. It was a moment of madness I'll never forget. Our sticks and pipes were useless against guns, batons and dogs, but logic did not stop us. And then something strange happened. The soldiers started backing away, fear in their eyes. Behind us a momentum grew and the victory washed away my fear of men with guns.[10]

Students returning to class on 18 June to re-register after a long closure 'became victims of police violence when they were batoned, man-handled, and tear-gassed, following an altercation outside the administrative block'. The day became known as 'Black Wednesday'.[11]

Medical students at the University of Natal, trainee teachers at the Springfield College of Education and UDW students were supported by the NIC leadership. A Committee of Ten was formed with Zak Yacoob as chair, and included Jerry Coovadia and D.K. Singh. Desperate university authorities forbade non-students from entering the campus from the beginning of May. June saw NIC executive members George Sewpersadh, M.J. Naidoo, Farouk Meer, Rabi Bugwandeen, Paul David, A.S. Chetty and Thumba Pillay detained under the Internal Security Act. They were held at Modderbee Prison in Benoni. Several hundred students were also detained, and many shops in Durban were closed on 16 June, two days before Black Wednesday.

Sewpersadh recounted his prison experience:

[The] first time we were detained was in 1980. We were kept in solitary confinement. Rabi Bugwandeen, Farouk Meer, Thumba Pillay, and I were kept at Umbilo Police Station. It was very unpleasant there because we were four in one cell ... After fourteen days we were taken to Modderbee Prison, that's where we all lived in one group. We were about 80 to 100 people together ... people of all races and we stayed there and it was much easier there because we were able to mix about with people.[12]

It was a shock to the community to see the NIC leadership, most of whom were professionals, detained for what amounted to supporting a student boycott. Such harsh measures indicated the effect that the boycott was having in mobilising people in the Indian community, and the state quickly reached for its weapon of choice: repression. Yet, as detained student leader Yunis Shaik reflected, his detention afforded him time for inter-generational bonding and lessons in politics:

> That was quite a difficult experience because you really didn't know whether you were going to be released, not going to be released, whether you'll sit for the exams, won't sit for the exams. But it was good on the other hand because my political education underwent a qualitative transformation. I had an older generation there who shared with us an entire nation's history of struggle. So I got to locate the struggles we were in at the time to the struggles that went before. I got connected to a whole range of people and families who were involved in the movement at the time. I also got exposed to different political thoughts. It was an oral history that had to be handed down. This intergenerational contact meant that we could start raising community issues and engaging in community struggles, so you could take the struggle out of the university into the communities.[13]

NIC and student leaders were given a raucous welcome by around a thousand supporters waving banners and singing freedom songs when they were released from Modderbee in August, having spent nearly two months in detention.

Many students coming out of the 1980 experience began to actively engage in the DHAC's struggles, working closely with the community and the NIC. A new cadre of student leaders emerged who were to play a crucial role in the NIC and in the broader political environment. Among them were Alf Karrim, Yunis Shaik and Moe Shaik in Durban; and Kumi Naidoo, Lenny Naidoo, Kovin Naidoo, and Maggie Govender and Charm Govender in Chatsworth. Sharm Maharaj recalled the role of UDW students in Phoenix:

> University students from UDW are part of the Phoenix history; they assisted us on the campaign trail and we had marches and motorcades and what have you. The students played a role in shaping the Civic Movement in Phoenix. I can remember a time when the SRC used to

bus in students who were what they call residential students staying in hostels, organise them and brought them to do surveys, to help us campaign, to do all sorts of things, be part of the public in terms of protests and so on.[14]

Charm Govender had enrolled for a BSc degree at UDW in 1980 but dropped out during the boycott. He maintained that the education boycott had a greater impact among Indians than Soweto 1976:

> 1980 was very important. I think if you look at the [political activist] community, there are quite a number of people that came out of that generation. '76 created a wave where people joined MK and so forth, but '76 had not entirely touched the Indian community. There was a symbolic boycott on this campus [UDW], but it wasn't widespread. 1980 ran into the community as well. When the students here were baton charged, it was the parents' committees that rallied behind them and said 'no, what you are doing is in fact wrong'. It was a good learning experience for the Indian community as a whole, but one must also understand that a large part of the student community were from the middle class ... so when these boycotts took place, the people that rallied around were the middle class, and if you look at the leadership of the parent committees, they were professionals. What happened here did not have the reverberations in the Indian working class, except by way of them hearing anecdotal stuff about what happened here.[15]

Like Yunis Shaik, other student leaders recounted how the boycott and imprisonment shaped their understanding of the struggle against apartheid. For Alf Karrim, it became clear that the struggle would be 'a protracted one' requiring 'a lot of discipline', and that Africans had to be at the centre of the drive for liberation. He appreciated that while liberation should benefit the working class most, the anti-apartheid struggle had to take 'a national democratic approach' that included everyone interested in challenging apartheid. Karrim articulated the two-stage revolution: 'Our overall belief was in a non-exploitative, a non-oppressive society, and we believed that that was a long-term process. Our immediate goal was a non-racial democratic government.'[16]

Karrim emphasised the importance of all classes participating in the struggle, while Govender and Shaik pointed to growing class divides in the rubric 'Indian', as professionals carved out a niche in the economy and adopted lifestyles different from those of working-class Indians. The latter were restricted mainly to the clothing, leather and textile industries and in niche areas such as waiting tables at white hotels. However, their positions were under threat from mechanisation, cheaper African labour and imports. Yunis Shaik and a few university-educated activists would try to bring life to unions organising mainly in the clothing sector in the 1980s.

Trade unions

The non-racial union movement, led by the South African Congress of Trade Unions (SACTU), had conducted a serious debate in the 1950s over the relationship between unions and political organisations. As with political organisations in 1960, the union movement itself was 'effectively crushed. Although never officially banned, its leadership was decimated by arrests, detentions, and bannings', while African workers were prevented from organising.[17] The union movement was resuscitated in a serious way with the Durban strikes of 1973. These strikes ushered in a spate of unionism, with 176 unions registered by 1976. As a result, the government appointed a commission under Professor Nic Wiehahn to examine labour problems in South Africa. The 1979 Wiehahn report led to African unions being granted some leeway to organise legally for the first time since the 1950s.[18] Indians and coloured workers were permitted to establish registered unions, as they were governed by the Industrial Conciliation Act of 1956.

Through its concessions to trade union organisation which would bring workers into a legal framework, the state hoped that a labour aristocracy would come into being, mitigating militancy and furthering the divide within the black community. Instead the opposite happened. Hesitantly at first, but with increasing commitment, unions began to engage with issues beyond the factory gates.

Two broad positions characterised the debate among black unions in this period: 'workerist' and 'populist'. Workerists, organised into the

Figure 5.1: The 1973 strikes in Durban sparked a new wave of anti-apartheid struggle that would involve students, workers and the banned underground liberation organisations. (Courtesy of African News Agency)

Federation of South African Trade Unions (FOSATU) in 1979, emphasised shop-floor strength and democratic processes, including mass political action. They were wary of multi-class movements which, in the words of FOSATU's general secretary Joe Forster, would be 'hijacked' by elements in 'the popular movement'.[19] 'Community unions' or populists, on the other hand, scorned this position as 'syndicalist' as it cut workers off from community struggles. They saw their challenge as bringing together the struggles at the factory and in the community.[20]

However, FOSATU was increasingly pushed into responding to events beyond everyday organising on the factory floor:

Unionists were increasingly subject to state repression to which FOSATU and other unions were compelled to respond ... By 1984, when the United Democratic Front was leading the opposition to the parliamentary proposals, FOSATU joined in calling for a boycott of the elections ... The militancy and class rhetoric of many UDF activists in the following years further eroded the unionists' suspicions of the Charterist movement. Although FOSATU ... continued to refuse to affiliate formally with the [UDF], the distinction between union organising and popular opposition became less clear as the stayaways and other forms of opposition expanded.[21]

With the formation of the Congress of South African Trade Unions (COSATU) in December 1985, unions moved almost completely into the Charterist camp, thus increasing support for the ANC and its allies.

According to Yunis Shaik, several young Indian activists became involved in the union movement. In 1984 Shaik joined the Garment Workers' Union, whose membership grew to 100 000 by the late 1980s. The clothing sector employed Indians in large numbers, which Shaik described as 'particularly important because it's working-class people, it's Indian women, and my own thinking was that if you win women over into the political struggles of the time they will commit their sons and daughters to participate. And hence, we went into this union.' There were parallel developments with some 'Indian boys joining the ANC, preparing for the military life [and] Indian boys getting involved in trade union work'. Shaik mentioned the likes of Jay Naidoo, who became general secretary of COSATU, and Jayendra Naidoo, who became the first director of the National Economic Development and Labour Council (NEDLAC), among others. 'So we fanned across in the Labour Movement and we were entering the ANC's underground.'[22]

Johnny Copelyn, in his account of his time in the trade union movement, emphasised the particular agenda of 'deployed' cadres such as Yunis Shaik:

> Once he was inside the union Yunis began to bring in cadres who were either ANC members or at least were ANC aligned. Soon enough [the] union decided to employ A.J. Moodley as an organiser. Naziema Jappie was recruited as an education officer ... Later the team was strengthened by bringing in Maggie Govender as an organising secretary and Pregs Govender, initially as a media officer. Finally, Elsie Nair, stoic wife of Billy, was brought in as an administrator.[23]

Copelyn argued that 'the point about all these folk is that they were all brought into the union by Yunis on the basis that they could be relied upon to promote the key instruction of the ANC at the time in relation to trade unions: "Unite under COSATU".[24] As we will see later, however, there were machinations among some of the cadres brought in, as people like Pregs Govender refused to simply 'toe the line'.

It is difficult to discern the kind of attention that people like Yunis Shaik were able to give to building shop-floor structures and union education, given that he was playing so many roles: as a union organiser, and within the NIC, UDF, and ANC underground. The 1980s were a heady time, as mobilisation was ongoing, and the ANC was making more demands on people like Shaik to provide support as comrades infiltrated the country. Conditions were also difficult in the labour market as employers pushed to hire African workers at lower wages, replacing Indian workers. The young activists set themselves the task of building a non-racial working-class consciousness. But ethnic identity was an incredibly strong glue.

In terms of their economic status through the 1980s, Indians in the workplace had come to occupy what has been referred to as an in-between character. Trevor Bell found that there was a general tendency for Indians rather than Africans to move upwards into skilled positions, due to their higher level of educational attainment.[25] In terms of earning capacity, for example, 42 per cent of economically active Indians earned over R16 000 per annum in 1984. This was a relatively small figure compared to 83 per cent of whites, but considerably higher than the 14 per cent of coloureds and 5 per cent of Africans with this earning capacity. At the other end of the spectrum, while 13 per cent of Indians earned less than R5 000 per annum, 48 per cent of coloureds and 62 per cent of Africans fell into this category.[26]

This led to Indians being described as a 'middleman' minority, but this characterisation is complicated by the high proportion of working-class Indians in South Africa. It is this latter sector that activists like Shaik were focusing on. Many of these workers had little in common with affluent Indians as far as lifestyle was concerned, yet they too substantially identified and were identified with middle- and high-income earners as 'Indians'. Many Indian workers were singled out as a minority in the 'middle' in the political landscape because of the semi-skilled or supervisory positions they held *inside* of the factory plant. These distinctions did not substantially differentiate them from African workers, if at all, and the gap with middle-class Indians was wider. However, when these distinctions in the workplace were tied to separate Group Areas, separate schools, and separate newspapers and radio stations, a vivid group identity coalesced.

The differential economic rewards of being in the 'middle' of the productive and social machine may not have been significant enough in and of themselves to hive off Indian workers from African workers. But when this differential was tied to factors outside the factory gates, there emerged a powerful ethnic identity, as opposed to identity around class constructs.

Widening protests

Some NIC activists were involved in trade unions, and NIC-linked students generally supported a populist position and multi-class movements like the UDF. Yet the leadership of the NIC was overwhelmingly from the professional class. George Sewpersadh, Rabi Bugwandeen, D.K. Singh and M.J. Naidoo were all lawyers; Jerry Coovadia and Farouk Meer were medical doctors; Pravin Gordhan was a pharmacist. The issue of middle-class leadership was periodically raised, but not in any sustained way. Often, the sniping around class was overwhelmed by the fact that the state was bent on co-opting people as ethnic/racial groups, and so the battle against apartheid was joined in these terms.

The education boycott gave the NIC a foothold among the Indian masses through parents' committees and regular community meetings, as parents were concerned about the impact of the boycott on their children. Increasing student involvement in the struggles waged by the NIC was instrumental because students acted as the foot soldiers of the various campaigns, providing essential human power to reach into the community. Student activism grew increasingly important in building an extra-parliamentary anti-apartheid culture that also grew into a challenge to the NIC old guard as the 1980s wore on.

From the time of its revival, the NIC always saw itself as part of the Congress tradition, joining with the ANC and its allies in support of the Freedom Charter. However, overt identification was not possible in view of the ANC's banning. In 1980 the ANC attempted to use the 25th anniversary of the adoption of the Freedom Charter to popularise its programme. The NIC linked up with this campaign by establishing a committee to request the release of political prisoners. In March the Release Mandela Committee (RMC) was formed under the chairmanship of NIC executive member Paul David: it was an early example of NIC involvement in resistance activities beyond its immediate constituency. Together with ANC veterans such as Archie Gumede and Griffiths Mxenge, the committee sought to raise the ANC's popularity by highlighting the plight and suffering of its long-detained leaders, with Nelson Mandela being the face of the campaign. The committee was also conceived as a means to generate African political leadership and promote the Charterist movement. In May the RMC organised a mass rally calling for Mandela's release. It was a huge success, with more than 5 000 people attending to support the call.

The NIC made a telling contribution to the Anti-Republic Celebrations Campaign (ARCC) of 1981. In early 1981, Pretoria announced the holding of a month of celebrations commemorating the 20th anniversary of South Africa's declaration as a republic. The ANC saw this as an opportunity to unite the pockets of resistance that periodically sprouted and then retreated. Responding to this call, the NIC swung into action. The ARCC included figures such as Archie Gumede, M.J. Naidoo and George Sewpersadh. Through the NIC's established links with civics and with the aid of tertiary students, school students who were central to Pretoria's celebration plans were mobilised by the ARCC and the NIC to boycott the celebrations. Hundreds of schoolchildren were expelled for boycotting classes and were only permitted to return in 1982 after a long court battle. Many of these students became activists at university. Kovin Naidoo, then in Standard 8, was involved in the protests:

> We said no, 31st May must be a normal day, we're going to come to school. [The school officials] obviously refused, so we went on boycott. It was initially successful and then they threatened the students with expulsion and a lot of students returned to class. We didn't and 25 of us were expelled from school [Chatsworth High]. We were not allowed back to school that year. We went to court and kind of won the case – they allowed us to write exams but they refused to allow us back into school for that year. We spent that year at home.[27]

Propaganda pamphlets and graffiti with slogans such as 'Racist Republic No, People's Republic Yes' were circulated and painted in schools and elsewhere to rally support. Students delegated for performances withdrew, athletes boycotted events and festival workers resigned, dampening Pretoria's festive mood. The success of the ARCC campaign is evident in the government's response: M.J. Naidoo, Pravin Gordhan and Yunus Mohamed, among other NIC members, were detained. In the final analysis, the NIC's contributions to the RMC and the ARCC were not only important in building the resistance momentum and popularising the ANC. They were also crucial in fostering interracial politics and solidarity since these committees and campaigns cut across the racial divide. These links, however, remained largely at the leadership level.

Still, as the ANC began to reassert itself in the 1980s, recently released Robben Islanders were returning to the fray, and the anti-apartheid movement was becoming a global phenomenon, the NIC began linking with networks that would consolidate into the MDM. In this resurgence Pravin Gordhan paid homage to the impact of the old on the new in the form of returning political prisoners:

> They were the bearers of history, bearers of experiences, bearers of anecdotes, bearers of Congress culture, 'this is how you say things, this is how you analyse things', they were bearers of inspiration, because you could relate to them as heroes, and there were not many heroes at the time.[28]

The next chapter examines the galvanising of opposition to the SAIC elections of 1981. This mobilisation was boosted by a cadre of students schooled in the boycotts of 1980, hardened by the experiences of detention and drawing lessons from older comrades who had weathered the 1960s and 1970s.

6 | Lenin and the Duma Come to Durban: Reigniting the Participation Debate

The Soweto rebellion brought to the boil a number of challenges confronting the apartheid state. Internally, political and economic crises were feeding into and off of each other. Externally, a burgeoning anti-apartheid movement was hurting the regime through a disinvestment campaign and a growing sports boycott. The Nationalists attempted to deal with these challenges through a series of reforms. At the core of their effort was a renewed drive to facilitate an urban African middle class, to give greater recognition to trade unions, and to create 'representative' bodies for Indians and coloureds.[1]

Alongside these reforms, Bantustans would be encouraged to accept 'independence' in the hope that an African middle class centred around civil servants with job security and business people feeding off contracts provided by these 'governments' would buy into the NP policy of separate development. Similarly, the state hoped to co-opt Indians and coloureds into the broad apartheid project of complete racial segregation. How would the NIC and the broader Indian community respond to these blandishments? Simply put, the ostensibly settled debate over rejectionist participation was reignited – only this time discussions crossed the oceans, capturing the attention of exiles in the leadership of the Charterist movement.

The SAIC was set up in 1968 as a fully nominated body of 25 members. From 1974 its membership was increased to 30, with half the members appointed by government and half nominated by members of other Indian local government structures, such as LACs. Due to pressure from SAIC members, the government passed legislation in 1978 providing for the election of 40 members and 5 nominated members. The government was concerned that the election would be delegitimised before it even got off the ground if the voter turnout was low. And so the carrot of full elections was accompanied by the stick: a fine would be imposed on those who failed to register. By June 1978, 71 per cent of the 360 000 eligible Indian voters had registered.[2]

The SAIC's failure to get concessions from government on issues such as trading rights and work opportunities led some members to moot a boycott of the organisation at a Council meeting in early November 1978. However, one member, H.N. Naran, made an impassioned plea for the Council to resume work:

> I think generally when you have a very big family, when you are a businessman, when you are a professional man, and when you fall out with somebody, or if you don't get your desired results, you still try to get best terms, and it is in this light that I would suggest that we continue with the functions of this Council ... By just giving up, we are not going to get anywhere; we will have no place to go and talk to; we will have no place to negotiate.[3]

Naran acutely summed up the dilemma of the SAIC. Many of its members were traders who had suffered as a consequence of the Group Areas Act and were sensitive to forced relocations. However, once their protests failed, their modus operandi was to lobby behind closed doors in language that was circumspect and fitted in with the prevailing ideology of separate development. The chairman of the SAIC moved a resolution that read simply: 'Council now resolves to return to normal work and functions.' The resolution was carried by 16 votes to 8, with 3 abstentions.[4] However, SAIC executive member J.A. Carrim warned in 1979:

> This generation of Blacks and Indians and Coloureds in this country is the last generation that the Government is going to be able to talk to, to find accord and a peaceful dispensation to ensure peace and stability. The time is fast approaching when even the moderate elements of

institutions like the SAIC and other sister bodies, are despairing because of the lack of initiative on the part of the Government.[5]

The SAIC elections were originally scheduled for 26 March 1980. Forces opposed to the election began to organise within the Indian community, but they did not speak with one voice. For example, NIC vice-president Farouk Meer, addressing a meeting of the Kharwastan Civic Association in March 1979, argued against participation since no member of the SAIC or LAC had made 'incisive gains' on behalf of the people. Meer also warned against rejectionist participation. Those who said that they were joining the SAIC

> to wreck it had in fact now become a part and parcel of it. Such individuals only delude themselves that they can radicalise apartheid-created institutions and will either end up frustrated or will be reshaped by such institutions ... The true radical would demand the wrecking of racial domination itself and the founding of an unsplintered South Africa devoid of tribalism.[6]

Meer urged Indians to boycott the elections: 'A vote for any candidate in the SAIC elections is a vote for apartheid, racial domination, inferior housing and all the ills that plague our society.'[7]

While Meer propagated an intransigent approach, the *Leader* newspaper reported in May 1979 that the 'left wing' of the NIC had proposed that the organisation participate in the elections, in direct opposition to the 'old men of the NIC'. The two 'left wing' members identified in the article were Pravin Gordhan and Yunus Mohamed, who 'head a group which is as yet behind the purdah [screen] and which seems to be based in Merebank and Phoenix'. However, the Phoenix Working Committee (PWC), headed by Roy Sukuram, distanced itself from the call.[8] A meeting of the PWC had resolved that it 'was a civic body and should not be used as a political platform, whether for participation or not'. According to one report, Mohamed and Gordhan 'immediately severed association with the PWC although they had been associated with the PWC since its inception and were the boffins behind Roy Sukuram'.[9]

An editorial in the *Leader* lamented that the Indian community could not get 'any kind of substantial and meaningful pabulum on the subject. Cases for and against participation remain at the doctrinaire and the dogmatic stage.'[10] Behind the scenes there were intense debates about whether or not to participate in the elections. Gordhan reflected in a 2003 interview that the changing political terrain called for new ways of approaching the 'struggle':

> That [military struggle] was the dominant theme of the time. There was no doubt that we were faced with a tough regime which had narrowed the space in which one could operate within the legal terrain, that the military underground processes needed to be at the forefront of the overall political strategy ... but the important thing is whether there was an ability to embrace new things that were happening at the time, and new things were beginning to happen.[11]

The 'new things' included political initiatives by the government which required a response. As Gordhan recounted:

> The issue of participating in the SAIC elections came up. The question was whether it was reactionary or indeed strategic to use that particular avenue and platform to mobilise various sections of the community. We were basing our approach on theoretical stuff that we had read about, Lenin and the Duma and similar experiences. Part of that debate was about saying let's draw a distinction between principles, in principle we need to destroy apartheid and replace it with a democracy and introduce the Freedom Charter as a programme, and the question of tactics which could be using an avenue like this.[12]

Yunus Mohamed contended that

> you don't just reject the participation strategy ... You actually have to logically look at the balance of forces ... You take a principled position, but if you are coming from a Congress position ... it is either a strategic or a tactical issue ... We persisted with the debate and really pushed people, and there was some sort of vilification.[13]

In exploring why Gordhan and his faction within the NIC considered participation, Yunus Carrim argued that they were using

> Lenin and the Duma, and the tactical issue about participating as a tool for mobilising a conservative Indian community ... to give a sort of defensive buffer against security police detention and raids and so on and to use the structure, presumably to prevent it [from] functioning properly. They thought that given the events of the late fifties and sixties, where the leadership was reduced to dormancy because of police intervention, things were picking up in the seventies, but it was clear that you needed cover to organise, mobilise ... it was a tactical issue for them.[14]

It is not clear how relevant Bolshevik participation in the Duma was in the South African context. The NIC were not exactly Bolsheviks, although some of its leading cadres would be accused of styling themselves as Leninist professional revolutionaries imbued with an advanced consciousness that they would bring to the masses. This elitist form of operating would in time contribute to accusations of the existence of cabals working to control the struggle effort. At the same time, the NIC was part of a broader mass movement to which it was accountable, and it had to acknowledge that it represented a racial minority whose position was hotly debated within the ANC. In other words, unlike the Bolsheviks, the NIC was not beholden only to itself, as the debate about participation illustrates. It is noteworthy that the example used was that of the Bolsheviks, whose name came to be associated with the seizure of power, rather than the Indian National Congress (INC), India's nationalist movement, which in its early days had participated in the structures set up by the British Raj.

At the same time, the issue of participation and boycott as a matter of tactics rather than principle had a long history in the ANC. Proponents of rejectionist participation provoked debate about tactics and strategy, rather than simply accepting a reflexive boycott position that characterised some left organisations. Boycott as principle often led to a militant abstentionism rather than a search for innovative ways to mobilise people to engage with the changing political terrain brought into play by a state trying to reorganise and consolidate its rule.

Gordhan's argument that 'the military underground processes needed to be at the forefront of the overall political strategy' is revealing, given that the NIC claimed to be staying close to Gandhian traditions of non-violence. Was this just a convenient front for people like Gordhan who supported militant action? Like other groupings in apartheid South Africa, the NIC could not have embraced the armed struggle openly, as the organisation would have been banned and faced other repressive measures. Moreover, different ideological strands coexisted around the question of resorting to violence to advance the liberation movement. This was clear when the ANC first debated this issue in earnest in 1960. Thula Simpson provides a fascinating insight into that seminal meeting of the Congress Alliance where the possible turn to armed struggle was debated, with Nelson Mandela and Albert Luthuli at the fore:

> Luthuli chairs ... In the ensuing debate, J.N. Singh [of the NIC] says: 'Non-violence has not failed us, we have failed non-violence.' Mandela responds that non-violence *has* in fact failed ... In the early hours of the following morning, Yusuf Cachalia [of the Transvaal Indian Congress] says ... 'Let's not decide to use violence. They will arrest us, they will throw us in jail, they will slaughter us.' To this M.D. Naidoo [of the NIC] answers – referring in particular to some of his colleagues in the Indian Congress – 'well, you people are just afraid of militant action, that's all' ... He concludes by saying: 'Ah, you are afraid of going to jail, that's all!' The proponents of non-violence are livid at this comment, pandemonium ensues and the discussion goes back to square one ... At 7 a.m. ... the meeting ... gives Mandela authority to build the military organ.[15]

This division between those who could support a military option and those who stuck firmly to non-violence ran through into the 1970s and 1980s. There would be some crossover, where those committed to non-violence would give sanctuary to those who were involved in armed struggle, but would disavow it themselves. More importantly, as some in the NIC, such as Gordhan and Moe Shaik, got more involved in the underground, they met in closed groupings, developing an above-ground camaraderie that was perceived, as Pregs Govender's memoir attests,[16] as a cabal. This faction was seen as acting outside the democratic processes of the NIC and seeking to impose its mandate on the wider internal Charterist movement.

Rumours of a participation lobby and of ructions inside the NIC broke into the public domain. According to media reports, an NIC meeting had been held in secret to discuss participation in the SAIC. M.J. Naidoo responded angrily that 'leakage to the press of a private meeting, giving the impression of a solid movement in favour of this new thinking, smacks of tactics one would expect from one's enemies and not from one's friends'.[17] The 'Young Turks' or 'rebels', as they were termed in newspaper reports, were identified as Krish Govender, Yunus Mohamed and Pravin Gordhan, who had allegedly convened a meeting with certain NIC executive members to convince them to participate in the SAIC in order to prevent 'non-entities' from gaining access to power.[18]

A local newspaper reported that at the last minute the organisers had informed all the members of the executive that the meeting had been cancelled, except for NIC president George Sewpersadh and vice-president M.J. Naidoo. However, Naidoo and Sewpersadh rejected participation. The NIC provincial organiser, A.H. Randeree, issued a statement asserting that the NIC

> categorically dissociated itself from the recent manoeuvres by those who are considering participation in the new dispensation for Indians. The secretive approach to discuss the issue leaves much ground for discontent. Having invited a large body to their meeting, they suddenly cancelled the meeting when it was realised there was a lot of opposition within the community to the new proposals. Then, in clandestine fashion, attempts were made to drag two senior officials of the NIC to their way of thinking [but] they voiced their total rejection of the new dispensation.[19]

This statement did not shut down the rumour mill. According to newspaper reports, disgruntled NIC members were forming a Congress Party and would field 30 candidates who, if elected, would hand over their entire salary for anti-apartheid activities.[20] M.J. Naidoo challenged 'the people behind this party to stand up and identify themselves so that the public can see who they are'.[21] Following an urgent meeting of the NIC executive on

6 May 1979, Sewpersadh issued a statement that there was 'no reappraisal by Congress in regard to its policy of non-participation in the SAIC', which was 'created by, and will be in the control of, people who believe in oppression of the Blacks. In the circumstances, it can only be a machinery of repression, and not of liberation.'[22]

The participation debate did not die there but led to an incredible set of events that drew in the ANC in exile. Rejectionist participation was discussed when the ANC's NEC and Revolutionary Council (RC) met between 27 December 1978 and 1 January 1979. At the meeting, a commission of six members – Thabo Mbeki, Joe Slovo, Moses Mabhida, Joe Gqabi, Joe Modise and president Oliver Tambo – was constituted to investigate rejectionist participation. The commission produced a report for the next meeting, held in Lusaka on 9 March 1979. For Joe Gqabi, this debate would have brought back memories of his time on Robben Island. There he had got into a heated debate with Mandela on the approach to Bantustans: 'Should the ANC oppose them entirely, giving them no legitimacy at all, or should it or its surrogates support strategic participation and consider forming opposition parties to contest the elections in those states?'[23] According to Padraig O'Malley, Gqabi took the former view, Mandela the latter.

With regard to Indians and coloureds, the commission met with Yusuf Dadoo and Reg September respectively, who agreed to convene meetings of 'cadres engaged in work among these communities in order to make recommendations on this question'. Mac Maharaj was co-opted by the commission to gauge the feelings of Indians.[24]

The commission's view was that government institutions served only 'to divide the black communities', and therefore every effort should be made to 'mobilise the masses to make the institutions unworkable'. The commission noted that, while working within the system, Buthelezi refused 'independence' for KwaZulu, and the Coloured Labour Party adopted 'obstructionist tactics' which made the Coloured Representative Council ineffectual. Among Indians, however, 'there is a consistent and traditional rejectionist mood in relation to the SAIC'. The report called for respect for the different approaches without labelling anyone a 'sell-out'.[25]

Mac Maharaj recounted in 2003 that when he was secretary of the ANC's internal wing, a meeting was convened with Thumba Pillay and

Figure 6.1: Yusuf Dadoo (*left*), pictured here with Aziz Pahad while both were in exile in London. (Courtesy of 1860 Heritage Centre)

Pravin Gordhan around May/June 1979 because divisions within the NIC were 'becoming acrimonious'. Maharaj identified key people on each side: Thumba Pillay was in the forefront of the group favouring a boycott, and Pravin Gordhan was seen to be leading the faction favouring rejection-ist participation. Maharaj arranged for Pillay and Gordhan, accompanied by Roy Padayachie, to visit him in London. Neither side knew that the other would be there. He also invited NIC stalwart I.C. Meer, who was in London at the time in order to visit his son Rashid, who had been forced into exile in 1976.[26]

Maharaj met with each group separately, and thereafter both groups met with Dadoo, Aziz Pahad and Frene Ginwala, all ANC officials of Indian ancestry. According to Maharaj, 'Dr [Yusuf] Dadoo says, "It appears to me that it will be more divisive to go for rejectionist participation than boy-cott. There are too many people on the boycott side who are going to be unbending and besides, as a tactic, it makes sense." I.C. Meer and Thumba

Figure 6.2: Mac Maharaj, pictured here at a 2008 forum on racism. (Courtesy of 1860 Heritage Centre)

Pillay agreed that 'it would be the boycott line'. Dadoo's parting advice was: 'Don't confuse the people. Speak one language.' A resolution reflecting the agreement was drafted and signed by Dadoo and Maharaj.[27]

In a 1990 interview, Maharaj explained the happenings in London in some detail to the journalist and academic Howard Barrell, who also served on the ANC's intelligence underground:

> I said: Let's start the discussion from first principles. I know one of them – the PG [Pravin Gordhan] grouping – I actually taped; and the fucking *ous* protested later on. And I screwed them up. First principles; we last come to the question of whether boycott or this [rejectionist participation]. And from first principles, I move them to the position: Can we agree as a principle that the central question is involvement of the masses and maximum unity? Agreed. Then after that whether it's rejectionist participation or boycott is unimportant. Each group agreed to that.
>
> No, then they said: No, we want the letter signed by Doc [Dadoo] and Mac [Maharaj]. So we signed it. And we sent it back. And the chaps

returned home. In the letter of course we said: 'However, in assessing the problem, we think that the best way to achieve maximum unity is to opt for boycott.' And this was because, in my assessment, PG [Pravin Gordhan] and company were hardworking, dedicated people, like all, but they were more loyal, more disciplined. And you could ask your more disciplined to bend. The others were Congress, but less disciplined. To ask them to bend was to ask more.

But it was recognised that we cannot just move one step right into position. So, the letter did say in the last paragraph that, however, we would advise, recommend – but final decision is yours on the ground. We recommended Boycott. Now, as it happened, PG and them sent a letter of protest – after they got home – because they ran into shit. When they reported to their unit, the unit says: You guys went there and sold out.

So, when they woke up to that, they wrote a letter of protest to Swaziland to say that I had misled them; I had come with a predetermined movement position. And they were wrong. I was armed with rejectionist participation. I happened to be in Swaziland when the letter arrived. And I immediately replied. And I said: 'Comrades, when I terminated your discussion, there were two reps on your side; in the session with the two of you, when we finally concluded, we had a joint meeting and we resumed, I asked you then honestly to make a criticism of the two weeks, and be free, I said; and you fucking *ous*, each of you stood up and praised me; I said that's on record ... They shut up.[28]

As disciplined Congress members, the Gordhan group were prepared to bend, not necessarily because the other side won the debate, but in order to ensure that the centre held. Yousuf Vawda, an NIC executive member and future law professor at the University of KwaZulu-Natal, made this very point when he argued that the 'political arguments for participation were not effectively countered [by the ANC]' but that Gordhan agreed to the resolution in the interests of unity. 'In my view the singular contribution of the ANC in that debate was the appeal to unity, which resulted in all points of view closing ranks around an anti-SAIC participation position.' Vawda also maintained that the pre- and post-1976 phases in the participation debate

> were of a qualitatively different nature. In the early period, there was very little organisation at the mass level. Leaders were proposing participation out of reasons of fear (safe platform to speak out) and visibility (not being eclipsed by conservative leaders). The 1979 discourse, on the other hand, was informed by significant national and local events: the Soweto uprising, the experience of activists conducting community-based campaigns on civic and other issues, and the skills that emerged from building mass-based community structures. These campaigns were of necessity local, and did not overtly

Figure 6.3: Yousuf Vawda, who was involved in civic structures in Phoenix, was among those activists open to participation in government-created structures for strategic reasons. (Courtesy of Gandhi-Luthuli Documentation Centre)

challenge the political regime. The point of departure for this later discourse was of a strategic and tactical nature – how to increase political consciousness and extend the mass base through engagement in the political sphere, utilising state-sponsored institutions to achieve these objectives. The debate was not about participation per se, but about exercising those strategic and tactical initiatives – a point lost on most commentators. This partly explains why the protagonists of the participation debate were among the most effective advocates and campaigners of the Anti-SAIC and Anti-Tricam [Anti-Tricameral Parliament] campaigns.[29]

The need for unity was not just an NIC matter but also involved the ANC. Moreover, given the huge fissures in South African society, it was noteworthy that the NIC, by managing to stay together, provided leadership in the 1980s on a range of issues in the new apartheid townships. Once a collective position was reached on the participation issue, Gordhan and his group, as disciplined cadres, were prepared to support it even though they had previously supported a different position.

Yusuf Dadoo's letter to Fatima Meer, written on 12 June 1979 following the London meetings, shows that the question of mass support was also key to understanding why the boycott position ultimately prevailed:

> My Dear Sister,
> I have been following with great interest the current debate and arguments over the question of participation in the elections, and of course it is being discussed widely. The ideal would be a total boycott. This option, as a political rather than moral issue, turns on how effective it can be. From your letter, your opinion is that it could not be sustained – that people will go to the polls, and therefore our attention should be directed to determining the character of the result. However, what is not very clear from the debate is what those elected are to do. Paying salaries into NIC will absolve them from mercenary motives, but what else? Is their going to use the institutions of apartheid, for whatever motive, not in itself going to give it credibility? How is one going to avoid that?

There is another option which should be considered, which might meet some of these points. One could seek election on a negative platform, i.e. 'Choose us to reject the institution.' Then, once elected, the new 'councillors' should not attend or participate in anything at all. This could lead either to a non-functioning of the body – possibly new elections or the appointment of replacements – which would make it lose its credibility as a democratically elected body (one needs to look at the legislation carefully). This option is also full of pitfalls – one would need to be certain of wide support – because otherwise the failure to win would be interpreted as positive support. However, in our view, it is something that needs to be considered by those on the spot.

Divisions, expulsions, exclusions, etc. only serve our enemies. Though it will not be possible to see you, please do what you can to assist representative views to be brought and discussed personally. Also discuss the suggested option, and also advise on what suggestions are being put forward on the attitude of councillors after election. This in our view is the real key – & only when that is clarified, can the question of participation be resolved. Keep well and greeting to all.
Y[30]

Dadoo here displays extraordinary acumen despite having spent almost two decades in exile. A haunting line about participation – 'one would need to be certain of wide support' – suggests that activists were not absolutely certain about the feelings of the majority of Indians. Despite Meer seeming to indicate that people might be attracted to vote, Dadoo, as a member of the ANC carefully surveying the options, was leaning towards boycott (as Mac Maharaj explained).

Mewa Ramgobin, a close ally of M.J. Naidoo, felt otherwise. In a letter to fellow NIC member A.K.M. Docrat on 1 August 1979, he maintained that the NIC 'should put up candidates, even nominate banned and house-arrested people' who would have to sign a pledge rejecting the SAIC as an institution, return all monies earned to the community, and campaign for

single representation based on the Freedom Charter. In essence, my view is based on my assessment of the situation in the country.

Whilst it will allow us, in cooperation with the community, to reject the system and have a nationwide mobilization, it will also facilitate us to restrain the collaborationist element in the community from being elected.[31]

That Ramgobin could contemplate participation was a measure of the angst that some in the NIC felt about both the potential gains made by the ANC and the NIC's challenges on the ground following the post-1976 crackdown. Was it also a recognition that the state could so easily take people like him out of circulation through bannings and that participation might afford some protection? For once, Ramgobin and his supposed nemesis the 'cabal' were on the same side.

After an NIC executive meeting at the end of August 1979, George Sewpersadh announced that the organisation had 'resolved internal differences' and agreed that the SAIC should be boycotted. There would now be 'greater involvement of Congress in problems that immediately confront the community to meet the challenges of the times'.[32] Following the lead of the South African Council on Sport (SACOS), whose 'double standards' resolution of 1977 expelled any person who participated in government structures, the NIC also resolved that anyone involved in the SAIC in any capacity would be expelled from Congress.[33]

Pravin Gordhan, Yunus Mohamed and Krish Govender issued a separate statement affirming their compliance with the direction of the NIC following 'intense and healthy' discussions:

We were very much part of these discussions and have initiated the move to reassess the traditional position of progressives on this question. We see the need at this point to categorically state our view. After due consideration we firmly believe that the SAIC election should be boycotted and in this regard to commit ourselves to the NIC programme ... In view of the state onslaught it is imperative that all progressives unite under the banner of the NIC. We are grateful to our president, Mr George Sewpersadh, whose open, honest, and mature approach has contributed tremendously to the resolution of the differences within the NIC and we pledge our support for his leadership.[34]

Figure 6.4: Activist and lawyer Yunus Mohamed also advocated rejectionist participation. (Courtesy of African News Agency)

The fact that the three felt a need to issue a separate statement was indicative of how serious the question of participation had become. The involvement of the ANC also showed the ties that were developing between some NIC activists and the banned ANC and MK in exile, a topic taken up in later chapters. Clearly participation was a serious enough issue for it to involve the top brass of the ANC. Possibly because things are remembered and forgotten differently as circumstances change, Paul David recalled the debate as a stage-managed affair:

> It was all designed to get the ideology right first ... The one thing that Lenin taught us is that for a tactic to be acceptable it must not only be politically correct, it must be accepted by the masses of the people. And we knew that the mass of the Indian people were not going to accept participation. Pravin and Yunus would never support participation because of all the problems and insults that would come

from the Indian community. Because we had painted the SAIC as traitors! But the debate had to happen to sharpen the ordinary person's thinking about political tactics. The political armament of the ordinary activist grew during that period. They could debate their position against anybody ... There was a semblance of a division in the NIC. But there was no division. We came out of that more united then we were before.[35]

The weekly column 'Tales from Gondwanaland', written anonymously but widely known to be the work of Pat Poovalingam, summed up with biting sarcasm the dilemma of the NIC with regard to participation in the SAIC:

We had the hilarious spectacle of a strictly and genuinely bona fide non-racial organisation being almost split into separate but entirely Indian sections by its great debate as to whether or not to take part in the SAIC elections. Let's do it, said M.J. Naidoo ... until Big Brother from London (Dadoo) said he mustn't. Let's do it, said Yunus Mohamed. Then all these good members of the Indian racial group, as good non-racial members of a wholly non-racial body which by sheer accident has only Indians as its office-bearers, finally decided not to take part in the election of the Indian Council.[36]

While Poovalingam could point to conundrums and somersaults, the reality was that in weighing up political options the NIC had to consider both its base in the Indian community and the broader Congress Alliance to whose aims it swore allegiance. With the ANC banned, the NIC not only reflected the views of the Indian community, but was a public demonstration that the Congress Alliance and its vision of a new South Africa, encapsulated in the Freedom Charter, was still alive. The attraction of using state structures to confront the state was ultimately trumped by the importance of maintaining unity, both within the NIC and in the broader ranks of the liberation movement.

The issue settled, the NIC turned its energies into a vigorous anti-SAIC election campaign, with many of the once pro-participation lobbyists leading the charge. The recent 'converts' were the most zealous in this regard.

7 | The Anti-SAIC Campaign of 1981: Prefigurative Politics?

O nce the NIC had settled on boycotting government institutions, it operated like a well-oiled machine. This is clearly demonstrated by the sheer number of pamphlets and letters it distributed within the Indian community to persuade potential voters to boycott the July 1979 LAC elections. Ten thousand personally addressed letters were sent to the residents of Durban warning that LACs were mere advisory bodies whose advice was 'left on the shelves to collect dust'.[1] This was a trial run for the main event: the campaign to delegitimise the SAIC, particularly by organising a boycott of the upcoming SAIC elections. These were originally scheduled for 26 March 1980 but were subsequently delayed until November 1981.

In July 1979, the Anti-SAIC Committee – consisting of M.J. Naidoo (president), Dr Korshed Ginwala (vice-president), Thumba Pillay and R. Ramesar (joint secretaries), Farouk Meer and Perry Pillay (joint treasurers), as well as A.H. Randeree, D.K. Singh and Marie Subramoney – circulated 9 000 copies of a newsletter named *The Call*. This name deliberately harked back to times past. *The Call for Freedom and Justice* newsletter had first been published in the 1940s by Cassim Amra. He was a member of the radical NIC faction that won hegemony under the leadership of Monty Naicker and led the NIC into an alliance with the ANC in the 1950s.[2]

The four-page newsletter contained messages of support from Nokukhanya Luthuli, widow of Chief Albert Luthuli; Dr Nthato Motlana, chairman of the Soweto Committee of Ten; and Hassan Howa, president of the South African Council on Sport (SACOS). It also contained a

Figure 7.1: Thumba Pillay (*left*) listens intently as Marie Naicker, widow of Monty Naicker, addresses an anti-SAIC rally in Durban, *c.* 1979. (Courtesy of African News Agency)

critique of the SAIC by Dr A.D. Lazarus and, significantly, a contribution by Obed Kunene, editor of the Zulu newspaper *Ilanga*, which was aligned to Mangosuthu Buthelezi's Inkatha movement. This is important, given that relations between the NIC and Inkatha would deteriorate dramatically over the next decade.

The line-up of contributors cut across racial boundaries. Nokukhanya Luthuli, wife of the former ANC president and winner of the Nobel Peace Prize who was instrumental in crafting the alliance between the NIC and the ANC, was a revered figure in her own right. Motlana, a medical doctor, had emerged as an influential figure post-1976, while Hassan Howa had galvanised the anti-apartheid sports movement with the slogan 'No normal sport in an abnormal society'. A.D. Lazarus was a venerated figure in education, having headed the iconic Sastri College.

M.J. Naidoo told *Daily News* political reporter Graham Linscott that the NIC believed in a new constitution based on the Freedom Charter, 'one-man-one-vote in a unitary state', and 'freedom from all discrimination, a free market system, and various subsidiary rights such as equal education and equal opportunity'. Any other proposal was 'a sham to entrench the existing privileged position of the whites'.[3] This mishmash of issues paid homage to the Freedom Charter while arguing for a free-market system. Naidoo did not spell out what 'equal opportunity' would mean in a context of centuries of accumulated privilege. His statement was symptomatic of the NIC: strong on its opposition to apartheid but vague on alternatives. Part of the reason for vagueness was the need to appeal to all sectors of the Indian community.

The build-up to elections opened political spaces that normally would have been viciously closed down. The Anti-SAIC Committee took full advantage of this singular moment. The 1980 education boycott introduced a new layer to anti-apartheid activities and the anti-SAIC propaganda efforts began to reach younger Indians. Kovin Naidoo, then a student at Chatsworth High School, described the impact of his involvement in the anti-SAIC election campaigns:

> Farouk Meer was in my house one night with all the parents, saying how bad it is, what happened, and then said you've got to come to NIC meetings. That's how we got involved; people like Maggie Govender, Shoots Naidoo and Charm Govender and Roy Padayachie played a big part in our lives. We were the kids, they were the university people, and for that year we basically did fieldwork in almost every house in Chatsworth. It's a bloody big township but every Saturday, every evening, [we were] visiting people, telling them not to support the local government elections, explaining to them the importance of non-racialism. At night we would use spray cans to spray 'sellout' on the houses of candidates' walls, at the train station, the swimming pool. Our lives really changed.[4]

A number of other campaigns fed into heightened anti-apartheid activism: the education boycotts, the Release Mandela Campaign, the campaign for cheaper bread, the boycott of red meat in support of abattoir workers who had been dismissed, and protests against the 1981 assassination of Griffiths Mxenge, who had served on the executive of the Release Mandela Committee. Charm Govender recounted that a message was received from the ANC to drape activists' coffins in ANC flags, and supporters clandestinely did so.[5] These moves helped to achieve 'symbolic identification with the ANC':

The hoisting of ANC flags at funerals became widespread ... Identification with the ANC was also made through the multiple ways in which Nelson Mandela was projected as the legitimate leader of the people of South Africa. This was often done in the context of campaigns for his release.[6]

Pravin Gordhan noted that some of these campaigns witnessed cross-race organisation for the first time:

In '79/80 we had our first links with the African community, particularly Lamontville ... By 1980 you had the launch of the Release Mandela Campaign, which had a committee in Durban which we were part of. Between '78 and '81 there was a very slow but systematic struggle against the local affairs committees. Similar struggles were taking place against Bantu or Community Councils. So you had activities sort of based in Indian areas on the one hand but non-racial linkages beginning to develop at the same time, because many of us had a non-racial perspective (a), and (b) we were informed by an ANC perspective which recognised the leading role of the African people. Plus Indian, Coloured, democratic whites, recognised that building alliances was quite crucial, but more importantly [they] recognised activists per se don't bring about change. They are merely catalysts. And that you've got to find pockets of opportunities, which enabled you to organise, whether it's high school students, university students, whole communities on transport issues, rental issues or as political issues began to come to the fore in 1981 – the SAIC elections.[7]

Gordhan refers to issues that were to become lightning rods for internal criticism as the Charterist movement grew. The idea of 'the leading role of the African people' was to haunt the Mass Democratic Movement, as some Indian activists were accused of dominating its politics and acting as gatekeepers. Moreover, the notion that 'activists per se don't bring about change' is ironical, given that there would be sharp criticism that some elements in the NIC were directing campaigns and promoting certain kinds of leadership – indeed, acting as some kind of Leninist vanguard, a cabal.

The government announced in February 1981 that SAIC elections would be held on 4 November 1981. Farouk Meer warned that the Anti-SAIC Committee would 'intensify its campaign to discourage Indians from voting. We believe the vast majority of Indians do not accept the SAIC concept and the November polling is going to show the Government once and for all what the will of the silent majority is.' Y.S. Chinsamy, chairperson of the Reform Party, retorted that the election would provide a means to test leadership, and 'prevent any Tom, Dick or Harry taking on the mantle of "community leader".[8]

In time the NIC formed four regional Anti-SAIC committees: Pietermaritzburg and Northern Natal (chaired by A.S. Chetty); North Coast and Northern Durban (Paul David); South Coast and Southern Durban (Reverend Michael Coopan of the Anglican Church, Chatsworth); and Central and Western Areas of Durban (D.K. Singh). These committees organised regular meetings across the province in the lead-up to the elections. Jerry Coovadia, writing on the eve of the elections, insisted that he would not vote:

By voting I will have betrayed my hopes for a democracy within an unfragmented South Africa ... My future and those of my family lie with Africans, Coloureds and whites and I will refuse to sanction, by my vote, an exclusion of the African majority in this determination ... Must I compound the perilous state of Indian politics by helping to usher in a band of faceless men who have little to offer except the noise of their shallow rhetoric?[9]

The SAIC was determined to show that it was not a toothless body that could only garner support through patronage. It passed a resolution mandating its executive committee to meet with Prime Minister P.W. Botha to express 'the growing frustration and dissatisfaction in the Indian community vis-à-vis the S.A. Indian Council' and to ask for a 'clear directive' with regard to the community's 'desire to participate in

Figure 7.2: Jerry Coovadia (*left*) of the NIC and Paddy Kearney of Diakonia with a list of the 189 persons arrested in the lead-up to the 1981 elections. (Courtesy of African News Agency)

the sovereign institutions of the Republic'. Without such undertaking, holding an election 'would be an exercise in futility'.[10] The NP did not appear to be listening. SAIC members were frustrated when they left the August 1981 meeting with Botha, as he refused to countenance requests for even minor adjustments to apartheid policies. One Council member summed up the feelings of the delegation: 'We were humiliated. Every member of the delegation felt they should have walked out that day ... The first time I tried to take up the cudgels on behalf of the delegation, he said: "look, no cross-talk".[11] A frustrated Joe Carrim, on resigning from the SAIC executive, described it as 'a glorified complaints department treating symptoms instead of the disease'.[12]

Botha, who had replaced B.J. Vorster as prime minister in 1978, made it clear that he regarded Indians as 'better off' in South Africa than elsewhere in Africa or even India. He vowed that there would never be 'one man, one vote' under his watch, and claimed that under Nationalist rule the Indian community 'was making significant progress in most directions and was benefiting through economic opportunities'. Like a cat that had spied the spilt milk, M.J. Naidoo pounced on Botha's intransigence and the SAIC's failure to shift Nationalist policy, advising SAIC members 'to lick their wounds and join the liberation struggle'.[13]

In the face of a state determined to keep the reins of political and economic power in white hands and apartheid's racial boundaries intact, the SAIC failed in its efforts to extract concessions from the government. This failure created profound bitterness in communities who feared that their livelihoods and homes could be summarily wiped away by a stroke of the pen. A member of the SAIC, in urging people to vote, pleaded:

> The extremist politician may gain the confidence of the public and may experience a feeling of euphoria ... but in all his efforts to bring about social and political reforms there will be but one pathetic outcome: the immiseration of his people. To pretend that an aggressive approach would bring results is to deceive oneself and awaken deception in the electorate.[14]

The SAIC approach, which, in its most benevolent form, sought to mitigate the excesses of apartheid, came up against the ceiling imposed on the professional classes, the forced removals of traders, and a working class bitter that it had been forced to the outskirts of the city. In those outlying areas, transport costs rocketed, and cramped accommodation meant that as children turned into young adults, space and privacy were at a premium.

The state resorted to a variety of tactics to disrupt election-boycott activities. An anti-election meeting scheduled for 26 June 1981 was banned. The Durban City Council ruled in October 1981 that anti-SAIC election posters could not be put up in public places because the by-law only permitted posters that 'furthered' activity in an election;

posters calling on people not to vote were thwarting election activity.[15] The state also arrested activists such as Moe Shaik, Yunus Mohamed and Pravin Gordhan in the lead-up to the elections. Gordhan recounted his experience:

> I was married and had a daughter, at the time 4½. They arrived at 5 o'clock in the morning. They searched the place for about an hour. At about 6:30 or so they take you away. The next thing you are sitting in a cell. C.R. Swart [Police Station]. You suddenly have gates crushing on you and you are left alone and then you start thinking about what information they might have, what likely explanations you might offer, anything that I knew was in the public domain, and I had a firm resolve that I wouldn't give them the name of anybody. And I didn't. A lot also depends on personality, your ability to survive things ... The police had a way of appearing calm but are threatening. They had a sense of authority and power ... a complete command over you. In the first day nothing happened. You are left to stew a bit. Anxiety, concern about what issues were gonna be raised and I suppose rehearsing in one's mind how one would avoid cracking up, avoid giving them certain information.
>
> I had a beard and long hair at that time so they pulled my beard and cut it and forced me to drink water, that sort of stuff. I was pulled out again at night. In the night they stripped me completely, then they put the [telephone] directory directly in my outstretched arms and then two minutes later you can't hold your arms straight and you just let go. They can do what they like. Because I wasn't a physically strong guy so I wasn't going to be pretending to be macho. It was up to them. Then I caught up to their games. I drank all the water they gave me. They made me urinate on the floor, clean it up, walk around without any clothes. All this to humiliate you.[16]

Arrested at the end of October, Gordhan was imprisoned in solitary confinement for 161 days. He suffered an acute eye infection and was moved to Brighton Police Station and then Durban Central even though the doctor advised that Gordhan be admitted to hospital. Eventually, in March 1982, he was hospitalised, but he was moved back to C.R. Swart on about 10 April. Upon his release on 15 May, he was banned for the next 13 months. He also lost his state job.[17] Gordhan had to take antidepressants, but surviving detention, he reflected, 'gives you self-confidence. It tells you [that] you can take on those challenges and it gives you more spunk to do a bit more work.'

Elections were held on 4 November 1981. Six candidates were unopposed and 81 candidates fought for the remaining 34 seats. Of 360 000 Indians eligible to vote, 297 000 or 84.6 per cent had registered. The call for a boycott was broadly heeded: just 10 per cent of registered voters cast their ballots. Yunus Moola, a Council member, conceded that the low turnout showed that 'the people ... want direct representation in a single parliament'.[18]

The Reform Party had initially decided to participate in the elections but subsequently withdrew. Party leader Y.S. Chinsamy stated that while he 'remained committed to negotiation as a strategy ... the present climate made it unbearable for him to enhance the credibility of the SAIC'. He thus joined Sonny Leon of the Coloured Labour Party, Mangosuthu Buthelezi of Inkatha, the Dikwakwentla Party from Qwaqwa in the Free State, and the Inyandza Movement of KaNgwane in forming the South African Black Alliance.[19]

The vacuum left by the Reform Party was filled by the National People's Party (NPP) under the leadership of ex-Reform Party member Amichand Rajbansi. The NPP became the majority party and took over the executive, with Rajbansi as chair. The challenge, Rajbansi said, was to 'prove to the community that we are an effective voice. I will say on issues like Cato Manor, Pageview, Clairwood and Grey Street – a wide spectrum of the interests of the Indian community – will lie the future of the SAIC.'[20] The 1982 SAIC sessions were marked by constant appeals to the government to grant the Council some victories to enable it to win the 'hearts and minds' of the people on the streets and alleviate some of the hardships endured by Indians, but these were not forthcoming.

The white Nationalists' intransigence frustrated the SAIC's attempts to enhance its credibility. After the elections, the organisation remained much as it had been in 1978, when Council member Abram-Mayet proclaimed that the SAIC had been 'reduced to a body which can merely pass resolutions on to the authorities. While they pass the motions, the motions go down somewhere in the sewage drain.'[21]

Rejection of the SAIC did not necessarily translate into support for majority rule. Three wide-ranging surveys conducted among Indians during this period indicated that a large percentage of them were concerned about majority rule. The surveys were conducted by the Buthelezi Commission in 1980, under the supervision of Professor Lawrence Schlemmer of the University of Natal; by the Johannesburg *Star* newspaper in August 1981 as part of a national black politics poll; and by Markinor, among 200 Durban housewives who were polled in February 1980.[22]

In analysing the data, political scientist Craig Charney proposed that the political attitudes of Indians were a response to their 'middleman' position between whites and Africans. He identified four broad tendencies: 'Leftists' (10–15 per cent of Indians) supported radical positions on nationalisation of industry, 'one person, one vote' and sanctions against South Africa; 'Left-liberals' (25 per cent) favoured 'one person, one vote' but also a capitalist economy; 'Liberals' (40 per cent) favoured capitalism and minority group vetoes over socialism and majority rule, but rejected apartheid-based politics and movements that operated 'within the system'; and 'Conservatives' (15–20 per cent) were suspicious of power-sharing with Africans and were willing to participate within apartheid structures. Charney held that 45 to 50 per cent of Indians appeared to favour power-sharing rather than straightforward majority rule and supported capitalism over socialism.[23]

Against this background it says much for the anti-SAIC forces that they could pull off a boycott of major proportions. What is occluded in Charney's analysis, but significant for understanding the political context, is the coming to the fore through the 1980 education boycotts of a layer of activists who forged a working relationship with older activists central to the NIC in the 1970s. This encouraged a turn to community and trade union organising.

The SAIC elections were a sharp rejection of both the Indian proposers of participation and the government's attempt to control the reform initiative. Alongside this the Nationalist government faced an economic crisis and an assertive anti-apartheid movement. How would the regime respond?

The state was caught in the crossfire of contradictory demands. Replacing white with black workers and supervisors, for example, would have halved the wage bill, but pressure from white labour restricted the full reorganisation of productive processes. An indication of the difficulty facing the NP was its loss of seats in the 1981 elections to the extreme right-wing Herstigte Nasionale Party (HNP). HNP leader Jaap Marais spoke to white fears as he criticised the government for repealing petty apartheid laws, engaging in 'wealth transfer' from white to black South Africans and proposing a new multiracial dispensation.[24]

Worsening economic conditions resulted in greater militancy among the African working class. Beyond the factory gates, resistance in African townships led to the growing rejection of community councils at the level of local government. There were many resignations from councils, and where elections were held, voter turnout was usually very low.[25]

Few imagined P.W. Botha as a reformer. In Parliament continuously from 1948, he 'had been on the far-right wing of South African politics'.[26] His 'Total Strategy' aimed to head off mounting economic and political challenges. Botha engaged in reform initiatives, central to which was the limited recognition of black trade unions and urban rights for some Africans. The 1979 Schlebusch Commission had recommended the formation of a President's Council as an official multiracial advisory body to replace the Senate, and Botha set about centralising power in the Office of the President. This structure would give a 'more equitable share in the central decision-making processes of the country' to Indians and coloureds, who, unlike Africans, did not have separate homelands for their political development. The premise was that the one-man, one-vote, winner-takes-all formula was 'unsuitable in the circumstance of South Africa with its remarkably heterogeneous population'.[27] Hence the 'tricameral' proposals, which allowed for limited coloured and Indian participation in central government. The key reform was separate assemblies for Indians and coloureds: the Tricameral Parliament, which was established in 1984.

In a position paper, the NIC criticised the proposals for being an 'imposition' which did not attempt to 'meet the demands of democracy'. The proposals reinforced apartheid, as they were race-based and 'cynically expand the White base of oppression to take in Indians and Coloureds as partners' but failed to address socio-economic inequities in the country. The latter are 'underpinned by a panoply of repressive legislation', Group

Areas, Bantustans and the migrant labour system. The NIC remained committed to the Freedom Charter and was adamant that it would not 'collaborate with the government in its evil schemes' or 'compromise our principles'. The document concluded that the NIC would continue to strive for unity: 'while Freedom Road is strewn with difficulties we look forward to the peace that is at the end of that road'.[28]

What stands out in this response is the NIC's assessment of the role of the middle class:

> The section of Indians who are most vulnerable to the high talk of 'consociational democracy' and therefore are most likely to participate are those whose economic position is favourable. The middle class is in peril. They can be seduced into accepting that the new proposals mean security and benefits for themselves and translate this misconception into a belief that what is good for them is good for the Indian people as a whole and indeed for the country altogether. This is not true as the majority of Indians are mainly working class. Our task is to dissuade the professionals and business interests from being sucked into the Apartheid machinery.[29]

The NIC document also attributed Afro–Indian tensions to the presence of an Indian trading class (so-called passenger Indians):

> Our argument is that the dominant influence of this trading class on the political, social, and economic life of Indian South Africans exaggerated the differences between Indians and Africans and acted as an impediment to black unity.[30]

The NIC had been working for black unity since its revival in 1971, and the tricameral proposals threatened to 'fracture' this unity.

While pointing to the danger of the Indian middle class being co-opted, the NIC was positive about the allegiance of the working class. History would show that it was the working class that would be concerned about its future in a new South Africa. With their position in factories threatened by Africans hired at lower pay, and faced with escalating costs for basic services in the townships, working-class Indians longed for security. This yearning proved fertile ground for a 'system' politician like Rajbansi.

Fatima Meer made an acute assessment of the new dispensation in an article published in 1983:

> The Nationalist hand has been forced by three sets of pressures. The first two ... are inherent in rising black demands, both middle and working class, expressed in a range of rhetoric and in periodic eruptions of almost unmanageable violence, and in the demands for reform from South Africa's allies and business partners ... The West is not asking for any radical change – in fact, radical change does not serve its interests. The West seeks to preserve capitalism in South Africa ... The West believes that the underlying threat to white domination is the rising expectations of the black elite which, if not gratified, will lead to the fuelling of a revolution which may destroy their investments. To forestall that, the blacks need to be incorporated into the white bourgeoisie.
>
> The Afrikaner dilemma is that in the process ... [they] will lose their own hegemony and identity. How can they overcome the spectre of past ignominies and insecurities, the memory of poor whitism which only 50 years ago threatened to decimate the Afrikaner Volk into the black mass? The third pressure [thus] comes from within Afrikanerdom itself. It emerged with the first signs that the Nationalist Party was making some concession to alien demands, that in its subscription to modernisation it was subordinating the interests of the Volk to those of international capitalism ... While appearing to respond to these pressures, the constitutional Bill in fact evades all of them and concentrates primarily on protecting the vested interest of the ruling party ... Restrictions drain the legislature of practically all self-determination and replace [it] with the obligation to become the lackey of the Nationalist government.
>
> It is a partnership in the horrible acts of apartheid that is being offered to the Indian and Coloured people, and who worth his salt would accept that? The Bill is, in effect, the culmination of the 1950 Group Areas Act, which provided for self-government in the racial zones ... The danger is that if the Bill is implemented, apartheid will gain a new legitimacy and all extra-parliamentary opposition will be met with even greater repression than now.[31]

Despite Meer's cogent critique, the move to offer greater powers to coloured and Indian representatives in Parliament marked a real shift in NP thinking and was a response to concerns that the SAIC had raised through the 1970s. The tricameral dispensation represented an attempt to transition from informal to formal co-option of Indians and coloureds.[32] Despite obvious limitations, giving increased power to Indians and coloureds over 'own affairs' provided those who served in the Tricameral Parliament with the potential to increase their powers of patronage. They could rub shoulders with those to whom they often had to plead for concessions which were just as often shunned. It would also reinforce and enhance a potentially loyal cohort of civil servants.

While these shifts were taking place within the NP, the SAIC found that the apartheid state continued working in its well-worn ways. Early in 1983 the SAIC was informed by Stoffel Botha, the administrator of Natal, that the residential community of Clairwood was to be rezoned as an industrial area.[33] The decision was a major setback, as the SAIC had lobbied the government intensively to hand Clairwood back to Indians. This was one of the oldest Indian communities in the city and an area of great symbolic significance.

The SAIC had also spent considerable time lobbying the government to agree to building the Oriental Plaza in Durban to house traders displaced by the Group Areas Act, as well as those whose businesses had been lost when a fire destroyed the historic Victoria Street Market in 1973. However, on 14 February 1983, the SAIC was informed by minister of community development Pen Kotze that plans to build the plaza had been scrapped.[34] Another issue that emerged in the SAIC was the question of Indians bringing in foreign brides, a practice that the Nationalists had banned in 1953. Council member A.E. Arbee complained that the SAIC's failure around these issues took away their 'credibility ... How do I face that Piet Retief community when I went to them to support me and to prove to them by negotiation we will achieve what we can in the form of our bread and butter political issues?'[35]

The SAIC did win some concessions in 1983: Kotze agreed to a section of Upper Church Street in Pietermaritzburg being designated a free trading area; the minister of law and order agreed to more police stations in Phoenix and Lenasia; and Grey Street was declared a residential area for Indians after a decade of struggle.[36]

Meanwhile, the NP's attempts at reforming apartheid seemed to be gaining traction. White South Africans approved a referendum on the tricameral proposals by a two-thirds majority on 2 November 1983. The existing white chamber, the House of Assembly, was to be carried over into the new dispensation. Despite the SAIC's criticisms of the constitutional arrangements and earlier blustering against the proposals, Rajbansi indicated at a meeting addressed by Botha at the Durban City Hall on 14 November 1983 that he would give the new constitution 'a fair trial'. Botha reneged on his promise to hold referendums for Indians and coloureds because he feared defeat for his government's policy.[37]

As if on cue, a myriad of anti-apartheid organisations geared up to challenge the proposals. This mobilisation united organisations that rejected the proposals as much as it created a divide between the Congress-aligned supporters and those of BCM and other leftist groupings. Two broad groupings, the United Democratic Front (UDF) and the National Forum (NF), emerged as a direct response to the reform initiatives. While the UDF was sympathetic to the ideals of the banned ANC, the NF looked to the spirit of the BCM and more left-leaning groups such as the Non-European Unity Movement.[38] The NF made a clear commitment to socialism, but being infused with sectarianism and dogmatic Marxism, it failed to attract a mass base. The UDF, on the other hand, following a massive launch on 20 August 1983 and a commitment to embracing a broad grouping of people, proved more durable over the long run. The NP would discover that once it embarked on steps to reform, it could neither control the process nor put a lid on it. The spectre of revolution, however, would see implacable foes reaching back to reform.

In the mid-1970s sociologist Kogila Moodley published an essay titled 'South African Indians: A Wavering Minority'. With considerable nuance she argued that how Indians reacted to the political conjuncture depended

on the nature of the assurances and type of security that the more sizable African subordinate group offers the wavering minority, as well as the kind of concession to Indians that the ruling group is willing to grant to prevent a threatening subordinate alliance.[39]

Moodley underestimated the zeal of a broadening group of Indian activists in pushing back at government attempts at co-option and in building a cross-racial anti-apartheid resistance. Sponsoring an anti-SAIC network in 1981 was to prove a masterstroke because it drew in constituencies beyond the NIC base, and forced those who chose to participate to contend with voices beyond the Indian community.

In many senses, the anti-SAIC campaign was prefigurative of the politics to come with the arrival of the UDF.

8 | Botha's 1984 and the Rise of the UDF

The UDF played a pre-eminent role in opposing apartheid and hastening its demise. Activists from the NIC and the Transvaal Indian Congress (TIC) were central in the formation of this national front designed to broaden and deepen resistance to the apartheid state. Spurred by the Nationalists' reform drive, the UDF's influence spread across the country. While it captured headlines for its national campaigns, the UDF was crucial in spawning street-level structures in townships that were at the heart of grassroots struggles.

Trevor Manuel recounted that the idea for the UDF emerged during his meeting with Pravin Gordhan on a visit to Durban in December 1982: 'We were talking about civics and the question that arose was, what is the next step? [Pravin Gordhan] said, why don't we go for a broad front, a kind of united front? ... The trick was to take the social capital on the ground [and] "somehow extract political capital out of it".'[1]

The two agreed to make the call for such a federation at a forthcoming conference in Johannesburg in January 1983, to revive the TIC.[2] Twenty years later, Gordhan said that the increased activism in the 1980–1983 period lent itself 'to the intensification of internal, so-called legal, mass activity and clearly anybody watching that from within or outside the country would be asking the question: how do you strategically take that forward?'[3]

In a 1988 interview Jerry Coovadia observed that the UDF was possible only because so many community-based struggles had taken place in the period following the Soweto uprising. This grassroots organising prepared the ground for the UDF, which 'had to be a federation of these many groups; tactically, it would be harder for the government to contain or ban a welter of groups, even if they banned the UDF itself'.[4]

Several NIC activists, interviewed at different times, corroborated Manuel's account, albeit with slight differences of emphasis. In the Transvaal, although the TIC had not yet been revived, the Transvaal Anti-SAIC Committee (TASC) was formed under the leadership of Dr Essop Jassat in June 1981. The possibility of calling for a united front was raised at the 1983 TASC conference.Thumba Pillay recalled:

> The formation of the UDF was discussed in NIC circles first. We went to the relaunch of the TIC and some of us spoke and chaired meetings. [The Reverend Allan] Boesak [then head of the World Alliance of Reformed Churches] was particularly prominent at the time so we thought he would raise this question of a united democratic front. And the UDF Declaration – it is something along the lines of the Freedom Charter – was drafted in Newcastle, the night before we arrived in the Transvaal for that meeting.[5]

According to oral testimony, those who helped to draft the UDF Declaration in Newcastle included Jerry Coovadia, Paul David, Zak Yacoob, Thumba Pillay and Farouk Meer.

Murthie Naidoo of the TIC had a slightly different recollection. He stated in a 2016 interview that the idea of a united front was mooted at a meeting between Transvaal and Natal activists in Newcastle:

> This was round about the time when Boesak was quite prominent and he had made some very, very good anti-apartheid statements ... And it was then decided that we will have this massive Anti-SAIC rally at the City Hall ... a no-vote rally. And Allan Boesak will be invited to speak. He [made the] call for a united front.[6]

The idea had broad appeal, as the ANC itself was keen to resuscitate above-ground legal political structures within South Africa. There was growing sentiment within the anti-apartheid movement both inside and outside the country that the exclusion of Africans from the tricameral dispensation, rather than dividing the struggle, could be a catalyst for unity in calling for the rejection of the new system. In an address on 8 January 1983, ANC president Oliver Tambo proclaimed 1983 the 'Year of United Action' and called for 'one front for national liberation'. The ANC, he said, was determined to 'bring under its revolutionary umbrella all actual and potential allies, inspire, activate, conduct, direct and lead them in united offensive against the enemy'.[7]

Boesak's call for a united front on 23 January 1983 set in motion the process for establishing the UDF. Regional UDF structures were soon set up countrywide, starting in Natal on 14 May 1983. The executive committee of the Natal group included Archie Gumede (president), Jerry Coovadia (chairperson), Virgil Bonhomme (vice-chairperson), Rabi Bugwandeen and Victoria Mxenge (treasurers), and Yunus Mohamed.

The TIC was formally reconstituted after the January meeting, and held its first general meeting at the Ramakrishna Hall in Lenasia on 1 May 1983. One of the speakers was Zak Yacoob of the NIC. His lengthy speech summarised the position of the Indian Congresses and the future UDF on the national question – that is, whether the post-apartheid South African nation was to be constituted on the basis of race or territory and therefore include all who lived in it. Yacoob warned that there was 'considerable debate and confusion in the ranks of patriots about who the oppressed are'. The broader Congress view was that Africans, Indians and coloureds 'of whatever class are victims of "naked racial oppression"' who had to 'act together and in unison create something new with its own dynamic'. The movement 'had room for democratic whites, however few they may be'. Yacoob was frustrated that 'ill-informed individuals' were critical of the Freedom Charter because it recognised national groups.

That there are Indians, Coloureds, Africans and Whites [national groups] is a self-evident and undeniable reality ... The failure to recognise the existence of national groups and ... heighten the positive features of each to weld these together [into] a single national consciousness ... smacks of the most retrogressive brand of intellectualism ... Our practical task is to bridge the gap between theory and practice ... and enable the oppressed people to act jointly in the process of change. Without this, befuddled politicians are reduced to facile rhetoric and sloganizing ... The movement for change is best facilitated by enabling organisations around issues which concern people in their daily lives: issues such as low wages, high transport costs and poor housing.[8]

Yacoob was proposing the basic Congress position that saw both racial and ethnic identity as imposed from above, while acknowledging its impulse from below. But Yacoob also brought to the fore a conundrum that faced the anti-apartheid struggle: how to imagine a South African-ness that at once recognised race and transcended it.

These heady developments must be understood in the context of the repression that accompanied reform. In July 1983 the full executive of the NIC met for the first time in 15 years, as the banning orders on people such as Mewa Ramgobin, George Sewpersadh, Pravin Gordhan and M.J. Naidoo had been lifted.[9]

Launch of the UDF

A month later, in August 1983, the national launch of the UDF took place in Mitchells Plain, Cape Town. According to Ramgobin, Cape Town was a deliberate choice

because Boesak, in terms of a national figure and a Martin Luther King of an orator, had made his mark; because he had catalysed the idea; and we chose the least developed area in terms of the Congress Movement so that it can have a psychological thrust ... an impetus for the whole region.[10]

Daya Pillay, who was one of those who went to the launch from Durban, recounted:

I was part of a convoy that drove up ... six buses and three cars ... It was an amazing experience being for the first time in such a huge crowd of people who had such an intense vibe. There was more emotion in the event than structure and a rational unfolding of a sequential programme.[11]

Sharm Maharaj of the PWC went as a member of the Durban Housing Action Committee (DHAC):

> We mobilised several busloads of people from Phoenix to say the public must launch this, because in the end it mustn't be just banned again by the State, and if a few political activists pitch up there, then surely there'll be trouble ... The atmosphere was electric. It was the first time we were becoming involved in a nation-wide launch of a political organisation ... I recall Alan Boesak speaking at the launch. You have charismatic speakers, but to whip up the emotions of people, I have never seen somebody as good as him.[12]

In his speech Boesak said that the demands of the UDF were not 'conferred or derived from the state, but you have to go back beyond the dim mist of eternity to understand their origins. They are God-given ...' He said that the UDF rejected the constitutional proposal because it 'kept all the race laws – the pillars of apartheid – intact'. South Africans opposed to apartheid would not be 'satisfied until justice rolls down like waters and righteousness like a mighty stream'.[13] Among the resolutions passed were a demand for 'cheap, nutritious food and other essentials'; a repeal of the Group Areas Act; support for workers 'in their struggle for a fair share of the wealth they produce'; condemnation of the 'imperialism' of the British and US governments, which supported the constitutional proposals; recognition of the rights of women; and a call on women's organisations to join in the struggle to end 'race, class, and sexual discrimination', and for South African troops to withdraw from South West Africa (now Namibia).[14]

For the first time since the 1950s, the country witnessed an extensive gathering of anti-apartheid forces as African, white, coloured and Indian political leaders, civic bodies and student activists came together into a broad-based national mass movement. Ramgobin emphasised that 'the launch of the UDF was a launch of the people's initiative of South Africa. Every cent expended at the launch and its preliminary work was either from the pockets of the proponents of the UDF personally, or elicited from the community; it was a community project.'[15]

For Yunus Mohamed, the UDF brought ordinary people from various spheres into the anti-apartheid movement.[16] This was affirmed by Ela Gandhi, who said that the formation of the UDF was one of the 'defining moments' in South Africa's history, as there 'was unity of religions ... civics, and we brought all the races together, in one united front'.[17] Sharm Maharaj recounted that the police viewed the UDF as 'the internal organ of the ANC'; but as he saw it, the UDF 'was an umbrella structure' that 'brought together the SANCOs [South African National Civic Organisations] and the civics and so on'. Among the people of Phoenix, 'we had a groundswell of support and enthusiasm of people who said, "yes, we want to be part of this movement"'.[18] Jerry Coovadia stated in 1989 that in his view the UDF was the most appropriate structure at that juncture in the anti-apartheid struggle:

> Apartheid's influence extends all over: in housing, education, welfare, political representation etc., so people feel most immediately the national oppression of the apartheid regime. This is the rational basis for bringing all groups of people into one organisation, whether they be the petty bourgeoisie, academics, businessmen or the working class. Amongst us there are different classes and groups, but we believe that the interests of all groups and classes are served by the removal of apartheid ... Our strategy recognises the key role of the working class while at the same time acknowledging the substantial part played by all the other sectors of society. A coalescence of these broad-based struggles will establish a springboard from which the final leap to freedom will be made.[19]

The influence of the external ANC on the activities of the internal UDF was raised as an issue by critics. Pravin Gordhan, a central figure in multiple Congress organisations, reflected that while there was broad synergy, decisions were mostly made by activists on the ground.

> There's always great difficulty in operating from afar when there's intense mass activities happening even if that afar is just in another province. It's those who are closest who have to make quick decisions

about tactical choices or initiatives that they actually have to take. They can take into account strategic perspectives which guide one broadly, and I think that's where you had an interesting synergy between strategic perspectives that were emerging from the ANC outside, perspectives that were emerging from people inside, and a kind of new chemistry beginning to evolve itself about how you engage with tactical initiatives within a particular context to build that particular process.[20]

Ramgobin maintained that while seeking continuity, the UDF in its formative stages 'had this tight balance to maintain. We didn't want to alienate people and we didn't want people to have a misconception that this is the ANC in disguise.'[21] It is for this reason, Ramgobin explained, that the UDF did not formally adopt the Freedom Charter at this stage:

> Some of us investigated the possibilities of going to establish a front on the basis of ideological unity. We thought in the long term it would be correct, but in the short term it would alienate a lot of people who are marginal or uncommitted to the Freedom Charter but are committed to fighting the Tricam[eral proposals]. And on that basis we succeeded in mobilizing hundreds of these organizations. It might have defeated our objective if we had put the cart before the horse, but as time went on it became very clear that ... there was a need nationally to have a cohesive organizational position based on a particular kind of ideology. So we had no problem because by then, realistically speaking, only organisations that stuck by the UDF were those who had a historical association with the Charterist position.[22]

The UDF officially adopted the Freedom Charter in 1987 to underscore its commitment to the Congress tradition.

There were murmurings about control of the UDF by Indian activists. Jeremy Seekings observes that

> the Natal UDF was still constrained by the lack of prominent African leaders. Moreover, several of the leading African charterists were not Zulu ... providing Inkatha with ammunition to throw at the UDF ... Many of the younger African ANC supporters were suspicious of the

UDF, seeing it as an NIC initiative, and sought instead to be involved in the ANC's military underground.[23]

One of the UDF national presidents, Archie Gumede, had a long relationship with the NIC and worked with Yunus Mohamed. Jerry Coovadia made it clear that while Gumede was 'old, sometimes gets overwhelmed by the immediacy of events', and while Gumede and the other national president, Albertina Sisulu, did 'make mistakes', NIC activists 'understand that UDF leaders must be Africans'.[24] Likewise, Ramgobin recounted that when he was being nominated for president, 'I said you are talking bullshit. It is wrong. It's got to be under the leadership of the African people. That is the tradition, and declared position'.[25] Gumede, in Coovadia's view, was the appropriate choice since he was 'the only senior African old Congress person in Natal'. Younger people found him 'acceptable, because of his ANC links, basically honest, admired for his courage, very committed to the Freedom Charter'.[26]

While the national presidents were African, NIC members such as Sewpersadh, Coovadia, Ramgobin and Mohamed were high-ranking office bearers. Crucially, Ramgobin and Cas Saloojee of the Transvaal were national treasurers, while Mohamed was treasurer in Natal, meaning that they were in control of resources.

NIC activists dismissed the idea of Indian dominance. Charm Govender argued instead that 'the perception of people I worked with is that ... the Indians who were around had serious political skills, that they learned by participating in the work of the NIC', which was one of the few organisations 'that people could galvanise around'.[27] Yunus Carrim suggested that NIC members' prominence in UDF leadership structures was likely due to the fact that 'many of the more senior African leaders ... were on Robben Island or in exile or banned'.[28] The accusation of Indian control, however, would get stronger as the decade wore on.

The UDF in Natal

In the lead-up to the launch of the UDF in Natal, Security Branch police raided the offices of Farouk Meer. They confiscated 18 000 NIC posters, which were deemed 'undesirable' because they contained photos of Boesak and Ramgobin. The NIC managed to distribute 5 000 posters with the words 'Congress Says No to Rajbansi and Botha's New Constitution'. A further 30 000 posters were handed out calling on Indians to 'Stop Rajbansi Now!' and 'prevent him from training our children to die for apartheid'; this pamphlet had a photograph of a dead man with a rifle. According to Farouk Meer, Rajbansi was 'being singled out for attack because he epitomised the SAIC. We have decided this time not to pussyfoot around with attacking the SAIC but to go for the man himself.'[29]

Singling out Rajbansi was a tacit recognition of his impact in the public domain. Unlike his suave contemporaries in the Solidarity Party – mostly businesspeople and professionals who were adept at structured meetings where a deal could be negotiated – Rajbansi was a bruiser. Born in 1942, he matriculated from Clairwood Secondary and attended the University College for Indians on Salisbury Island. He worked with great aplomb as a public relations officer for the milk industry, and was a soccer referee and sports administrator, holding the presidency of the Southern Natal Football Association. Rajbansi won his first Southern Durban LAC election in 1970 and was elected to the SAIC's executive committee on 26 November 1974. He was chair of that committee from 1981 until its dissolution in September 1984. Rajbansi had the uncanny ability to talk the language of the street while at the same time swanning around with the president of the apartheid republic. Together with his wife of the time, Asha Devi, who was always resplendent in a colourful sari, Rajbansi brought vigour and verve to the SAIC. His ability to make political somersaults and somehow land on his feet served him well during the apartheid years as well as in the post-apartheid period.

The UDF was officially launched in Natal at Durban's Orient Hall on 14 November 1983. P.W. Botha was holding a meeting that same evening with a group of invited Indians at the Durban City Hall.[30] Earlier that day several NIC leaders were arrested for taking part in a placard demonstration outside the building where P.W. Botha was scheduled to speak. Those arrested included Mewa Ramgobin, Farouk Meer, George Sewpersadh, M.J. Naidoo, Zak Yacoob, Ela Gandhi and Fatima Meer. The demonstrators' placards read: 'Equal rights for all', 'Indians will never accept apartheid', 'Botha's deal has no appeal', 'Indians, Africans and Coloureds stand united' and 'SAIC – apartheid stooges'.[31]

At his City Hall meeting, Botha raised the spectre of the expulsion of Asians from Uganda in 1972, an event that clearly impacted local Indians.

Figure 8.1: Anti-tricameral protest meetings drew large crowds across the country. (Courtesy of Gandhi-Luthuli Documentation Centre)

Botha was playing on or nurturing fears that under African majority rule Indians would be expelled from South Africa or at least treated poorly, as was the case in Uganda, and that they were better off under white minority rule. He said that the new constitutional proposals represented a further recognition of the permanence of Indians in South Africa.[32]

Referendum

Although the NIC emphatically rejected the new constitutional arrangements, the issue of boycotting the upcoming referendum on approving the tricameral proposals was not clear-cut. Charles Nqakula from the Border region of the UDF, who left the country shortly after this period to join Operation Vula (discussed in Chapter 11) and would become a cabinet minister in the post-apartheid ANC government, was clearly critical of the Natal UDF position. He recalled in his autobiography that at a UDF council meeting in 1983, the Natal delegates proposed that Indians be allowed to participate in the tricameral elections in order to gauge

the UDF's popularity among Indians in Natal and across the country. They said that they would use their seats as a battering ram to make the system unworkable. We could not understand why politically mature people such as our Natal comrades would want to associate themselves with such a fraudulent exercise. They included stalwarts such as Archie Gumede and Mewa Ramgobin.[33]

While Nqakula misremembers the NIC position, assuming that they proposed to stand for the Tricameral Parliament when the issue was whether or not to vote in the proposed referendum in order to reject the proposals, this debate nevertheless threatened the unity of the UDF. The matter came to a head at a special national conference held in Port Elizabeth in December 1983. At the conference, those who advocated participation in the referendum, led by the Natal region, were labelled 'sell-outs' and outvoted by 55 to 45.[34] In Yunus Mohamed's recollection, the NIC had a 'fairly uniform position' over participating in the referendum since 'it wasn't participation in a dummy institution ... In the referendum, it is giving an opinion, rather than being involved in a longer, ongoing process.'[35]

The Natal UDF mandated Curnick Ndlovu, an African comrade just released from Robben Island, to present its case in Port Elizabeth, in part to reduce resentment against Indians.[36] Mohamed recalled:

The Natal Region was called moderates, because of our position on the referendum ... We had our own kind of joke: Natal always seemed to be a kind of more participative vision; the Western Cape had a non-collaborationist tradition. It was heated in the Lenasia meeting ... we decided, it's obviously such a major issue, let's go to PE ... It was not the only issue but it became the only issue, fairly heated.[37]

Mewa Ramgobin also related his disappointment over the Port Elizabeth decision:

Western Cape politics was basically Unity Movement [NEUM] oriented. On the question of a referendum, we could never get the Cape with us. We said that the referendum would be a mobilising factor, more important than the election campaign ... to tell people about the system. It would have given us greater potential for mobilisation and we'd have been less vulnerable in terms of repression ... That was the first time I suffered high blood pressure because ... we just couldn't carry the day in Port Elizabeth ... We adjourned it to the Pretoria executive meeting. We couldn't even carry it there.[38]

Thus the issue of participation was raised in Lenasia, debated further in Port Elizabeth and eventually defeated in Pretoria. That NIC leaders were keen to participate in a referendum was also made clear by its president, M.J. Naidoo. In February 1984, two months after the Port Elizabeth meeting and before the forthcoming executive meeting in Pretoria, Naidoo spoke at the Krish Rabilal Memorial Meeting in Durban. He asserted that it was important for Indians to emphatically reject the tricameral constitutional proposals:

The question about the referendum is, isn't that a racial referendum? And if it is, how can you participate in it? Ladies and gentlemen, I say yes, indeed it is racial. But we are gonna ask the people to reject that racial system. Now, there is a difference between participating to make it work and participating to reject it. I want to say that the only way in which you can reject the Indian parliament is, we say in the referendum 'NO'. If we do not say 'NO', we will be forced to have this Indian chamber put on our heads whether we like it or not.[39]

Naidoo saw the referendum as an opportunity for a 'no' vote that would delegitimise the tricameral initiative and further African–Indian solidarity. In the swirl of debate, not much store was placed on the consequences of losing the referendum. In any event the situation was resolved by the state calling off referendums among coloureds and Indians.

These conflicts had long-term consequences, as the factions claimed authority from different ANC connections in exile. The Border group claimed authority from Lesotho, while the Durban group claimed a line to Swaziland and London. These claims later fed into allegations of attempts at control that were mired in issues of racial identity, since mainly Indian activists pushed the participation position, while African comrades opposed it.[40]

Figure 8.2: *From left*: R. Ramesar, unidentified, Farouk Meer and M.J. Naidoo addressing an NIC human rights/anti-tricameral meeting. (Courtesy of 1860 Heritage Centre)

The UDF held together despite the bruising debate, and launched an ambitious national Million Signature Campaign in early 1984 to galvanise opposition to the tricameral elections. The campaign was a training ground for young volunteers across the country who busied themselves collecting signatures. They went door-to-door in the townships to talk with residents, highlighting bread-and-butter issues such as high bus fares, rentals and rates. While the target of a million signatures was not met, this mobilisation allowed the UDF to run open political campaigns while attracting new activists.

Patsy Seethal and Fatima Carrim, two NIC activists in Pietermaritzburg, recounted how they picketed outside factories to distribute pamphlets on weekdays and spent their weekends mobilising the community.[41] Roy Sukuram contended that the work of the PWC was critical in mobilising Phoenix against the tricameral elections: 'We made one thing very clear ... do not come to Phoenix if you are advocating SAIC.'[42] Kumi Naidoo, who cut his political teeth in the school boycotts of 1980, recalled the campaign in Chatsworth:

> On the days of the elections we would go up to the polling booths and ask questions and try to arouse as much protest as possible. There were lots of policemen around so we had to be careful how we did that. It would be done by raising questions as if we were supporting one candidate or the other ... The tricameral election wasn't so straightforward because one or two of the people that stood for elections were anti-SAIC people in the past. In Chatsworth one of the persons that spoke at our anti-SAIC rally in 1981 was a candidate in 1984.[43]

The NIC big guns also made their presence felt. Billy Nair, M.J. Naidoo, Mewa Ramgobin and Fatima Meer addressed an anti-tricameral meeting in Port Shepstone in July 1984. The presence of Billy Nair, who had

Figure 8.3: Fatima Meer, next to R. Ramesar, addressing an anti-tricameral meeting. (Courtesy of 1860 Heritage Centre)

been released from Robben Island in February 1984, gave the campaign a huge boost. Gordhan stated in a 1986 interview that Nair's presence was 'like Nelson Mandela returning ... authentic leadership. Here was a person who was active in the '50s, paid a heavy price for his commitment, having gone through all the fires of apartheid.' Nair was seen to 'offer clear and gutsy leadership' and 'was not going to compromise', unlike the 'Rajbansi's and J.N. Reddy's of our community who were busy compromising left, right and centre'.[44]

The Freedom Charter

At the Port Shepstone meeting Fatima Meer described the Nationalist government as 'a sinking ship making its last pleasure cruise'.[45] This was one of the few meetings that she was invited to address. Though she was always associated with the NIC/UDF/ANC in the popular mind, NIC members were upset that she did not openly embrace the Freedom Charter. In a mid-1980s interview with Julie Frederikse, she related an incident in which she told a student researcher that she respected the charter of the BCM's National Forum as well as the ten-point programme of the Unity Movement, adding, 'There's nothing sacrosanct about the Freedom Charter.' The NIC interpreted her comments as being anti-Freedom Charter. When some executive members visited her at Natal University to invite her to become a member of the executive, one of their demands was that she 'must commit to the Freedom Charter'.[46] On 22 July 1983 she wrote to those who had visited her – Mewa Ramgobin, M.J. Naidoo, Jerry Coovadia, Zak Yacoob and Thumba Pillay – indicating that she was 'greatly honoured' by their visit but politely declining the proffered executive position:

> There is no single group in the province today with which I could serve the cause which we commonly share more effectively than with you. I do however have inhibitions ... Frankly I was surprised that commitment to the Charter now constitutes a pre-requisite to membership of the Natal Indian Congress. Without having the benefit of the considerable discussion that must have preceded your arrival at this position, my reaction is to question its wisdom ... My own view of the Freedom Charter is to see it as serving a symbolic active engagement.[47]

Fatima Meer told Frederikse that the NIC executive punished her for this stance:

> The first meeting they had where they were welcoming back a whole lot of people whose banning orders were removed – in one big sweep – I was at that meeting, my first public political meeting – they welcomed everybody who had been unbanned – meticulously left me out and I'm in front and I see a note going to the chairman and, you know, clearly there were people who were saying: 'Well, why [is she] not being welcomed back into the fold' – and eventually the chairman could not ignore these notes, so he sort of said, 'There's also here the wife of I.C. Meer, Fatima Meer, and we also welcome her' – suddenly I became the wife of somebody. And that's when the vendetta started – at the national launch of the UDF in the Cape they wanted me to be one of the key speakers. I would have joined without any problems whatsoever, but they said I was not acceptable as a speaker because I rejected the Freedom Charter ... I consider myself as part of the liberatory movement, and I consider Congress and UDF and PAC and NEUM and AZAPO, all of them, to be part of the liberatory movement. That is the difficulty that everybody has with me.[48]

The NIC's original 1971 membership form did not mention the Freedom Charter, but an amended form, post-1980, included the words 'I accept the principles of the Natal Indian Congress as set out in the Freedom Charter' and a list of the Charter's clauses.[49] Making acceptance of the Freedom Charter a prerequisite for NIC membership may be regarded as ironical at one level. But this should be viewed in context. In the 1950s NIC activists had been deeply involved in canvassing for the demands set out in the Charter. An NIC meeting at the Bharat Hall in Durban on 28 August 1955 approved the formation of a National Joint Consultative Committee to popularise the Freedom Charter. Moreover, then NIC president Monty Naicker's New Year's message for 1956, published in *New Age* on 29 December 1955, stated that the Freedom Charter 'enshrines the hopes and aspirations of the millions of underprivileged peoples of the Union and in 1956 our main task will be to advance the cause of the Charter'. At the South African Indian Congress conference in 1956, Naicker reiterated that the Freedom Charter 'has become the guiding star of all South Africans of all races advancing on the road to freedom. In all our deliberations, decisions and actions, our main concern should be to make this great Charter a living reality.'[50] This adherence to the Charter was affirmed by Zak Yacoob in his May 1983 speech to the TIC in Lenasia, quoted above.

Elections

The elections for the Tricameral Parliament were held on 28 August 1984. The state arrested a number of UDF/NIC leaders in the days leading up to the election in an attempt to impose what it referred to as 'stability'. Ramgobin recounted in 1989:

> Nobody can deny the fact that the UDF became a household name in that period, until August of 1984, the 20th of August to be precise, because it was almost a year, the first anniversary, that we got arrested. The first grouping of people got detained – Archie, myself, George, MJ, Billy, Mama-Sisulu, Terror Lekota, Popo Molefe – the hierarchy of the UDF were detained. Until then the UDF grew with leaps and bounds. The UDF faced its first catastrophe ... the state just took away the top.[51]

Such arrests would cripple anti-apartheid activism in the second half of the 1980s.

Of 504 400 eligible Indian voters, 411 804 had registered. However, only 20.3 per cent of registered voters cast ballots, a total of 83 703.[52] According to official estimates, 30.9 per cent of coloureds voted.[53] Rajbansi's NPP won 18 seats and J.N. Reddy's Solidarity Party took 17 seats.

The tricameral dispensation came at a historical juncture when thousands of students were becoming politicised and most implored their parents not to vote. Many teachers had been forced to kowtow to the SAIC through the 1970s, even as they accused it of making political appointments and promotions. These teachers showed their displeasure by simply not voting for those perceived to be manipulating the system for their own ends. The political work of sports organisations through the 1970s and 1980s was also crucial.

A joint statement issued by the NIC and TIC concluded that the low voter turnout showed that 'the people had not been fooled by the

Figure 8.4: Graffiti and posters in support of the UDF and against the tricameral proposals, 1984. (Courtesy of Gandhi-Luthuli Documentation Centre)

Government's new deal' and that 'the anti-Tricam cause is just, our unity is deep-rooted and our determination to be free is unshakeable'.[54]

For his part, Rajbansi issued a statement that the low voter turnout was the result of 'fear and not because of any ideological boycott of the elections'. Solidarity's national chairman Pat Poovalingam also attributed the low voter turnout to intimidation: 'the country knows the poll was low because of intimidation by the right wing and the left wing'.[55] The accusation of intimidation was ironic, given that the apartheid state had violently broken up protests and arrested many opponents of the new dispensation. '[T]he rhino whip, tear gas, sneeze machines, plastic bullets, real bullets, detention orders, arrests, stone-throwing, petrol bombs, and concerted abuse – all the familiar accompaniments of non-White protest and police reaction – welcomed the dawn of consociational democracy.'[56]

The tricameral experiment would prove 'a disastrous failure that actually hastened the end of apartheid' because it was rejected by black

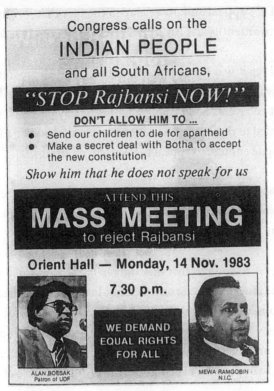

Figure 8.5: Poster advertising a UDF meeting, 1983. (Courtesy of Gandhi-Luthuli Documentation Centre)

South Africans and led to a right-wing revolt within the NP. Andries Treurnicht destabilised the party by leaving with his followers to form the Conservative Party.[57] Ironically, the strategy pursued by the NP, which was to weaken by division, was visited on the ruling party itself.

Tom Lodge views the NIC as playing a central role in the resurgence of the public profile of the ANC from the late 1970s.[58] NIC activists worked courageously to bring the Freedom Charter into the public domain and to campaign for the release of Nelson Mandela, as well as conducting the anti-SAIC and anti-tricameral campaigns. Jerry Coovadia stated that the NIC/UDF 'had overwhelming support from the people, in the sense that they never went to vote, so for that project, we were immensely successful'. Coovadia conceded that thereafter 'we did lose support because it became difficult to organise'.[59] Some NIC activists began to forge links with the ANC in exile and would be instrumental in building the underground.

Part of the UDF's appeal and power lay in the fact that it refused to be tied into any narrow identity. As Anthony Marx points out in a seminal study:

> Its central tenet was nonracialism ... The United Democratic Front's priority [was] broad mobilisation over conceptual purity. To achieve the widest adherents and avoid antagonising any potential sources of funds needed to organise mass actions, it was in the UDF's interest to remain vague enough to appeal to a variety of groups.[60]

While there was a commitment to 'broad mobilisation', there was also a tendency to control, a point argued by Johnny Copelyn, who was centrally involved in the independent labour movement:

> NIC cadres in the unions that they did not control operated as a secret cabal in the movement. Worse, it was not in the least bit clear whether these groups were committed to drawing their mandates from the workers they were supposedly leading or whether their commitment was to an underground vanguardist group who knew better. At best they gave the impression of being a very hyped-up mixture of the two.[61]

In an echo of Fatima Meer's experience, when Copelyn questioned the Freedom Charter's vagueness on fundamental worker rights he was, like others of this ilk, 'labelled ... a problematic person, a syndicalist who wanted only to isolate workers from the national liberation struggle and who had no respect for the people's leaders'.[62] These threads of underground, vanguard, cabal emerge in the chapters to come.

The next chapter examines a dramatic event in the history of the struggle: the occupation of the British Consulate by senior NIC/UDF leaders on the run from the Security Branch. It was a moment of inspiration that galvanised international attention at a time when the apartheid state was desperately trying to win support for its reform drive. The incident also provides startling insights into the factions within the NIC, forged by sharp debates over political and ideological differences, which sometimes even cut through marriage and friendship.

9 | Letters from Near and Afar: The Consulate Six

O ngoing and intensifying anti-tricameral protests in 1984 prompted the state to marshal its repressive arsenal. Activists across the country were detained in an effort to stem mobilisation. An NIC court application resulted in some of those detained in the lead-up to the elections being released on 12 September 1984, but the state immediately issued orders for their rearrest. Among those released were six senior leaders of the NIC/UDF: Archie Gumede, George Sewpersadh, Mewa Ramgobin, M.J. Naidoo, Billy Nair and Paul David. In a dramatic move these six activists took refuge in the British Consulate in Durban on 13 September 1984. This occupation would span three months, as the last of them only left the Consulate on 13 December 1984.

The immediate aim of the Consulate Six, as they came to be known, was to attract maximum international publicity because P.W. Botha was to be inaugurated as state president on 14 September.[1] Ramgobin's short press conference following the occupation revealed this intention:

> I appeared at the door just below the British Consulate seal and, to the clicking of cameras, read out my hand-written statement as to why we were in the Consulate ... Those few minutes provided the democratic movement in South Africa with invaluable international exposure for weeks on end. Having upstaged his inauguration, I don't think P.W. [Botha] ever forgave us.[2]

While Ramgobin may have overstated the impact of the group's actions on Botha's inauguration, the incident certainly created a buzz in the country and once more dragged the apartheid state's heavy-handedness into the international spotlight.

The occupation proved a masterstroke, as it demonstrated the resilience and unity of purpose of these veteran activists. There also appeared to be smooth coordination between the Consulate Six and their families and fellow activists on the outside, who provided both personal and political support.

A closer look suggests that the plans for occupation were somewhat hastily put together. This is hardly surprising under the circumstances, but it meant that long-term strategies and goals had not been worked out. As we will see, the correspondence in this period between Mewa Ramgobin and Ela Gandhi reveals a complicated and insightful picture of intertwining family strains and bitter recrimination over political ideology and tactics. Their letters show how in a small organisation like the NIC, with its mingling of political objectives with family and friendships, activists under personal stress and operating in repressive conditions lent themselves to debates that left deep scars. Bonds that appeared tight from the outside were often tenuous, and the wounds were often more painful because they were inflicted by kith and kin.

The occupation

As the Consulate Six saga unfolded, what was originally planned as a sit-in became an 'occupation'. Paul David's recollection of events is that on the advice of their lawyer Ismail Mahomed, they went into hiding in La Mercy, on the north coast of KwaZulu-Natal:

> The six of us had a discussion together with other leaders of the NIC, Pravin and Thumba ... and we said, yes, we'll get sanctuary in the British Consulate but not just to evade arrest but as a sign that we are opposed to arrest without warrants, detention without trial. We were driven in two cars by doctor friends of ours, Joey Govender and his partner, D.V. Naidoo, to the consulate and we pretended we were on business, managed to get in to see Phyllis Orr, deputy consular general in Durban. She thought the conversation was over, but we told her, 'No, we'd like to stay on for a little while.' At first, she said, 'you're

welcome', and then we broke the news to her and she said, 'Are you all now in occupation of the consulate?' We could have chosen some other country not as hostile to us, but we chose the British Consulate because we didn't like Britain's stand on the ANC generally.[3]

While the activists did not expect full-on British hospitality with tea and scones, neither did they anticipate the frosty response they received from the consular officials. According to David:

> We were kept in the reading room. Conditions were harsh; goodness me, they wouldn't give us a mattress, they wouldn't give us bedding. We had to sleep on the dusty carpet floor. That room hadn't been cleaned up for a long time. For bathing, they took us after hours to the toilet. There were no showers; we had to bath in a hand basin and I taught the fellows to have a bath with a face towel! We used to air-dry. They allowed us one meal and to keep breakfast things ... We used our shoes as pillows. We were given a chemical toilet that we covered with shelves.[4]

This led Mewa Ramgobin to suggest in jest, 'We made a mistake. We should have gone to their homes and not to their offices. At least we would have had beds to sleep, and toilets to use. Here we didn't have beds and toilets to use.'[5]

According to David, they were able to meet some NIC officials:

> The British allowed us medical visits and the medical people were our friends ... Farouk Meer, Jerry Coovadia, Khorshed Ginwala ... Jerry was Mewa's doctor, and one day Simon Davey, who was the consul general, opened the door and said, 'Mr. Ramgobin, your paediatrician is here to see you.' And I remember I said to him, 'Lucky I didn't choose Joey Govender, he's a gynaecologist.' Yes, we had our moments there![6]

Farouk Meer, NIC executive member who visited the Consulate as a medical doctor, described the occupation as a 'spectacular success':

> There were thousands of people [outside the building]; the streets were clogged ... and the security police were waiting to detain them.

And the television people were parked outside. We even arranged for a clandestine interview with the people occupying the Consulate with British television, and that was shown internationally. We smuggled equipment when I went to see them, and we gave these guys the speakers and through the speakers we were then with the British journalists/TV people. They stood at another building overlooking this building, and the interview was carrying on.[7]

These captivating descriptions obscure an important part of the story of the sit-in-turned-occupation. Although the decision to enter the Consulate was fully supported by the NIC/UDF, the events that subsequently unfolded were hotly debated. There were tensions over tactics and

Figure 9.1: Mewa Ramgobin, with George Sewpersadh, reading out a press statement after occupation of the British Consulate, 13 September 1984. (Courtesy of Mewa Ramgobin and Iain Edwards)

between factions pulling in different directions. Much of this is revealed in the correspondence between fellow activists Mewa Ramgobin and Ela Gandhi, who were also husband and wife.

Letters between Ela Gandhi and Mewa Ramgobin

Ramgobin's letters, compiled by Iain Edwards,[8] were crucial in deepening our understanding of the Consulate occupation. We wrote to Ela Gandhi to solicit her perspective on the event, but she politely demurred, replying on 25 September 2020: 'The NIC had a large executive and perhaps if you want another view you should ask some of the other executive members so that this is not seen as a family issue but rather a cooperative democratic view.' While her response is justifiable, those members of the executive whom we approached were unable to clarify issues arising from this correspondence.

The correspondence between Ramgobin and Ela Gandhi is a window on the human element in the world of activism and reveals divisions produced in the cauldron of struggle. The letters resonate with a palpable tension, giving the reader a sense of the personal as political and the political as personal. According to Edwards, Ramgobin's letters show, 'in compellingly powerful ways, the desire to continue being both husband and father and also breadwinner. These letters are the finest examples of what banning, house arrest etc. mean to the people involved. These should never be flattened into all-heroic chronicles of struggle.'[9]

In a letter to Ramgobin on 26 September 1984, Ela Gandhi reported that a mass meeting in Verulam had attracted around 800 people, and was addressed by Dullah Omar, Jerry Coovadia and ex-Robben Islander Curnick Ndlovu. She intimated that the NIC executive discussed what the six activists should do next. It appears that Ramgobin favoured negotiating an exit with the British and South African authorities, while Ela Gandhi's preference was to take the case to court as a way of exposing apartheid and its system of arbitrary detention to a global audience. She wrote:

> Have we achieved what we want – International focus – yet? Engaging the Govt. – to an extent. [Relations between] S.A. and [Britain] only beginning to deteriorate. Before this aspect becomes more intense

both Br and S.A. would like to end impasse – what better way than to enter into a little quiet agreement? World focus is on the outcome of the case. Everyone is waiting – if court is in our favour – [minister of law and order] Le Grange loses face. If court is in their favour S.A.'s vicious system will be further exposed. But if no judgement is given and a compromise is made what do we gain?[10]

Ela Gandhi acknowledged the strain that the sit-in was placing on activists, as it 'sharpened our tempers, our tolerance is waning, our sensitivity is rising'. She called for all to act sensibly 'to try to check this trend, so that emotions can remain under control and we can think and work systematically'.[11]

In his reply to Ela Gandhi on 28 September, Ramgobin made the case that exiting the Consulate would be the correct line to take. He took issue with those who sought to label him an 'opportunist', singling out 'P.G.' (Pravin Gordhan?) as one of those figures:

I have a point, and politically a workable one, but I have abided by a decision taken outside ... [It was in] the quiet and intimacy of political colleagues only that I came to the conclusion that the plan was an effective (I believe it still is) one. Then, there was unanimity ... It was I who sent to elicit the views from the outside. Who met, how they met, what courtesies were exchanged or not exchanged, who agreed or disagreed I do not know. What I do know was that ... it was disturbing because of the attitude of especially P.G. ... I'll never tolerate anybody, even P.G., in this case, to use words like 'opportunist' to describe me or my political assessment. It is precisely because I do not want to appear as an opportunist politician ... that I took the opportunity to demand a triumphant departure for our struggle.[12]

While the sit-in had placed the British and the South Africans 'in a spot', Ramgobin was circumspect with regard to its deeper impact. He argued in the letter of 28 September that Britain and South Africa had the 'ability to resolve their long-term interests. Do we have the ability and the resources to maintain a momentum to change their long-term interests, from the

Consulate and the propaganda emanating from here? No, I say.' Ramgobin was of the view that Indians as a minority could only play an 'ancillary' role in the anti-apartheid struggle, and that 'change in our country can be effected, in essence, by our African counterparts'. He ended his letter cynically by stating that he would remain in the Consulate if Ela Gandhi thought that that would 'advance' the cause, but 'do get a frank opinion of our fellow comrades and people, in whose name I am doing, whatever I am doing'.[13]

Ramgobin questioned the sit-in-turned-occupation which, in his view, had been intended as a short-term strategy to upstage P.W. Botha's inauguration. But those on the outside saw the political possibilities flowing from the publicity, especially on the international terrain, and wanted it to continue. When Ramgobin refers to the African majority, it is not clear whether he is pointing to their muted involvement in the leadership of the mass movement and to the heavy burden placed on Indians as a minority, or whether it is a backhanded criticism that those on the outside had not successfully mobilised Africans. Was this a heartfelt critique or merely an excuse to bring the occupation to an end?

In a letter dated 2 October 1984, Ramgobin stated that the court appearance of the Consulate Six later that day would show that they were willing to subject themselves to the 'jurisdiction of the courts here (no matter how repugnant the laws of the land)', unlike the apartheid regime which 'encouraged lawlessness' by allowing the 'Coventry Four' to escape from the judicial process in Britain. This was a reference to the four businessmen whom the NP government was refusing to extradite to the UK in connection with arms smuggling to South Africa. Ramgobin admitted to going through 'a serious and painful emotional dilemma'. He wrote that it was

> no help for a conscience in agony, to learn that we should stay here, or any other place, until we have won. Because, very honestly I do not know when and how we reach our victory. That we are gaining fortitude, in respect of propaganda, raising the level of consciousness here and abroad, mobilization etc. there is no doubt. But, to ever believe that the struggle is going to be waged from here, indefinitely, turns across my own political perception.[14]

Ela Gandhi's reply on 4 October 1984 informed Ramgobin that the NIC executive disagreed with 'the question of termination of the campaign. This I think is largely due to the fact that you are away from the community ... events have escalated and the objectives as well as the campaign moved on a much wider level.' The occupation had generated widespread support. More importantly,

> at present a point of concern is the timing of your exit from there. Zak [Yacoob] has been able to spur on International interest ... The British community is also being pressurized to support us and to apply pressure on the Govt. It is these pressures that have resulted in withdrawal of charges, unbanning of Beyers N. [Naudé] and the present silence.
>
> With all these external pressures mounting, we need to keep up the internal pressure ... Understandably the problem is how long. Like when trying to push a heavy piece of furniture, if pressure is applied simultaneously by the whole gang it moves, one by one it can't move, withdrawing pressure on one side while the other continues, doesn't help either. A premature withdrawal can have the effect of popping the balloon ...
>
> While we are just as anxious to rescue normal family life, we feel that this emotional aspect must not be the deciding factor in what must be done. Likewise I think that it would be indeed very sad if your leaving the consulate is determined by emotion. There are tensions, there are serious constraints, there are also the barriers placed by the British and South Africans to hamper your spirits. To succumb to these is a serious defeat for us ... [I]f you come out now deep down you will know that you have failed and will always have to live with that ... try to exert that degree of discipline and control that you will not only make us proud but you will feel pride in yourselves.[15]

This letter relies on a mix of political reasoning and personal cajoling to appeal to Ramgobin's sense of himself. In contrast to Ramgobin's view, the 'revolutionary leadership' saw leaving the Consulate as amounting to failure for himself, the community and the struggle.

NIC executive member Farouk Meer argued retrospectively that the occupation of the Consulate was intended to achieve four objectives:

> Firstly, there was the Koornhof Bills; we popularise the Koornhof Bills [which were to bring the Tricameral Parliament into effect]. We popularised the UDF because the UDF was still in its formative years; it hadn't become internationally recognized as it subsequently became. Then there was the Vaal Triangle uprising at the time – and we exposed the whole Section 28 regulation, which allowed for preventative detention. So if you looked at these four issues, we felt why let these guys go back into prison like sitting ducks? Let us have a spectacular impact.[16]

In the name of the 'revolutionary leadership', Ela Gandhi took a similar line in an undated document to 'Mewa and All', in which she addressed M.J. Naidoo and George Sewpersadh directly:

> Sew, I know how you and M.J. feel. Let me tell you that today I was in Pietermaritzburg at a meeting at the University. Everybody there was praising you guys and asking how you all are. Now I want you to put yourself in my position and if people asked 'how are the guys' are their spirits high? Would you say no! The guys want to 'pull out'? ... How are you going to explain your exit now and the split? I am very much aware of your tensions, your distrust or lack of confidence in us, but if you do come out let me tell you clearly that you will have to answer a lot of questions from a lot of quarters and this can really finish us.[17]

These words reveal a growing division over tactics. While the tone of the letter is one of reproach, it also shows that Ela Gandhi understood that those in the Consulate felt a lack of trust for those making decisions on the outside. The letter ends in both a pleading and a warning that 'if you do come out let me tell you clearly that you will have to answer a lot of questions from a lot of quarters and this can really finish us'.

Ramgobin wrote to Ela Gandhi on 4 October 1984, apparently shortly after she had visited the Consulate. There is a hint in the tone and content that the differences between them went beyond the political:

> That you were shocked and hurt at my attitude, this afternoon, I have no doubt ... I do not believe that any one person or side has the monopoly of ability to assess situations. As for me, I have neither posed as a leader nor have I pretended to be anything more than what I am. I am what I am regardless of who thinks what of me – including you and our children ... Before I end (yes I am so upset) let me refer to your letter sent to me and the guys in here. Write to us, and especially to me, if you wish. But, in your writing to me, if you are going to take the liberty to use words like 'abandon the fight,' 'un-leader like,' 'unplanned,' 'irresponsible,' 'impulsive,' 'overwhelmed by emotionalism,' etc. etc., then I think you shouldn't do so at all. You may, and you do, have a view of your own, but I'll not allow you or anybody else in the Exec. to cast aspersions on my political work. God knows it is tough enough to place all these above-going thoughts on paper, but it is tougher to know that such views are put on paper as two pieces of paper, without the courtesy of an envelope, handed to Jerry [Coovadia] to hand to me![18]

Many in the NIC would have smiled wryly at Ramgobin's remark that he did not 'pose' as a leader, since it was often asserted by interviewees that he regarded leadership as his due and had a grand sense of his centrality to the liberation struggle. Still, words like 'abandon the fight' and 'un-leader like' must have stung all the more painfully, given the conditions that prevailed in the Consulate. Ela Gandhi and the crew outside, however, were convinced that the occupation had to continue and that much was at stake in this eventuality. Yet, despite the unhappiness of forces on the 'outside' with his position, Ramgobin was determined to exit the Consulate.

The duelling between Ela Gandhi and Ramgobin did not end when he left the Consulate. In fact the rapier cut more sharply following his departure. When the NIC described Ramgobin's stay at the Consulate as 'satyagraha', referring to Mahatma Gandhi's strategy of non-violent resistance, his response to Ela Gandhi on 15 February 1985 was brutal:

Are you really so 'under-read' on Satyagraha? I don't know ... Always remember that pre-requisite to Satyagraha is advance notice, openness, honesty and honour. You know, I read in the press that Farouk Meer in his 'Gandhi Memorial Lecture' had said that the Consulate sit-in was Satyagraha. I must confess that I did laugh at that assertion.[19]

Ramgobin considered the continued occupation of the Consulate and Zak Yacoob's negotiations with minister of police Louis le Grange as un-Gandhian, and claimed that he had been forced to take actions he disagreed with.

> ... you talk of sacrifice and fearlessness and Gandhi-ism. I have never boasted to be even the dust on Gandhi's feet ... Suffice for the moment: Nobody and nobody has acted in Gandhi-ian fashion – let's not labour the point anymore. REMEMBER ALL OF YOU. I DON'T WANT TO BE TREATED AS A POLITICAL BUM ... I refuse to be a puppet on a string held + swayed by others.[20]

If Ramgobin was a puppet, who were the puppeteers?

Ramgobin left the Consulate on 6 October 1984 with George Sewpersadh and M.J. Naidoo. It is not clear whether their departure had the blessing of the NIC executive, but probably not, given the tone of the communications between Ela Gandhi and Ramgobin. The *New York Times* reported on 7 October that Sewpersadh 'wrestled with a security police officer while his colleagues climbed into a car parked nearby. Other police officers then moved in to block off escape routes while the Consulate Three argued with the police that they had no right to detain them before a court ruling, scheduled for Monday, on an appeal against their detention orders.'[21] Nonetheless the three were rearrested.

The NIC gave a different spin to the story. The *New York Times* reported that the three had surrendered in order to see whether South Africa would extradite the Coventry Four, and that three of the men were remaining in the Consulate to expose Britain's 'dismal failure to act against the South African Government'.[22] As the correspondence between Ramgobin and Ela Gandhi reveals, this sleight of hand was stage-managed by the activists on the outside.

The sparring and acrimony refused to abate. In a letter to Ela Gandhi written from prison in Pietermaritzburg in March 1985, Ramgobin situated his insistence on exiting the Consulate as Gandhian by his announcing, in advance, a specific date on which he would leave:

Going to the Consulate was for only one day, agreed by all. We gave the [Simon] Davey man and [another Consulate official] an undertaking – we gave him our word and I was nominated spokesman. We went in to get some 'temporary' immunity so that a.) the [British] Ambassador will negotiate an interview on our behalf with Le Grange or the [prime minister] to put forward certain demands; b.) to deflect the inauguration of the State President ceremony and place emphasis on detentions; c.) and to come out into public life with a 'gusto'. These were all and no more. We departed from our original undertaking ... I must be the first one to confess that it was un-Gandhian.

You and others were in consultation about our continued stay ... Did you or anyone else tell anybody at the consultation that 'Mewa considers the continued stay un-Gandhian' esp. with all the press publicity, advertisements with Bapuji's [the Mahatma's] photograph counter-poised with [George Sewpersadh's] and the word Satyagraha used so freely? Did you tell them that at least my conscience was at zero level? Did you tell them that before our departure, I asked that it be made public a day before that we were going to leave, and not leave with newspapers to hide our faces and women's arms to pretend that we were couples! In my case I was asked to leave with Daya [Pillay?] in my arms. Is this more Gandhian? ...

I for one did not go in there to stay there 'for as long as necessary,' or until all detention orders were withdrawn. If you agreed with the others that we should remain there, I can't and couldn't do anything about it BUT it is my RIGHT to defend what I consider RIGHT, MORAL and good ... It is from Bapuji that I have learnt ... the meaning of Satyagraha and absolute trust and honesty among colleagues ... If you, Ela, think (and it appears you do) that my present position and attitude in the struggle is farcical (your word), you then have the right and the duty to the oppressed masses to warn them against the likes of me. Yes, one day when I come out I'll see and know why your heart cries out, for you see what I can't from here.[23]

One feels here the sense in which Ela Gandhi's position cut so deeply with Ramgobin. In suggesting that she and a faction in the NIC were bent on 'punishing' him, Ramgobin returns to his theme of a small group wanting to stage-manage events in which people like him were reduced to mere props. But finally there was some concession from Ramgobin: 'Yes, one day when I come out I'll see and know why your heart cries out, for you see what I can't from here.'

The occupation continues: October–December 1985

Paul David, Archie Gumede and Billy Nair remained in the Consulate until December 1984. It was an inspired form of spectacle politics and brought the three a global platform from which to air their views. The British threatened to expel them. Approaches to the French government were rebuffed. The NIC was informed that neither 'international legal principles nor the local situation' warranted French government intervention.[24] According to their lawyer, Zak Yacoob, the West German and US governments also refused to give the men refuge. Moreover, their families and Yacoob as their legal representative were denied access to them. Most staff were removed from the Consulate.[25]

Ursula, Paul David's wife, claimed that mail was not handed to her husband and the others.[26] Edwards notes that consul general Davey 'understood the power of media' and denied the men 'access to British newspapers which were not deposited, as was customary, in the Consulate reading room whilst the six were staying there'.[27] The attitude of the British government is unclear because documents pertaining to this affair, including correspondence between Botha and British prime minister Margaret Thatcher, remain classified. According to Edwards, the British National Archives, under national rules, had opened the collection on the Consulate affair in mid-2015, but when he requested access to the collection, 'a section of the previously open collection was re-sealed until 2051'.[28]

It is worth noting, however, that during a tour of Europe a few months before the sit-in started, Botha had met with Thatcher on 2 June 1984. Also, in a letter to Labour MP Robert Hughes dated 29 October 1984, Thatcher wrote that Britain had initially accommodated the men on 'humanitarian grounds'. However, she noted that the Natal Supreme Court had subsequently rejected the appeal of the three for their detention notices to be withdrawn, and their remaining in the Consulate would serve no purpose. Thatcher went on:

> They had indulged in political activity, which is clearly an abuse of Consular premises ... In view of this, and given the growing disruption to the Consulate's work, we have had no choice but to take measures designed to end further exploitation of our premises for political purposes and to reduce considerably the Consulate's work ... It is regrettably the case that our ability to communicate with the South African Government on broader issues is at present inhibited by the situation in the Durban Consulate.[29]

In December 1984, Zak Yacoob led a delegation to meet with barristers in London and with the Red Cross in Geneva to discuss the British ban on access to the men.[30] Yacoob was met in London by Mike Terry, executive secretary of the British Anti-Apartheid Movement (AAM). Although the British government refused Yacoob's request to meet with a minister, he did meet with John Johnson, assistant undersecretary at the Foreign Office. Johnson informed him that the ban on contacts between the trio and the outside world would remain because of the clandestine set of demands they had given to visiting British Labour MP Donald Anderson.[31]

In the face of sustained international media coverage, the South African government withdrew its detention notices, and Gumede, David and Nair left the Consulate on 13 December 1984.[32] The police rearrested Gumede and David, while Nair 'was carried shoulder-high through the streets by the enthusiastic crowd, some six thousand strong'.[33] They, together with other leaders in the UDF were charged and brought to court in what came to be known as the Pietermaritzburg Treason Trial.[34]

Figure 9.2: *Left to right*: Paul David, Archie Gumede and Billy Nair on leaving the British Consulate, 13 December 1984. (Courtesy of African News Agency)

Behind the spectacle of the Consulate occupation lay a hidden world of intrigue and recrimination, bringing to the fore deep cracks and fissures over strategy and tactics in the NIC that engulfed long-time comrades and split families.

The aftermath

Five of the Consulate Six (Mewa Ramgobin, Archie Gumede, George Sewpersadh, Paul David and M.J. Naidoo) were occupied for most of 1985 defending charges of treason in the *State vs Ramgobin & Others*, popularly known as the Pietermaritzburg Treason Trial. The indictment, 587 pages long, was delivered on 25 April 1985. The charge was that in the previous four years they and the other accused (16 in all) had acted to 'further the aims of banned organisations (ANC and SACP) to over-throw the State' and were therefore guilty of high treason, which carried the death penalty.[35] Essentially the charge was that '[t]he Natal Indian Congress (NIC) and Transvaal Indian Congress (TIC) ... through their identification with the Congress Alliance, which shared the same violent objectives of the Revolutionary Alliance, were committed to the tactical programme of the latter'.[36]

When the trial opened in October 1985, Ismail Mahomed, acting for the accused, dismantled the evidence of the key state witness, Izak Daniel de Vries. De Vries, a doctoral candidate at the Rand Afrikaans University (now the University of Johannesburg), was presented as an 'expert' on revolutionary theory. But according to one report, he was 'so completely discredited by Mr. Mohammed's [sic] cross-examination that the Attorney-General decided even before the cross-examination was completed to discontinue the prosecution against the first 12'. On 9 December 1985, Natal Attorney General Mike Imber formally announced that charges had been dropped against 12 of the 16 trialists. The remaining accused – Thozamile Richard Gqweta, Sisa Njikelana, Samuel Kikine and Isaac Ngcobo, all members of the South African

Figure 9.3: Pietermaritzburg Treason Trial, 1985. (*Centre front*) Advocate Ismail Mahomed with (*from left*) George Sewpersadh, George Naicker, Leonard Gering (wearing glasses, between and behind Naicker and Ramgobin), Mewa Ramgobin (arms folded), Cassim Saloojee, Thumba Pillay (spectacles, chin on hand) and Essop Jassat (*extreme right*). (Courtesy of African News Agency)

Allied Workers' Union (SAAWU) – were set free on 23 June 1986, when the state withdrew all charges.[37]

In scenes reminiscent of the Treason Trial of the 1950s, the 1985 trial attracted great international attention. As in 1956, after much huffing and puffing by the state about a conspiracy to violently seize power, the courts found that the 'evidence' did not pass muster. While the state had effectively banished those charged from everyday politics, they were also provided with a platform to express their views and garner even more support for the struggle.

The NIC was at the centre of the occupation of the British Consulate. This remarkable episode exposed the apartheid state to international scrutiny and drew the British government directly into the spotlight. Less known are the deep divisions it brought about within the NIC itself.

Figure 9.4: Mewa Ramgobin, shortly after his acquittal in the Pietermaritzburg Treason Trial, raises his hands in salute as he makes his way to the platform to address a UDF rally, 16 December 1985. (Courtesy of African News Agency)

Rather than suturing these wounds, the crumbling of apartheid and the unfolding transition to democracy would deepen them.

Ela Gandhi and Mewa Ramgobin were both to serve in the first democratically elected Parliament, but the marriage that had withstood the years of bannings and state persecution was to slowly erode and eventually they went their separate ways. Struggle wounds are often more painful than state repression. Almost 35 years after the Consulate occupation, Ela Gandhi's response that the issues between her and her husband should not be 'seen as a family issue but rather a cooperative democratic view' is haunting.

Meanwhile the apartheid government's co-opting of coloureds and Indians through the Tricameral Parliament and the arrest of large numbers of activists failed to curb protests. The next chapter examines the intensifying opposition to apartheid and the state's drastic response.

10 | Inanda, Inkatha and Insurrection: 1985

The government had hoped that co-opting coloureds and Indians as junior partners of the apartheid state, as well as facilitating a settled urban African population with access to an industrial relations machinery, would create the conditions for political stability and economic recovery. Instead, the UDF pushed back against state control in many townships and began establishing alternative forms of power.

The government responded by declaring a partial state of emergency covering key areas in the country on 22 July 1985, the first since 1960. On 24 July, two days after the emergency was declared, Oliver Tambo called on South Africans to 'make apartheid unworkable and the country ungovernable'.[1] The partial state of emergency expired on 7 March 1986, but as resistance continued, the state of emergency was implemented nationwide on 12 June 1986 and would continue in Natal until October 1990.

The state of emergency served as a lightning rod for dissent and confrontation. Protests grew more violent, and consumer boycotts and other grassroots resistance intensified. While the state of emergency acted to escalate the anti-apartheid struggle, it also brought to the surface conflicts with deep roots in the histories of local communities, including racial tensions in Inanda, and led to the arrest of large numbers of activists. Under these circumstances, the NIC found it difficult to maintain the support it had enjoyed among Indians in the first half of the 1980s. Moreover, its internal divisions would become public and its organisational weaknesses exposed.

Violent protests that drew in workers, students and the unemployed erupted throughout South African townships. They were sparked by myriad issues that included low wages, high levels of unemployment and exorbitant transportation costs. Robert Price labels these protests an 'insurrection', such was the ferocity of the revolt against apartheid authority.[2] Fatima Meer placed young people at the heart of the 'insurrection' in African townships:

> The townships are charged today with the explosive energy of the youth who form the single most populous group and who are neither at school nor in formal employment ... They are under constant police and military surveillance, and subjected to brutal attack from both the state and state-instigated black vigilantes. They organise through fragile, makeshift structures ... [engage in] consumer and rent boycotts and set up street barricades and take on the military and the police and suspected informers.[3]

The states of emergency gave the Security Branch the power to ban meetings and organisations and to detain people without trial. The police were indemnified against prosecution for most of their actions and strict media controls were imposed. The 'mass violation of human rights and a state of officially sanctioned lawlessness', as Christopher Merrett describes it, reduced 'the power of the courts to protect the welfare of those detained ... The main advantage for the state was the ability to act rapidly with little fear of being called to account by members of Parliament or the judiciary.' Ten thousand people were held in 1985; 12 144 had been imprisoned by 7 March 1986 at the end of the partial emergency; and 30 000 were detained under the nationwide emergency declared on 12 June 1986.[4]

Detentions bit hard into personal relationships. In June 1986 the newly married couple Sundra and Timay Reddy, along with Maggie Govender, Vishnu Naidoo, Hinderen Naidoo and Patsy Pillay, were some of the NIC activists arrested in Chatsworth. Maggie Govender described her arrest as

> a major eye-opener in the community because the police came heavily armed. They surrounded the school [in Chatsworth] with military vehicles. This was June 17th. I had, every year since I started teaching, stayed away from school on June 16th as a point of principle. I was teaching. [The policeman] jumped up and said 'you are arrested

under the State of Emergency'. I had a Head of Department who was progressive, Rex Aiyer, and he went to the staff to say this is what happened. Two of the children ran to a relative's home to tell them. This is important because while this was happening the police were sending people to my home [so] my mother-in-law burnt everything that looked political and my husband [Charm] had come home; they told him to leave. My son was one year and one month and he was breastfed. They didn't allow me access to my son. His breast-feeding had to stop. I was kept in solitary confinement. After three months and a few weeks I was released without charge.[5]

Maggie's husband, Charm Govender, went into hiding, and Roy Padayachie, who eventually escaped to London, evaded arrest. Most detainees were released in late August. Thinking that he was off the police radar, Charm returned to work in December 1986 and was promptly arrested. Locked in a cell at C.R. Swart for 23 hours a day, he was subjected to police beatings. He was released in June 1987 after almost six months in detention. While her husband was in prison, the authorities punished Maggie

Figure 10.1: Maggie Govender (*right*), seen here at a rally shortly after the unbanning of the ANC in 1990. (Courtesy of Gandhi-Luthuli Documentation Centre)

Govender by transferring her from a school close to her home to one in Umzinto, 45 minutes away by car. She described it as 'straight political intervention and victimisation'.[6]

Among the incarcerated was Yousuf Vawda. His story illustrates how arrests and detentions impacted anti-apartheid activism. When his colleagues were arrested, Vawda went into hiding for almost six months in the latter part of 1986 at great cost to himself and the movement. 'I was running a solo [legal] practice so it was quite a strain ... financially crippling ...' Vawda was arrested immediately when he resurfaced in January 1987, and spent the next six months in prison. He was warned that he would 'rot' in jail. When the matter went to court, although there was no evidence against him, the conservative judge 'reserved judgment and the matter went on for months ...' Through an awaiting-trial prisoner, Vawda managed to get word of his arrest to the then judge president of Natal, John Milne, who was regarded as 'liberal'. With no advance notice, Vawda was released on 12 June 1987.

In June 1986 the Security Branch carried out an all-night sweep in Pietermaritzburg, apprehending around 40 people. Long periods of uncertainty followed for the detainees and their families. Among those detained were Chota Motala, Yunus Carrim, Yusuf Bhamjee and A.S. Chetty. Chetty, who was the chairperson of the UDF's Pietermaritzburg branch, had been imprisoned during the 1960 state of emergency and during the education boycott in 1980. He was arrested once again on 12 June 1986 and held for 98 days at New Prison, Pietermaritzburg. Chetty kept a detailed diary, now in the Alan Paton Centre and Struggle Archives at the University of KwaZulu-Natal. His diary offers rare contemporaneous notes on the interior life and thoughts of an activist caged in solitary confinement:

Sunday 29/06/86: Remembered that it is the Annual General meeting of the Sri Siva Soobramoniar Marriamen Temple. I hope that Saras [Chetty's wife] and Bala [Saras's brother] go for this meeting. Will be anxious to know what the elections are, particularly that of President. Wonder whether Jessie [Chetty's daughter] and Thegie [Jessie's husband] are still at home and whether Vijay [Chetty's son] and Daya [Vijay's wife] came home. Wondered also whether Kamy [Chetty's daughter] came back from Harare. I hope she went because she deserved that holiday. I suppose the house would be full of visitors. I hope also that all those who were detained including C.D. [Moodley] and party are released for their own sakes. Concerned about C.D. and the girls, how are they coping? Hope also that the office is managing. Sister Kleynhans enquired as to when I will be released. I said I have no idea, only when the 'State of Emergency' is over ... Everything seems so quiet. I pray it won't be too long ... It is approximately 12 noon. Am trying to read. Cells open at about 3:00 pm. Took a shower. Am showering daily. If I don't I find it difficult to sleep. Heard that the four guys from Sobantu had to sign [?] in terms of the 'State of Emergency'. Their release is also in abeyance. Peter [Kerchhoff; Pietermaritzburg activist] is still being held in Solitary. I keep praying for him. Thought of Saras practically the whole day. I really miss her. I suppose it is because of our very close attachment and love for each other. I will definitely give her a better life when I come out, because I gave serious thought to whether I am going to continue my present life of struggle. I owe it to her and must try and take her for a long holiday. There is no doubt in my mind that I have to make the remaining days of my life worthy of her. I have gone too old now too carry on ... I am all alone in my cell. I keep thinking about [fellow activists] Vasu [Chetty], Visagan [Naidoo], and [Francis]Grantham in their respective cells ...[7]

Inanda

The detention of so many activists proved a severe test for the UDF and NIC. The challenge was compounded both at the ideological level and organisationally by an outbreak of anti-Indian violence in Inanda on 8 August 1985. Inanda, a township 30 kilometres north of central Durban, adjoins the Phoenix Settlement established by Gandhi in 1904, and is a place where Indians and Africans had been neighbours for half a century.[8] The violence was sparked by demonstrations against the assassination of UDF leader Victoria Mxenge in Umlazi on 1 August 1985, allegedly by a government 'death squad'. Within a week an estimated 63 people were killed and around a thousand were hospitalised. Initially the targets of the attacks were government administrative buildings and staff. On 8 and 9 August the attackers turned on Inanda, some 30 kilometres from Umlazi.[9]

Many Indians were driven from their homes, shops were looted and demolished, and the Phoenix settlement, where the NIC had been revived in 1971, was almost totally destroyed.[10] Gandhi's restored home, Sarvodaya, the clinic which played an important role in providing relief to the local African community, the museum, the printing press where *Indian Opinion* had been published, and the Kasturba Gandhi School lay in ruins.[11] Within a week, there were over 2 000 Indian refugees in the adjoining Indian township of Phoenix. There were many tragic stories. One was of an African domestic worker, Voice, and an Indian bus driver, Bobby Jugdeo, who had married in 1963 and had seven children. As agreed, the boys had Indian names (Bhandlal, Ram and Vishnu) and the girls English names (Priscilla, Queenie, Cherry and Helen). Enjoying a cordial relationship with their Indian and African neighbours, Voice and Bobby were 'bewildered' when they were forced to flee Inanda, their home and livestock destroyed in the rampage.[12]

Indian refugees fled Inanda on trucks and bakkies with whatever they could salvage, 'running the gauntlet of stone throwers, leaving their homes to the mercy of looters and arsonists'.[13] The way in which

Figure 10.2: An Indian-owned service station up in flames during the August 1985 riots in Inanda. (Courtesy of African News Agency)

Figure 10.3: A convoy of trucks moves toward Inanda, carrying refugees hoping to salvage something from their ransacked homes. (Courtesy of African News Agency)

Figure 10.4: Indian self-protection group on the lookout for further attacks. (Courtesy of African News Agency)

the House of Delegates (HOD) – the Indian branch of the Tricameral Parliament – outpaced the NIC in responding to the crisis demonstrated a stark reality. The HOD had the resources of the state to call upon, the very state that many accused of fuelling antagonisms between racial and ethnic groups.

Amichand Rajbansi, chairman of the HOD Ministers Council, reacted swiftly. When the refugees arrived in Phoenix, Rajbansi addressed them at the Greenbury Community Hall on immediate relief and measures to retrieve their belongings. The HOD arranged for the South African Defence Force (SADF) to send armoured cars to accompany refugees in their search for their belongings, while HOD offices in Verulam, Pietermaritzburg, Chatsworth and Phoenix became collection points for food, clothing, blankets, toys and other relief. The education department was instructed to make alternative arrangements for learners at schools in Phoenix. Rajbansi met with Inkatha officials, including Oscar Dhlomo, the minister of education and culture in the KwaZulu Legislative Assembly. They agreed that all sides would show 'restraint' and work together to 'bring about peace and stability in the area'.[14]

Rajbansi came under attack from UDW students who, on 6 August, displayed banners on Higginson Highway in Chatsworth protesting the SADF's presence in the township. In a letter to the *Daily News* on 12 August 1985, Rajbansi wrote that the newspaper's report of 7 August on the subject was incorrect. He insisted that he did not bring in the army on his own accord:

On the nights of August 7 to 10 I received a massive request for the SADF to hurry to protect Indian areas. While most of the requests came from the Phoenix/Inanda area, there were also many from Reservoir Hills, Verulam, Marianhill and Chatsworth. They also complained that the SADF units were insufficient. The SADF units came to Phoenix and Chatsworth at the request of the Indian people. Why did the Indian people not rebel against them? Deep down in their hearts they wanted the SADF because of the circumstances the Indian community was placed in. They wanted the SADF units to come fast. Even now I am receiving pleas that the SADF should remain until absolute calm is restored.[15]

Such efforts from the so-called sell-outs increased their standing in the community, Rajbansi's in particular. Sharm Maharaj of the PWC recalled a particular memory of Rajbansi in Inanda:

> I have photographs about the kind of role Rajbansi actually played. On the day, he was using [P.W.] Botha's hat. You know, P.W. had this funny bowler hat, [by] which you can distinguish him. Between Rajbansi and J.N. Reddy, they believed that they were Botha also, and they from time to time used this hat. I have a photograph of Rajbansi standing on a Hippo [armoured personnel carrier] of the South African Defence Force during the riots that were happening in Inanda.[16]

In spite of Rajbansi's tragicomic hat, his role, backed by the state, was substantial and could not be wished away. Sharm Maharaj conceded that

Figure 10.5: Amichand Rajbansi (*right front*), then chairman of the House of Delegates Ministers Council, was popular among the Indian working classes. Seated to his right is his then wife, Asha Devi. (Courtesy of African News Agency)

he and fellow activists had to work with those they normally would have classified as apartheid puppets.

The Black Sash, a human rights group established in 1955 by and for liberal white women, set up a crisis committee with various Natal-based organisations (excluding Inkatha) on 14 August, and assisted both Indian and African (mainly UDF-supporting) victims of the violence. According to the Black Sash's report:

> Hundreds of people came from Inanda in need of food, clothing, housing, comfort, money. We tried to interview them ... but soon realised that most of them were frightened, confused and hungry and unlikely, at that time, to be able to make the picture of what had happened in Inanda any clearer ... Most of the burnings of houses, killings and beatings were carried out by unidentifiable groups of people, generally the 'amabutho' who are closely linked in people's minds with Inkatha.[17]

Mewa Ramgobin blamed 'third force' elements for the attacks:

> Inanda was an island in the apartheid scheme of things. Institutions like Phoenix Settlement and the Indian community had to be driven out in 1985 by the forces of apartheid. It was an island of hope, an island of peace and an island of non-racialism. It was an island of co-existence.[18]

Perhaps due to concerns about the broader political repercussions of Afro–Indian tensions, it was hinted by unnamed NIC activists that Indian vigilantes were behind the final burning of the Phoenix Settlement on the 9th so that Africans would not have access to it. Sita Gandhi, Manilal's eldest daughter, was apprehensive about this suggestion and asked private investigator C.K. Hill to investigate the incident. Hill found that 'there is no justification for the lie that Indians did the burning'.[19] The circumstances surrounding the destruction of the Phoenix Settlement await a more substantial investigation.

Deeper probing of the socio-economic realities on the ground provides a more complex picture than Ramgobin's allegations of a third force.

There were up to a million people living in Inanda in the mid-1980s, drawn there by the shortage of housing in newly built African townships and the deterioration of rural areas in KwaZulu. Some had gravitated to Inanda from Cato Manor in the 1960s and 1970s because they could not be accommodated in KwaMashu or Umlazi. There were high levels of poverty and little in the way of service delivery. The thousands in informal housing lived in squalid conditions. The drought of the late 1970s and early 1980s exacerbated an already dire health environment. The poor saw their immediate problem as the mostly Indian landlords and shop owners.[20] Politically the situation was complex: there were supporters of Inkatha, the UDF and trade unions living there; the KwaZulu Legislative Assembly had a strong influence in the area; and many of the residents had links to rural areas.[21]

All the complex causes of the Inanda violence cannot be unpacked here; the main concern of this chapter is to examine the impact of the conflict on Afro–Indian relations. The state had insisted all along that it could only support development in the area once Indians moved out so that land could be incorporated into KwaZulu, which was controlled by the IFP. According to a late 1980s study by Fatima Meer on resistance in African townships, Indian tenants were willing to move in return for subsidised housing, while Indian landlords and shopkeepers demanded adequate compensation. It followed that the KwaZulu government, the central state, African residents and business interests had a stake in the removal of Indians. It is alleged that at a meeting called by the Inanda Liaison Committee at the end of July 1985, African speakers argued that the refusal of Indians to sell the land was blocking development for African people.[22]

Much of this is, of course, hearsay. But as Kumi Naidoo argues, Inanda 'exposed the serious organisational weaknesses of the NIC. Its leadership was distant from the people affected by the riots, and it had no influence or grassroots presence in the area that could calm anxieties.'[23] While this analysis has plausibility, it brushes over the circumstances that were on the boil in Inanda. And once the violence began, it is difficult to imagine how the NIC could have intervened to convince people not to flee, given that its members were already on the defensive and in some cases on the run as a result of the arrest of most of its leaders.

However one may seek to understand and explain the attacks in Inanda, the festering memories of Durban's Afro–Indian riots in January 1949 were reignited, feeding into fears of anti-Indian violence. The 1949 riots were extremely violent, resulting in 142 deaths, the loss of hundreds of businesses, and around 40 000 Indian refugees, some of whom did not have access to housing for almost a year. Fears of renewed violence would intensify during the years of transition to democracy and continue into the post-apartheid period. Many Indians saw the conflagration as a racial attack despite NIC-aligned activists' efforts to underplay the racial dimension. Inanda created challenges for the NIC/UDF leadership, as their promise of a non-racial South Africa seemed to be no more than a pipe dream. Academic explanations of the Inanda violence, while instructive, were outweighed by the psychological impact of the violence on Indians as negotiations to end apartheid unfolded. It was a fertile field in which to sow fear of African majority rule.

The absence of a significant NIC presence in addressing this crisis was noticeable. While many of its leaders were arrested or banned, and the NIC lacked the resources Rajbansi could deploy, the failure to play a more public role was seized upon by opponents to question the extent of NIC support of, and concern for, working-class township residents. Graham Spence, political reporter for the *Daily News*, observed in 1988:

> The NIC has failed on one basic issue – that of allaying the insular Indian community's fears of group security if an African majority were in power. Many Indians tacitly support the Group Areas Act not necessarily because of racism, but rather [out of] a fear of being swamped by blacks. These fears were fuelled significantly by the 1985 Inanda riots. The NIC is aware of this concern and the major thrust of their mobilisation campaign is to persuade the community that their future security in fact lies with the African majority. By all accounts, it could be a difficult task.[24]

What is not properly acknowledged in this assessment is the impact of repression on the activities of cadres who were underground for extended periods, crippling the NIC's organisational ability at a crucial time. Some of those not in detention feared being targeted and refrained from overt political work. Crucially, state repression also created a climate of fear which made it difficult to encourage a new layer of above-ground activists to join the NIC. The lesson for the mass movement, Richard Levin warned in 1987, was that

> the 'heady optimism' which governed the conjuncture ... has given way to a pragmatic realism which recognises that the final push to national bourgeois democracy is neither imminent nor just around the corner. The systematic quality of the 1986 state of emergency (renewed in June 1987) has demonstrated the limits of an exclusive mobilisation strategy, and the lesson learnt is that there is no substitute for patient and rigorous organisation.[25]

Inkatha

In the years after the Inanda riots, virtual war broke out in African townships, a conflict which pitted Inkatha, the KwaZulu homeland structure and the central state against supporters of the UDF. The Inkatha–NP alliance, as Ari Sitas has pointed out, 'sought to "normalise" the townships and to roll back the United Democratic Front's street mobilisation'.[26] The causes of the violence are multiple and complex, but the conflict was also fuelled by state-sponsored 'third force' elements.[27]

There was a broader context to the conflict between Mangosuthu Buthelezi and the NIC. As a cultural movement, Inkatha had contact with the ANC, and even projected itself as the ANC's internal wing. However, these links began to break down once Buthelezi formed the Inkatha Freedom Party (IFP) as a political organisation in 1975. As the breach between the ANC and Inkatha began to widen, a federal option for KwaZulu/Natal was given serious consideration.[28] The NP government considered a federal system for South Africa so that KwaZulu-Natal would no longer be a Bantustan but, along with Natal, become a separate province. This would allow KwaZulu-Natal to implement policies that diverged from those in other provinces. Buthelezi was amenable to such moves and established the South African Black Alliance (SABA) with Y.S. Chinsamy of the Reform Party. Criticism from the NIC in particular mostly met with a venomous response from IFP politicians.

In 1980 the South African Sugar Association had commissioned University of Natal economist Jan Lombard to examine the viability of a

Natal 'solution'. Following this, the Buthelezi Commission provided a report which recommended a federal option for KwaZulu/Natal.[29] Chinsamy welcomed the proposals, as all 'minority groups, including Indians, were well protected'.[30] The NIC rejected the report. Thumba Pillay issued a statement that the report was unacceptable given the NIC's 'unalterable commitment' to the Freedom Charter, 'which subscribed to the philosophy of democratic rights in a unitary state'.[31]

With the region facing common problems like drought and unemployment, the governments of KwaZulu and Natal began to cooperate on various levels, eventually leading to the KwaZulu Natal Indaba of 28 November 1986. The regional solution proposed by the Indaba was rejected by the NIC. Mewa Ramgobin argued that the Indaba was 'initiated by the dying NPA [Natal Provincial Administration] and an economically non-viable KwaZulu authority, in cahoots with commerce, industry and agriculture'. The NIC view was that

> the ANC had to be central to any resolution to South Africa's problems. After all, with its resurgence ... the ANC has not only caught the imagination of the vast majority of black people, but also the attention of the State itself, big business, white and black theologians, white students, white academics, artists, and politicians, from Lusaka to Dakar ... The KwaZulu/Natal thrust will become a major destabilising factor in the national thrust for a non-racial, democratic South Africa ... The Indaba [was] the seat of counter-revolution.[32]

This comprehensive rejection affirmed that the ANC was pivotal to any resolution of the conflict in South Africa, and showed the value of the NIC in keeping alive and putting into the public domain the ANC's commitment to a unitary non-racial South Africa.

However, the NIC's stance also put the organisation in Inkatha's cross hairs. Buthelezi accused the NIC of 'being provocative and irresponsible and a danger to the Black community':

> I would like to appeal to all oppressed people in Natal to put this coterie of frustrated black middle class in their place. They do not represent the majority of the Indian people. They represent only themselves

and their brand of elitism which, if we do not snuff out, will retard our struggle for liberation ... They remind me of a child who plays with a timebomb, disregarding warnings that what he is playing with is dangerous and explosive. Clearly such a child would be a danger not only to himself but also to all who are around him: This is exactly the position of the NIC. They are a danger to each and every one of us and we have to deal with them jointly to defuse the bomb in their hands.[33]

NIC president George Sewpersadh responded that it was unreasonable to believe that 'a small community can cause violence in the townships, or anywhere else'. Instead, he stated, the government was responsible for the oppression of Africans. Moreover,

the KwaZulu Legislative Assembly is unable to challenge the Government and is turning its anger and frustration against the Indian people. In utter frustration, the KwaZulu authorities are trying to hide their own inability to bring about the necessary changes in the country by attacking and blaming the NIC.[34]

One can discern how this war of words emerged. The NIC was seen as one of the prime drivers of the UDF. Inkatha was locked in deadly combat with the UDF, especially between young people from each group who had taken to fighting pitched street battles against each other. The Inkatha leadership periodically identified the NIC leadership as instigators of violence and racial tension. This prompted vigorous responses from the NIC. Pravin Gordhan, for example, argued in 1986 that Buthelezi 'has not hesitated to say Indians must not forget 1949 whenever he has been criticised by Indians and he amongst other people [has] been instrumental in reinforcing that fear element amongst Indians'. In Gordhan's view, Inkatha was a 'violent force' which had eliminated its opponents, and made it necessary for activists 'to exercise some discretion in the manner in which one articulates oneself'.[35] Paul David recounted:

[At] a UDF meeting we had in Pioneer Hall in Durban in early 1984 to welcome Billy Nair back from prison, two busloads of Inkatha supporters came, escorted by the police! The police were saying it's a peaceful demonstration. As they got off they had assegais [spears] and knob-sticks as big as my head. And they charged. There was no escape for us in the hall. One of the people in charge of security for the delegates had a firearm and shot the first fellow through the head. And he was shouting to the people in the hall: 'Come here, pretending you got guns.' That's what saved us.[36]

The IFP's relationship with the ANC turned frosty and broke into open warfare when the UDF began to mobilise in former IFP strongholds. John Nkadimeng, a member of the ANC's NEC, warned aggressively in 1986:

> It is clear that the puppet Gathsa [Buthelezi] is being groomed by the West and the racist regime to become a Savimbi [the Angolan guerrilla leader] in a future free South Africa. The onus is on the people of South Africa to neutralise the Gathsa snake, which is poisoning the people of South Africa. It needs to be hit on the head.[37]

The IFP's defence of Zuluness during this conflict, Jeremy Seekings argues, was not contested by the UDF:

> The character and concerns of the UDF in Natal meant that opportunities were not seized ... Archie Gumede later expressed regret that 'the UDF divided Zulus'. His implication was that this was not inevitable: the UDF should have shown that it was not anti-Zulu and contested Inkatha's claim to represent all Zulu-speakers.[38]

Generally, Congress activists were reticent about a language of mobilisation that focused on Zuluness, which was seen as reinforcing ethnic and tribal consciousness. The union movement, on the other hand, had shown that workers could have both a worker consciousness as well as a commitment to their Zuluness, and that this double consciousness did not deter a militant defence of class interests at the workplace.[39] Sitas suggests that Zulu workers were influenced in many instances

> by segregationist rhetoric, that they were a distinct group (from the Amapondo and Indians) and that Zulu workers constituted a separate

culture ... Many see Inkatha as a cultural movement that revived a pride in the past, which was in danger [of being] destroyed. They also had a unique pre-history, adjacent to petty-bourgeoisie, traders and shop-keepers, who in turn clashed with Indian interests over attempted monopolies or racially exclusive markets.[40]

It is beyond the scope of this book to examine the myriad explanations offered for the allegiances to the UDF/ANC and IFP. But violence escalated as the IFP lost the urban African areas. ANC/UDF forces mobilised the defence of communities and counter-attacks, which fuelled more violence.

The violence in the townships around Durban and Pietermaritzburg continued through the 1980s and into the 1990s. Indian and coloured townships and white suburbs were mostly spared this violence. Consumer boycotts were a feature of African townships across the country at this time, but were not characteristic of Indian areas. When Jeremy Seekings asked Yunus Mohamed why these boycotts were not successful in Natal, he was told that it was because of the Inkatha violence in African townships. Why not Indian areas, Seekings asked?

I think we didn't even consider it ... Predominantly one would look at the African areas. I mean, you know, it is the first time it is actually striking me that should we have tried it out in these other areas? Could we have had a differentiated policy of just doing it in the Indian and Coloured areas? I don't think actually that that thought crossed people's minds in that form.[41]

The fact that consumer boycotts were not even considered underscores the different conditions that prevailed in African and Indian areas. Consumer boycotts across the country contained an element of coercion, with the threat of violence. There would have been an instant pushback from the Indian community had the NIC tried similar tactics. In any event, if white businesses were boycotted, would that not strengthen the hand of the Indian trading class, many of whom had traditionally shown allegiance to the SAIC and HOD?

Attempts to organise youth into a non-racial alliance also floundered. When 1985 was declared International Youth Year, the UDF formed the

International Youth Year Committee as part of its efforts to broaden the organisation. Khetso Gordhan was among those involved in organising, but he recounted that the movement split into two at a camp in Durban in February 1985. Some Indian youth wanted to form a separate national organisation; others, including Gordhan, felt it was premature to do so and that the youth should continue to work through the UDF.[42] Pregs Govender, for example, recalled that

> [at a] turbulent Youth Forum meeting at Diakonia, a woman I had known since our days together as students loudly announced to some youth attending the meeting that 'there are some in the UDF who are anti-UDF, like Pregs Govender and Kumi Naidoo' ... Unaware of her allegations, I walked about with my name tag prominently displayed ... I am sure that this young woman and others like her did not appreciate the full consequences of destructive labels or the intangible viciousness of whispering campaigns, social ostracism and lost reputations.[43]

Such splits dented efforts to involve Indian youth, although it is worth wondering whether young Indians would have got involved in any substantial way, if the example of education is anything to go by. Kumi Naidoo pointed out that Lulu Johnson, president of the Congress of South African Students (COSAS), stated in 1986 that they should not allow the '"Coloured" and "Indian" ... education systems to be treated as separate entities of our struggles'. Indians and coloureds were called upon to make their systems ungovernable, but as Naidoo recognised, Indian and coloured education systems 'for the most part did remain separate and were noted for their "stability"'.[44]

Even where the Indian youth formed organisations with political intent, such as in Chatsworth, they named it 'Helping Hands', to 'play down the political content of their activities, forestalling the possible alienation of their parents and the "scaring away" of potential members'.[45] Naidoo emphasised that it was difficult to organise youth across race lines:

> The attempt to develop a non-racial, democratic youth culture met with a variety of problems. The major obstacles were the structural divisions brought about by apartheid, the manoeuvrings of Inkatha,

and the repression of the state. The subjective weaknesses in organisations included cultural and ideological differences; gender discrimination; inadequate leadership skills; a general lack of organisational resources; and inter- and intra-organisational rivalry.[46]

While these are valid points, the irony is that they were made by a younger, seemingly more radical person critical of the established NIC leadership – and yet they sound so similar to the justifications given by the elder generation for retaining the 'I' in the NIC.

Writing in 1987, Sitas wrote that within the NIC and UDF 'unity and camaraderie occurred at the leadership levels of Indian and African communities without it having any resonance at the grassroots'. That 1949 was so easily 'revived in popular memory' showed that 'it has not been actively buried'.[47]

In the midst of the Inanda attacks, P.W. Botha delivered his historic 'Rubicon' speech in Durban on 15 August 1985. A global audience waited intently for him to announce an end to apartheid and the freeing of Nelson Mandela. Instead he rejected demands that apartheid be overturned. The speech led to the collapse of the rand, a further shrinking of the South African economy and intensification of the country's international isolation. Given Botha's intransigence, guerrilla warfare, which was taking place simultaneously with the above-ground activism discussed in this chapter, aimed to intensify political protest. But the armed struggle also held the key to the possibility of a negotiated end to apartheid. It is to this that we now turn.

11 | Building Up Steam: Operation Vula and Local Networks

W hile members of the post-1971 NIC publicly embraced Gandhi and his principle of non-violent resistance (satyagraha) on every possible occasion, they did not openly criticise the activities of Umkhonto we Sizwe (MK), the armed wing of the ANC. When it was put to Jerry Coovadia that there appeared to be a contradiction between some activists' involvement in MK and the organisation's public endorsement of Gandhi, he responded:

> We saw the armed wing of the ANC. We saw how things were going
> in the country. We saw the fights between the cops and all of us.
> We saw the violence of the struggle. To us, to think of satyagraha in
> that context just didn't seem right. Gandhi was fine for India ... but
> we were looking at Cuba, looking at Vietnam, looking at all those
> struggles and there comes Gandhi and he didn't sound right for us.[1]

In a 1968 call for Indian youth to join MK, Yusuf Dadoo explained that passive resistance was a method, not a principle, of the Indian Congresses:

> Passive resistance was never the ideology of the organisation,
> although it had been used as a method of struggle since it was intro-
> duced by Gandhiji in the early part of this century. The principles
> of Satyagraha as enunciated by Gandhiji were never accepted as a
> creed by the Indian people. It is true that in the [South African Indian
> Congress], as a national organisation representing all interests and all

viewpoints, there are some leaders – like Dr. G.M. [Monty] Naicker and Nana Sita – who implicitly believe in Gandhian principles and who have lived by them; and of course we honour their convictions and their sufferings for their convictions.[2]

Indian activists joined MK from its inception and a significant tranche of NIC members supported the building of ANC underground structures. NIC activists such as Ebrahim Ebrahim, Billy Nair and Sunny Singh were among the first to be imprisoned on Robben Island for MK activities. Even the most Gandhian of Gandhians in the NIC, George Sewpersadh, defended the turn to armed struggle when he said:

> I never really joined the armed struggle, but I was never opposed to it. The ANC, when it was banned, it couldn't operate here in South Africa and the people had no other alternative but to be involved in armed struggle. So I think from that point of view it was justified.[3]

While some NIC activists were painstakingly building underground structures, others were keen to engage the enemy more directly and immediately. The 'Lenny Naidu Unit', for example, was formed towards the end of 1984 by young activists in Bayview, Chatsworth. Two operations were carried out in the township. A limpet mine was placed outside the home of HOD politician Amichand Rajbansi on 4 August 1985, and the magistrate's court was bombed on 13 December 1985. The bombing of Rajbansi's home was executed by Lenny Naidu, Derek Naidoo, Jude Francis, David Madurai and Raymond Methraj (Sakloo). According to Derek Naidoo, the cell unravelled within weeks when a member of the unit was arrested. Naidoo, unit leader Vejay Ramlakan and Jude Francis were imprisoned on Robben Island.

Lenny Naidu did not live to see post-apartheid South Africa. Naidu attended Chatsworth High, where he was involved in the school boycotts of 1980 and anti-Republic Day protests in 1981, and was a member of Helping Hands. He attended UDW in 1983 but dropped out to focus on anti-apartheid activism. When police raided his home during the state of emergency in 1986, Naidu went into hiding and then into exile. He received military training in Angola, and from there went to Swaziland. On 8 June 1988, Naidu, Lindiwe Mthembu, Makhosi Nyoka and Nontsikelelo Cothoza entered South Africa and were gunned down by the apartheid police on the road between Houtkop and Piet Retief. Thula Simpson details how three of the apartheid policemen responded after the initial ambush:

> When Frederik Pienaar searches the car a slight problem emerges. There are no weapons in the vehicle or on the persons of the deceased. After a discussion by the policemen about what to do, Lieutenant Ras tells Eugene de Kok he has a pistol and hand grenade. Ras places Lenny Naidu's hand around the pistol and fires shots. He then gives two hand grenades to Pienaar, who deposits them in the group's carry bags.[4]

Naidu's mother, Neela, who went to Swaziland with human rights lawyers Daya Pillay and Sarojini Pillay to collect his body, described the funeral as follows:

> We took it [Naidu's body] here to the Temple Hall [in Chatsworth]. From there the police were [everywhere], machine guns, they had helicopters and the graveyard was cordoned, they didn't let anyone go inside. But African people from other townships, they all came, 25 busloads, they jumped over the walls of the graveyard, they put an ANC cloth on the coffin, the Brigadier [just] stood there ... we couldn't have the last rites [burning camphor], and they were chasing all the people from there [but] the African people stayed behind. They buried the coffin and they were toyi-toying over there. And then they came home, they had supper with me ... Cyril Ramaphosa, Terror Lekota, he was here. They were toyi-toying, singing, and that's how Lenny's life came to an end.[5]

It emerged at the TRC that the security police had infiltrated MK's network and that Naidu's 'comrade' driving the car was an askari (a former ANC cadre turned by the apartheid regime) who drove them to the Security Branch ambush.[6]

Some NIC activists were part of an MK cell that linked up with Operation Vula, whose main aim was to smuggle freedom fighters into South Africa. Yunis Shaik's 1980 arrest as a student leader convinced him of the need for armed struggle. He went to Swaziland and met with Mandla Judson Khuzwayo, who had been imprisoned on Robben Island and worked as a researcher at the University of Natal before becoming an ANC commander in Swaziland. Shaik recruited his brother Moe and his friend Jayendra Naidoo into what came to be known as the MJK unit. Their first handler was Swaziland-based Ivan Pillay, followed by Ebrahim Ebrahim, who was based in Mozambique as a member of the ANC's Politico-Military Council after spending 15 years on Robben Island.[7]

Ivan Pillay grew up in Merebank and stated in a 2002 interview that he became politicised at high school in the early 1970s. He was attracted to Black Consciousness but subsequently gravitated to Congress and MK when he met a former Robben Island prisoner, Sunny Singh. Pillay was part of an underground cell in Durban which unravelled in 1977. He then fled to Swaziland, where he met MK commander Judson Khuzwayo. In 1985 he moved to Zambia, where he reported directly to Oliver Tambo as project manager of Operation Vula.[8]

Pravin Gordhan was also in contact with the ANC from the late 1970s. He related in a 2003 interview that 'there were dead letter boxes in South Africa where we would have stuff dropped off, and that would be reports about activities that we were involved in or feedback on questions that we might have raised and suggestions about propaganda that needed to be distributed locally. And so, we were what you might call a mass mobilisation and propaganda outfit.'[9] These activists were operating at two levels: the legal mass mobilisation and the illegal underground.[10]

Ebrahim Ebrahim returned to South Africa in January 1985 to canvass views on the upcoming ANC conference to be held in Kabwe, Zambia. The police got wind of his presence and tried to arrest him in early June. Yunis and Moe Shaik and Gordhan helped him to escape. Moe Shaik was arrested during the state of emergency. Shortly thereafter Yunis, along with his and Moe's father and brother Chippie, was also arrested, as was Shirish Soni, another member of their cell. Moe and Yunis Shaik's mother died while they were in detention.[11]

Figure 11.1: *Left to right*: Brothers Moe, Schabir and Yunis Shaik were active in MK and trade unions in the 1980s. (Courtesy of 1860 Heritage Centre)

For most of the period from 1986 to 1989 Moe Shaik was underground, organising the intelligence section of the ANC. He was sent to East Germany in 1987 for training in intelligence and thereafter recruited ANC/UDF/NIC members such as Claudia Manning, Selina Pillay, Kamilla Naidoo and Clifford Collins, together with London-based Shaheen Bawa, to establish an ANC intelligence unit. Some of them went to the Soviet Union for training. These activists became part of Project Bible, which specialised in counter-intelligence that aimed to detect who from the MDM was working for the apartheid regime. They uncovered several alleged plots to kill ANC operatives.[12]

The second half of the 1980s was a difficult time for the NIC and its leaders. Hounded by the security police for their work with the UDF, NIC activists also faced a House of Delegates that was given increased powers over Indian life. At the same time, for some NIC members, involvement in an underground organisation and the armed struggle took up considerable time and resources. A number of key NIC activists became involved in the underground project Operation Vula.

Operation Vula

Operation Vula was a secret project initiated by Oliver Tambo to create structures that would allow senior ANC leadership in exile or underground to locate themselves in South Africa.[13] These 'cadres involved in special operations' were being brought into 'one underground revolutionary network', according to one of its operatives, so that they could 'be mobilised if talks with the government failed'.[14]

It remains unclear whether Operation Vula aimed to situate senior ANC leaders in the country to prepare for insurrection, or whether it was a back-up strategy in case negotiations failed or an attempt to coordinate and provide direction to internal anti-apartheid structures. Arguably its purposes changed as the terrain of struggle shifted decisively to negotiations.

Operation Vula was part of a change in MK strategy. The ANC's 'Strategy and Tactics' document adopted in Morogoro, Tanzania, in 1969 followed guerrilla warfare tactics as adopted in Cuba, where a weak force was pitted against a stronger one, and the expectation was that the programme would initiate mass resistance. Prior to 1976, it was difficult to undertake military operations within South Africa from Zambia and Tanzania, as Mozambique, Angola and Rhodesia were under white rule. MK therefore found it tough to make the impact it hoped for within the country in the 1960s.[15] Raymond Suttner argues against periodising MK's activity and effectiveness, as 'there were ruptures in continuities and continuities in ruptures'.[16] However, the independence of Angola and Mozambique in 1975 opened new possibilities.

The ANC NEC resolved in 1978 to combine armed activity with 'legal and semi-legal internal activity in order to spur general mass uprisings'. But MK activity in the early 1980s prompted a swift response from the apartheid regime, which launched raids on Mozambique and Angola. MK suffered a blow when Mozambique signed the 1984 Nkomati Accord with the Botha government, which barred MK activity on its territory.[17] The ANC resolved at its 1985 Kabwe conference to build an internal underground that would mobilise 'people's power' in the townships to produce a national uprising.[18] The conference also endorsed the view that 'whites must be made to feel the impact of MK's armed actions to a greater extent'.[19]

According to Pravin Gordhan, by June 1986 a core of activists was operating at both a mass level and the underground: 'we were not living at our homes ... so security people wouldn't be able to pick us up. A whole lot of detentions had occurred in that period so we evaded the emergency detentions.' The evading of arrest had an impact on mass work, which was further relegated to the back burner as the activists attempted to establish a single ANC underground structure in Durban that would be responsible for political and military activity.[20] Activists on the ground did not always have a full understanding of what was going on. According to Gordhan:

I can't say I understood the full scheme. It was about preparing the conditions for more senior people to come into the country, creating internal capability to steer the struggle with very senior people, being on the spot ... There was a clear debate going on and discussion about what insurrection means in terms of an armed rebellion, about what needs to be prepared for that. But given the nature of underground work, not all of us knew everything, and a lot of that resided I think in [Mac Maharaj's] head and in [Siphiwe Nyanda's] head and those that they were accounting to ... My role was organising units on the ground, organising propaganda. A print shop had been established, and [I was busy] keeping my connection to above-the-ground organisations alive and creating additional facilities within the country ... I was the major person responsible for arranging for people to go to Botswana and bring arms into the country.[21]

For Gordhan, Vula was in line with ANC policy of multiple pillars of struggle:

This was a period of very intense battle between internal ANC structures and mass structures and quasi-underground structures and the state at all sorts of levels. Community organising in African areas really took off the ground, street committees emerged, street battles emerged, people's power was being spoken about. There was combat taking place between communities and the armed forces, and the UDF itself ran all sorts of boycott campaigns, national stay-away campaigns, COSATU was active in that process as well, so you had a very intense state of hyperactivity.

The central question all the time was: how do you seize power? What are the organisational forms that needed to be evolved, what kind of capability needed to be created, what kind of political and military training needed to be offered and what strategies and tactics needed to evolve in order to seize political power? That's the direction all of this activity fed into. By then the four pillars were fairly clear as well as a broad strategy that we were pursuing ... so you kept the mass activity alive, you kept the underground alive, you kept the military activity alive, and you kept the external mobilisation alive.[22]

Gordhan recalled that, on getting word from his handlers in 1986, he sent Yousuf Vawda to meet Mac Maharaj in Mauritius.[23] Vawda returned with instructions to get a safe house and car ready for an operation to bring senior ANC members into the country to help create political-military structures on the ground. Among those who returned to Natal were Maharaj himself (in August 1988), Siphiwe Nyanda and Ronnie Kasrils.[24] Ivan Pillay explained the aim behind this move:

The ANC never had a member of the NEC inside the country since the 1960s ... There's nobody giving political leadership as an organisation inside the country. The closest you've come as a political leadership was the UDF. So providing political leadership, especially for the African people, and some political cohesion was a huge problem. The Indian community was always slightly better off in that we had the NIC and it continued right up to when the ANC was unbanned. So they played a role in pulling a lot of those people together.[25]

It is no coincidence that the accelerated drive to insert exiled leadership inside the country occurred at the same time as negotiations with the apartheid regime were beginning to unfold. There was much to see if one scratched beneath the varnish.

Vula was active in Natal between August 1988 and May 1990, providing logistical support for the conflict in KwaZulu-Natal. Moe Shaik's unit provided the intelligence component of Operation Vula. According to Moe Shaik:

Vula's influence spread into the mass democratic movement, the trade unions, the activities of MK, and – via London and Lusaka – to the involvement of international sympathisers. It even spread into Nelson Mandela's quarters at Victor Verster [Prison], giving him the benefit of confidential contact with the exiled leadership ... Everyone was imbued and infected with a purpose and action ... a common mission.[26]

When Vula unravelled, 40 people, including Gordhan and Billy Nair, were arrested on 12 July 1990. According to Gordhan,

[I was] detained on 12 July 1990 together with Anesh Sankar. I was supposed to meet him at the secret flat which Charles Ndaba, who was one of the people who was killed by the police, had access to. When I get there I have a gun at my head, there's a policeman waiting. So effectively that was the beginning of the detention. I was then removed to Newcastle on the Friday and then on Sunday evening to Bethlehem in the Free State. I was interrogated for 3½ months. No lawyer. I was tortured but not too badly. I was suffocated for about 45 minutes or an hour by a chap called Hentie Botha. He put the balaclava over your head and then rubber tubing over your mouth and nose, but your body would be wrapped in a blanket and rope of some kind so you can't move ... I managed to get a message out and so there was a court application in Durban ... You must remember what you had is a situation where the police knew a hell of a lot. It surprised me how much they knew ... They killed two people, so clearly something happened there, and secondly in raiding everybody it appears – subsequently anyway, I didn't know at that time – that they had a fair amount of information. I was spinning a yarn, so to speak, trying to explain my involvement, and clearly they knew much more than I was telling them ... I didn't panic. This was my third detention so I had a fair amount of experience in how to deal with them. I was held in 1981/82 for 5½ months and in 1985 for a month.[27]

These detentions were taking place when the ANC was unbanned and Mandela was setting up formal negotiations with the apartheid regime.

Gordhan joined others who were charged with terrorism as part of the Vula Eight: Siphiwe Nyanda, Susanna Tshabalala, Dipak Patel, Anesh Sankar, Billy Nair, Mac Maharaj, Raymond Lala and Catherine Mvelase.[28]

Mac Maharaj was of the view that because Vula was uncovered just prior to an important negotiations meeting, the ANC did not 'robustly acknowledge' it as an ANC operation. Mendi Msimang, the ANC's chief representative in Britain, claimed on television there that Vula was a 'maverick' operation. When the Vula Eight eventually appeared in court after six months in detention, Maharaj ruefully recalled that no one from the ANC NEC or SACP Central Committee attended the court hearing. The accused were granted bail but the ANC did not provide them funding. Instead their legal representatives, Zak Yacoob and Yunus Mohamed, went around Durban to raise the R300 000 bail for the Vula operatives.[29]

The trial started in January 1991 and was then adjourned due to the political negotiations that were gathering momentum. On 25 March 1991 President F.W. de Klerk granted indemnity to the entire group.[30] In a frank assessment, Gordhan stated that Vula was not around long enough 'to make a significant contribution ... The period we're talking about was largely a preparatory period where you were beginning to build up steam as opposed to driving a locomotive.'[31] Gordhan himself quickly abandoned the notion of the seizure of power as he stepped into a pivotal role in negotiations that saw the speedy suspension of armed struggle.

Ivan Pillay, on the other hand, although critical of the delay in getting leaders into the country, made a more positive assessment:

> In the little time that was there, we sent in a lot of weapons, we carried out some action, we did a lot of propaganda work, we did a hell of a lot of political work ... pulled together lots of people, UDF, church leaders, all sorts of people, and gave greater cohesion and impetus ... On the intelligence side, we made headway in penetrating the SA Intelligence structures. It's one of the rare times we had managed to recruit people from within the security services and we were receiving reports directly from their archives.[32]

Pillay does concede that the situating of ANC leaders happened when the endgame was in sight. Much of the internal ANC's work turned to ensuring that the ANC was the major player in talks about talks with the apartheid regime. This effort was to prove spectacularly successful.

On the armed struggle, Janet Cherry points out that the quest to bring in 'guerrillas to transform the township uprising into a seizure of state power' did not materialise:

> By the time the security police had brought the township uprising under control [by October 1988], MK had lost its bases in Angola and Mozambique, and was still struggling to smuggle guerrillas across the border. [When the] ANC managed to send underground leadership into SA in August 1988, the masses were never armed; by my reckoning, MK was desperately trying to establish a presence inside South Africa. Yet at the very point that it was able to do so, the Soviet Union began [in January 1989] applying pressure on the ANC to negotiate with the regime.[33]

This critique of the effectiveness of MK should not undermine its symbolic significance and its role in allowing the ANC to gain hegemony over other anti-apartheid forces. Raymond Suttner argues that

> MK's actual military power was not what was attributed to it by many activists. But its very presence, the existence of a military arm of the ANC which attacked apartheid targets, was an important element in establishing ANC hegemony over the anti-apartheid forces in general ... Although one cannot claim that MK had the capacity to overthrow the apartheid regime, there is little doubt that many people cherished this hope, that MK inspired them greatly, and that its existence and the military achievements that it did secure were an important element in ANC hegemony being consolidated ... Military forays were important in the perception of the ANC as the force that would bring freedom.[34]

Of the Vula group, Moe Shaik went back into hiding for almost a year until he was granted indemnity in June 1991 with the likes of Ronnie Kasrils, Charles Nqakula, Janet Love and Ivan Pillay. Shaik joined the negotiation process and was nominated by the Communist Party to serve on the intelligence subcouncil of the Transitional Executive Council, which shaped the new intelligence structures of South Africa. In 1994 he became chair of the committee set up to amalgamate the intelligence services of the country: these were the National Intelligence Service, ANC, PAC, Transkei Intelligence, BOP, Ciskei and Venda.[35]

After 20 years on Robben Island, Billy Nair had been released in 1984. He immediately plunged into UDF work and was central to mobilisation against the tricameral proposals. This activity put him back on the radar of the Security Branch. Evading arrest during the states of emergency, Nair signed up with Operation Vula and was arrested on 12 July 1990. Nair insisted in a 2002 interview that it was the ANC's restraint in the period after 1990 that eventually paved the way for a negotiated peace:

> They [the apartheid regime] tried to use force, they tried their tricks to sabotage negotiations. We then hit back with a complete stoppage of work. Total. Nobody worked in South Africa for three days and then we said, well, you go any further, we're going to go also a step further ... We had activists throughout the country, we had arms throughout the country. We decided to restrain ourselves not to use them at all even when in 1993/1994 the State ... [was] slaughtering us. We said no, we don't use the weapons that we've got. No hitting back, nothing. Let the peace process continue, let the negotiations continue and we were quite determined about that.[36]

It is questionable whether the ANC really had arms and capacity 'to hit back'. In any case the 'steam' of struggle, to borrow Gordhan's word, was already congealing at the station of negotiation. Billy Nair became a member of the ANC interim leadership group in 1990 and joined the National Executive Committee in 1991. He served in Parliament from 1994 to 2004.

Pravin Gordhan received indemnity in March 1991, and in November 1991 came to represent the Natal and Transvaal Indian Congresses in the Convention for a Democratic South Africa (CODESA) process. He then became part of the management committee and turned his attention to ensuring that the locomotive of negotiation would not be derailed. He was

Figure 11.2: Pravin Gordhan (*standing*), pictured here with Nelson Mandela, played a key role in CODESA talks. (Courtesy of African News Agency)

appointed CODESA chairperson in January 1992 and was involved in the negotiations to end apartheid in South Africa. He went to Parliament as an MP in 1994 and served until February 1998. In March 1998 he joined the South African Revenue Service (SARS) as deputy commissioner and became commissioner in November 1999.[37] Gordhan was to become a leading figure in the efforts to unseat Jacob Zuma as president of the country after allegations of sustained corruption surfaced.

The price of secrecy

State repression and counter-mobilisation during the state of emergency forced many NIC/UDF activists underground as open resistance became impossible. This meant that there was a great deal of secrecy, which in turn created tensions in the public work of the NIC, as it appeared to some members that they were being left out of discussions. As a result, accusations of cabalism appeared. These claims went beyond the NIC and were alleged to have entered the MDM. Charles Nqakula, for example, recalled that at a UDF/COSATU meeting with the ANC, including

Oliver Tambo, on 21 March 1988, 'the question of disunity once more dominated the discussions. One of the causes of the friction, the MDM leaders told the meeting, was the emergence in the people's structures of what they defined as "cabalism" – factionalism especially in the Transvaal and Natal.'[38]

Did Vula play into the narrative of an Indian cabal dominating and even manipulating political decisions and promoting carefully selected cadres? When Oliver Tambo gave command of Vula inside of South Africa to Mac Maharaj, the latter raised the issue of his race/ethnicity:

> ... O.R., I have a question to ask you ... I'm going to do what you're asking me to do, but why is it you are sending me among others to the province of Natal, where there are very, very serious racial tensions, and you are not sending an African member of the NEC?[39]

Whatever Maharaj's initial questioning of his deployment, once inside the country he was quite combative in exercising his power and calling on the authority of Tambo when he was challenged. He got into a stand-off with Harry Gwala, an ex-Robben Islander and a legendary figure in resistance politics. Gwala, based in the Natal Midlands, had decided to take on the IFP in a bloody head-to-head battle. According to Maharaj:

> Gwala was paranoid that the ANC's structures in Natal were cor-rupted by an 'Indian cabal' and apoplectic when he learned that the ANC had chosen an Indian to organise its underground structures inside the country. Gwala, whom the comrades held in high esteem for the tenacity of his war against Mangosuthu Buthelezi, was in real-ity a high-risk threat to the struggle he embodied. I made numerous attempts to arrange a meeting with him through intermediaries. He ignored everyone, but we eventually met ... I was conciliatory and cooperative. But Gwala kept none of the agreements we made ... As I recall this incident so many years later, I can laugh it off. But there was nothing funny about it at the time ... He was trying to lobby support against me by alleging I was part of an Indian cabal. He thought that Natal was his territory ... He didn't want interference from 'outsiders' in his area.[40]

Gwala likely saw Maharaj as trespassing on his territory by making independent contact with his people and drawing them into Vula. It would therefore have been reasonable for Gwala to see this as a deliberate attempt to undermine him. One can imagine Maharaj, with all his political capital and buttressed by the fact that he had the ear of Tambo, using this to bring people into his orbit of influence. What is occluded in Maharaj's account is that it was Gwala to whom people turned for respite when they felt under attack from what they saw as the cabal. Pregs Govender recounts how more than once she relied on Gwala for protection and counsel when ANC underground operatives attacked fellow comrades.[41] And both Yusuf Bhamjee and Yunus Carrim mentioned that they enjoyed a relationship of trust with Gwala.

Maharaj, it must be remembered, was relying on the likes of Pravin Gordhan and Moe Shaik as part of his internal network. In Johannesburg he made contact with Ismail Momoniat of the TIC, who became, in Maharaj's words, 'indispensable to Vula'.[42]

Maharaj's mode of operating would have reinforced the notion of a cabal seeking to control the movement and working with carefully selected people. By raising the issue of his ethnicity with Tambo, Maharaj clearly showed he was sensitive to the issue. But while he was incognito, carrying on incredibly dangerous work that required him to rely on people he could trust, sensitivity was not his priority.

Nothing exemplifies the use of networks in the Indian community more than the case of Schabir Shaik, the brother of Moe Shaik, who was recruited to find ways to provide finance for underground work in the country. In Moe Shaik's words:

> Schabir came up with a working solution – the hawala system. The hawala system was as old as the hills. It is a way of conducting fund transfers across borders without using the conventional banking system ... In South Africa, especially among the Indian merchant class, there were vast sums of cash, called 'ooplang', undeclared to the tax authorities. This cash flowed outside the conventional money system. Using the hawala system, for example, Dealer A in Lusaka could instruct Dealer B in Durban to make cash available to me. Dealer B would then have a line of credit with Dealer A that he could realise as cash or property in another country.[43]

Schabir Shaik 'was also involved in trying to purchase companies in the United States and the United Kingdom and opening franchise outlets in South Africa as a way of laundering money. Some got off the ground; some didn't.'[44] It was in this role that he met Jacob Zuma. Their relationship was to end in post-apartheid South Africa with Schabir Shaik's criminal conviction for corruption in what was termed a 'mutually beneficial symbiosis' with Zuma.

The role of key Operation Vula figures in the quest to establish hegemony – in particular, the isolating of some leading ANC cadres who had been released from prison and the attempt to position others – led to pushback and acrimony from forces that saw Operation Vula as undermining their position. As much as this conflict and rancour was about ANC politics, it was also about battles fought within the UDF and the NIC.

One can see how, with even the best intentions, the 'tightness' of cadres led to gatekeeping – deciding who would be brought in and who would be left out – which fed into the notion of a cabal. What did this mean for the mass organisations that had sprung up and were nurtured through the 1980s? Were they simply to be siphoned into an ANC machine? What would this mean for the NIC, which saw its leading cadres consumed by underground work and fulfilling orders from on high? Moe Shaik argues that '[f]rom the top down the ANC was constituted in a manner that reflected its non-racial character'.[45] In the bubble of the armed struggle and intelligence gathering, that may well have been the case. But the progressive voice – consumed in the exigencies and emergencies of the transition with the prize of power in sight – was heard less and less above ground in places like Chatsworth and Phoenix.

The end of the 1980s saw the terrain of struggle change dramatically. In 1985, responding to the declaration of a state of emergency, Oliver Tambo declared:

> Our own tasks are very clear ... we have to break down and destroy the old order. We have to make apartheid unworkable and our country ungovernable. The accomplishment of these tasks will create the situation for us to overthrow the apartheid regime and for power to pass into the hands of the people as a whole.[46]

Five years later, the Pretoria Minute of 6 August 1990 announced that armed struggle had been suspended. The ANC was determined to show that it could govern. This meant producing conditions for stability by bringing key personnel into the negotiating room. During this challenging period the state sought ways to weaken and disarm the liberation movement, while those within the ANC jockeyed for influence and position. These complexities made it a time for tight control by those in leadership, as much as it was a time to appeal to the broadest layers of 'the people'.

Those who opted to build the ANC's capacity for armed struggle within the country had to work in secret while maintaining lines of communication with those in exile. They were often forced to follow a double agenda, as they were public leaders of the NIC. This modus operandi fed into the allegations of cabal, while the recruiting of key NIC members into underground work also limited the organisation's ability to provide political direction to a community that needed assurance as the demise of apartheid loomed.

12 | Between Fact and Factions: The 1987 Conference

The NIC was certainly not a tight grouping of activists all reading from the same script. It was criss-crossed – some might say double-crossed – with leadership splits, personality clashes, and contestations over tactics and strategies, the fallout from which reached into the broader liberation movement. The issue of a cabal within the NIC, with accusations of secret meetings and factions, captured public attention in the mid-1980s. There are contested narratives as one follows different groupings, ideological streams, and generational- and personality-driven impulses, although it is difficult to pin down exactly who belonged to the different factions and how they operated.

In examining this issue, we took cognisance of Yunus Carrim's contention that there is little to be gained by 'personalising political events'. He explained:

> I am no abstract structuralist, but there should not be too much of who said what to whom. Yes, that is important, that is the stuff of politics, but one has to also look at the context and the questions should be: What was the policy? What was the strategy? What was the set of tactics that underpinned action?[1]

There were differences over strategy and ideology, but can personality be totally ignored? For example, I.C. Meer shared office space with Mewa Ramgobin in Verulam. Iain Edwards observed that the two 'spoke, argued, and lunched nearly every day, each on their side of a stable door, the top half open. Yet Meer never mentions Mewa Ramgobin once in his memoir.[2]

209

Are there are lifelong enmities in this observation? What drove it?'[3] Edwards, who conducted interviews with Ramgobin and with MK soldier and Robben Island prisoner Natoo Babenia, was struck by the deep-seated 'sectarianism' within the NIC:

> Both the otherwise mild-mannered Natoo, and Mewa, known for his divisive public and behind-the-scenes behaviour, would often say 'Don't talk to so and so, he's a sell-out, stooge ... can't be trusted ... is involved with ...' As an outsider I can't help [but] wonder whether there is something deeply historical about this feature of politics. What are its roots? Why has it proved so enduring? Does no-one realise its destructive capacities?[4]

Where did the impulses come from that made some in the NIC personae non gratae, while others were treated with suspicion and kept on a tight leash? Was there a shadowy group or groups that sought to pull the strings, and to what end?

Some NIC executive members denied the existence of a cabal. Thumba Pillay described the idea of a cabal as 'a figment of somebody's imagination. It never existed, but in the NIC, like in every organisation, some people were more active than others and the perceptions emerged that these active people were taking the decisions.'[5] Paul David also described the cabal as

> a figment of most people's imagination. It was never there. The cabal accusations came simply because some of us that were accused – Pravin, Yunus, Farouk, Jerry, Thumba, and myself – I was the supposed convener of the cabal – were friends and would have dinner with Jerry, with Thumba, we'd raise discussions and because we were political people, what the hell would we talk about but politics and mostly tactics, strategy and things like that. It was not an organised group. We were the closest of friends and we had commonality between us as individuals and as a group.[6]

David added that, ideologically, the younger NIC members 'were to the left. I'm a communist, Pravin was, Thumba would show great obedience to the Communist Party ... We gravitated together because we would be to the left of people like Mewa and Sew [Sewpersadh], DK [Singh].[7] Similarly, Coovadia argued in 1988 that the old guard 'couldn't accept the more energetic younger people who had come into NIC with ideas of making it more a mass organization, have more youth involvement. This threatened some of the older dilettantes who ... were entrenched ... and relied too much on rhetoric rather than analysis.[8] Yunus Mohamed, in rejecting the allegations of cabal, made 'no apologies for being active and for being able to do the work'. Critics like M.J. Naidoo, he said, preferred 'press statement leadership'.[9] Mohamed's sarcastic comment suggests an element of contempt among younger recruits for the older leadership, who had their own style of political conduct nurtured from the late 1960s.

Even if one concedes David's point that they were not a formally organised group, these 'leftists' clearly saw themselves as a separate grouping ideologically. David did not elaborate on what 'to the left' meant in everyday politics, but it is instructive that there was little class and ideological difference between them, as all were professionals who took the Freedom Charter as their guide. However, contemporary letters to the press suggest that there were perceptions of 'centre' and 'left' in the NIC. One letter observed that 'the more conservative members [of the Indian community] ... have difficulty in coming to terms with the increasingly powerful left-wing faction'.[10] 'Congress Watcher' noted that 'the basic conflict in the NIC at present is between those who support Gandhian democratic ideals and those who have veered too far to the left and abandoned democracy'.[11]

The Consulate affair in 1984 (discussed in Chapter 9) left bitter divisions. Ramgobin referred to splits within the NIC in a March 1985 letter to Ela Gandhi from prison, where he was awaiting trial for treason:

> About NIC I am sorry and despondent that things are bad out 'there' ...
> I hold no brief for anybody ... Don't you know that I wanted to sever
> my relationship, politically, with both NIC and the UDF from the
> time we were in the Consulate? ... Your stormy meeting with Rabi
> [Bugwandeen] and D.K. [Singh] must have been sad and not at all
> necessary ... It is a pity that Congress Exec is ... characterized for so
> long by two factions; which division for far too long has permeated
> the ranks of activists, too.[12]

In a subsequent letter to his daughter Asha in the same month, Ramgobin was even more forthright:

> I want to, always wanted to, belong to Congress, not to factions led by X or Z within Congress. Your mummy is identifiable as belonging to one such faction. And this saddens me. She has her own rights but my rights are being commented on.[13]

This letter is the clearest outright assertion that the NIC was spilt into factions. Although the lines were not always clear-cut, it appears that Yunus Mohamed and Pravin Gordhan formed one axis with the 'leftists'. How they were differentiated from the likes of Ramgobin, M.J. Naidoo, D.K. Singh and Rabi Bugwandeen is not entirely clear. George Sewpersadh was admired across the 'factions', which was seen as both a strength and a weakness. Some suggested that generational differences were exacerbated as new layers of activists began to find their voice.

By the mid-1980s, the former student leaders and community activists now involved in the NIC were demanding a voice in how the organisation was run. As debates about internal democracy intensified, accusations that a clique was in operation came into the open when the NIC held a workshop at the Aryan Benevolent Home in Chatsworth in October 1987, followed by a provincial conference on 27 November.

Yunus Carrim wrote at the time that the 'thrust for the conference had come largely from activists who had been involved in the anti-tricameral protests of 1984'. These activists were concerned that 'the extent of organisational work they did was not matched by the degree of control they had over the organisation, particularly its executive'. They felt that 'there was unnecessary factionalism and there were accusations of domination by a "cabal"'. The aim of the conference was to make the NIC more democratic and to review its strategy in view of the changing political conditions. Due to the state of emergency and 'the controversial nature of some of the issues being discussed', the conference was open only to delegates and observers from NIC branches and fraternal organisations. Carrim agreed with Farouk Meer, NIC general secretary, that it was a *'closed* not a *secret* conference'.[14]

It appears ironical that even though one impetus for the conference was the allegation that the NIC was run by a small grouping, the meeting was a closely controlled process. But, as Charm Govender explained, their options were limited by political conditions. The meeting could not be 'publicly advertised. We had people whose task was to secure the conference so that if police were seen anywhere, people like Moe Shaik, Pravin Gordhan, Roy Padayachie, Billy Nair, Yunis Shaik could be escorted to safety before the police could apprehend them.'[15] Nevertheless, newspaper reports on the 'cabal' increased in the aftermath of the 1987 conference.

The NIC executive appeared to be aware of its failings. Farouk Meer's secretarial report, presented on 29 November 1987, pointed to some of these:

> Lacking in long-term approach and planning to our activity, we are often open to criticism for being too issue-orientated; Inability to convert the NIC into a truly mass organisation; Lack of cohesion amongst activists resulting in the organisation being unable to advance; No on-going programme of political education at mass, activist levels; Inability to check collaborators making inroads e.g. Tongaat by-election; Inability to address insecurities of Indian masses and to affect low-level political consciousness within the community and particularly in relation to questions of majority rule; Quality of our activists – deficient in spirit and militancy resulting in an inability to agitate and organise the masses for a more active role in the struggle.[16]

The conference elections ousted M.J. Naidoo as president and executive members Rabi Bugwandeen, R. Ramesar and R.B. Chaudhray. George Sewpersadh was elected president, with Mewa Ramgobin, Paul David, S. Govender, Billy Nair, A.S. Chetty, Hassim Seedat, Jerry Coovadia, Ela Gandhi, Zak Yacoob and Farouk Meer elected to the executive. In a letter to the *Daily News*, 'NIC Feminist, Merebank' bemoaned the fact that the executive continued to be dominated by men, a trend that runs throughout NIC history.[17]

M.J. Naidoo went on the offensive. He told the *Weekly Mail* that 'the election was a sham. I am talking about six or seven people who in the past referred to themselves as the "think tank".'[18] It is noteworthy that Naidoo was not re-elected while Ramgobin and Sewpersadh, with whom he had been holed up at the British Consulate and imprisoned during the Pietermaritzburg Treason Trial, survived. Carrim believes that Sewpersadh was a 'compromise choice to unify the different strands. Also, I think, to prevent [the rise of] Mewa Ramgobin, who wanted to be the president of the NIC. Mewa is a buddy of George, and I think it would have been hard for Mewa, for all his ambitions, to take on George. Anybody else, he would.'[19] Coovadia described Sewpersadh in 1988 as 'an old school type liberal: big on due process, civil rights and liberties, human rights. People respect his length of service in politics. This really counts for a lot among us. His long and consistent involvement, sacrifices. We don't look for charisma, in fact we're suspicious of it.'[20]

If the choice of Sewpersadh for president was a manoeuvre to outflank Ramgobin, then prior planning would have been necessary to ensure that Ramgobin could not, would not, stand against Sewpersadh. Given Ramgobin's seminal role in the revival of the NIC, it was presumably felt that he could be prevented from becoming president but not completely ousted.

By now the word 'cabal' was in common public use. At an NIC Verulam branch meeting on 4 February 1988, Paul David stated that it was being 'misused' and was 'misleading'; he appealed to members to avoid using it. Ramgobin reported that at the request of the NIC executive, he had written to the press in his personal capacity to dismiss allegations of the existence of a so-called cabal in the NIC.[21] Ramgobin stated in the letter:

> I must remind my fellow South Africans that although I did revive the NIC, George Sewpersadh was elected the president of the organisation in 1971 ... Had George's nomination and unanimous election as the current president not been made by Billy Nair, I would have personally had the pleasure of nominating him. To those who say that George is the nominee of a 'cabal', I want to say that he has strong views and is unlikely to be anybody's puppet.[22]

While debunking the idea that Sewpersadh was a puppet of the cabal, Ramgobin simultaneously put the issue of the cabal in the public domain. He was a wily, tireless operator and, almost on cue, he told Sewpersadh in a letter written a month later, on 10 March, that Farouk Meer's executive report at the November 1987 meeting had attacked him personally. He described the practice where individuals were 'targeted' as 'part and parcel of the practice of "Cabalism"' and called on Sewpersadh to get the executive to discuss this 'anti-organisational conduct'.[23]

Ramgobin always led from the front and was ready with an acerbic put-down to any opposition from the ranks. Through his involvement in the Release Mandela Committee (RMC), Ramgobin had begun to build linkages with African comrades, which would prove important in his internal NIC battles. Notably, Jeremy Seekings makes the argument that the RMC 'was intended as an Africanist counterweight to the TIC [and NIC] within the broad Charterist movement and the UDF'.[24]

There were several strands of tension within the NIC. One that was particularly discernible by the late 1980s was between members who had their base in Chatsworth and were jostling for control with what they saw as the entrenched city-based professional middle class. Charm Govender identified this as a 'factionalism [comprised] essentially of a Pravin Gordhan apparatus and a Roy Padayachie apparatus'. He believed that this may have had its origins in the leaders' contact with different ANC factions in exile.[25] Additionally, Gordhan had his base in Phoenix and Padayachie in Chatsworth. Phoenix-based Roy Sukuram described Padayachie as 'unofficially the leader of Chatsworth'.[26] Coovadia described the differences between Gordhan and Padayachie as 'personal':

> Both of them probably felt that they were senior enough to provide the leadership. Roy was caught up in Chatsworth, in a school set-up. He had a much more academic style of speaking and addressing issues, whereas Pravin had this intellectual strength, but he was still very down-to-earth. He didn't speak in ideological terms. He explained things easily and there wasn't an issue for which he didn't have an answer.[27]

Paul David described Gordhan and Padayachie as

> two strong personalities. Roy as a debater was formidable, Pravin too, but they were both very individualistic, very forceful characters. It was not over doctrine, it was not over theory, it was personality ... Within

the NIC, Pravin emerged as a central figure, not just because he was clever, not just because he knew his politics, not just because he knew the history of the NIC, but because he matched that with work.[28]

Charm Govender's recollection points to small groups operating within the NIC:

> There were people then who were close in the Chatsworth group and referred to the Phoenix group as a cabal. That was a word that [A.K.M.?] Docrat used to describe Pravin Gordon and his group. So, everyone says, 'oh, this is what the cabal's view on it is and this is what our view is.' But [our] practice was just the same, the groups meeting in secret, groups trying to engage in machinations against each other, and it did have a destructive effect because now you dislocated the struggle to make sure that the influence of the other was reduced ... The divisions were very sharp and took the form even of antagonism and disrespect.[29]

Govender recounted, for example, that he was initially reluctant to work with Gordhan when Billy Nair put them in the same Communist Party cell because 'we had not a very good relationship up until then'. When he objected, Nair responded that the 'basis of your difficulties is a personal one, there is no difference in ideology between you, now you'll have to work together and just get this thing sorted out'.[30] Nair's comment of 'no difference in ideology' reinforces the idea that divisions, rather than having deep ideological strains, were more likely to have been generated by particular links with exiles, geographic location and the operation of egos, all of which were intensified in the cut and thrust of everyday politics.

M.J. Naidoo's ousting raised issues of language, ethnicity, religion and regionalism. Like the majority of working-class Indians, Naidoo was of South Indian background, whereas the leadership was mainly North Indian. This was one of the rare occasions that the issue of North Indians and South Indians as a basis of division was raised openly within the NIC, and while it had origins as far back as indenture, this division prefigured cleavages that would emerge in post-apartheid South Africa.

According to Kumi Naidoo, M.J. Naidoo's ousting was seen by working-class Indians as the removal of a fellow 'south Indian Tamil-speaking Hindu of indentured roots ... [in favour of Hassim] Seedat and [Hassan] Mall, who were of north Indian, Muslim and merchant class roots'.[31] When this was put to Yunus Carrim, he was sceptical:

> Yes, there are inevitable cultural and socialisation aspects to all of us, but it did not play a role [in M.J. Naidoo's ousting]; it was a class issue as well. South Indians, because they disproportionally represent the working people, and Hindi-speaking Hindus represent, in particular, business people and professionals. Class differences played themselves out more as a reflection of the structural conditions rather than a conscious decision to use ethnicity as a criteria [sic] to marginalise people. If you look at the student community that became quite dominant, often they were more middle class. Those who could take part in politics were proportionately less among those from a working-class background. There are all those complex permutations that explain why the effect was that some South Indians got marginalised and ousted, but that it was a conscious decision, I think, is nonsensical.[32]

Carrim added that he was part of a group which insisted that A.S. Chetty, a South Indian from Pietermaritzburg, be one of the deputy chairpersons alongside Mewa Ramgobin and Jerry Coovadia, who had been nominated: 'We said, no, who has got a longer history in the struggle? Jerry or A.S.? We stuck to our guns, so they changed the constitution there, which I am not even sure was allowed, and there were three deputies.' Carrim pointed out that Thumba Pillay, also a South Indian, was on the executive for over three decades.[33]

Pregs Govender points a finger at the operation of a cabal in the 1980s, noting that 'criticisms of the cabal became more pronounced: of its centralised and undemocratic manner of decision-making, its lack of respect for working-class leadership, the ethnic lines on which it organised, the chauvinism and sexist attitudes, its control of resources and patronage of areas and individuals who were loyal'.[34]

Criticism that the middle-class character of the NIC leadership made it insensitive to the everyday issues of its working-class constituency rankled some members. In a 1986 interview, Pravin Gordhan

Figure 12.1: Kumi Naidoo (*left*), seen here with Walter Sisulu. (Courtesy of Gandhi-Luthuli Documentation Centre)

responded to this allegation by pointing out that one had to distinguish between the 'class background of the individuals and the class positions they take'. While the working class would be the 'major benefactor' of the struggle, the NIC's responsibility was 'to develop meaningful working unity amongst all classes within the oppressed groupings' so long as 'the direction of their organisation is maintained'. The aim, Gordhan said, was to get 'in both numerical and qualitative terms the maximum number of people into the people's camp. Ostracising any class would mean that we are wilfully letting the enemy take away a part of our community.'[35]

Mewa Ramgobin responded to the issue of class by stating that he was 'not sorry' if the NIC was not 'very conclusive in our projection of a working class grouping. When did we take the decision, the ANC or the NIC,

Figure 12.2: Pregs Govender, a student leader at UDW and ANC MP (1994–2002). (Courtesy of Gandhi-Luthuli Documentation Centre)

to exclude any one class from the national democratic struggle? Each plays a significant role in the emancipation of all. [The NIC] was not declared a working-class party.'[36]

Similarly, when 'Oppressed' criticised the class composition of the leadership in a letter to the press, Farouk Meer responded:

> The NIC certainly does not represent the so-called elitist class in the community. Objectively, in housing and education, welfare and health, Indians are more privileged which creates more separation from vast majority of oppressed people. Majority of Indians reject apartheid, but fear of majority rule has increased. The minority syndrome has a materialistic basis. The overall economic position does lend to the possibilities of neutralisation, fear and group feeling.

Our concern has always been to improve the living conditions in Chatsworth, Phoenix and all areas where the majority of our people live. 'Oppressed' attempts to deflect the responsibility for oppression and exploitation to people who have managed, despite apartheid, to become professionals and are therefore more privileged than the majority of South African Indians. If class is the sole criterion for participation in peoples' struggles many leaders would have had no role to play ... Nelson Mandela, Mahatma Gandhi, Nehru, Bram Fischer, George Sewpersadh were all lawyers; Naicker, Dadoo and Neto were doctors; Messrs Kaunda, Nyerere, Cabral have distinguished academic backgrounds. The class origins of these individuals and those that are associated with the NIC and other democratic organisations have not impeded their contribution to the struggle for democracy.[37]

While Meer's and Gordhan's points are well made, being middle class brought with it social and cultural capital that gave activists a position of influence relative to those with a working-class background, who sometimes felt elbowed out of networks of power. Phoenix activist Roy Sukuram was critical of the fact that at the 40th anniversary commemoration of the Phoenix Working Committee in 2018, middle-class activists were given greater recognition than former working-class activists from the township.[38] The overwhelming majority of Indians had found homes in Chatsworth and Phoenix, where issues of transport, drugs, alcoholism and gangsterism were everyday circumstances unknown to the established middle-class leadership of the NIC. This disconnect would have consequences when the NIC sought to solicit support for the ANC at the end of the decade.

Another criticism of the NIC's supposed class amnesia came from those involved in building an independent union movement. Johnny Copelyn recounted that when activists such as Yunis Shaik entered the unions, they were determined to enforce the leadership role of the ANC at the expense of worker control.[39] For such activists, it appears that those who proposed building a non-racial, independent working-class movement – one that was wary of alliances with multi-class organisations – were working against the national democratic revolution.

One of the ironies of the criticism of the NIC's middle-class leadership is that many of the young critics were themselves leaving behind the working-class roots of their parents as they graduated with professional qualifications. While nothing prevented them from building mass-based organisations beyond the gaze of the NIC, this proved a difficult task. For example, Helping Hands, the organisation started by young activists in Chatsworth, operated more or less as an NGO and faced criticisms of being a tightly controlled grouping rather than having a mass orientation.

There were many alleged factions in the saga of the cabal. Fissures involved 'town' versus the new townships of Chatsworth and Phoenix, different lines of communication to various groups in exile, egos, family tensions and younger university leaders against the established leadership. Certainly there was a feeling that rather than critical thinking, the best attribute for underground work was loyalty – not to question but to accept orders from on high. For Pregs Govender, there was a recurring pattern:

> There were some in the NIC who said they were anti-cabal, yet, with few exceptions, many replicated these same patterns when they took positions as leaders. Later on, changes occurred in the leadership of the cabal, but this was not accompanied by any fundamental critique or alternative model of power and leadership.[40]

While not referring specifically to a cabal, Surendra Bhana notes the NIC's organisational shortcomings and distancing from the mass of Indians in the 1980s:

> In the last few years its structures remained too centralised, and its leadership much too removed from the rank and file to build a base of mass support. Having to answer to an ill-defined, loose constituency of supporters, the leaders did not face the rigours of accountability. They tended, therefore, to impose from above, rather than structure from below through the medium of 'town hall' type meetings.[41]

Was Bhana's criticism of a centralised leadership without a sense of accountability too harsh? In mitigation, as Coovadia argued, the closing of space for political organisation and outright repression made it 'dangerous to meet openly'. Many were operating under the constant threat of detention and for some the charge of treason.[42] Nor should we ignore the power of deeply personal bonds that were woven in the work of the underground. Moe Shaik, in reflecting on his detention and that of his brother Yunis and friend Shirish, writes hauntingly:

> Yunis endured his torture drawing on inner resilience ... He said nothing. He suffered his torture in part for the glorious ideals of the struggle but more because of his commitment he had made to Pravin [Gordhan]. Under torture, resilience is not born of ideals but of love and loyalty to others. Torture is endured to protect human love. For Yunis it was for Pravin. For Shirish and me it was for Yunis.[43]

Yunus Carrim, one of those in the NIC leadership who was critical of the cabal in the 1980s, is more sympathetic in hindsight. In a 2019 interview, he maintained his opinion that

> there was a Cabal, [but] I am more understanding about why it existed and less critical of what they did. I didn't know then that they were so linked to the external ANC, that most of them were concurrently participating in underground struggle. I don't know why people who were there in that structure refuse to accept the Cabal existed. Surely, the issue is to say, yes, there was a group that existed. Cabal may be too strong a term for it, but a group did exist and these are the reasons: a) we were operating in semi-clandestine conditions; b) the legal structures [of the NIC] were dormant ... really, up to 1987 at least; c) in those conditions of semi-insurrection you couldn't actually only have those legal, overt structures, but [you also needed] a steering thing; d) furthermore, from the mid-80s onwards the townships were flaring, African people were now beginning to take centre stage all over the country, you had to connect with African people and the younger generation seemed more at ease, more able to do this ... so connections between Indians and Africans took place outside the formal structures and decisions had to be made; e) people inside the NIC had links with different people in the broad ANC in exile.

The internal structures, the legal structures, could not connect with the ANC in the way semi-clandestine, semi-underground structures would. Knowing now what I do know, there are some things that are utterly remarkable about that group. It is not whether they should have existed or not. In that context, it was inevitable. If you were going to get things done, then some structure like that was inevitable.[44]

Carrim's argument, written from the perspective of an NIC insider who was never fingered as part of a cabal, is arguably the most cogent explanation for the existence of one. On the other hand, Carrim, advantaged by his location in Pietermaritzburg, might have had a less benign view of the cabal if he had felt marginalised in the way that others contend they did. Pregs Govender is one of many who, when they sought to carve their own paths within the anti-apartheid movement, were slandered and set upon by what she and many others saw as a cabal of Indian men using their connections with the ANC as a weapon of control. She writes, for example, of how an ANC operative

asked me to write reports on important figures in the movement: the general secretary of Cosatu, Jay Naidoo; the general secretary of Numsa, Alec Erwin; ... I'd laugh at the jokes of this comrade from university days but was stunned by his impatient anger when I kept replying, 'We are fighting the state, not each other. Our priority should be monitoring and reporting their atrocities.'[45]

Carrim seems not to recognise the depth of hurt of those cast as outsiders by this tight grouping or the price paid by those labelled as 'problematic'. Some cynics might argue that Carrim's understanding is due to his being a high-ranking member of the SACP with its democratic centralism, the prototype of cabalism. There are possibly other factors that account for why Carrim's position is less critical. One is the way in which people associated with the cabal, such as Gordhan, came to the fore in the fight to remove Jacob Zuma from the presidency in the post-apartheid period. Another is the way the notion of the cabal is being used opportunistically by the Economic Freedom Fighters (EFF) and associated racial chauvinists.

The banning of NIC leaders certainly affected the organisation's capacity to mount campaigns to boycott the HOD. One stark example is that in the 1984 election, the voter turnout in Tongaat was a paltry 6 per cent; in an October 1987 by-election in the same community, there was a 38 per cent poll.[46] Soon after this election, ousted NIC president M.J. Naidoo said that he was 'convinced of plans for NIC-backed participation' in the HOD, instigated by the cabal, and he could 'no longer keep silent'.[47]

Farouk Meer described Naidoo's statement as 'devoid of any truth'. It was, he said, 'intended to ... present the organisation as one lacking in discipline and principle'.[48] George Sewpersadh told reporters that NIC executive members had given a signed undertaking that they did not hold such talks, and that if anyone was found to have done so, he or she would have to 'appear before a disciplinary inquiry and face expulsion from the organisation if necessary'.[49]

The fact that Sewpersadh mentioned that there were signed undertakings meant that the red flag raised by Naidoo could not be dismissed out of hand. In a June 1988 interview, Jerry Coovadia explained that those in favour of participation argued that 'radical' parties had participated in the system elsewhere; that Congress regarded boycott as a tactic and not a principle; and that participation would afford new opportunities to mobilise the people and get hands on resources.[50] After the Indian Congresses met with the ANC in Lusaka in October 1988, Coovadia issued a communiqué on 10 October stating that the issue of participation in the municipal elections later that month had been discussed. However, the decision was taken not to participate, as the ANC was concerned that a high turnout would give the Nationalists the impression that there was support for its structures and 'help perpetuate the apartheid regime'.[51]

In the wake of the tricameral elections and the raising of the ante against those deemed to be 'collaborators', it may have appeared that the boycott of government institutions had become the norm. Yet the issue was far from dead. In the context of the state crackdown, renewed debate about participation appeared in publications such as *Work in Progress, Transformation, South African Labour Bulletin* and *Weekly Mail*. Some in the NIC latched onto a speech by UDF leader Archie Gumede in which he insinuated that participation should be reconsidered, as tactically it offered more than a boycott.[52]

In response Guy Berger, who served time in prison for his anti-apartheid activities, insisted that the benefits of participation would be offset by increasing 'confusion and dislocation' in the movement. Participation was not actually taken up as an option and the 'culture of "non-collaboration"' remained the 'response to apartheid as well as its institutional changes', but the issue was debated.[53]

Following the 1987 conference, the NIC attempted to extend its influence in the Indian community. A branch was opened in Verulam and another in Merebank. The NIC sent a delegation to the COSATU congress at the University of the Witwatersrand on 14 May 1988. In a report to the NIC executive, the delegation noted the strong emphasis on unity, but expressed concern that there was 'No visible presence of "Indian" workers or Unions with Indian Workers, even though several "Indian" organisations were present. NIC needs to have an on-going program re: Trade Unions especially so because so many NIC senior activists hold key positions in Unions.'[54]

The minutes of an NIC leadership workshop on 6–7 August 1988 underscored concern about mobilising Indians in support of majority rule. Delegates noted that separation under the Group Areas Act had 'devastating political effects in respect of joint actions against apartheid and Unity'. While the UDF had 'created a new positive climate', the racial violence in Inanda in 1985 'affected the current mood of Indian people'. State repression compounded the problem by 'weakening existing structures in the Community'. At UDF level 'there was little sense of belonging' among Indians. The minutes further stated:

Objectively, in housing and education, welfare and health, Indians are more privileged, which creates more separation from vast majority of oppressed people. Majority of Indians reject apartheid, but fear of majority rule has increased. The minority syndrome has a materialistic basis. The overall economic position does lend to the possibilities of neutralisation, fear and group feeling.

The NIC's economic, social, educational and collective political experiences [help the organisation] to build leadership and organisation in all other areas. There are some negative aspects of this, e.g. accusation of 'Indian lead' [led?]. NIC determined to defeat State's attempt to divide and rule. Cosatu needs our urgent attention. Being in Cosatu – which has adopted FC [Freedom Charter] – greater potential for Unity and ideological thrust towards non-racialism ...

Militancy among Indian Youth is not on the same level as African Youth. Un-governability, people's courts etc. seem not to click with/ among Indians even among youth, even though nonracialism is the declared vision through NIC. There is the lack of coordination between Indian and African civic demands/struggles. The same level of resistance, boycott of schools etc. as an area of struggle, between Indian and African is missing.[55]

The NIC was finding it difficult to transcend the African–Indian divide as community, student and civic campaigns, while espousing non-racialism, rarely breached racial boundaries.

By the late 1980s whispers of talks with the apartheid regime filtered through the ANC's internally based ranks. More and more demands came for upping the presence of the ANC, gathering intelligence and providing greater coordination for the underground. Some of the leading lights of the NIC were drawn into this world of underground structures, where they built their own networks in the ANC. This not only fuelled the notion of a cabal pulling the strings from afar, marginalising some and promoting others, but also meant that these NIC members spent less time addressing the issues raised at the August leadership workshop. Moe Shaik's biography, for example, reveals in detail how intelligence work for the ANC consumed his time and also how he recruited mainly younger people who might have played a pivotal role in the NIC.[56]

As this chapter has shown, through the 1980s there were many lines drawn within the NIC, reflecting fissures that would seethe and fester and play themselves out in new terrains. We pursue these different lines of march in subsequent chapters which deal with the endgame of apartheid and the future of the UDF and the NIC.

13 | 'Caught with Our Pants Down': The NIC and the Crumbling of Apartheid, 1988–1990

NIC secretary Farouk Meer wrote at the beginning of 1989 that whites had been 'brainwashed, cajoled and bullied into a false sense of fear and apprehension, mistakenly seeking security and privilege with the tenuous protection of security forces, big business and Nationalist politicians'.[1] He was not optimistic that an end to centuries of racist and exploitative rule was imminent. But within months of his statement, the Berlin Wall came crashing down and the international terrain changed dramatically, with major implications for local politics.

Elements within the apartheid regime regarded the changing context as a favourable environment for negotiations. As apartheid spy boss Niël Barnard put it:

> [With] the disintegration of the Soviet Union as a world power ... [the] implication for South Africa was that the USSR's military and financial support to the MPLA [ruling party] in Angola, and particularly to the ANC, was set to decline, which meant the ANC would become more vulnerable ... In a nutshell, the weaker the ANC was, the more advantageous it was to negotiate with them.[2]

What Barnard did not mention was that with the fall of the Soviet Union, the West could no longer be drawn into the argument that apartheid South Africa was a bulwark against communism, thus weakening the Nats' ability to solicit support internationally. In short, dramatic changes in geopolitics made both the ANC and the NP more amenable to sitting around a table.

Fatima Meer observed acutely in 1987 that P.W. Botha, fearing 'Afrikaner strife', had failed to make the 'necessary intellectual leap to real change' and continued 'worshipping the carcass [of apartheid]'. While observers believed that 'the Afrikaner will never give up', Meer argued that there was 'no special mystique about the Afrikaner', who had long 'parted company with his tough frontier forebears'. The Afrikaner attitude towards blacks had not changed, but because they had 'accumulated so many creature comforts' they would 'ultimately bargain to save some of them rather than lose all'.[3]

As Barnard observed, the fall of the Soviet Union had an immediate impact on the ANC and the SACP. With the Soviets 'abandoning the "no win" Cold War', there was declining support for 'any further protraction in South Africa's guerrilla warfare'.[4] Even before this, the ANC had sensed that it could not defeat the Nats militarily. The ANC had largely evacuated from Mozambique after the Nkomati Accord was signed in 1984, and the civil war in Angola sputtered on. Destabilised by the apartheid regime, the so-called Frontline States – Angola, Botswana, Lesotho, Malawi, Mozambique, Swaziland, Tanzania, Zambia and Zimbabwe – were encouraging the ANC to continue negotiations. In a revealing slip, ANC secretary general Alfred Nzo read out a policy document to journalists on 18 January 1990, stating that the ANC 'did not have the capacity within our country to intensify the armed struggle in any meaningful way'.[5]

Some in the ANC also feared that the internal rebellion would spiral out of control. Anthony Sampson noted at the time that 'some members of the ANC, which had called to render South Africa ungovernable eighteen months before, were beginning to worry that it might become ungovernable by anyone'.[6] Joe Slovo of the SACP explained: 'There are manifestations which we don't like, as kids begin to say: what can we do today? I've never relished the escalation of violence ... It was the only option, the last option: and we want to get out as soon as possible.'[7]

From the mid-1980s, a series of meetings took place between local organisations and international groups, as well as between South Africans of different political persuasions. An NIC/UDF delegation met the Commonwealth Eminent Persons Group in early 1986. There were moves by various political groups and individuals to meet with the country's white business leaders. Iain Edwards writes that 'much to the chagrin of some UDF colleagues, in 1987 [Mewa Ramgobin] addressed two such discreet and unpublicised meetings – in Durban and Johannesburg. Soon he was making personal introductions between very senior business and UDF leaders, some of these being his fellow former treason trialists.[8] In 1985 the ANC met with Gavin Relly, chairman of Anglo American Corporation, and other bigwigs of monopoly capital in Lusaka, where Relly sensed that the ANC realised 'the need for free enterprise'.[9]

Lusaka

As the contours of a negotiated settlement began to take shape, a number of South African groupings made the trek to Lusaka to meet with the ANC. It is in this context that members of the Indian Congresses were

Figure 13.1: The NIC/TIC delegation of October 1988 was one of the largest to meet with the ANC in Lusaka. *From left*: Cassim Saloojee (TIC delegation leader), Joe Slovo (ANC executive member and SACP leader), Jerry Coovadia (NIC delegation leader), Hassim Seedat (president of the M.L. Sultan Technikon Council) and Pat Samuels (president of the Teachers' Association of South Africa). (Courtesy of Faizal Dawjee)

invited to Lusaka in October 1988 to be briefed by the ANC. The delegation comprised 52 Indians, which included members of the NIC (led by Jerry Coovadia) and the TIC (led by Cassim Saloojee), as well as academics, business people, media representatives, and members of trade unions, religious organisations and civics.

The formal outcome of the 7–9 October 1988 meeting was a joint communiqué issued by the ANC, NIC and TIC on 10 October. The statement noted that the ANC was 'indispensable to the process of seeking a peaceful solution' in South Africa and called for the release of political prisoners and the lifting of the state of emergency.

Given the fear of African majority rule and anxiety over the spectre of communism which existed among many Indians, the communiqué gave the assurance that the ANC was a national liberation movement that included 'all classes and strata of the oppressed people and democratically-minded whites' committed to the Freedom Charter. The ANC believed in a mixed economy that would aim 'to eliminate social inequality based on race'. It supported sanctions and disinvestment to pressure the apartheid regime.

The issue of the cultural boycott, which had an impact on religious and cultural practices, was raised by the Indian delegation. Delegates mentioned that temples could not get priests from India, and artistes were prevented from visiting, which had a negative effect on the ability to inspire young people to join traditional dance and musical groups. The ANC was seen as the main obstacle to ending the cultural boycott, a point members of the HOD who were part of the delegation were quick to highlight. The ANC delegates conceded that the boycott of apartheid South Africa should not extend to 'the cultural expression of the oppressed people of South Africa'. It was agreed that Indian bodies could consult with the democratic movement for redress, since the ANC's position was to respect and allow the expression of different cultures, religions and traditions. The Indian delegates, in turn, pledged to sustain and even increase the Indian community's contribution to the anti-apartheid struggle.[10]

When the delegation returned to South Africa, Jerry Coovadia observed that delegates' fears of majority rule were eased as a result of the meeting:

When the South Africans met the exco [NEC], which consists of members of all race groups, all their fear about African dominance evaporated because if the ANC could have such an integrated executive who so obviously saw each other as comrades and not people belonging to certain race groups, they realised their fears were groundless.[11]

Charm Govender contended that many cultural and religious leaders changed their view of the ANC: 'people came back with new notions about the Eastern Bloc, about the ANC, about communism and so forth. It was a very enriching experience for those who went.'[12]

The NIC organised a report-back meeting in Durban on 16 February 1989, which was addressed by Harry Gwala, Jerry Coovadia and Rama Reddy, president of the South African Soccer Federation. Coovadia told the meeting that NIC leaders were willing to talk to the white Nationalists when political prisoners were released and exiles were allowed to return home, but not with right-wing Afrikaner parties who were 'fascists', nor with parties in the HOD who 'did not represent the people'.[13]

In the context of the ANC meeting with big capital and Mandela's meetings with the apartheid regime, Coovadia's insistence that the NIC was not prepared to talk to members of the HOD appears out of sync with the direction that the ANC was taking. The hard line towards the HOD is also difficult to fathom when one considers that the delegation to Lusaka was a heterogeneous group of Indians from various backgrounds. It would appear that some NIC leaders were consumed by the fight for hegemony within an ethnic enclave, wanting to be the sole voice of Indians as the transition unfolded. After all, they had fought rearguard battles through the 1970s and early 1980s to head off threats from the BCM, the Non-European Unity Movement and 'workerists'.

Mother India

Leaders of religious and cultural organisations pushed for a relaxation of the international boycott. They had kept institutions alive through the frozen isolationist years of apartheid and now saw the possibility of a thaw. When the delegation returned from Lusaka, a steering committee was established to facilitate dialogue on this issue. Members were R. Padayachie (chair – NIC); K. Mohan (National Hindu Youth Movement); P.V. Lakhani (Hindu Maha Subha); B.J. Garach (Kathiawad Hindu Seva Samaj); U.E. Meer (Bazme Adab);

Figure 13.2: Delegation to India, May 1989. *From left*: Fred Gona, Charm Govender, Cassim Saloojee, Yunus Carrim and Reggie Vandeyar. (Courtesy of 1860 Heritage Centre)

D. Naidoo (Natal Tamil Vedic Society); Kiren Satgar (National Hindu Youth); and K.J. Gokool (Hindu Development Trust).[14]

The NIC grasped this opportunity as a way to be seen delivering to the community. Through its boycott of government structures, the NIC had been hamstrung in the actual delivery of material benefits. The close relationship between the ANC and the Congress Party of India could potentially deliver an important dividend in a way that the HOD could not match. An NIC/TIC delegation comprising Yunus Carrim and Charm Govender (NIC executive members), Cassim Saloojee and Reggie Vandeyar (president and vice-president of the TIC) and Fred Gona of COSATU visited India from 5 to 10 May 1989, the first official visit by the Indian Congresses to the 'motherland' since Monty Naicker and Yusuf Dadoo had visited Gandhi and Nehru there in 1947. The NIC issued a statement indicating that while it had advocated a total boycott in the past, it now recognised the need for teachers and artists to 'enrich Indian culture locally' and would make a request to the Indian government to allow them to visit South Africa.[15]

Yunus Carrim sent faxes to South Africa informing NIC members and the local press about the visit. A fax dated 8 May 1989, to Brijlall Ramguthee, editor of the *Post*, reported that the delegation was accompanied by the ANC representative in India, Mosie Moolla, and had been given a 'rapturous' welcome. The delegation's meetings with MPs, anti-apartheid solidarity groups and trade unions had attracted considerable media attention.

Carrim's telex to Roy Padayachie, passed on to Farouk Meer, reported that the delegation had met with government officials on 5 May. These officials had indicated that they had a blacklist of collaborators with the apartheid regime dating back to 1984 and were willing to act against them. On 8 May the delegation visited the Blue Bells School to see first-hand the anti-apartheid programmes for schoolchildren. This was followed by lunch in Parliament with the group Parliamentarians for Action for the Removal of Apartheid, followed by a press conference, after which the delegation met with academics whose work focused on South Africa.

The delegation also met with India's prime minister, Rajiv Gandhi. In a fax to the *Daily News* on 12 May, Carrim reported that Gandhi had told them that 'nothing short of adult suffrage in a single parliament for all South Africans will satisfy India that South Africa has changed'. The prime minister was pleased to learn that a statue of Mahatma Gandhi was being erected in Pietermaritzburg in time for the 100th anniversary of his eviction from a train in the city. He quipped, 'I hope you have changed the situation by 1993 so that we can participate in the opening ceremony.' The prime minister called on Indians in South Africa to 'participate more actively in the Great SA Liberation struggle'.

Carrim made some overall observations about the visit:

(i) Repeatedly told it's very good to meet real, live S. Africans from inside the country. India meets ANC people but first time people from within. (ii) Lots of interest in Reggie Vandeyar – served on Robben Island (1964–1977) – house arrested and banned for 10 years. Seen as a colleague of Nelson Mandela – enormous interest about when he is going to be released. (iii) Following TV, Radio and press reports. Lots of groups here have contacted government asking if they could meet us. (iv) Press curbs in S.A. mean people feel a thirst for knowledge about what's really going on. (v) Gandhi's link with S.A., largest group of Indian descent outside S.A., successive Indian PMs personal interest in S.A., Legend of Mandela, Link between Apartheid and British colonialism makes us a very important cause for India. Even have a somewhat romantic picture of us. Constantly refer to us as Freedom Fighters.

In an article in the *Post*, the delegation described the visit as an 'overwhelming success' and explained why they were received so positively.

> Firstly, because India is vigorously opposed to apartheid laws ... Secondly, the 900 000-strong Indian community in South Africa constitutes the largest grouping of people of Indian descent outside India – and the South African delegation was seen as being representative of their interests ... Thirdly, Mahatma Gandhi started his political career in South Africa – and the delegation was repeatedly told that India owed an enormous debt to the South African liberation struggle. The fact that Gandhi founded the Natal Indian Congress also gave the South African delegation considerable status ... Fourthly, successive Indian Prime Ministers – Jawaharlal Nehru, Indira Gandhi, Rajiv Gandhi – have taken a personal interest in the anti-apartheid course and the South African delegation met top Indian officials ... Fifthly, India's support for the anti-apartheid course ... has considerably enhanced its prestige in Third World and international forums ... Sixthly, the mass democratic movement inside the country has won for itself enormous credibility since the launch of the UDF and COSATU. The two Indian Congresses are an integral part of this broad democratic movement and have played an integral part in its development.[16]

The report noted that the delegation was 'swept off its feet by the reception it received. No immigration formalities; chauffeur-driven cars; accommodation in the fanciest hotels; smooth access through the airports; special guided tours of historical and cultural sites; regular appearance on television, over the radio and in newspapers; meetings with the Prime Ministers, M.P.s, top government officials.' The delegation felt 'ill-at-ease' at some of the luxury but were assured that they were only being treated in the same way as any foreign government delegation that was 'close to India'.

The Indian government regarded the national democratic movement as a 'government in the making'.[17]

Discussions covered a wide range of issues: Indian citizens being permitted to visit relatives in South Africa; trade and sports links; scholarships for South African students; and the revitalisation of Tolstoy Farm and Phoenix Settlement. It was agreed to allow 'genuine' cultural and religious contact on the following basis: 'only bona fide cultural and religious organisations not supporting the apartheid regime may initiate such contact'; such contact was to be endorsed by the national democratic movement and the Indian government and was not to be made for private commercial gain; and Indian nationals visiting South Africa could not support the apartheid regime. The delegation saw the agreement as a 'moral and ideological gain' and as 'opening a new terrain – that of diplomatic relations – for the two Indian Congresses'.[18]

One can imagine the exuberance and confidence that ran through the returning Indian Congresses' delegates. It must have been overwhelming to be feted across India and given the status of diplomats after years of organising under constant surveillance, repression and the threat of detention. To be recognised as gatekeepers with the power to open doors to those deemed 'bona fide' and able to red-card others was a remarkable change of fortune. Most importantly, the elevated status of the delegation held the potential to draw in a wider local constituency.

The NIC warmed to its task of becoming a patron in cultural and religious matters. The call for a denial of visas for HOD-linked politicians appears petty amid the broader political developments of the time. It was not clear whether this ban would also include people working in the police services or serving in the armed forces, which would affect many working-class Indians. Charm Govender was candid about the consequences of the visit to India: the agreement reached there 'elevated the legitimacy of the NIC and TIC in the Indian community because when religious organisations had bona fide requests, we would be in a position to make it possible for their religious leaders to come to South Africa'.[19] NIC activists hoped that this would garner kudos from Indians and soften fears of majority rule that might negatively affect Indian cultural and religious aspirations.

Mandela freed

Through its use of musicians, actors and other celebrities, the Anti-Apartheid Movement (AAM) in Britain had successfully projected Nelson Mandela as a global icon and the de facto leader of the liberation movement. It was clear that he would be at the centre of any discussion about a future South Africa.[20] Mandela had been moved from Robben Island to Pollsmoor Prison in Cape Town in 1982, and he was transferred to Victor Verster Prison in 1988. From June 1986 he had been meeting in secret with the minister of justice, Kobie Coetsee. Beginning in May 1988, Mandela met with an NP negotiating team headed by Niël Barnard, chief of the National Intelligence Service (NIS). Barnard reports that he and his team were 'comforted' by the discussions:

> It was reasonably certain that the ANC, with Mandela at the helm, would not introduce a classically communist policy of class struggle and large-scale nationalisation. When Thabo Mbeki and the leaders of the external wing of the ANC became part of negotiations, it soon became clear that they were committed capitalists.[21]

While Jerry Coovadia may have waxed lyrical in earlier days about the commitment to socialism, it was clear that the ANC had shifted ground from a radical economic policy.[22] Mewa Ramgobin stated in 1989, before the collapse of the Berlin Wall, that the Congress movement would have to reconsider policy, given that 'when one looks at the global picture and the so-called liberalisations that are taking place in the Soviet Union and in China, [with] Gorbachev ... talking about the co-existence of two economic systems, the capitalist and the socialist, there is an admission that socialism cannot exist without people'.[23] Fatima Meer wrote tellingly on the negotiations in early 1990, stating that with 'the withdrawal of Soviet ambitions for a socialist state in South Africa in the immediate future, whites really do not have much to fear. In the ultimate analysis it is the black left that will be compromised.'[24]

Mandela continued to engage in talks with senior government officials, which culminated in a meeting between him and President P.W. Botha. On 5 July 1989 Mandela and Botha met at Tuynhuis, the Cape Town office of the president. Mandela recorded in his autobiography that 'there was no turning back'.[25] Botha's poor health led to his replacement by F.W. de Klerk in September 1989. This speeded up the drive to a negotiated settlement. De Klerk later revealed that this acceleration was intended to show 'that we were not negotiating under pressure, but from the strength of our convictions'.[26]

In the following months Mandela began to receive a stream of visitors at Victor Verster Prison to sound out their views as well as to ward off suspicion and dissent when word got out that he was negotiating with the government. Chota Motala, a long-standing NIC member from Pietermaritzburg, was one of the invited visitors. He and his wife, Rabia, spent five hours with Mandela on 11 November 1989. Mandela showed them around what Rabia described as a 'very nice' house and treated them to lunch. Mandela and Chota spoke of many things – family, health, the global political situation – but they dwelt mostly on the political violence in Pietermaritzburg, which was of grave concern to both men. It was clear to them, Rabia recounted, that change was inevitable.[27]

I.C. Meer recounted the visit that he and Fatima Meer made to Mandela in May 1989:

> We found him [Mandela] in excellent form and were surprised to see how comfortably he had been set up. He enjoyed taking us around his 'house' – to his bedroom with its queen-size bed. He opened a cupboard and displayed his wardrobe befitting a gentleman of presidential rank. He showed us his exercise room. We sat down to lunch, served by his warder, who also acted as his butler. Nelson indicated that he was having talks with government ministers. I came away convinced his release was imminent, and negotiations on the cards.[28]

Fatima Meer remarked on Mandela's accommodation with astonishment:

> I was absolutely flabbergasted by the manner in which he had been imprisoned, and I realised then, it became quite clear to me, that the Nats, whom we had thought were totally unchangeable and unmovable, were in fact changeable and moveable. It became very apparent to me that they saw him as a crucial factor in the future of South Africa.[29]

The sense of change was not limited to the liberation 'elite'. A.K. Babal wrote to Fatima Meer on 17 October 1989:

> Dear Behenji, *Namaste*
>
> Many of us look forward to you and your husband for guidance regarding political matters. You all visited Mr Mandela recently. Did Mr Mandela tell you all that we must now go back-slapping with Buthelezi, HOD and HOR [House of Representatives] guys? Forgive me for thinking on these lines, what other conclusion can we come to? ... Those who oppose Congress are jumping for joy as you are now giving them credibility, especially the HOD and HOR, who have earned sin-money doing very little or nothing ... What do we do now? Once you were 'Buthelezi's sister', then you fell out with him, now I suppose he will have to adopt you again! You people are leaders, please don't fool us common folk with things like this. Many people use the common folk to gain their ends, and dump them. We don't expect you to do so, having worked long and hard with common folk. But we cannot help coming to this conclusion. You educated people and leaders please 'get your act together' and give us proper direction.[30]

The boundaries of collaborator and non-collaborator were being turned upside down and would quickly become blurred in many cases. The ANC was talking to the apartheid regime, Mandela had walked his own path for a few years as he met with the dreaded NIS, and the NIC was consorting with religious and cultural leaders once seen as bastions of conservatism. It was as exciting as it was perplexing. Those in the resistance movement within the country were unsure what the next moves of the government and the ANC would be. Official visits to Mandela and the meetings with the ANC in Lusaka all pointed to some dramatic breakthrough. But the repressive arm of the state still operated, and for the NP – and in fact for most white South Africans – the spectre of African majority rule was difficult to countenance.

Through the 1970s and 1980s, resistance ebbed and flowed and the NP swung between compromise and confrontation and then back again. In early 1990 these impulses from above and below merged dramatically.

When South African president F.W. De Klerk made his move, it was with surprising speed that caught activists and political commentators unaware.

On 2 February 1990, without much fanfare, De Klerk unbanned all political organisations, including the ANC, PAC and SACP. Mewa Ramgobin recalled the moment of the announcement of the unbanning of the organisations:

> We knew that De Klerk was going to make a statement, but we didn't know what statement he was going to make. And because my office in Verulam was like a common room with a very large number of the leadership there, the Ismail Meers', the George Sewpersadhs', and the Paul Davids' and all these guys, we all gathered in my office and borrowed a television to listen to De Klerk. To be very honest, we were caught with our pants down when he announced the unbanning of the organizations. Even though we had been to Soweto by then and received the Walter Sisulus and the Govan Mbekis at the reception, to have the ANC [and] Communist Party unbanned on the heels of that, suddenly jolted us into a reality unvisualised.[31]

With this news barely digested, De Klerk announced that Nelson Mandela would be freed on 11 February 1990, little more than a week after the announcement of the unbanning of the organisations. Reality would be visualised as Mandela's 'march to freedom' from Victor Verster Prison 'proceeded in the brilliant sunshine and saturated colours of the high Cape summer. History, myth, and deliverance combined to make this theatrical moment one of the world's great spectacles.'[32]

Away from the cameras and the euphoria of a possible negotiated settlement, the country was consumed with ongoing political violence. Conflicts involved not only the state and its opponents in the extra-parliamentary arena, but also long-running feuds between black political organisations, most notably the bloody township battles between the ANC/UDF and Inkatha. Indeed, violence had 'become diffuse to the point of incoherence'.[33] Padraig O'Malley noted that 'more South Africans – almost 14 000 – were killed during the four and a half years following the release of Mandela in February 1990 and his inauguration as President of South Africa in May 1994' than during the apartheid era.[34] South Africa appeared unique in one respect: 'Many societies are deeply marked by political violence and in many others a culture of negotiation is firmly rooted. In few, if any, violent societies, however, are so many negotiations going on and no other society which negotiates so readily and so extensively is as violent.'[35]

Reminiscent of India's 'non-violent' ousting of the British, South Africa's 'peaceful transition' occludes the loss of life that came with it. Ela Gandhi described the coming end of Nationalist rule as a 'bittersweet moment':

> It was really a wonderful moment for us. I was fortunate that I was chosen as one of the people who went with Mama Sisulu and all the leadership of UDF to see Mandela in Pollsmoor the day before he was released [and moved to Victor Verster], and so we got a real insight into the whole set-up, why the release, what was happening, and all the problems with the unbanning of the organisations, the return of the exiles, there were lots of refugees ... I went to Pietermaritzburg and saw the refugees there, and it was heartbreaking. The families that were broken, the homes that were razed to the ground, the people that were murdered, orphaned children. So, whilst we had joy on the one hand ... it was a bad time.[36]

Beyond the violence, there were important questions to be answered about the way existing anti-apartheid organisations would respond to the changing circumstances. As mentioned at the start of this chapter, Farouk Meer indicated that those supporting apartheid were lulled into a false sense of security: they were 'brainwashed'. How would Indian South Africans respond to the rapidly changing circumstances? Would the NIC, buoyed by the boycott of the HOD, the visits to Lusaka and India, and the ANC's insistence on a peaceful transition and non-racialism, be able to carry the Indian masses with it? Or were they also 'brainwashed', filled with 'fear and apprehension'?

14 | Snapping the Strings of the UDF

The unbanning of the ANC raised questions about the future of the NIC/TIC as well as of the UDF. There were murmurings that the UDF would redefine its focus to concentrate on socio-economic issues while the ANC focused on political negotiations. Some put forward the idea that the NIC could become a cultural body. Yunus Mohamed, then regional secretary of the UDF in Natal and a member of the NIC executive, indicated in a 1990 interview that the UDF would 'restructure' itself to remain relevant in the changing political context.[1] He lamented in 2002 that 'it would have been good if the UDF had remained. I argued that position openly, but ... there was a climate of suspicion and the decision was to close the organisation.'[2]

Why was the UDF disbanded with such haste?

Some within the ANC saw the UDF as their creation. However, even though its programmes were important in popularising the Freedom Charter, the UDF had gathered its own identity, momentum and home-grown leadership.[3] Those who did not want to see the UDF simply disband were portrayed by some within the ANC as part of a reactionary cabal. In an open letter to Walter Sisulu, Aubrey Mokoena, a key member of the Release Mandela Committee (RMC) and the UDF, who wanted the UDF disbanded, explained: 'It has always been our understanding that the UDF was a *front* of organisations and *never* an organisation in itself. However, certain functionaries of the UDF cherished ambitions and aspirations that ... the UDF should exist as a parallel structure to the ANC.'[4]

Writing in 1989, Jerry Coovadia waxed lyrical that a strong heterogeneous internal movement 'will be the foundation on which democracy will be built in South Africa ... because the ANC has made it clear that it is not a government in exile. It has said that it will accept the freely expressed wishes of all the people of South Africa.'[5] Coovadia's romantic view seemed to be oblivious to the dangers of the ANC's democratic centralism and the UDF's adoption of the Freedom Charter in 1987, factors which created the conditions for 'the centralisation of the [Mass Democratic Movement] under the national leadership and the reduced concern for accommodating alternative views'.[6]

Those within the UDF who felt a need to maintain independence from the ANC were undermined from within by members who were keen to disband the organisation and join the ANC. This conflict over the future of the UDF, accompanied by the jockeying for positions within the ANC, was further complicated by allegations of a cabal operating within the national liberation movement. The cabal was said to have had its origins in the NIC and TIC, had dominated the politics of the UDF and had spread into the ANC underground.

On 24 September 1989, a meeting called by the nebulously titled group 'Concerned Activists' was held at the University of Natal. This meeting appears to have been crucial in the discussion of the cabal and its implications for the ANC. Although shrouded in the mists of time and subsequent realignments of post-negotiation politics, it got to the heart of the charge sheet directed against those insinuated to be part of a cabal.

Mewa Ramgobin was present at this meeting. According to a report in his files – which he possibly prepared, although this is unclear – the meeting was convened as the result of conversations 'between four people who discussed a series of allegations being made about individuals and racial groups in Natal'. Discussion among the 20 activists in attendance led them to determine that the UDF was 'distorted, both organisationally and in terms of leadership'.[7]

The participants concluded that the UDF had a 'built-in minority preventing organizations coming into their own, not empowering them, etc.'. This leadership, it was alleged, was dominated by Indian men, with Africans 'expected to provide the "masses" to support these actions'. Resources were 'disproportionately located in Indian areas', where those in control did not 'clearly account' for their use.[8] The control of resources was a recurring theme throughout the UDF's history. As Jeremy Seekings points out, the UDF was receiving significant funding which 'affected the internal politics of the UDF ... seen in the cabal allegations. [Azar] Cachalia, national treasurer from 1985, freely admits that he had considerable autonomy to decide whom to pay and whom not.'[9]

A five-page document, of which page four is missing, typed by Ramgobin after the meeting contains some clues about how he viewed the cabal. To that document was stapled a six-page fax, made up of documents from Peter Mokaba, then president of the ANC Youth League, which was sent to Ramgobin on 23 September 1992.[10] This suggests that Ramgobin was working with or was at least in contact with ANCYL members. One of the ironies of Ramgobin's communications with Peter Mokaba was that the latter stood accused of being an apartheid agent and was investigated by the ANC in 1989. Later Mokaba played a key role in Thabo Mbeki's quest to succeed Mandela.[11]

In the document that he prepared, Ramgobin listed Mac Maharaj, Pravin Gordhan, Ebrahim Ebrahim and Yunus Mohamed as the core of the cabal, with an added comment 'fractions of the CP'. According to this document, Maharaj was key to the struggle for power between internals and externals: 'Mac from one fraction of Exiles continues/consolidates links with internal fraction.' This internal fraction was linked to the Operation Vula network, in which Billy Nair and Pravin Gordhan were central. The document reported that there was a lack of openness, with tension fuelled by the stand-off between Maharaj and Harry Gwala. Among Ramgobin's many allegations were that Yunus Mohamed had described Nelson Mandela as a 'ceremonial' leader; Jerry Coovadia was alleged to have said in Lusaka that the ANC was 'out of touch with reality'; the NIC/TIC had a 'disproportionate' influence on the UDF; there were unwarranted 'attacks' on Roy Padayachie of Chatsworth; the NIC had allegedly refused to meet with Govan Mbeki; the Reverend Mcebisi Xundu, who served in various parishes in Natal and the Eastern Cape, as well as in community organisations and was a member of the UDF, had been 'displaced'; Gordhan was viewed as being allied to ANC secretary general Alfred Nzo; and Ebrahim Ebrahim was seen to have very close links with the UDF. Billy Nair was identified 'as part of the problem', with a note: 'Struggle against CABAL – B.N. elimination'. The document concludes: 'Question: It's not in the nature of these activists to remain in the twilight. Therefore are they in strategic think tanks within the key cabal operations within the ANC?'[12]

This document, although incomplete, provides a valuable snapshot of the machinations in the UDF/ANC/NIC/TIC as the transition to democracy unfolded, revealing historic differences playing out on new terrain. There are dots that can be connected to other documents. Ramgobin's document overlaps with the account from Maharaj (who was scathing in his assessment of Govan Mbeki's activities after his release from Robben Island), tallying with the accusation of the NIC's refusal to meet with him.[13] While Ramgobin thought that a local leader like the Reverend Xundu was 'displaced', the same Reverend Xundu comes under criticism from Maharaj, who refers to him as 'divisive', with 'an authoritarian streak coming from Govan'.[14] The alleged 'attacks on Roy' suggest that the notion of cabalism had its genesis in the internal fights of the NIC. It subsequently mutated into the broader politics of the UDF and the ANC, and then, swinging around as fissures emerged within the ANC, made its way back into the NIC and UDF.

The ANC had much to deal with. The NP, which still controlled the state apparatus, was keen to be the hegemonic role player in negotiations and was involved in a myriad of alliances and destabilising missions. Within ANC ranks there were backroom intrigues as members attempted to position themselves amid the difficulties of operating in a new and changing terrain. In the face of these challenges, the insinuation of an Indian cabal as the engine room of the UDF was raised with sufficient frequency for the ANC to set up a commission to look into the matter.[15] The outcome was a confidential document titled 'Report and Recommendations of Commission on the Cabal', dated 14 March 1990. This report named Pravin Gordhan, Zak Yacoob, Alf Karrim, Yunus Mohamed, Farouk Meer, Jerry Coovadia and Billy Nair as being part of the cabal, with African activists such as Diliza Mji, Sikhumbuzo Ngwenya and Curnick Ndlovu identified as being under their 'influence'. Cabal members were also identified in the Transvaal and Western Cape.[16]

The basis of the Commission's work appears to be the initial report of the 24 September 1989 meeting. The Commission argued that a cabal of Indians and whites 'manipulates strategy, lacks democratic practices and stifles free and open debate necessary for the growth of organization and for the advance of the struggle'. Interestingly, the Commission's report states that the problem was 'publicly disclosed' following the 1987 NIC conference. The report found that the emergence of the cabal was facilitated by

> a phenomenon of so-called advanced activists. People took upon themselves the task of strategizing for all and sundry (the NIC, UDF regional and on a national level via national contacts) and imposing their will on others. A consequence of this was that those who disagree with such strategies are often labelled as nationalists, mavericks, old guard, etc. Over a period of time, this has led to the ousting of senior activists in the struggle from their leadership positions which were subsequently taken up by members or supporters of the Cabal. Senior NIC activists like MJ Naidoo, RB Chaudhary, Ramlall Ramesar and Rabi Bugwandeen were subjected to the manipulating style of Cabal ... [Comrades] Govan Mbeki and Ahmed Kathrada have been informed of the problem and have, in the process of further investigating it, already spoken to ousted NIC members, namely MJ [Naidoo], RR [Ramesar], and RB [Bugwandeen].[17]

The report made the following recommendation:

> BEARING in mind the 'ethnic' composition of the Cabal, their vested interests as well as their perceived power base, it would be naïve to think our consultations with the Cabal would have a real impact on them as regards their cooperation within broad democratic structures ... We must embark on a strategy which should be aimed at isolating certain individuals and at the same time undermining their power base. Our aim should be to make them feel comfortable in their positions while we prepare to finally rid our structures of them ...[18]

Raymond Suttner soberly insists that we go beyond 'gossip' when analysing allegations of a cabal. He notes that it is important to 'explore the conditions under which these allegations emerged and the extent to which they might have reflected ideological differences'; examine whether one group in fact controlled the UDF; and take into account the political orientation

245

of the accusers and the accused. The allegations, Suttner adds, must be 'located in the underground conditions of the time when normal processes of consultation could not take place'.[19]

While the author(s) of the cabal report are not definitively known, various anti-Gordhan factions in post-apartheid debates have falsely attributed authorship to high-ranking members of the ANC to increase the report's credibility and to settle political scores. When MP Floyd Shivambu and the Economic Freedom Fighters (EFF) accused Gordhan of being part of this cabal, they insinuated that the report was written by Mac Maharaj, which he vehemently denied. Maharaj told a reporter for the *Mail & Guardian* that he had 'no knowledge of, or participation in, the preparation of this so-called report'. He described it as a 'very strange document to [appear] in March 1990 – just after the ANC, MK and SACP were unbanned'. Moreover,

> PG [Pravin Gordhan], and many of the names, irrespective of their race, that appear in the document were active comrades in different arms of the struggle ... Insofar as this purported report maligns any of the people named in it, it is a complete distortion of the reality. It is a misuse of the document to dub Pravin as a mischief-maker and a cabalist.[20]

As every allegation became public, attempts to follow the threads of the cabal proved frustrating, taking twists and turns depending on the politics of the time. This is clearly exemplified in the figure of Mac Maharaj. He had been fingered as one of the central players in the cabal, was then cited as the alleged author of the report exposing the cabal, and was finally named as the person who exonerated some of the alleged masterminds!

Many of the allegations that found their way into the Commission's report had been circulating as rumours through the second half of the 1980s. Yet it is jarring that the report, written just a month after the unbanning of the ANC and the release of Mandela, brazenly named people as cabalists just as the state security apparatus, with its myriad of dirty tricks, was keen to sow confusion and doubt.

It is also significant that those alleging cabalism appeared to be positioning themselves in the ANC, using the same modus operandi of cabalism as the so-called cabalists. Were those who felt set upon by the so-called cabal in the NIC through the 1980s the source of the Commission's allegations? Ramgobin appears to have been a key figure in the peddling of the cabal line, together with M.J. Naidoo, Ramesar and Bugwandeen, who had been ousted from NIC leadership in 1987. Ramgobin's critique of the cabal as a group dovetailed with that of Aubrey Mokoena: they had worked together in the RMC, and it is not inconceivable that they were now trying to influence emergent ANC structures and leadership through their allegations.

As its leading cadres returned from exile, the ANC began to place them in official party positions in various provinces to strengthen its presence and carry its programme into existing and newly sprouted structures. In Natal some forces within the ANC were intent on sidelining certain NIC/UDF members. The NIC submitted a memorandum to the Southern Natal Regional Interim Committee (RIC) of the ANC on 10 May 1990, expressing concern that the RIC had organised a meeting for 4 May in the old Indian area of Asherville and Springtown without consulting with or even informing the NIC, which was invited 'almost as an afterthought'. NIC secretary Farouk Meer 'was informed at midnight two days before the meeting'. The invitation had led to disagreement among ANC organisers, as some did not want to invite him. The NIC was attacked at the meeting as an 'ethnic' ('racist') organisation. While the ANC claimed the prerogative to establish branches wherever the RIC considered it necessary, the memo maintained that the way the meeting was called 'contradicts the guidelines given by the ANC which emphasises the need to work with existing organisations and natural allies'.[21] The NIC memorandum further stated:

> The NIC has promoted the ANC within the Indian community and has fought for and defended its alliance with the ANC and African people throughout its history. Now that the ANC is unbanned, the NIC seeks to find the best possible way to continue in this fine tradition of securing the support and participation of the Indian people within the National Liberation Struggle. We are cognisant of the fact that the leading role in this process cannot merely be proclaimed but must be won in the best practice of advancing the mass struggle.

In our historical tradition we have demonstrated in our campaigns that we fulfil such a role and are even more determined, now that conditions are available to advance the ANC legally, to continue to play that role.[22]

Because of its history, the NIC had expected to be anointed the vanguard of the ANC in Indian areas, but its role came to be muddied and then directly challenged. It was deeply disturbing that an organisation that had kept the ANC flag flying, produced many leading cadres of the anti-apartheid movement and resisted challenges from other movements to its progressive role in the struggle was now scrambling to justify its credentials.

There was pushback against the alleged NIC/UDF cabal, and this was disconcerting to activists:

An unsigned Report on ANC Southern Natal Convening Committee (3 May 1990) concludes that 'the present committee is dominated by individuals who have a history of opposition to the leadership of the UDF in Natal (the "cabal") and it would appear that all efforts have been made to avoid associating the new CC [Convening Committee] with the "cabal".' (p 7); The CC asked the UDF not to open an office next to the ANC as 'they were two separate organizations and should maintain a distance from one another.' (p 7); and 'There appears to have been a deliberate move to leave out of the committee those comrades who have been involved in the building of the mass and underground structures over the past few years.' (p 8). Indians predominated in the building of these structures.[23]

Countrywide there were reports of UDF members being marginalised. The *Sunday Times*, for example, reported on 25 November 1990 that with the exception of the Western Cape, the ANC had 'purged' most UDF members from its offices and replaced them with returned exiles and former Robben Islanders.

The ANC's Southern Natal Regional Congress in mid-November 1990 saw a culling of UDF leaders from the regional executive. Among those removed were Nair and Gordhan, both Operation Vula trialists and UDF and NIC executive members. Prominent NIC members such as

Farouk Meer, Jerry Coovadia and Paul David were all omitted, as were national UDF co-president Archie Gumede and Natal UDF chairman Curnick Ndlovu. Former UDF interim convenor Patrick 'Terror' Lekota was replaced by former Robben Islander Jeff Radebe. Notably, Ramgobin was the only NIC person elected to this committee.[24] He appeared to be dealing with his adversaries – the 'cabal' – by hitching his wagon to a star in the form of Radebe, thus ensuring his place on the ANC election list.

It was a remarkable comeback for Ramgobin, who was not central to underground structures, while people like Gordhan and Nair found themselves marginalised. Ramgobin had nurtured relationships with those who were close to Thabo Mbeki and he seemingly prevailed when all appeared lost. For his part, Radebe delivered a paper at the conference on behalf of Robben Islanders in which he described the UDF as 'plagued by in-fighting, factionalism and uneven distribution of resources'; failing to 'involve the masses in the decision-making process'; and being conspicuous by 'the absence of African leadership'.[25]

Presented by a figure fresh out of Robben Island, Radebe's paper was a devastating critique. What were the sources of the evidence that Radebe presented? Was he reading from someone else's script? It would appear that there were a few individuals and groupings that fed into the allegation of cabalism. One was Harry Gwala in the Natal Midlands. Gwala had a tempestuous relationship with Mandela while on Robben Island, and on his release his connections with Durban NIC members were frosty, in part because of his differences with Maharaj and because those who felt disadvantaged by the 'cabal' sought his support. There was also exile politics to consider. People such as the Thabo Mbeki-aligned Pahad brothers, Essop and Aziz, were increasingly alienated from the Gordhan group, who had aligned themselves with Maharaj and consolidated their connection through Operation Vula. These divisions were reinforced by the distance between Maharaj and Thabo Mbeki (and by default the Pahads) that, according to Zarina Maharaj, went back to the early exile years: 'Thabo was beginning to sense a threat from Mac. Mac upstaged him in all these meetings.'[26] There were also the old NIC stalwarts who felt under the whip from Gordhan and company, as well as younger activists such as Pregs Govender, who makes the allegation of cabal openly in her 2007 autobiography.[27]

Radebe's assessment is open to scrutiny. The ANC underground had certainly played a major part in ensuring that ANC/UDF comrades could defend themselves on the ground in the 'war' against the state and Inkatha. In many cases, they were able to push back the IFP and establish their own local leaderships. When this conflict was at its height in the 1980s, Radebe was on Robben Island; he was released only in 1990. He failed to acknowledge that some of those accused of cabalism had spent a great deal of time building the structures of Operation Vula under the most dangerous circumstances.

Natal UDF leaders forcefully dismissed Radebe's claims. Archie Gumede described the comments as 'ill-informed ... That paper was written with no knowledge of what had been happening in Natal under the UDF.'[28] Gumede pointed out elsewhere that the UDF was made up of over 600 youth, labour, civic and student organisations, and that the affiliates were 'totally autonomous, they operate their own communities. The UDF itself does not have the machinery to supervise the activities of its affiliates.'[29]

Jerry Coovadia stated in a 2019 interview that the 'idea that the UDF was controlled by an Indian cabal arose ... I'm pretty convinced ... from the Black guys I knew ... and then they had the MJ's [Naidoos] and all of the others'. Coovadia was adamant that until these allegations were levelled, 'I really didn't even know the meaning of the word cabal. To them it was really important to isolate us as some sort of small pressure group without the legitimacy of a popular organisation.' Coovadia added that people like Gordhan and Nair subsequently became key cogs in the ANC. 'Why did that happen if they were considered to be part of the cabal?' he asked, and responded that it was 'because the cabal definition wasn't grounded in solid people and positions and organisations, and it was almost an epiphenomenon of that period'. Coovadia further suggested that some middle-class African leaders used race to position themselves as a cover. 'They needed to find a way out of their own inaction, because they did nothing, so it suited their purpose to label us as a cabal', and they found convenient allies in the aggrieved NIC leaders who had been ousted in 1987.[30]

The UDF announced in March 1991 that it would formally disband on its eighth anniversary, 21 August 1991. The UDF as an organisation did not join the ANC, but individual people did, while some civic organisations wanted to continue operating independently. Although there were some discordant voices, many of the UDF leaders were flattered by the call to join ANC delegations, and in any case they had regarded the unbanning of the organisation as their life's work. This is evidenced by the ease with which well-known UDF figures such as Trevor Manuel, Allan Boesak, Murphy Morobe, Dullah Omar, Valli Moosa, Popo Molefe, Beyers Naudé and Cheryl Carolus drifted, without a backward glance, into the ANC's sensitive negotiations teams.

In Natal, the critique of the cabal and the allegation of Indian dominance left people such as Jerry Coovadia, Paul David and Farouk Meer devastated and they receded from the overtly political sphere. Others were more resolute and remained pivotal in the ANC – ironically through their membership of the NIC/TIC in the first instance – representing the Indian organisations at CODESA. In fact, some of those associated with the label 'cabal', such as Gordhan, Nair and Maharaj, made the parliamentary lists, with Maharaj becoming minister of transport in Mandela's cabinet. Maharaj's relationship with Mandela and Sisulu would have smoothed this appointment even if there had been attempts to marginalise him. But, given the antipathy between him and Thabo Mbeki, his and Gordhan's entry into the upper echelons of the CODESA negotiations is striking. It was made all the more significant by the fact that Vula communications indicate that those in underground structures were bypassed in ANC interim structures in the southern Natal region and 'found themselves in the political wilderness'.[31]

The 1991 ANC conference

The ANC held its first full conference in South Africa since 1959 at the UDW campus on 2–6 July 1991. It was here that Nelson Mandela was formally elected ANC president, replacing the ailing Oliver Tambo. Charm Govender attended the conference and recounted its significance:

> There was a bruising battle between internals, externals, the political, ex-political prisoners. Very interesting for us to see what was going to happen with the election of the Secretary General. Our preferred option was for Cyril Ramaphosa to be Secretary General because he's an internal, he's in close relation to the trade union and an able

person. The exiles' contender for that post was Jacob Zuma and the election results were announced so that Cyril Ramaphosa won the round. Jacob Zuma became Assistant Secretary General. So it was a big triumph for us, the 1991 conference.[32]

Govender's summation makes for interesting reading, as he speaks of factions. The conference was followed by what Mark Gevisser describes as 'a palace coup' in the first week of August 1991. At this time Mandela was on a visit to Cuba, and Mbeki and Zuma were attending a conference in England. Ramaphosa convened the National Working Committee in their absence and replaced Zuma as head of intelligence with former UDF leader Lekota. Ramaphosa himself replaced Mbeki as head of negotiations.[33] Aziz Pahad, a close confidant of Mbeki, recounts in his memoirs:

> even I to this day fail to appreciate why Mbeki and Zuma were replaced, especially since both were actively involved in every critical phase leading up to negotiations ... There was a view that provoked wide public debate that the emerging power struggles were symptomatic of growing cleavages between internal members of the MDM and the ANC in exile, as well as perceived ideological rifts between nationalists and communists within the Alliance ...The fundamental question was: who was engineering these tendencies and how would we be able to combat them?[34]

The concern about factionalism is ironic coming from Pahad, given that he had attached his star to Thabo Mbeki, and the reaction to Operation Vula, where Maharaj felt that the operatives had been abandoned by the ANC, had exacerbated matters. Maharaj, for example, singled out Pahad for attack at an ANC NEC meeting while he was awaiting trial for Vula activities: 'My attack was brutal ... Thabo hadn't raised a voice to refute all the wild talk.'[35] Suspicions reigned that Chris Hani and Joe Slovo supported the ousting of Mbeki and Zuma.[36] Thabo Mbeki was initially in the pound seats. It is difficult to imagine Maharaj being brought in by Mbeki and assuming a central role at CODESA, given the animosity between them. That antipathy is apparent in Maharaj's biography *Shades of Difference* by

Padraig O'Malley, who writes: 'Most insiders I have spoken to swear there is bad blood between Mbeki and Mac ... Some mentioned that Mac supported Cyril Ramaphosa over Mbeki as head of ANC's negotiations team in 1991.'[37] It is not coincidental that Maharaj became spokesperson for Jacob Zuma when the latter ousted Thabo Mbeki and assumed the presidency in 2008.

Mbeki's ousting certainly smoothed the way for Maharaj. Slovo and Maharaj became part of the Ramaphosa inner circle and 'there was a hardening of attitude towards Mbeki by the ANC's new secretary-general'.[38] Sydney Mafumadi recounted that when the tension between Mbeki on the one hand and Slovo and Maharaj on the other was becoming obvious, he approached Ramaphosa to mediate, and was shocked at the response: '"Mac and Joe accord me due respect. Thabo has not shown me that respect at all!" From this moment, Mafumadi told me, it was clear to him that Ramaphosa "had made up his mind that, in the context of the tensions that existed, there was a side to take".'[39]

This 'respect' translated into Maharaj becoming a key adviser to Ramaphosa, the ANC's chief negotiator.[40] Gordhan also played a crucial role as the transition unfolded. However, Charm Govender's idea of triumph was short-lived, as the strategy of pushing Ramaphosa for deputy president of the ANC was ultimately defeated.

An African political commentator wrote in 2010 that 'every African needs his Indian', citing as examples Mandela's relationship with his lawyer Ayob Ismail and Jacob Zuma's connection with the Gupta family from India.[41] To turn that maxim on its head, the jockeying for power within the ANC revealed how important it was for persons of Indian origin to attach themselves to African leaders. The danger was, of course, that their fortunes were linked to those leaders' political fortunes. When Mbeki assumed the presidency in 1999, the Pahads were in and Maharaj was out, and for a time Gordhan was reduced to a parliamentary backbencher. When Zuma became president in 2008, the Pahads exited the stage and Maharaj and Gordhan returned. After falling out with Zuma, Gordhan was sent packing, but when Ramaphosa came to power in 2018, Gordhan was back. It is a script for a tragicomic play in which it would appear that every Indian needs a chief and every chief an Indian.

In a haunting excerpt from Maharaj's biography, O'Malley provides insights into the place of the Indian in the liberation movement:

> In the paradoxical and contradictory ways apartheid worked, whites like Joe Slovo occupied a more privileged place in the struggle than Indians. 'Struggle whites' ... brought skills, world-ranging experiences, special insights into the ways in which the regime thought. They were to be listened to. 'Struggle Indians' were not seen in the same light. When Mac [Maharaj] was invited to the RC [Revolutionary Council] to attend meetings in order to brief it on the activities of the IPRD [Internal Politics and Reconstruction Department, set up to organise a political underground in South Africa], he was not asked to sit beside IPRD chairman John Motsabi but behind him. One can hardly imagine Joe Slovo being treated in a similar way.[42]

Whatever the veracity of the way in which white comrades were treated, the idea of the Indian sitting just behind African leaders lends itself to all kinds of interpretations, one of them being that of the Indian knowing his place in the ANC's non-racialism of a special type. There is also the image of the Indian pulling the strings. The Indian as manipulator. The Indian as cabal. The 'sitting behind' position forced upon the Indians becomes evidence of guilt.

Politics, Eric Louw reminds us, 'is more than approaches or ideals; it is ideals in interaction with real conditions'. State repression of the 1980s may have resulted in activists 'who were at heart democrats being compelled by circumstances to put "democracy" on the back burner. The alternative to this would be to concede defeat.'[43] Suttner agrees that under conditions of

> extreme repression ... internal democracy took a knock and those who could adapt best to such conditions undoubtedly had greater influence. Under state of emergency conditions ... accountability was difficult to sustain and, where attempts were made to do so, activists in semi-underground conditions had their security compromised ... The range and boundaries of debate tended to expand and contract, according to security or perceived security considerations.[44]

Billy Nair's story is typical of many activists of the period. As he explained:

> From 1985 or early 1986, a number of us ... went underground. The
> police could not catch us now. We were quite determined about that.
> I went throughout South Africa, hiding all over, staying for a week or
> two weeks, depending on the safety or otherwise of a particular place.
> A number of us went through that and ... I surfaced only [at the] end
> of 1989, when the government was now on the carpet, it was releas-
> ing political prisoners, Walter Sisulu, Kathrada and Raymond Mhlaba
> and others were released. I was in Soweto welcoming them. That is
> the first time that I came out after three and a half years![45]

Given the state of repression and mounting involvement in Operation
Vula, it was not feasible for Nair to engage in open, democratic politics.
It is difficult to see how people like Nair would have been able to account
to the masses in a democratic manner or, for that matter, to dominate the
agenda of the UDF. In considering allegations of cabal, cognisance must
be taken of the broader issues at play. These revolved around the internal upsurge that threw up new leadership, the underground, the politics
within the UDF, and the exiled ANC.

When it was unbanned, the ANC was determined to envelop the UDF
and thus ensure that the ANC would provide the leadership core in South
Africa. It is important, however, not to see this in dichotomous terms: the
years of underground work meant that there were many points of conflu-
ence between the internal and external movements. And as the UDF faded,
many of its leading lights positioned themselves with varying degrees of
success within the ANC.[46]

As discussed in the next chapter, the NIC enjoyed a slightly longer
shelf life.

15 | Digging Their Own Grave: Debating the Future of the NIC

As the political environment changed dramatically, what would become of those old warhorses – some would say Trojan horses – of the Charterist tradition, the Indian Congresses?

Many activists within these organisations had paid a heavy price to keep the Freedom Charter in the public domain, helping to build the ANC's underground structures and supporting the armed struggle. Others saw their professional careers ruined as they suffered detentions and banning orders. They also faced down criticism for persisting with the 'I' in the NIC. From within the very organisation they had helped to build, the UDF, they faced the slur of cabal. Through all this they had defended the NIC/TIC as a surrogate of the ANC and representative of its ideals.

The unbanning of the ANC in February 1990 caught NIC leaders on the horns of a dilemma. They had sacrificed their lives for this moment, and many became members of the ANC legally for the first time. But what about the Indian community as a whole? How best to carry Indian South Africans into the new dispensation that was fraught with ongoing violence and threats of re(dis)tribution?

Differences of opinion emerged within the NIC once the ANC was unbanned. Mewa Ramgobin was one of the first to enter the fray, stating in a 1990 interview that the unbanning of the ANC meant that 'there may be a limited lifespan for the NIC, especially as the democratic movement is now seeking to build non-racial constituencies for the creation of a future non-racial, democratic and united South Africa'.[1]

In a speech delivered at an NIC meeting in Ladysmith on 29 April 1990, Ramgobin warned:

> An indefinite lifespan for the NIC is neither in the interests of the Indian Community nor will it be in step with the new historical forces operative in our country. Since we in 1971 were bold enough to demonstrate the need for the re-emergence of the NIC, let us be bolder enough, now, to demonstrate that our historical role has been played, and therefore we will suspend all activities under its auspices and add to the glory of the ANC by facilitating for the first time in its own history, in formal terms, to make it a truly non-racial political formation, to which we commit our own destiny.[2]

While Ramgobin had suffered hammer blows from the 'cabal', including from his own wife, he remained an important voice. His pivotal role in reviving the NIC meant that his views carried weight within both the Indian community and the ANC. Yet his resolve in calling for the effective dissolution of the organisation soon after the unbanning of the ANC was surprising. He himself had admitted that the unbanning of the ANC and the release of Nelson Mandela had caught the NIC with their 'pants down', and that the government's and media's portrayal of the ANC as 'the bad guy' made it difficult to recruit Indians into the organisation.[3]

Farouk Meer was more circumspect. He indicated that the NIC would disband once it had completed its task of acting as facilitator for the ANC in establishing branches in the Indian townships.[4] NIC executive member Yunus Carrim echoed this view when he said that the NIC would 'phase out so that its dissolution is part of an overall campaign that ensures that a significant strata of the Indian community is drawn into the ANC'.[5] Meer and Carrim seemed to believe that, given the effects of apartheid which thrived on racial fears, it would be best to bring Indians into the fold of the ANC through the midwifery of the NIC.

However, M.J. Naidoo, a Ramgobin ally who had been ousted as NIC president in 1987, supported the call to disband the NIC. He said that ordinary people were sceptical of the

> vibes emanating from the NIC ranks, such as the NIC should phase itself out (whatever that means), the NIC structures are debating

the issue ... The impression must not be given that [the NIC] is reluctant to subordinate its interests to [those] of the ANC and the national
interests or that it is unwilling to relinquish its control over progressive politics in Natal or that it is reticent about handing over control
of funds to ANC leadership ... It is in the best interests of the Indian
community to work with the ANC under its umbrella. The NIC, as
NIC, cannot play a role in this regard.[6]

Through the 1970s and 1980s, Ramgobin and M.J. Naidoo were central
figures in the bitter battles against BC adherents for the NIC's right to
operate as an ethnic organisation. Naidoo was president of the NIC as a
separate entity even as the UDF was making ground as a non-racial movement. Now, seemingly overnight, he saw no value in the organisation at
a time of heightening political tensions in Natal between the ANC and
the IFP, and growing anxiety among the Indian masses. Naidoo's statement was biting, embodying the language that accompanied the allegation
of cabal. He warned that the NIC should not convey the idea, through its
insistence on continuing to exist as a separate racial organisation, that it
was 'reluctant to subordinate its interests to that of the ANC ... or that it
is unwilling to relinquish its control over progressive politics in Natal or
that it is reticent about handing over control of funds to ANC leadership'.
These were the charges of 'cabal' levied against the leadership of the NIC
since 1987.

The euphoria following the unbanning of the ANC and the excitement
at the possibility of openly joining an organisation that had been declared
illegal for so long are understandable. Yet Naidoo's and Ramgobin's seemingly rushed conclusion to disband the NIC raises questions of whether
their recommendation was based on their reading of the present conjuncture or on their own cold-shouldering by the NIC. Did they have a
genuine sense that their life's work had come to fruition? Or were they
motivated by a belief that the NIC was the captive of a small group of
people who had played a role in marginalising them, and it was now time
for a payback?

The NIC and TIC met in the northern Natal town of Newcastle in
June 1990 to decide on their future. Ramgobin argued at the meeting that
disbandment would strengthen the hand of the ANC at the negotiating

table. How it would do this was not explained. The decision was taken to reconvene at a meeting that would include the ANC.[7]

It was not all animus and tension in this period, as old comradeships between the ANC and NIC veterans were rekindled following the unbanning. Mandela, who was then deputy president of the ANC, made a trip to Natal during which he visited Pietermaritzburg and addressed a large rally on 7 October 1990.[8] In welcoming Mandela to the city, local NIC leader Chota Motala said he was overjoyed that they finally belonged to a common organisation. What was unique about this gathering, Motala said, was that it was 'the first time when all of us sit here as members of one single organisation – the ANC – and there has never been any doubt whatsoever in the minds of many of us that the ANC is the best instrument we have to achieve the goal of a truly non-racial and democratic South Africa'.[9] Motala did not raise the issue of the role of the NIC/TIC.

The ANC, NIC and TIC met in Lenasia on 8 December 1990.[10] Many NIC luminaries were present, including George Sewpersadh, Farouk Meer, Mewa Ramgobin, Thumba Pillay, Zak Yacoob, Pravin Gordhan, Yunus Mohamed, Hassim Seedat, Alf Karrim, I.C. Meer, Roy Padayachie and Yusuf Bhamjee. Ismail Momoniat of the TIC explained that the meeting had been called following the establishment of ANC interim committees to decide the fate of the Indian Congresses. Ismail Vadi, a TIC delegate, explained in September 2020 that delegates faced three key questions:

Did the NIC and TIC have a role to play in building the ANC which had just been unbanned? What was the best way to build non-racialism within the ANC? How could social and economic inequalities around issues of housing and education, where there were significant disparities, be addressed – through ANC/TIC/NIC branches or people's organs like civic structures or trades unions? ... The most advanced members within the community supported the ANC in sizeable numbers, but the less politically advanced saw Indians as a racial minority and had their own fears and reservations about majority rule. The NP spoke of Group rights which appealed to many. While it was easy to form a political structure for the advanced, the challenge was what to do about the working class, which lacked a strong trade union consciousness. The Tricam had a foothold in the Indian community, and the question was whether the NIC and TIC could be vehicles for politicisation.[11]

Alfred Nzo, ANC secretary general, stated that he supported a memo sent by the NIC to the ANC's internal head, Walter Sisulu, on the role the NIC could play in helping to build the ANC. Nzo 'regretted' that the Natal ANC Regional Executive Committee (REC) members were not present, given 'that Natal has a large concentration of the Indian community'.[12] This non-attendance cannot be seen in isolation from the swirl of allegations about the cabal raised by some within the ANC in Natal. There was also the open letter from Aubrey Mokoena to Walter Sisulu asserting that 'the cabal is a secret clique of activists who had been perceived as doing good work on the surface, but with a hidden double agenda'.[13]

There were intense debates over disbandment; over whether special provision should be made for Indians in the new constitution; how best to attract Indians to the ANC; what class stratification meant in terms of Indian consciousness; and the impact of Jeff Radebe's critique of the influence of Indians in the Mass Democratic Movement. On the question of disbandment three options were discussed: disband immediately; continue indefinitely; or be 'phased out, contingent upon certain conditions subject to the processes of consultation'.[14]

Ramgobin argued firmly in favour of immediate disbandment on the grounds that the policies of the NIC, TIC and ANC were similar; Indian formal membership of the ANC was higher than Indian membership of the NIC; the continued existence of the NIC and TIC would hamper nation building; the Freedom Charter contained provisions to accommodate uncertainties among Indians; and it was 'presumptuous' of the NIC and TIC to believe that they could be the vehicles to build the ANC by attracting Indian members.[15]

Roy Padayachie supported this position. He observed that although historically Indians had 'always been on the side of the liberation movement, yet currently there is vacillation and uncertainty'. The attitude of Indians appeared to be shaped by 'upsurge and down surge of the violence, and the way the ANC was presented in the media'. He also said that 'the ANC has drawn a larger section of the Indian people into its ranks than the NIC/TIC, though neither the ANC nor the Indian Congresses had succeeded in making inroads amongst the working classes'. The ANC had attracted the support of the educated Indian youth and 'a broad middle class who had much to lose, and for whom political stability was essential'.[16]

Mac Maharaj concurred that there was limited Indian support for the ANC: business people were opportunists and their support for the ANC was self-serving; intellectuals were initially excited by the unbanning of the ANC but disillusion had set in because of violence; and the Indian working class had concerns over affirmative action.[17]

Yunus Mohamed stressed the importance of class stratification within the Indian community, observing that few workers were joining the ANC. He disagreed with Cassim Saloojee's assessment that positive responses to fund-raising in the Transvaal were a sign of support for the ANC. Like Maharaj, he saw this as self-serving. Mohamed described it as 'unfortunate' that Natal ANC REC members, who were peddling the cabal line, were not present. He also stated that 'the Robben Island letter' that was read by Jeff Radebe at the ANC's Southern Natal Regional Conference had 'aroused anti-Indian sentiments'.[18]

Several participants dismissed talk of Indian 'uniqueness' and advocated the immediate disbanding of the NIC/TIC. Essop Pahad stated that all communities had 'unique characteristics' and that the specificities of Indians should 'not be exaggerated'. The socio-economic shift within the Indian community meant that the larger middle class 'does have something to lose, therefore the issues of political stability and the violence were of serious concern' to them. In a challenge to a long Congress tradition, Pahad asserted that the concept of 'national groups' impeded the 'quest to develop a common nationhood'.[19]

Jessie Duarte, formerly of the UDF and now a member of the ANC's Interim Leadership Core, warned against 'creating a cocoon for Indian people to retreat into', as that would 'entrench this conservatism or racism'. She insisted that continuation of the NIC/TIC would consolidate the perception of minority group interests.[20] Aziz Pahad warned that cabalism and racism made the task of recruiting Indians into the ANC difficult. The challenge before them was to develop Indian political consciousness through 'a united, non-racial movement through the ANC which represented the image of non-racism. The NIC/TIC could not tackle this separately from the ANC.'[21]

Figure 15.1: Joint NIC/TIC meeting in Johannesburg, 8 December 1990. (Courtesy of Ismail Vadi)

From the vantage point of the present, one can sense the tension in the discussions, given the bad blood between Essop Pahad and Mac Maharaj born out of exile politics, and between Pravin Gordhan and Roy Padayachie/Mewa Ramgobin internally. Essop Pahad, for example, made a statement on 17 December 1990: 'In June this year, Comrade Mac informed both the ANC and the SACP that he intended to retire in the middle of December. He indicated that his retirement was related to personal reasons. But everybody knows that Comrade Mac is not very well.'[22] When Padraig O'Malley alerted Maharaj to this statement, his riposte was, 'Essop was neither in the Politburo nor the NEC; where he got his "facts" from one can only guess.'[23] There was little love lost between them.

To hear about cabalism from Aziz Pahad, who had spent decades in exile, must have been a bitter experience for an internal activist like Pravin Gordhan. But this did not prevent Gordhan from providing an acute analysis of the challenge of mobilising Indians:

We have already absorbed all those who were close to the ANC. As we engage in campaigns, membership will increase; there was disillusionment with the ANC as the ANC was unable to provide a vision and was unable to end the violence; De Klerk was doing a good job; the violence and crime was increasing and the state was exacerbating the violence; there was a perception that the ANC NEC was making decisions without involving its membership; the House of Delegates was incapable of asserting political leadership; and provided we are able to adopt the mass approach, we could mobilise Indians into the ANC.[24]

Gordhan warned that the ANC was hamstrung by the 'struggle for power in our ranks and greater interest in acquiring positions within the ANC than the desire for advancing the movement'. The cabal issue and the Vula trial were being used by ambitious individuals to further their positions. If this was not stopped, he cautioned, 'the assassination of political opponents within the movement was likely'. Gordhan said that he detected clear 'evidence of anti-Indianism and Zulu chauvinism' within the ANC in Natal, where the ANC REC had 'developed an exclusive approach'. The UDF and NIC were not allowed to function adequately, individuals such as Billy Nair had been sidelined and cliques within the ANC interim leadership structure had deliberately excluded certain people. Gordhan questioned the factual basis of the 'Robben Island Paper' and underscored the 'deliberate and damaging leaks' made to the press prior to the conference.[25]

Gordhan's intervention was a robust counter to the accusation of cabalism. He appeared particularly irritated that he and Billy Nair, having just emerged out of Vula, had to defend themselves against attacks from the very people who had failed to support them at their trial. Gordhan, alleged mastermind of a clique of cliques, swung that back to the accusers, pointing to the manufacturing of untruths by tight groupings to marginalise him politically.

Maharaj reminded delegates that they were meeting 'first-and-foremost as the ANC, and that the disbanding of the organisations [NIC/TIC] was not the issue'. They had to work out ways to mobilise Indians and 'demonstrate in our present times the vision of non-racialism in our practice'. The question of disbandment should be taken to the branches, where a decision could be made.[26] Maharaj was cautioning against a hasty decision, although his call to go back to the branches was hollow, given that the NIC had very few functioning ones.

Steve Tshwete, ANC NEC member who had served time on Robben Island with Billy Nair, emphasised that the task of mobilising Indians was the duty of 'the entire revolutionary alliance' and not that of the NIC/TIC alone. He was critical of the composition of the ANC REC in Natal, which, in excluding Indian activists, was not exhibiting that the ANC 'belongs to all'.[27] Walter Sisulu stated that it was 'especially unfortunate that the Southern Natal ANC RILC [Regional Interim Leadership Committee] was not present. The discussions on racism were vitally important.' Aubrey Mokoena's open letter on the 'cabal' was 'causing more damage than good' to the movement and Sisulu warned that 'all unprincipled ideas must be eradicated. Sisulu questioned "What is this thing called 'cabal'?", and if there was any evidence for its existence, this should be thoroughly examined.' Like Maharaj, Sisulu did not think it necessary to make a hasty decision about the future of the Indian Congresses. He proposed a further meeting, with the Natal ANC members in attendance, so that 'serious discussion' could be held over strategies for mobilising Indians and the obstacles faced by NIC/TIC activists within the ANC.[28]

The discussion laid the divisions bare but left key issues hanging in the air. It must be remembered that this debate had to take into consideration that negotiations would involve parties that formed the tricameral system and governed the Bantustans. The ANC felt that, given the numbers game at CODESA, the NIC and TIC should continue strategically in order to secure a place at the negotiating table. As Ismail Vadi explained:

> Sisulu, Kathrada, etc. had no idea as to the form of the negotiating structure. Pretoria and Groote Schuur Minutes dealt with bigger issues but who would sit around the negotiating table? When you looked at the table, there was the ANC and [SA]CP, the PAC was ambivalent, on COSATU it was not clear if trade unions could partic-ipate. On the other side you had the NP, the Tricam, the Homelands, etc. So in a sense, the table was unbalanced. The ANC needed to strengthen its hand at the negotiating table. It was decided for this reason that the NIC/TIC must be participants. The older delegates said, 'Hold on, we want non-racial movements, but look at other stra-tegic considerations.' In principle we are all ANC, but the decision to dissolve was left unresolved as there were so many factors at play. The TIC and NIC in fact sent delegates to technical committees at CODESA which needed specialist skills.[29]

Figure 15.2: Meeting of the NIC/TIC with the ANC at UDW on 17 March 1991. *From left*: I.C. Meer, Dullah Omar and Aziz Pahad. (Courtesy of Faizal Dawjee)

NIC/TIC national executives met again at UDW on 17 March 1991, with an ANC delegation that included Walter Sisulu, SACP general secretary Joe Slovo, Alfred Nzo, Thabo Mbeki (head of internal communications), and Southern Natal ANC chairman Jacob Zuma. They resolved that the NIC and TIC should not disband but use their existing structures to mobilise support for the ANC.[30]

This decision served only to increase the focus on the NIC's continued existence and did nothing to quell debate and criticism. Reporter Viven Bissetty described the announcement as a 'bombshell' in a context where the UDF was disbanding.[31] The ANC Youth League was also critical of the decision and issued a statement asserting that

> no ethnic or racial group, no matter how well intentioned, should ethnically prepare itself to join the ANC. The League views the decision as a strategic error that might lead to polarization of the national liberation forces. It is our view that more effort should be concentrated towards building the ANC into a cohesive and truly non-racial movement.[32]

One of the ironies of the Youth League criticism is that the Congress Alliance had seen the need to organise along racial lines since the 1950s, leading to criticism through the years that they were not non-racial but multiracial. The NIC had been defended through the 1970s and 1980s as operating within the Congress tradition of the four-nation thesis. Now the Youth League wanted to wish that history away. What lay behind this tack? In part it may have been the relationship between Ramgobin and Peter Mokaba, president of the Youth League, as discussed in the previous chapter.

A week after the decision of 17 March, Bissetty spoke with various leaders about the role of the NIC/TIC. HOD politician Amichand Rajbansi said that the decision not to disband 'had certain political consequences and elements of political dishonesty'. It aimed to 'deceive the Indian community by using the minority bait to lure them into the folds of the ANC'. NIC secretary Farouk Meer insisted that his organisation's sole concern was 'to mobilise the Indian community, either to become members of the ANC or, failing that, to support its policies ... rather than to search for NIC membership or minority privileges or rights'. Meer was adamant that the NIC/TIC were unfairly criticised since 'the decision not to disband was decided jointly with the ANC, and if people wanted to attack ... they should attack the ANC as well'.[33]

The future role of the NIC was one of the issues debated at the ANC's first full conference in South Africa since 1959, held at UDW on 2–6 July 1991. Delegates agreed that the NIC should help muster support for the ANC in the run-up to elections and thereafter be phased out. The conference also resolved that as part of the strategy of defeating the NP, an alliance of all anti-apartheid forces, the 'Patriotic Front', would be launched at a three-day conference scheduled for the end of October 1991.

On 14 October 1991, Farouk Meer sent out a circular inviting the public to a meeting on 22 October to gauge their political preferences in advance of the planned conference. Meer explained:

This initiative is consonant with the concern voiced by Nelson Mandela on the participation of minority groups within the ANC ... The future of the NIC can only be decided after consultation with the community. For the present there is agreement and also because of our participation in the Patriotic Front that the NIC should continue to play a political role to represent the interests of the Indian community within the broader democratic society. We are agreed that this is an interim role that will cease once a democratic constitution is in place.[34]

The Patriotic Front conference was attended by the ANC, COSATU, the PAC, the SACP, the NIC and TIC, some homeland parties, and many cultural and religious organisations. The outcome was an agreement that gave the ANC and forces opposing the NP government the mandate to demand that formal talks take place on an equal footing rather than kowtow to the NP agenda. AZAPO and Inkatha chose not to be part of the Front, while the PAC soon dropped out.

The feverish debate about the continued existence of the NIC was in one sense 'much ado about nothing' since formal NIC meetings were no longer being held and NIC members were forming ANC branches in Indian areas. Mewa Ramgobin, Paul David and Ela Gandhi were central to forming a branch in Verulam. Sharm Maharaj was involved in the ANC branch in Phoenix, where there was one branch for 400 000 people, while five ANC branches were established in Chatsworth. A branch was formed in Stanger, where Riaz Meer, A.Q. Mangerah and Edwin Pillay were active. In Pietermaritzburg, in the predominantly Indian areas to the north, two ANC branches were established. One branch was led by Chota Motala and the other by A.S. Chetty, both long-standing and experienced NIC leaders who commanded great respect among locals. Old Greytown Road, now Chota Motala Drive, was a convenient demarcation line: A.S. Chetty lived in the Newholmes area to the east of the road and Motala in Mountain Rise to the west. Motala's branch was called Northern A and included the largely middle-class areas of Mountain Rise, Allandale and Raisethorpe. Chetty's branch, Northern B, included mostly working-class Indians. Yunus Carrim lived in the city centre and was part of a third, non-racial branch.

These activists mobilised on behalf of the ANC as ANC members. This siphoning of senior NIC members into the ANC created a further challenge over addressing the fears of the Indian community. Former NIC leaders, now acting as ANC members, had to push the party line, which, as much as it tried to be sensitive to minority fears, was also geared to formulating policies that appealed to the African majority and winning their votes in an election. The gap that was created between activists and the masses as the NIC leaders made haste into the ANC was to come back to haunt them, although it is difficult to imagine what spaces they had for implementing an alternative strategy.

After numerous preparatory meetings, the first plenary session of CODESA was held on 20 and 21 December 1991 at the World Trade Centre in Johannesburg. Nineteen parties attended,[35] with the black nationalist PAC and the white right-wing Afrikaner Conservative Party (CP) boycotting the talks. Participants included three 'anti-government' organisations – the ANC, the SACP, and the NIC/TIC (represented as one organisation) – and 15 'system' parties, including the Indian houses of the Tricameral Parliament.[36]

The NIC delegation included Pravin Gordhan, George Sewpersadh, Farouk Meer, I.C. Meer, Ela Gandhi and Billy Nair, while the TIC delegation included Cassim Saloojee, Reggie Vandeyer, Ramlall Bhoola, Feroz Cachalia and Essop Jassat.[37] Both the NIC and TIC were represented on the Working Group and Management Committee, which were formed to undertake negotiations. These commenced on 20 January 1992. NIC and TIC representation was to prove important for the ANC, as it was able to bring with it numbers and expertise and thus bolster its position in the negotiation process. Pravin Gordhan came to the fore at CODESA. A Declaration of Intent signed at CODESA committed the participants to work towards peaceful constitutional change. Gordhan chaired the Management Committee, one of whose members was Jacob Zuma, to oversee this process.[38] Gordhan was among the chairpersons on the planning committee of the multiparty negotiation process in 1993.

A referendum among whites on 17 March 1992 resulted in a 68.7 per cent 'yes' vote in favour of a negotiated constitution.[39] There were many twists and turns and delays still to come, but protracted negotiations eventually resulted in agreement to hold South Africa's first democratic elections on 27 April 1994.

For those in the NIC/TIC, this was a vindication of their life's work. But with elections fast approaching, they had one more challenge: to convince Indians to vote for the ANC. Struggle credentials would not be enough, and they had to find a way to dispel the fear of majority rule. While Mandela had shown statesmanship and made a determined effort to woo the Indian community, De Klerk had won plaudits for his efforts to end the political stalemate.

The likes of Pravin Gordhan, Billy Nair and Mac Maharaj, with decades of knowledge accumulated in the trenches of anti-apartheid resistance, came up against 'political animals' such as Amichand Rajbansi. Would struggle credentials trump those who had developed a public profile in participating in government-created bodies? Would the low turnout that characterised HOD elections translate into a positive vote for the ANC? Or would the fear of majority rule draw Indians into a broadening white laager that emphasised the protection of minority rights? These questions are examined in the next chapter as we analyse voting patterns among Indians in 1994.

16 | The Ballot Box, 1994: A Punch in the Gut?

Nelson Mandela was free. The ANC had been unbanned. The seeming speed with which this happened had caught many seasoned activists unawares. But excitement was tinged with uncertainty. An NIC memo to the Southern Natal Regional Interim Committee of the ANC, dated 10 May 1990, noted that as a result of visits to individual homes and formal and informal meetings to assess the 'political mood' among Indians, it was clear that 'widespread fear and confusion' existed in the community.[1]

The memo cited the immediate reasons for this anxiety as the 1985 violence in Inanda and attacks on Indians in the transport hub of Warwick Avenue in Durban during 1989. The memo made special mention of NP propaganda about the consequences of majority rule for Indians, the perception that the ANC was responsible for countrywide violence, and 'persistent inflammatory (anti-Indian) statements' from Inkatha. The memo argued that due to the weak level of political organisation among Indians, 'the absence of vigorous and decisive intervention by progressive forces' would result in Indians 'supporting an option (NP) that will bring about an end to apartheid and which at the same time addresses minority interests (defined as security)'. The memo called on the ANC's senior leadership 'to directly address the fears and misconceptions' which existed in the Indian community.[2]

The memo sought to identify the common-sense views of the mass of Indians at this historical moment, and the basis for these. The memo was an honest recognition of the vast divisions that existed between South Africans, and of the NIC's inability to assuage the fears of the Indian community sufficiently to garner votes for the ANC. Clearly the violence

Figure 16.1: Mrs Thrunagavalli Dixon garlands Nelson Mandela at a function in Chatsworth, November 1994. Ebrahim Ebrahim is standing on the right and Jeff Radebe on the left. (Courtesy of African News Agency)

between the ANC/UDF and the IFP, often fuelled by 'third force' elements linked to the apartheid state, impacted on the community, as many Indians lived cheek by jowl with Africans. However, there were other factors to take into consideration. The NIC was caught up in its own internal leadership battles. Moreover, as a result of detentions, bannings and involvement in ANC underground structures, the NIC's organic relationship with everyday Indian life was often distant.

While there was a close working relationship and friendship across race lines among many political activists, among ordinary people the effects of segregation, the Group Areas Act and other apartheid policies emphasised difference, which lent itself to anxiety over the future. Due to the rapid spread of higher education and increased economic mobility, Indians as a community were a completely different entity socially and economically in 1990 than they had been when the NIC was revived in 1971. Place became important, with the majority of Indians living in racially defined dormitory townships on the outer edges of the city. Many individuals only one generation away from parents who had worked in clothing factories or as hotel waiters had joined the middle class and were concerned about radical economic policies and affirmative action. The Cato Manor riots of 1949 and the violent attacks in Inanda in 1985 haunted the minds of many Indians, whose memories were brought into the immediate present amid the swirling rumours of planned attacks on Indians.

In Pietermaritzburg, for example, there were rumours of an attack which would take place on Friday, 16 February 1990. The attacks did not materialise, but the threat exacerbated existing trepidation in the community. A.S. Chetty, chairperson of the NIC in Pietermaritzburg, 'condemned those responsible for the rumours' and insisted that the 'oppressed people are all one in the struggle and the sooner we come together in unity the better'. Yunus Carrim explained that due to 'the destitution and desperation of people in the townships it is inevitable that violence should spill over into the Indian area and take a racial form ... In the long term we will have to act to ensure that people have adequate jobs and housing.'[3]

Anti-Indian pamphlets were circulated in the two largest African townships around Durban, Umlazi and KwaMashu. Written in Zulu, one of them was translated as follows:

These Indians are still bent [on] and committed to revenge the bitter uprisings of 1949 between Indians and Africans, in which the Zulus nearly destroyed Cato Manor in its entirety. At this moment the Indians are secretly planning to bring thousands of Indians from India to take over our jobs. Millions of these Indians are dying of hunger every day; these Indians want their children to take over the better jobs. These Indians are bribing union officials with money so that they can carry on calling for strike action.[4]

The bribe allegation was made in reference to strikes organised by COSATU, whose secretary general, Jay Naidoo, was depicted as being at the head of an Indian group controlling the union federation and instigating strikes that resulted in African job losses. This strike action was linked to the ANC-supported sanctions and disinvestment movement of the 1980s, which sought to cripple the NP government economically, a tactic that the IFP deplored.

T.R. Mthemba, editor of the Zulu-language newspaper *Ilanga*, wrote an editorial attacking the 'shadowy and sinister' NIC for allegedly fanning racial tensions by making 'inflammatory statements against those from whom it differs politically. The NIC will be placing Indian people in Natal on a collision course with the black majority if it does not stop making the most outrageous allegations against Inkatha and its leader Dr M.G. Buthelezi'. The editorial accused NIC secretary Farouk Meer of being aware that the ANC leadership had called for the murder of Inkatha president Mangosuthu Buthelezi. Yet 'those who serve with him in the NIC and what they clearly regard as their kindergarten, the MDM and the UDF' had failed to speak out against such threats.[5]

At an Inkatha mass meeting at King's Park Stadium in February 1990, Goodwill Zwelithini, king of the Zulu nation since 1968, publicly accused 'leading Indians' of 'fanning the flames of black on black violence'. He

Figure 16.2: Protests against Indians occupying Cato Manor houses, which the HOD had built for Indian occupation. (Courtesy of Gandhi-Luthuli Documentation Centre)

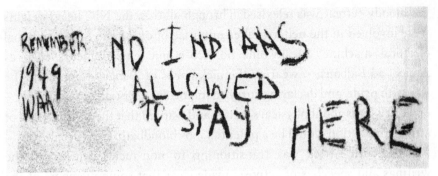

Figure 16.3: Threatening graffiti, such as this example in Cato Manor, added to the anxiety of many Indians. (Courtesy of Gandhi-Luthuli Documentation Centre)

warned: 'When Indian activists use Indian money to subvert the morals of the black children and turn them into young killing demons, there will be a very strong reaction.'[6] Farouk Meer accused Inkatha of fuelling anti-Indianism: 'The situation has never been as tense as it is now. Inkatha is losing support. Inkatha has been running an anti-Indian campaign and it's also coming from *Ilanga*. The message to Indians is quite clear: the UDF is trouble for you.'[7] Meer told reporters that the NIC had 'been told of attacks on Indians at Isipingo, Welbedacht and Pinetown and had heard that assaults were likely to be launched on the Indian community at Phoenix'.[8]

In March 1990 the NIC began to fan out its cadres to meet with members of the Indian community in order to curb their fears. Farouk Meer and Archie Gumede visited Welbedacht; Billy Nair, Jerry Coovadia and Farouk Meer spoke in Malagazi. In the same month NIC and UDF activists organised peace patrols in Durban's Warwick Avenue, where two Indian men had been stabbed to death and several Indian women robbed. Mosiuoa 'Terror' Lekota of the UDF and several NIC branch activists addressed the community in Tongaat in April 1990.[9]

Many Indians interpreted a 'home invasion' in Cato Manor, where Africans took occupation of houses originally built by the HOD for Indians, as a sign of things to come. Memories of the forced, violent expulsion of Indians from Inanda were fresh. Inkatha and the UDF/ANC continued their low-intensity warfare. Rumours of impending attacks on Indians were rife. The white right-wing invasion of Bophuthatswana and the bloody retreat was televised. Through all this, the NIC heavyweights were involved in the helter-skelter minutiae of oiling the ANC's national electoral machine. Meanwhile, politico-ethnic entrepreneurs such as Amichand Rajbansi – wearing the nicknames of 'Bengal Tiger' and 'The Raj' with pride, and declaring curry an important negotiating instrument – exploited fears about physical security and warned that the introduction of affirmative action would be a potential jobs bloodbath.

As South Africa was transitioning to non-racial democracy, the writings and speeches of activists made clear that some members of the movement were well aware of the deep divisions created by decades of divide-and-rule policies, and of the anxieties among Indians over major-ity rule. Moreover, promises of security, even when delivered by Mandela himself, were not enough to placate fears that had a long history.

Frene Ginwala, who served as Speaker of the National Assembly from 1994 to 2004, acknowledged Indian fears in a mid-1980s interview:

> There's no question that running through the Indians at all times there's always this fear, how does a minority cope – it's foolhardy not to address that and to assume that it doesn't exist, or somehow it's bad that it exists ... It's no good saying don't be afraid, because that doesn't solve anything. People have genuine fears – recognise the vulnerability of minorities that is almost intrinsic in that kind of society, and then deal with those issues ... You don't succeed if you demand commitment out of fear, or give people panaceas and say: 'No, everything will be fine' – because it won't be fine – minorities inevitably are scapegoats.[10]

But like most other Indian activists, Ginwala advised Indians that their best option was to embrace non-racialism and get involved in the UDF and ANC in order to shape policy:

> I say the extent to which you are part and parcel of the ANC, and part and parcel of the UDF, and part and parcel of the democratic move-ment, you determine policies, you set the agenda, and to that extent you're able to participate in making your future secure. The other way there's no way you can be secure, so the choice is not between security within a racist system and taking a chance outside, but with

a guaranteed lack of security in a racist system, and working towards achieving a security for everybody outside.[11]

While Ginwala and others seemed to grasp the fears of many Indians, the NIC-activists-turned-ANC-cadres were constrained in the way they addressed these issues. Did this constraint reflect activists' failure to come to grips with the tenacity of ethnic and racial identities because they were caught up in the euphoria of the ANC's unbanning and the 'non-racial' world they were privileged to occupy? Was it the case that they faced the nearly impossible task of reconciling the needs of the ANC's majority African base with the needs and fears of their Indian constituency?

Chota Motala stated at a public meeting in the early 1990s that Indians should 'discard old myths, the many untenable assumptions of the past, the old notions that people subscribe to, the prejudices totally unsupported'. The time had come, Motala said, 'for opening up our minds and our imagination to the vision of a new society'.[12]

Yunus Carrim, who was then a lecturer in sociology at the University of Natal and would feature high on the ANC provincial list as a candidate for Parliament, sought to provide 'the vision of a new society' in a memorandum that he circulated in early 1994. He argued that the ANC was best placed to serve Indians' 'material, ideological, psychological and spiritual needs'. He contended that from the time of Mahatma Gandhi, Indians had produced a host of outstanding leaders in the Congress movement. Many Indians had been killed or incarcerated in the course of their anti-apartheid activism, and it would be a severe betrayal of this long history of struggle not to vote for the ANC. Carrim pointed out that the ANC had a long tradition of non-racialism, and that 36 of the top 100 candidates on the ANC's 1994 parliamentary list were non-Africans, among them 15 Indians. The Reconstruction and Development Programme (RDP), Carrim argued, would radically alter the economy and improve the lives of the majority. Importantly, no party boasted the 'high calibre leadership' of the ANC. Moreover, of all the leaders only Mandela had the 'ear of the international community, including key bankers and investors', as well as support from India. Finally, 'It is precisely because Indians as a minority have fears about the future that they cannot vote for any party other than the ANC ... Surely it is in the interests of Indians to join the mainstream, instead of becoming more isolated?'[13]

The sobering reality of the Indian community's ambivalence towards the changing South Africa was acknowledged at the highest levels within the ANC. The ANC Negotiating Forum, made up of allies from various regions, met on 14 April 1992. Chota Motala was present at this meeting; he kept detailed notes and recorded the expressed concerns about the political role of Indians. According to his notes, there was little involvement of Indian youth in politics; Indians tended to be preoccupied with their own futures without contextualising their situation within the problems of the larger society; there was a need for Indians to carefully consider what the struggle had been about and what was morally and politically correct for the future; and the task of NIC activists was to 'unleash a programme of re-education of our community' since this 'crisis [had been] brought about by the collapse of critical thinking'.[14]

In Chatsworth, long-time activist Charm Govender noted that before the 1994 elections he could 'see the community displaying a lot of unease about having majority rule and they then, in the election, reflected this

Figure 16.4: Pietermaritzburg activist Chota Motala addressing an ANC meeting in the city. Seated on Motala's right is activist John Jeffrey, and to his left are Harry Gwala and Walter Sisulu. (Courtesy of Rabia Motala Archives)

unease by voting in a significant majority for the National Party'.[15] Paul David was forthright on this issue in a 2017 interview:

> While we managed to persuade communities to reject anything that the National government provided, they were still afraid of African majority rule. You could feel that in house meetings where there was a more intimate relationship. We thought we had managed to quell it, but it was there, you know, in the subconscious. But they [the ANC] wouldn't listen to this and I said, 'Well, it's our experience of the Indian community.' I was asked straight out by, may have been Jesse Duarte, 'Well, how do you feel?' I said, 'I was born into the ANC; the NIC was there for convenience for me.' 'Then how can you be arguing like this? We represent everybody.' I said, 'Yes, you will represent everybody, but canvassing for support is sensitive.' Look where the Indian community has gone. By and large they don't support the ANC.[16]

These assessments of where the majority of Indians stood constituted a challenge for the NIC. The organisation had justified its existence on the basis that it was operating inside the Indian community to create conditions for support of the ANC and its policies, and more generally working for a new South Africa. The boycott of government-created institutions led the NIC to claim to be the dominant force in Indian politics. Had its abilities been overestimated? What would Motala's 're-education' of Indians entail? Was the litmus test for a minority community's embrace of a new South Africa simply whether or not it voted for the ANC? Why was the debate about the continued existence of the NIC so bare of content and so weakly articulated?

Amid these many questions, events were moving quickly, with senior ANC/NIC activists preoccupied by the politics of the transition on the national stage and within CODESA. Leading NIC figures were absorbed in the final lap of negotiations, and some were drafted into the ANC's national election machine. Others, such as Mac Maharaj, were consumed by the 'dual power' that characterised the last days of apartheid rule, in which the ANC and the NP shared power in what was known as the Transitional Executive Committee. Moe Shaik, for example, details his role in setting up a new national security system. He was part of an ANC group that

> met with the leadership of the SADF at the naval base in Simon's Town. We flew into the then DF Malan airport in Cape Town and from there were whisked by military helicopters to the naval base. It was an impressive sight as the three helicopters flew in formation ... Awaiting us were squads of sailors and navy officers standing to attention ... That evening we had a long dinner which ended with a game of cards after much wine and laughter.[17]

The meeting Shaik describes took place on 23 April 1993, five days after the funeral of Chris Hani, the activist and SACP general secretary who was assassinated outside his home in Boksburg. His murder brought to a climax the tension and violence that marked the transition period. But the killing helped spur the decision to set a date for South Africa's first democratic election: 27 April 1994.

This world was a far cry from the streets of Chatsworth, where Amichand Rajbansi stalked the neighbourhood promising to defend the Indian and the constitution. The NIC saw him as a snake-oil salesman. Those who voted for him saw him as an irresistible snake-charmer.

The history of the NIC is replete with debates about participation in apartheid-created bodies. At each decision point, the organisation opted for the tactic of boycott. And each time, the NIC could claim victory, as the votes for apartheid structures amounted to a mere trickle. Now, as 27 April 1994 – Judgement Day – loomed, the life's work of NIC leaders would be measured. Most former NIC activists were campaigning as the ANC rather than as the NIC in support of the ANC. Would the majority of Indians make their mark for the ANC, the organisation to which the NIC had given its total allegiance?

The ANC swept to victory with just over 62 per cent of the vote, and formed a Government of National Unity (GNU) with Frederik de Klerk's NP (which took 24 per cent of the vote) and Buthelezi's IFP (10 per cent). Nelson Mandela became South Africa's first democratically elected president. Yet the NP 'succeeded in attracting nearly 1.5 million black votes, mainly from the Coloured and Indian communities in both

Figure 16.5: 27 April 1994: A historic day as Fatima and I.C. Meer and millions of other South Africans cast their votes for the first time for a democratic government of their choice. (Courtesy of 1860 Heritage Centre)

of which it was the most popular party. This represented over a third of its total support.'[18]

Tom Lodge estimates that in KwaZulu-Natal, the NP secured 45 000 votes in Chatsworth and a further 40 000 votes in Inanda and Lower Tugela, districts with a considerable Indian population. Indians contributed at least half of the NP's votes in Durban and Pietermaritzburg. Rajbansi's Minority Front (MF) received 49 000 votes, representing 10 per cent of Indian electors.[19] In the Chatsworth electoral area, results show that 19.42 per cent of eligible voters cast their vote for the MF and 44.6 per cent for the NP at provincial level; at national level 64.32 per cent of Chatsworth voters opted for the NP.[20]

In the National Assembly elections in Pietermaritzburg, 53.28 per cent of the electorate voted for the ANC, while the NP secured 20.94 per cent and the IFP 20.26 per cent. For the KwaZulu-Natal provincial legislature, 52.15 per cent voted ANC; 26.13 per cent voted IFP; 14.31 per cent voted for the NP; and Rajbansi's MF attracted roughly 2 640 votes, or about

0.77 per cent of the electorate. Yunus Carrim contended that the majority of Indians in Pietermaritzburg voted for the ANC. Instrumental in securing ANC support, he suggested, was the hard work of younger activists as well as the presence of Chota Motala, A.S. Chetty and other activists whom the Indian community had come to trust since the 1950s, and who worked hard to forge non-racial alliances and friendships with people such as Archie Gumede, Harry Gwala and Peter Brown.[21]

Despite the ANC's liberation tradition most Indians voted for the NP, as many in the Congress movement had anticipated and feared. The NIC's own assessment of the reasons for this, as contained in a March 1995 analysis, pointed to

> a) fear of African people and 'majority rule' and that there will be a backlash against Indians; b) lack of confidence that Africans can rule the country; c) the ANC's poor campaign strategy and insufficient work put in by activists; d) failure of community leaders supporting the ANC to carry their constituencies with them; and e) the legacy of the ANC-NIC difficulties in Natal since 1990.[22]

Caught between economically dominant whites and numerically powerful Africans, many Indians seemingly felt extremely vulnerable and did not regard the ANC as their political home. Some commentators have argued that class was important in determining voting patterns among Indians (and coloureds). Adam Habib and Sanusha Naidu show that the Indian vote was determined by their 'material vulnerability in the post-apartheid economy' over such things as jobs, access to housing and high levels of crime, resulting in the working class voting mainly for the NP.[23] Many Indian voters were attracted by the NP pledge to protect minority rights. Lodge underscores this point: 'Indians as a group were most uncertain about their political affiliations: polls suggested that more than half the Indian electorate were swing voters ... Working-class Indians and coloureds, middle-class whites, and a few middle-class Africans voted for the National Party.'[24] Lodge's assessment that more than half of Indians were swing voters indicates that votes were up for grabs and that the ANC campaign, and by implication the NIC/TIC, did not sufficiently address Indian fears.

In 2002, when Ela Gandhi was serving as an ANC MP, she explained Indian voting patterns since 1994 in the following terms:

> The very fact that a lot of Indian people and Coloured people voted for the National Party indicates that many of the people became comfortable in their townships. Prior to the '70s and the '80s, there were no Indian townships, there were no Coloured townships ... Indians were staying all over, and lived with African communities in Cato Manor and Inanda and other places. A lot of the poor Indians lived in Magazine Barracks in Durban, lived in wood and iron huts all over Malagazi, Inanda. So they knew what it was to live as African people were living. It was in the '70s and '80s that things changed. They [the Nationalists] felt we needed to co-opt these people [Indians] and they started building houses, removed all the shack settlements, brought Indian people into the built-up houses, built schools for them, gave them water, electricity which they never had in the shacks, and so people became comfortable with that ... Those schools would not compare with the white schools, but they were comfortable with it because it was better than what they had and then they had a slightly higher status than the African community had.[25]

This observation places blame on the same people who had boycotted the SAIC and the HOD, victories that the NIC had claimed. Ela Gandhi and other NIC critics of the behaviour of the Indian masses failed to self-critique their own shortcomings – harking back to the dramatist Bertolt Brecht's point in his 1953 satirical work *The Solution*: 'Would it not be easier ... for the government to dissolve the people and elect another?' It seems that many of the NIC leaders were living in their own bubble of the underground, Operation Vula, the UDF and machinations within the ANC. There is little recognition from Ela Gandhi of the divisions and acrimony within the NIC or of the denunciation of counter-voices which impacted on the NIC's effectiveness.

Ela Gandhi's explanation of what she sees as the co-option of Indians also conveniently passes over an important part of the forced relocation of Indians into Chatsworth and Phoenix: their *own* making of a life, their rebuilding of cultural, religious and sporting organisations and civic bodies.

Figure 16.6: Ela Gandhi, granddaughter of Mahatma Gandhi, was a member of Parliament from 1994 to 2004. (Courtesy of 1860 Heritage Centre)

To view Indians as simply 'co-opted' sees them as mere puppets pulled along by the string of the NP rather than as a people making sacrifices, building new lives, showing agency, making history. According to Thomas Blom Hansen, Ela Gandhi had in fact called on Indian South Africans in 1998 to apologise for benefiting from apartheid. This 'elicited a flurry of responses and reactions from leaders and ordinary Indians who felt hurt and offended'. Faced with a huge outcry she had to backtrack.[26]

Should Ela Gandhi's statement about working-class Indians be read as double standards? After all, the children of the NIC middle-class leadership often went to the best universities, secured scholarships and, like their parents, took on professional livelihoods. For NIC activists to claim the moral high ground and admonish the working classes can be construed as hypocrisy and as condemning the sacrifices of working-class people trying to build a better life.

Additionally, as the post-apartheid period unfolded, many of these same activists from the NIC/TIC took advantage of cadre deployment to sweep into positions as bureaucrats in local and provincial government.

This was at a time when the ANC government was imposing higher rents and electricity and water disconnections for non-payment. The costs of these services were escalating just when many Chatsworth and Phoenix residents were losing their jobs in the clothing and textile sectors as imports flooded the market. Residents lamented that the very activists who had led protests in the 1970s and 1980s against what they termed apartheid's anti-poor rent increases had now turned City enforcers, and led the charge to disconnect and evict the poor in the late 1990s and early 2000s.

In the words of one critic, who wished to remain anonymous, these activists-turned-bureaucrats 'flagrantly and shameless spat on the very scriptures of the struggle they once represented'. They were applying 'shock therapy' to the poor without the therapy. The deployed cadres, many of whom assumed office not because of ability but through political connections, were, of course, anaesthetised as their salaries doubled and quadrupled. Many leading activists of the ANC/UDF/NIC/TIC, taking advantage of Black Economic Empowerment (BEE) and the notion of a patriotic bourgeoisie, shamelessly cashed in. Others used their political networks and the state tender system to accumulate fabulous wealth with incredible speed.

The 1996 local government elections affirmed the pattern of 1994. The ANC enjoyed support among middle-class Indians, while the MF and the NP garnered the support of the working class, although there were nuances even within that class. According to Alexander Johnston and R.W. Johnson:

> The ANC had an entrenched position among the more educated and upper class Indian elites, with the MF's strength lying in the lower middle and working class ... Where the sense of threat was particularly strong the NP could still win Indian ward seats as well. Thus while the MF won a swathe of seats in middle income Chatsworth, the NP beat the MF handily in lower income Phoenix. The Indians of Chatsworth, living in the relative security of belonging to the largest Indian community in the country, felt more able to indulge their penchant for a separate Indian party, while the Indian population of Phoenix, which lives in the shadow of Inanda's large and turbulent

African population, clearly felt more inclined to cling to the skirts of the NP, with its national profile and presence.[27]

Johnston and Johnson argue that Indian voters were

> the most strictly endogamous community in the country and even within the Congress tradition insisted on the maintenance of the racially separate Natal and Transvaal Indian Congresses. The MF's strong party list vote suggests that a significant number of Indians do want to see a specifically Indian party. In that sense the MF is the real successor to the NIC.[28]

To argue that the existence of the Indian Congresses somehow reinforced or was symptomatic of 'the most strictly endogamous community in the country' is a perverse rewriting of history. It ignores the fact that African political organisations were banned in the country, that many Indians were leaders and members of unions and the UDF, and that out of the ranks of the Indian Congresses came some of the most consistent fighters for non-racialism, who saw their activism as laying the groundwork for the ANC. In that sense the fear-mongering MF, which took advantage of the anxieties of the Indian minority, was certainly not a successor to the NIC. The MF was a carry-over of the tricameral system, and its leader, Rajbansi, was able to attract votes by drawing on the HOD's record of building schools and creating jobs for Indian civil servants. NIC activists were precluded by the non-racial ideology of the ANC from competing in this terrain and could not generate racial fears as the MF could, while Rajbansi masterfully exploited these insecurities among the voters his party targeted.

Most Indians and coloureds did not vote for the ANC, despite Mandela's warning in January 1994 that 'Coloured and Indian votes for the National Party would betray the revolution'.[29] NIC activists contended that the NP's *swart gevaar* (black threat) campaign swayed the Indian vote. It is true that the NP did not spell out policy details but emphasised that it was 'a new party which had left its past behind', while the ANC, in contrast, 'was still locked in the past'. NP advertisements and speeches preyed on fears that the ANC 'was dominated by communists and that violence and disorder would be the outcome of an ANC victory'.[30]

Support for the Nationalists cannot be reduced to the party's political cunning. As Lodge observes, for whites, Indians and coloureds, 'considerations of racial identity often dovetailed with anxieties about security and welfare. Calling the election a racial consensus is simplistic ... In general, liberation parties paid little attention to the material preoccupations of the racial minorities until too late.'[31]

The NIC itself acknowledged as much, stating in a 1995 discussion document on its future:

> Some segments of Indian people – for example, big business, senior personnel at big companies, senior civil servants and sportspeople – have experienced positive changes. The majority of Indians however are alienated from the transition and feel increasingly marginalised – which is contributed to by the crime, violence, difficult economic conditions, deteriorating social services, the impact of informal settlements, and the effects of affirmative action.[32]

Nor did the organisation regard the outlook as optimistic:

> Indian feelings of marginalisation and alienation are likely to increase as the transition deepens and the ANC focuses more concertedly on the needs of the most disadvantaged and deprived people of our sector – the African people. In the circumstances Indian people are going to become increasingly aggrieved and could easily constitute a base for conservatism and reaction.[33]

The NIC approached its 100th anniversary in 1994, a few months after the heady inauguration of Nelson Mandela as president. Would it be a celebration or a funeral notice, albeit with the usual praise-singing?

Once more old questions were raised in new times. Was there a role for the NIC in a deracialised South Africa? Dr Kesaveloo Goonam, who had been NIC vice-president in the 1940s and had subsequently gone into exile, argued that it was 'time to let go. It [NIC] failed miserably in mobilising Indian support for the ANC in the election. People just no longer have any faith in the organisation.'[34] Others disagreed. Abdul H. Randeree, a long-time NIC official, felt that 'the movement still has a

Figure 16.7: NIC 100th anniversary march through Durban, 21 August 1994. (Courtesy of Hassim Seedat and Faizal Dawjee)

vital role to play, even in politics, and can make a valuable contribution to society in future'.[35]

Marlan Padayachee, in an article titled 'Has the NIC reached a cul-de-sac?', canvassed the opinions of activists. Among the views expressed was the suggestion that, in view of the transition to a non-racial democracy, the NIC should cease functioning and 'leave the political scene on a high note in its historic 100th anniversary year'.[36]

Thumba Pillay, Hassim Seedat, M.D. Naidoo (brother of M.J. Naidoo and a former Robben Island prisoner) and several other activists felt that it would be premature to disband the organisation. M.D. Naidoo said that 'the time has not arrived for the NIC to fold'. Naidoo, who had spent long years in exile, argued that while the ANC had been won over to non-racialism, there remained a strong Africanist trend in the organisation, and history had repeatedly shown that national liberation movements, once in power, tend to slide towards exclusive forms of nationalism.[37] As was his way, Naidoo was looking further into the future, beyond Mandela and the commitment to an inclusive nationalism born of nearly four decades of debate and struggle, to the dangers of racial chauvinism.

Only 150 people turned up for the march through Grey Street (now Yusuf Dadoo Street) to celebrate the NIC's 100th anniversary, and there was a poor turnout at the KwaMuhle Museum for the get-together that followed. Padayachee saw this as a clear signal that the NIC had come to the end of the road.[38]

Many were still reluctant to let go of their ties to the NIC, not only for emotional and historical reasons, but because they saw a need for it. The NIC executive prepared a document in March 1995 discussing whether the organisation should 'disband with dignity or be revived and restructured to play a clearly defined role'. One of the key arguments was that although Indians had voted for the NP, they would get little in return since the IFP was in control of KwaZulu-Natal and the ANC was in charge nationally. With the political vacuum among Indians being filled by Rajbansi, and NIC activists of the 1980s either 'absorbed in the ANC or withdrawn from party politics', consideration should be given to reviving the NIC, with the permission of the ANC and Tripartite Alliance, in a way that did not erode the already weak ANC branches in Indian areas. The document made clear that the NIC would not contest elections but would operate as part of civil society, with the aim of 'making Indians more sympathetic to the ANC and to make the ANC more responsive to the needs and interests of the Indian people'. But the document acknowledged that this would create other problems, with Zulus, Tswanas, Afrikaners and coloureds all wanting their own organisations. 'In what ways are Indians specifically different that they warrant a specific organisation for them?' the document asked.[39]

There is no evidence of a further meeting to decide the fate of the NIC. The organisation never formally disbanded but simply faded into the creases of history. Over the past quarter-century there have been periodic calls for the NIC to be revived, since Indians were being attracted to the former white parties and for a time to Rajbansi's ethnic party, but this was never seriously pursued. The South African political system of proportional representation means that one has to get on a party list to become an MP. Those Indians who were on the ANC list had to ensure that their message stayed within the boundaries of ANC policy, whereas Rajbansi and other ethnic brokers could openly preach an ethnic and racial chauvinism to attract votes. Those from the NIC who went to Parliament were caught up not only in advancing the policies of the ANC but also in the power machinations of that organisation. Ironically, this took NIC MPs further away from the constituency they had spent their lives trying to conscientise and prepare to play a role in a non-racial South Africa.

17 | Between Rajbansi's 'Ethnic Guitar' and the String of the ANC Party List

For the ANC, the years immediately following its unbanning were a mixture of excitement, vindication and turmoil. It had to deal with the negotiation process, the re-entry of exiles, and reconnecting with its internal allies and the underground. Alongside this, as elections loomed the organisation had to get on with the complex process of developing party lists.

In doing so, the ANC had to take account of those returning from exile, internal activists, and provincial and ethnic sentiments. It also had to create space for those who had once been part of government structures and had decided to join the ANC. The process was fraught with tension as individuals and groupings lobbied and positioned themselves to gain entry into national and provincial legislatures. The future of the NIC and the position of its leading cadres in the inner workings of the ANC were also thrown into the mix.

A number of NIC members served in the country's first non-racial Parliament, while others claimed to have paid a price for being fingered as part of the cabal within the UDF and NIC. Jerry Coovadia, for example, reflected on this time and his own ostracism in a 2019 interview:

> Once the ANC was unbanned, there was a lot of criticism of the UDF which hinged on the fact that it was believed that there was a cabal of Indians who controlled both the direction and the resources of the UDF. So that led to a lot of differences between the returning ANC, the trade union movement, and the UDF. Some of us who were

Indian in the UDF paid a price for that. And as the branches of the UDF fell away, and new branches of the ANC were created, many of us who had participated before – well, let me speak for myself, I was just too deeply wounded to participate in an organisation where my bona fides were being questioned. I wasn't the same sort of political animal that many of my colleagues were, like Pravin Gordhan and Zak Yacoob, or others who could take the political heat of the cut and thrust of political affairs. So it wasn't that I withdrew willingly, but it was my inability to face up with what was demanded of this period, where one had to fight off these types of accusations, which are deeply racist. As far as I was concerned, I had participated in the struggle for freedom because my conscience told me it was the right thing to do, and it was my innate sense of wanting freedom for all our people that drove me. I didn't make money out of it; in fact, it kept my career back. I thought that was obvious. However, those people who were willing to see it otherwise saw it in that way. I left politics more or less altogether and went back to medicine.[1]

While acknowledging Coovadia's sensitivities, one has to question his claim of not being au fait with the cut and thrust of politics, given the bloody fights inside the NIC and the marginalisation of some in the UDF, in both of which organisations he had held leadership positions. Coovadia himself was hardly a wilting flower, and had been known to throw demeaning labels at the BCM and NEUM in the 1970s. Was something deeper coming to the fore in his decision to withdraw? Was it that professionals had taken their leadership roles in the NIC and UDF for granted, without having to deal with the scrum of competition, and were now unwilling to engage in an open contest for positions? And if this racism/racial nationalism was directed against high-powered indi-viduals like Coovadia who felt it necessary to retreat from politics, how would ordinary Indians who did not have 'struggle credentials' to lean on feel about the re-racialisation of politics?

Yusuf Bhamjee observed, in what must rank as an understatement, that the 'politics of the time became somewhat hostile', but he was not sympa-thetic to those who felt marginalised. He noted that the task of choosing candidates for the provincial and national election lists was difficult for the ANC leadership, which had to strike a balance between its African, Indian, white and coloured constituencies, as well as the different religious, ethnic and class groupings among Indians. Bhamjee dismissed as conspiracy theories the claims of deliberate exclusion of particular individuals. He explained that each branch nominated members for the National Assembly and the provincial legislature, and forwarded the nominations to the provincial ANC, which in KwaZulu-Natal was chaired by Harry Gwala. Members from all branches voted for the final selection. According to Bhamjee, some of the office bearers in the NIC, UDF and TIC 'assumed that they would be accommodated in the ANC but felt marginalised and became politically reclusive. They were very senior comrades. I have tremendous respect for them. They led us very bravely and pointedly, and offered a lot of wisdom. But that is the paradox of politics.'[2]

While the process was branch driven, it is likely there was pressure by senior ANC leaders to select certain candidates. Bhamjee said there

Figure 17.1: *Left to right*: Activist Chota Motala, Dullah Omar (first minister of justice in the post-apartheid period) and activist Yusuf Bhamjee. (Courtesy of 1860 Heritage Centre)

was great disappointment in Pietermaritzburg because A.S. Chetty, who had devoted his life to anti-apartheid activism since the 1940s, was not made an MP.[3] Chetty was the number one candidate in the Northern B branch, Bhamjee was number one in the Northern A branch and Yunus Carrim topped the Central branch list.[4] Only Carrim ranked high enough on the ANC list to make it to the national Parliament. Bhamjee's ranking saw him enter the KwaZulu-Natal legislature, while A.S. Chetty missed out completely.[5]

There were also allegations that Fatima Meer, a close friend of Winnie Mandela and the first authorised biographer of Nelson Mandela, was side-lined because she was seen as non-conformist, prone to questioning the party line. As one NIC member from Pietermaritzburg (who requested anonymity) put it:

> Fatima Meer was considered a maverick. The NIC comrades in Durban did not see eye-to-eye with her. They were sitting very narrowly and thought that politics started with them, but Fatima was somebody like a Winnie Mandela, in a sense. They [Fatima and Winnie] had their own style of doing things and nobody could tell them anything. They [the Durban NIC] did not fully understand or grasp the value of Fatima Meer.

Fatima Meer was not one to follow party dogma, often responding spontaneously to various issues and situations, and through the 1970s and 1980s she reached out to different strands in the anti-apartheid movement. When Julie Frederikse asked her in 1985 about the possibility of an ANC majority government, she replied:

> God spare us a monolithic political solution, because that could destroy our freedom altogether. I mean you're talking about a one-party system which weighs down heavily on the people. I don't think that is what we want for South Africa. We'll have ANC in government, and we will have the ANC moderated by its opposition, particularly the opposition to the left, and there will be an opposition to the right.[6]

While some were happy to take their places in Parliament and make common cause with the changing political environment, Fatima Meer's support of the ANC was 'not unqualified'. In the post-apartheid period, her 'misgivings about the nature of the transition ... led her back to her earlier activist engagements' in the township of Chatsworth.[7]

Fatima Meer's husband, I.C. Meer, wrote in his autobiography that they had been informed by Ahmed Kathrada that her name was high on both the provincial and parliamentary lists, and that her lifelong friend Winnie Mandela had told Fatima that this was the case. It therefore came as a surprise when she did not feature on either the provincial or parliamentary lists. I.C. Meer wrote that 'Fathu was not one to push herself into any position, but her exclusion from the nomination lists upset me'.[8] While Coovadia felt that he was a victim of the UDF allegation of being associated with a cabal, some close to Fatima Meer believed that she was a victim of Congress members who were annoyed by her 'lack of discipline' and her refusal to officially embrace the Freedom Charter.

Although the earlier assertions by Kumi Naidoo of a North/South Indian divide within the NIC had not been given much credence, in the post-apartheid period there were suggestions that Roy Padayachie was appointed as a minister due to pressure for there to be a South Indian in the cabinet. One witness to these goings-on (who wished to remain anonymous) recounted that a South Indian business person, who was very close to then president Thabo Mbeki, complained that there were too many Muslims in the post-apartheid cabinet (Dullah Omar, Kader Asmal, Valli Moosa, Essop Pahad, Aziz Pahad), even though several of them were not practising Muslims and some were atheists. As the interviewee pointed out, 'The average person in Phoenix, Northdale and Chatsworth, doesn't see it like that. Asmal is a Muslim, as far as they see it, even though he is not a practising Muslim, so there was disquiet.' It was suggested that the most 'obvious choice was Pregs Govender, she was younger, she was a former trade unionist, she was a gender activist, and she is sharp'. But Pregs Govender was not deemed palatable to the ruling party because 'she was very feisty and independent, having raised issues of corruption in government and was persona non grata to those high up in the ANC'.

The most contentious issue was the accommodation of those who had formerly participated in government structures. While sworn enemies were reaching out to each other, some in the NIC were determined to take a hard line. Thumba Pillay, for example, recounted that in the lead-up to the elections, he was in a meeting with Mandela and 'raised the issue of welcoming into the ranks of the ANC former members of the House of Delegates and other collaborators with the apartheid regime ... He was not prepared to hear me out.'[9] Pillay was chairman of the Umgeni North branch, and recounted that this run-in was over Vivian Reddy and Baldeo Dookie, the latter from the former Tricameral Parliament. Reddy and Dookie were introduced as ANC members at a meeting at the Royal Hotel in Durban. Both men were suddenly in Pillay's constituency without his knowledge as branch chairman. However, 'Madiba virtually shut me up and I resigned as the chairman of that branch.'[10]

While Pillay may have been right to question the constitutionality of Mandela's intervention, his perspective is somewhat naive in terms of reading the changing political conjuncture. Elections were looming, KwaZulu-Natal was a highly contested province and the Indian community was clearly fearful of the ANC. It was believed that bringing in people who were seen as conservative or from outside ANC ranks would help assuage these fears and garner votes for the organisation. Apparently happy with compromises elsewhere in the country, as the ANC adopted a pragmatic posture on all kinds of issues, ranging from the economy to sport, the NIC could not countenance this in their own backyard.

Among HOD political figures, the most enigmatic was undoubtedly Amichand Rajbansi. Although he never achieved a high turnout in the tricameral elections and was the subject of ridicule by the NIC, Rajbansi enjoyed support among working-class Indians. He was accused of nepotism and a one-person commission of inquiry under Judge Neville James found in 1988 that he 'offered his close allies liquor licenses, influenced civil service appointments and promotions, and improperly influenced witnesses against previous parliamentary inquiries about his conduct in office'.[11] In January 1989 President P.W. Botha dismissed Rajbansi from the cabinet as minister of housing, and as chairman of the Ministers Council. Members of Rajbansi's National People's Party crossed the floor to join other parties. In typical fashion, he turned the corruption charge into a badge of honour: he was a victim, he asserted, of the apartheid government because of his outspokenness and defence of Indian interests. In the period from the unbanning of the ANC in 1990 to the elections in 1994, Rajbansi was the sole member of his party in the Tricameral Parliament.[12]

During the negotiations at CODESA, Rajbansi used every opportunity to be seen as a conciliator. This gave him a profile beyond the Indian community. Grabbing a photo opportunity when the right-wing AWB attempted to storm CODESA made him a larger-than-life figure. It helped that the NP and ANC were keen on drawing to their sides as many of the smaller parties at CODESA as possible. Throughout 1993 there was much speculation about with whom Rajbansi would throw in his lot. There were reports of him reaching out to the ANC as well as the NIC and TIC, but he made it clear he would never join the NP. Many would have scoffed at this sudden change after long years of consorting with the Nationalists, but that was Rajbansi's skill. He was adept at reading the political wind and riding it, often outflanking those in pole position. His February 1993 call to link up with the NIC and TIC was suitably provocative. He made the call on the basis that an African majority government would introduce affirmative action and job reservation to the detriment of minorities, and it was therefore important to have a strong party to represent Indians.[13] It made NIC-turned-ANC leaders cringe, but it allowed Rajbansi another opportunity to talk the language of standing up for Indians on issues that could potentially hurt them.

In September 1993 Rajbansi announced the formation of what he initially named the United Minority Front, but subsequently renamed the Minority Front (MF). He was widely applauded among Indians when he criticised the NP for not entrenching Indian religions in the interim constitution. Newspaper reports in early 1994 suggested that both the ANC and the PAC were trying to woo him. The *Daily News* reported on 2 February 1994: 'Ever the survivor, Mr Rajbansi had in recent months appeared to be moving closer to different parties at different times.' Eventually Rajbansi went into the election under the banner of his own party. He campaigned on issues relevant to Indians, such as customs officials harassing Indian women returning from India; the difficulties faced by Indian fishermen; and permission to bring Indian movie stars to South Africa as a sign of respect for Indian culture. The MF attracted 49 000 votes and obtained a single seat in the KwaZulu-Natal legislature in 1994.[14]

The attraction of Rajbansi was his fearlessness in clearly identifying Indians as a group whose interests he was prepared to defend. His simple but powerful message was that he understood Indian concerns and would speak up for them. In fact, former South African president F.W. de Klerk stated on 29 June 1996 that the more he listened to and saw Rajbansi,

> the more he looks and sounds like South Africa's new Indian Andries Treurnicht [former leader of the Afrikaner Conservative Party]. Somebody please go and wake [him] up ... and tell him this is the new South Africa. We are one nation and [he] must stop playing the ethnic guitar. All Indians are South Africans like me, there is no place for ethnic politics.[15]

Calling Rajbansi out for playing the ethnic card was somewhat hypocritical coming from De Klerk, who clung on to the notion of 'minority rights' until the ANC forced it from his hands and led him into a system of majority rule.[16] Still, it is true that while De Klerk tried to turn the NP into a non-racial party, Rajbansi saw the virtue of strumming the ethnic strings of his guitar, calculating that he could at least secure himself a seat, given the nature of the proportional representation system.

Rajbansi and others in government institutions had enjoyed an advantage through the 1980s because ordinary Indians could not escape the HOD. As Charm Govender pointed out, even though the NIC boycotted the HOD, there were always 'elements within the community who in pursuit of things like say a bottle store licence or butchery licence, would approach individuals within these structures to say, "can you facilitate this?"'[17] But as the years ahead would show, Rajbansi was more than simply a patron for the Indian working class. He was agile in raising issues that were of concern to Indians in ways that the political correctness of the NIC prevented it from doing. As the IFP and ANC squared off in KwaZulu-Natal, Rajbansi used his single seat to tip the balance in favour of the latter. He happily entered into an alliance with the ANC and served with some aplomb as member of the Executive Council (MEC) for Sport and Recreation in the province.

Farouk Meer noted in a 2012 interview the concern at the way in which the ANC included former Tricameral Parliament members:

> There's always a tongue-in-cheek guy who will tell you, 'You know what, the guys who took part in the Tricameral Parliament and who

collaborated with the [white] South Africans are better off today than you are, so you know, didn't you guys make a mistake?' And I say, 'No.' We made a principled stand. I think that was the correct stand. I think if my organisation today is letting me down and promoting collaborators and marginalising people like myself, I'd say, 'Well, tough.' The correct thing to do at that time was to do exactly what we did. And if history had to repeat itself, we'll adopt the same attitude, the same strategies as we did in the past.[18]

The ANC's embrace of select members of the HOD and other floor crossers clearly rankled NIC cadres who had spent years in the trenches. Still, many had professional careers to lean on, and a fair smattering of Indians from the NIC/TIC and exile made the party lists. Many others made the speedy transfer into government positions as the ANC activated its policy of cadre deployment. Some advanced quickly into top judicial positions.

Yunus Mohamed, who was a key ally of Pravin Gordhan and dropped out of politics in the post-apartheid period, mused about the contradictions of the ANC associating with Rajbansi but opposing the existence of the NIC:

> You've got an alliance with the Minority Front which mobilises in the Indian community, and the ANC's very comfortable with that. Yet it does not want the NIC to be revived in some way. There is a contradiction there. Is it not better to have somebody with whom the ANC has had, in the past, a principle alliance, where you've got people who don't have that kind of collaborationist history, and who have credibility?[19]

Phoenix-based Sharm Maharaj expressed similar sentiments: '[T]here was no point in saying that the NIC must just disappear then, and now you work with the Minority Front who basically work for the Indian community, it don't make sense, it don't make sense at all.'[20]

While Mohamed and Maharaj identify an important contradiction, they fail to confront a fundamental dilemma. If the NIC had sought to act like the MF, it would have had to put up its own candidates. What purpose would it serve if those candidates were not able to speak Rajbansi's racial language? One can see the logic of the ANC's alliance with the MF, as it did not impact on the ANC's own orientation as a non-racial party. At the same time the ANC could use the MF to swing power its way in a province like KwaZulu-Natal, where margins with political rivals were very narrow. The NIC, in contrast, would have had to remain loyal to ANC policies; hence, there was no guarantee that it would attract Indians votes.

It appears that former NIC activists misread the tenor of the times. The ANC had reached out to the IFP and Bantustan leaders, had accepted former members of the Security Branch within its ranks, and was prepared to envisage a unity government that would include De Klerk. The IFP and the ANC had fought bloody battles that resulted in thousands of lives being lost, and yet there was an attempt to find common ground and accept former IFP warlords into the ANC. Seen in this light, complaining about former members of the Tricameral Parliament looked like petty carping.

This is not how NIC activists saw it, however. On 1 December 1993 an ANC Natal regional executive meeting had discussed the acceptance of HOD/LAC members into the organisation. There it was reported that ANC branches with Indian members had been 'flooded with complaints and protests' about the ANC's acceptance of Baldeo Dookie as a member and reports about the possibility of Rajbansi also joining. Members had asked that the acceptance of HOD/LAC members be put on hold until the issue was discussed 'fully within the ANC and there is appropriate consultation with progressive organisations and influential opinion makers within the Indian community'. As a result, Harry Gwala wrote to ANC president Nelson Mandela on 2 December, with a copy of the letter also sent to Jeff Radebe. According to one source, the letter was actually drafted by NIC members in Pietermaritzburg. The letter began:

> Senior members of the Indian community have also called on me to express their disquiet particularly as the Umgeni North members of the ANC were not consulted when it was announced that Dookie's membership had been accepted and they learnt of it through the press. The entire members of some branches with a predominantly Indian membership have threatened to resign in disgust if Mr Rajbansi is accepted as an ANC member.[21]

The letter rejected comparisons of HOD members with homeland leaders and even apartheid-era assassin Dirk Coetzee. The principle, the letter argued, should be: 'in what way is our acceptance of controversial individuals as ANC members going to benefit the organization more than it disadvantages us?' Accepting Coetzee as a member, for example, helped to expose 'apartheid secrets' and weakened the state. Homeland leaders could strategically help to secure support. On the other hand, Dookie 'brought very little to the ANC and yet causes us to lose much. He does not bring any irreplaceable or invaluable skills or prowess and he certainly does not bring in any significant constituency.' Acceptance of people like him resulted 'in demobilizing and demoralizing our activists in the Indian areas, and undermining our attempts to mobilise Indians to support the ANC'.

The letter did not shut the door on HOD/LAC members being considered for ANC membership, but proposed that each application be evaluated 'on its specific merits and demerits'. It was also proposed that applications should be submitted at branch level so branch members could have full say in the decision, as they 'know the dynamics in the local areas and know the MPs' particular history'. Further, no 'undue press publicity and attention' should be accorded to those accepted as ANC members; it would be 'appropriate for the MPs to publicly apologise for perpetuating apartheid and acting against the masses'; and they should serve the ANC for a period of two to five years before being given positions in the organisation in order to show their 'loyalty' and 'commitment to serving the people and not just their self-interests'.

This letter illustrates the muddled thinking of some leading lights in the NIC as the transition unfolded. There was no principle for wanting to keep out HOD members; rather the consideration was whether they were going 'to benefit the organisation'. Many Indians saw some HOD participants as genuinely seeking to uplift the community. A number of those who served in the HOD/LAC had come from working-class backgrounds. On the other hand, some leaders of the NIC had become wealthy in the struggle years; they were ensconced in the suburbs, with their children often studying at foreign universities. The letter raises other questions: Who would vet the application? What would be the test for merit or demerit? The call for gatekeeping once more raised the spectre of a small group assuming that they had a monopoly on progressiveness in the Indian community – which in some quarters earned the label of 'cabal'. In a phrase that would come back to haunt NIC leaders, the document declares that to be in the ANC equates 'to serving the people'. This assertion ignored the fact that the ANC was replete with factions and ideological contestations. To assert some purist line only reinforced the quaint but out-of-step reality of many in the NIC.

Two decades later, Yunus Carrim offered points and counterpoints on HOD members:

I couldn't accept it [HOD members]. No, I didn't agree on that. Now, they said to us, the ANC leadership at the top, we are doing it with the [coloured] Labour Party. What justifies not doing it with the House of Delegates? You couldn't, from the ANC point of view, say no to the Rajbansis and Reddys if you were saying yes to the Hendrickses and the Holomisas. I think the reasons for our objections were partly emotional, but partly moral, partly strategic.

What upset people a lot was when Rajbansi was made an MEC. I remember [Thabo] Mbeki came to the Durban City Hall and said Rajbansi has a base, and you people are upset? When he said how is it that Rajbansi can go and get votes, and you can't, meaning the Indian activists, I remember getting up and saying, yes, it is very easy. We can't do what Rajbansi does. He goes to people and tells them, who is going to protect you against the African people? Who is going to protect you when another 1949 goes? How do we go to Chatsworth and Phoenix and Northdale and say that to the Indian people? That is completely against our principles. It is like the *swaart gevaar* story, in a different version. We can't do that.

Quite a few people came to me and said, actually, you gave a good argument, [but] Mbeki was quite ruthless in saying to us, if you want us to marginalise Rajbansi, deliver the vote. I was annoyed at him. It is not our responsibility, alone. It is all of us. In fact, it is primarily the responsibility of the African comrades, because Indian people don't want us knocking on the door and assuring them that non-racialism means all of us, and affirmative action means all Blacks. It means African people going there and reassuring them that their future is certain. They are not going to listen to me.[22]

Was this a case of short memories? Was not the very existence of the NIC justified on the basis of a need for Indians to organise Indians?

Carrim admitted that the antipathy which the NIC directed at former HOD members was stronger than was the case with

> Coloured comrades, who were in the UDF, in respect of the Labour Party being absorbed ... African comrades were much more generous, far more than even Coloured comrades. African comrades just forgot, many of them almost overnight, that the Bantustan leaders were so repressive, where these leaders were turning to the white state's military might to deal with activists in those areas. African people, in many respects, are remarkably generous, too forgiving in some respects and that also reflected not just towards whites, but also towards fellow Africans who served in these apartheid-era institutions. For them it was very startling, you know; they were a bit puzzled, couldn't understand, why Indian comrades were so upset about Rajbansi. What is the big deal?
>
> I don't know why Indians felt so strongly. I think it may be this thing of retributive justice versus restorative justice. In the ANC, there is a deep tradition of African social justice. You don't punish people, you rehabilitate them. On the other hand, we had a psychological block, morally, fuck them! They didn't pay a price. Rajbansi never paid a price, but then did the Bantustan people pay a price? No. Did anybody pay a price? Not the security policeman for sure. That is Mandela-ism. The great advantage of it is that it reduced the prospects of a civil war, but on the other side, maybe we went too far.[23]

Battle lines can be felt much more intensely within minority communities. Sigmund Freud spoke of the narcissism of small differences – the idea that communities or people in close relationships who show few outward differences often have the most abiding and deep divisions. Jerry Coovadia argued that this antipathy towards HOD members was perfectly understandable:

> I don't think it's anything specific to an Indian mentality of looking at things. There was a huge gap between what Mandela and them understood and what people like us on the ground did. We were

actually quite opposed to that sort of thing, and I think the ANC didn't understand that and they weren't working in these areas. It's easy, when you are Mandela, to forgive them, but we were on the ground and these were the guys who were giving us trouble in Chatsworth and Phoenix and elsewhere. They were the people who were reflecting the worst aspects of us [Indians], they were the people who participated in those elections, and so to us, they were the immediate enemy, short of the whites, the Boers, they were the immediate enemy within our ranks.[24]

There was also the issue of there being only so much largesse to go around. Indians constituted around 2 per cent of the South African population, and while there were many dedicated activists whose supporters were convinced that they deserved to be in Parliament, not everyone could be accommodated. Indians were well represented, some would say over-represented, in the early provincial and national parliaments, given the numbers and voting patterns among Indians. This was still a time in which resistance networks forged in struggle outweighed strict racial consid-erations. That would change as younger African members rose through the ranks, murmurings of an exclusive African nationalism acquired greater resonance, and the perks of office became the difference between unemployment and a comfortable middle-class life.

In speaking to activists about the 1970s and 1980s, we asked whether there was anything the NIC could have done differently that may have yielded different political outcomes. Yunus Carrim's forthright and insightful comments are detailed here because they capture most of the reflections of the more critical voices in the NIC:

It is easy to say in hindsight what the shortcomings were, but in politics things move very fast. The State was getting increasingly repressive. Events were tumbling one into the other. The re-emergence of mass activity amongst the African communities changed the trajectory of politics as a whole, and the NIC couldn't remain aloof. The arms struggle was intensifying. What could we have done better? First, I think we would have managed our differences internally better. The gap between the older generation and the younger generation could have been reduced.

Second, we could have managed the whole debate around participation or not in the House of Delegates better. It came to be seen too much as an unacceptable, morally repugnant thing, whereas if Pravin [Gordhan] and [others] communicated the tactical flexibility, it may have been more effective. But you couldn't say too much either, because then the State becomes aware of your strategy and tactics and there would be blocks put in your way, and then those who are competing against you, the Rajbansi or the Reddy types, would say, 'You see, these people have no intention of serving you, they are coming to destroy this structure', so you couldn't say all those things, but we could have done more to bridge the gap.

Third, I think that we should have managed our relationship with African comrades much better. We tended, because of our middle-class, more formally educated backgrounds, to dominate unduly the internal anti-apartheid structures, both at the level of the underground, political underground, and at the level of the overt mass movement, broadly speaking, the UDF. I think we should have entered the townships more. I would say our biggest failure was not to learn to speak isiZulu. To not be politically correct in our relationship with Africans alone, but to understand more the customs and traditions, the role of the traditional leader, the effects of the migrant labour system and the destruction of African families, the consequences of going through a Bantu Education system. I think we failed dismally to bridge the cultural barriers and we are feeling the effects of that now. Which is not to romanticise the relationship of Africans to Indians. For a progressive African not to know the difference between a Hindu and a Muslim, or between Diwali, Christmas, and Eid, is unacceptable also.

But look, we must not also ignore some of the obstacles. They were quite formidable. It was difficult to enter the townships after dusk, you know. The townships were much more monitored, roadblocks, semi-militarised. Also, African people, at that time, not now, tended to want to speak English, or just took it that you would speak English, that was a discourse of the UDF and the ANC. Nowadays, if you go to an ANC meeting, it is [in] isiZulu and rightly so.[25]

Carrim points directly to the possible roads not taken as much as he explains how the overwhelming demands of struggle did not allow much time to consider alternatives. While there has been much hand-wringing about Indians not voting for the ANC as reflective of their fear of African majority rule, Carrim shines a light on relationships between Indian and African comrades. Many of the African activists at the time were working class, while their Indian counterparts were professionals with substantial social and cultural capital. This sometimes led to resentment of dominance and gatekeeping by Indians, and provided grist for those keen to keep the slur of the cabal alive.

As Carrim observes, the ANC is a different organisation some 25 years into the post-apartheid era. It is overwhelmingly African and very few younger Indians are active at its various levels. While there is occasional talk of building non-racialism, the new African members of the ANC are less sensitive to this. Positioning by members to make it onto the party lists often means playing the race card.

At a time when Indian progressives should be showing their colours, the racial populism of the EFF, as well as the demeaning and belittling of senior Indian members of the ANC from within their own party and without, make many hesitate to enter the public domain. In the time of Mandela, the garnering of Indian support, while not crucial to the ANC winning the elections, was symbolically important. A quarter of a century later, the time for symbolism is past.

The ANC achieved an electoral victory in 1994. Many in the NIC likely had mixed feelings. Euphoria at the overwhelming Congress victory was tinged with disappointment that they were not able to deliver the Indian vote.

There was simultaneously a sense of defeat and victory, victory and defeat.

Conclusion: A Spoke in the Wheel

The NIC was revived in a city that was alive with resurgent anti-apartheid activity. Workers started to flex their collective muscle, and white university academics and students played supportive roles in building trade unions. The BCM engaged in discussion groups that drew on the ideological streams of Frantz Fanon, Jean-Paul Sartre, the US Black Power movement, and liberation theology, forming a heady mix of intellectual mutiny and militant bravado. French-educated philosopher Rick Turner sparred with Steve Biko over participatory democracy, race and whiteness. The NIC, drawing on the status of its founder M.K. Gandhi and the path-breaking generation of the 1950s, reignited the passions of Indian communities battered by forced relocations under the Group Areas Act. Those who tried to prod the NIC into dropping the 'I' were faced down and BC rebels walked their own path.

Despite concentrated and at times spectacular media coverage, the first years after the revival did not witness the coming of a mass-based organisation. Annual meetings drew fewer than a hundred delegates, while public meetings attracted a few hundred attendees, or perhaps a thousand people for a major current issue, such as the death of Ahmed Timol in 1971 and the Chatsworth transport disputes of 1972.

In the face of fiery internal debates over participation in government-sponsored organisations, the NIC held together even as it was drawn into legendary battles with those termed collaborators. Intense activism brought exhaustion, but new recruits schooled in classrooms of dissent entered the ranks. In 1980 university students joined the NIC, unions and, most spectacularly, community organisations. As Pravin Gordhan put it:

> If you look at all the people that were detained at that time, [they were] not necessarily ... connected to each other but many knew each other. That was a generation of late 20s and early 30s in age terms who were maturating in the political process, who had become involved in the labour movement, community activity, underground movement and mass political activity. There were massive student protests ... Round about '78/79 to about '81/82 was quite a hectic period in our struggle. That sweep [from the state] was, let's see if we can crush this thing because there was quite a wide range of people. But there were too many forces operational within the country and the movement was becoming too strong.[1]

Racial boundaries were crossed, although in limited ways, and solidarity was sharpened in joint struggle. The UDF, embryo of a non-racial movement, brought NIC leaders onto the national stage. At the same time, energy was siphoned into the ANC underground and armed struggle, work at once exciting and dangerous. Here the notion of cabal, used loosely within the NIC's internal battles, began to gain currency in broader politics, although it would be argued that secrecy was born of exigency rather than deliberately planned. Nevertheless, some used their social and political capital as ANC and MK cadres to win a debate or silence an opponent, to dam(n) rather than let different streams of struggle flow.

Pregs Govender wrote searingly of the closing down of alternative voices by a tight grouping of men who would brook no dissent. She also spoke of NIC activists fighting turf wars, recounting a debate at UDW in which trade unionists such as Alec Erwin and Bobby Marie met

> with a flurry of opposition from the floor. Much of it came from the important men (all middle class and Indian) from the cabal who attended and aggressively led the questioning of speakers. UDW, an ethnic 'Indian' institution, was their territory and Cosatu, a non-racial trade union federation, was not warmly welcomed.[2]

This contestation was linked to the struggle between the so-called work-erists and populists. As negotiations heated up, so the power of those with links to the exiled movement was used to burrow inside many a trade union either to split it or to win it over to the ANC. Johnny Copelyn, key player in the formation of COSATU, recorded:

> The overwhelming explosion of national liberatory politics gripped the movement from every corner of its activity. Jay Naidoo, general secretary of COSATU, had immediately on his election flown to Lusaka for consultations ... Subsequently, he announced publicly that COSATU was part of an alliance led by the ANC ... Increasingly, those like me, who were not ANC members, found themselves outsiders in a movement they had built and served loyally for years.[3]

Some in the NIC, with links to the underground, unions and ANC intelligence, held powerful positions in this environment and were charged with keeping the Congress wheel at the forefront of internal resistance. The secrecy of Operation Vula drew some into an inner circle, and as negotiations with the NP gathered pace, they were accused of acting as an Indian cabal, the minority spoke, that dominated the wheel of resistance. A critical evaluation of this resistance is the spine of this book. Even a cursory reading of the newspapers of the 1970s and early 1980s shows how the organisation was able to enter the public domain and put forward its anti-apartheid non-racial vision.

Farouk Meer noted that in the face of white minority oppression, Indian South Africans had a proud history of resistance:

> This was not done in conference rooms. The choice, made by us to resist apartheid and join the liberation struggle and play a vigorous, full and equal role in the struggle for liberation, was concretised in action, in actual struggle, in building unity through full participation with fellow oppressed South Africans ... In this way the NIC/TIC established a proud record of sacrifice, commitment and courage.[4]

While Meer raised the choice of a 'full and equal role in the struggle for liberation' as seemingly unproblematic, it was, as the pages of this book show, one of the central issues confronting the NIC. While the NIC was the only legal functioning part of the Congress Alliance in the 1970s, NIC activists almost always spoke in many ways for the whole Charterist movement. This influence, as Meer pointed out, was carried through the 1980s. If apartheid was a special type of internal colonialism, Indian South Africans carved out a special kind of history, one not repeated anywhere in Africa. The Indian Congresses and people of Indian origin in militant movements such as the BCM, trade unions and sports bodies stood shoulder to shoulder through the long years of racist white rule, demanding the vote for all South Africans.

Following the initial flurry of debates over non-racialism and participation in government structures in the early 1970s, state repression led to an NIC downturn, with activities confined to press statements and annual conferences. As the 1970s unfolded, the NIC began mobilising for anti-LAC and anti-SAIC campaigns, service delivery protests, and rent and education boycotts. These years also saw the formation of the Durban Housing Action Committee (DHAC), the Release Mandela Committee (RMC) and the Anti-Republic Day Celebrations Committee.

Focus on the tricameral structures from 1983 to 1985 sparked the formation of the UDF and mass campaigns that attracted thousands to meetings and heightened consciousness through anti-election door-to-door organisational work. The occupation of the British Consulate in 1984 garnered international support, but the detention of activists and declaration of states of emergency impacted on the NIC's and UDF's ability to maintain organisational coherence and keep mass activity going. This was brought home by the 1985 violence in Inanda, where the NIC struggled to respond to the crisis. This was a setback for the Congress movement as a whole, but while bent, the Congress wheel of a single united non-racial South Africa was far from broken. In fact, the racial conflagration and display of Zulu tribal and federalist impulses only served to strengthen the idea of a united South Africa. In this context, despite being put on the back foot by the Inanda violence, the NIC's opposition to federalism and the IFP was a courageous stance whose vindication was to come at CODESA.

At the level of mass mobilisation, contradictory impulses ate away at the NIC's gains in the aftermath of the anti-tricam mobilisation. NIC members who had shared the struggle trenches found themselves in conflicts where lines between the personal and the political were blurred. Letters between Mewa Ramgobin and Ela Gandhi, as well as contemporary newspaper reports, laid bare this low-intensity warfare. Some leading NIC/ UDF cadres were forced to operate under extremely repressive conditions, as Billy Nair's story shows. Innovative and courageous leaders, including Pravin Gordhan, set up the ANC underground. At the same time, members of the older generation felt alienated and marginalised, and some, like M.J. Naidoo, were forced off the political stage.

Younger activists, offering new energy and initiative within the Congress tradition, felt hemmed in and forced to follow a line of march that was handed down from on high. Pregs Govender recounted that efforts to set up a youth forum were destroyed by 'a handful of influential individuals linked to the cabal' who felt that 'their power base was being threatened'.[5] She also felt that she was a victim of 'destructive labels, whispering campaigns, social ostracism and lost reputations'.[6] Others could attest to similar experiences. The NIC spoke, it would appear, pierced not only those who worked the system but also those who sought to challenge the system beyond the confines of the NIC's gaze.

The narrative of cabal made public headlines in the second half of the 1980s, and there are several strands in this story. One came from within the NIC, with allegations that a small group of activists cohering around Pravin Gordhan and Yunus Mohamed sought to impose their authority on the organisation while marginalising the older leadership. As the ANC underground became more active and established links with exile luminaries, a tighter grouping with allegiances born of danger and secrecy emerged, and likely acted as a powerful group inside the NIC. There were also reports of a division between Roy Padayachie and Pravin Gordhan. That division may be due to personality differences, but it had an impact on the NIC, given Padayachie's location in Chatsworth, with the largest concentration of Indians in South Africa, and Gordhan's supposed influence in Phoenix through the Phoenix Working Committee. As a result, some younger NIC members and activists coming through the education boycotts chose sides, or they simply went their own way and built organisations such as Helping Hands.

Another strand in this narrative is the allegation that an Indian-dominated cabal was a controlling force in the UDF. Here Raymond

Suttner makes an important point: the ANC's focus 'on national liberation ... meant assembling people and forces from a range of sectors and communities', leading to 'a cross-class and cross-community alliance'.[7] Given their resources and easier access to cross-border travel, those of Indian origin had set up lines of communication with different groupings in the ANC. There was certainly a grouping around Mewa Ramgobin with links to African comrades in the RMC, and another around Pravin Gordhan, Mac Maharaj and their associates in the ANC underground and in exile. Pregs Govender contended there was a tendency for some younger members in the underground, flush with power and cash, to use their positions to 'persuade' others to submit to their authority.

'Underground' lines of communication came in handy when a position or action had to be pushed within the internal resistance when it was not yet aligned in any coordinated way with the exiled liberation movement. But this modus operandi was not all-pervasive: debates were won as often as they were lost, and a cabal could not always control impulses from below.

Towards ANC hegemony

Attacks on the spectre of an all-controlling cabal heightened as the ANC worked to build hegemony after 1990, with the need to turn the organisation into a disciplined machine with lines of authority becoming paramount. This was a turbulent period. Internal factions were linking up with exile forces and newly released Robben Islanders; the jostling for positions within the ANC was unfolding; negotiations were on a knife-edge; the 'third force' was baiting violence; and political alliances were constantly shifting. Fatima Meer criticised what she saw as the 'new political elite' in a 1992 interview with Padraig O'Malley:

> What is really happening is that it is the exiles and the important, VIP prisoners, who are constituting the political elite, and they haven't gone around taking sufficient cognisance of all the political formations that have developed over the years and that have become involved in the whole liberation process. The political elite that has cropped up has not cropped up through some sort of democratic process.[8]

Following Fatima Meer's line of thinking, the unbanning of the ANC and the release of political prisoners meant that the ANC expected to assume leadership and was ready to do battle with any who challenged it. Given the unwieldy nature of the internal forces, the ANC's rise to dominance was a remarkable achievement. It was made possible by the underground operatives who had built ANC influence internally and by the armed struggle, whatever its limitations. According to O'Malley, writing from the perspective of Vula operative Ivan Pillay:

> Perhaps, when the real history of the period is written, Vula's greatest contribution will be seen to have been its contribution to the ease with which the ANC returned from exile and simply appropriated the machinery of the mass movements. It could do so because Vula had done its homework.[9]

There were contestations for power all over the country, and the charge of cabal was undoubtedly used to settle old political scores. To successfully label one's enemies as 'cabalists' was to marginalise them, as the 'Letter from Robben Island' (discussed in Chapter 15) shows. Ironically, those who laid accusations of cabal often operated in a similar way themselves: building relationships with those in exile, seeking to put their candidates forward in interim structures, and smearing old adversaries so as to sideline them and move up the pecking order.

The women and men who cut their political teeth in the NIC, braved the underground, built non-racial networks, and used their class and race privilege to provide support to the internal forces of liberation might have earned criticism for their secrecy, or for their tendency to be scathing of different ways of seeing and organising. But such reproval does not detract from their courage and commitment. Despite internal divisions, many in the NIC made enormous sacrifices and their legacy cannot be wished away through the slur of the cabal. Jerry Coovadia, for one, was adamant:

> I think you should prune the NIC of all those views of being a so-called Indian organisation, a cabal, and go to the essence of what the NIC did. It stood for solid values. It stood for a socialism which may not have been articulated in detail, but at least made that possible. It influenced

COLOUR, CLASS AND COMMUNITY

many of us who would have just gone to waste in our professions, to get involved [in the anti-apartheid struggle] ... Now, to ignore all that [the NIC achieved] just because the BC doesn't like it, or the Black guys felt that we were a cabal, is totally unfair because the NIC made a contribution and that contribution has to be acknowledged. It was not an insignificant contribution.[10]

Those who led the revived NIC pioneered a remarkable journey of resistance to apartheid in the quest for majority rule. In the endgame of negotiations, the Indian Congresses took their place alongside their old ally, the ANC. It was hard to distinguish between the two, as their representatives swapped chairs, reached agreements in caucuses and stood unwavering in their commitment to a non-racial democratic South Africa. Being at the negotiating table alongside and oftentimes within the ANC's decision-making apparatus was a vindication of many activists' life's work.

CODESA consumed many of the NIC activists. But they had one more task: to ensure that Indians voted for the ANC. The 1994 elections brought to the fore the challenges faced by NIC ideologues and activists. They were in the engine room of the ANC developing policy and lobbying for leadership positions while simultaneously trying to create the conditions and language to carry the Indian vote. In these efforts NIC cadres were often overstretched, especially during the 1980s, when they were building the UDF and working underground for the ANC while keeping the NIC alive. The migration of key activists to build ANC branches was often at the expense of carrying a community that needed assurance. Many Indians, not sure which road to take, were swing voters. In the final analysis the NIC did not carry the community with them.

The NIC had led the charge against attempts at co-option by the apartheid government. The Group Areas that the system imposed had allowed the NIC to run tight campaigns and make those who chose to participate feel the heat of labels like 'collaborator', 'puppet' and 'sell-out'. Yet the success of the boycott campaigns did not translate into an embrace of the ANC. Some saw the NIC's failure to carry the Indian community as a rejection of the organisation itself, but this judgement is too harsh and does not take cognisance of the conjunctural politics at play. The end of apartheid came with surprising speed. In the final days the region teetered on the brink as the IFP threatened to pull out of the elections. The ANC in Natal was itself undermining the work of the NIC, while many of the NIC's most innovative thinkers were caught up in the ANC's electoral machine. Many forces were sowing suspicion and conspiring to vie for votes. The NIC was caught in the crossfire of building the ANC while trying to reassure an uneasy minority, and for once it could not find the language and where-withal to attract a sizeable constituency.

After bitter contestations through the 1970s and 1980s over the need to employ different strategies to mobilise Indians, with the insistence that cognisance be taken of the differential incorporation of racial groups into the body politic, the debate about the future of the NIC was surprisingly muted. Perhaps part of the reason for this lay in the NIC discussion document of March 1995, which laid out the seemingly impossible conundrum facing the organisation:

> In the past it was accepted as part of the national democratic tradition for Indians to be mobilized specifically through the NIC and for their specific interests to be linked thereby with the general interests of all the oppressed. This too was an aspect of the ANC's non-racialism. Given present conditions, the crucial question is: will such specific mobilization enhance or undermine nation-building?[11]

There was no ready answer, but it was a question which would recur.

In many ways, however, there could be no turning back to the NIC. Mac Maharaj, Ahmed Kathrada and Pravin Gordhan, having fought so hard to open the ANC to all racial groups, could not retreat once more into the NIC. The ANC recognised that the 'national question' was still to be resolved, and in the build-up to elections there had been the sponsoring of structures like the IWC (a forum for Indians, whites and coloureds) that would focus on these groups and speak to their fears and desires. But beyond the fuzzy notion of 'rainbowism' and 'unity in diversity', there was little debate and introspection around a broader South Africanism.

From the time of its revival, the NIC provided a political home for many young activists, as well as a base from which to move into community politics and, for some, into the armed struggle. Its leading cadres played a crucial role in the formation of the non-racial UDF, and in the

UDF's evolution into a powerful national movement that challenged white Nationalists' attempts to further divide the oppressed classes. This in turn generated ongoing rebellion, thus forcing the state to rule through emergency measures. Many NIC activists became key figures in the ANC.

Past present

There was always tension surrounding the ANC policy of non-racialism, on the one hand, and a multiracial political organisation with an insistence on African leadership, on the other. In the 1950s the ANC's multiracialism came under attack from an Africanist lobby. But through the 1960s, 1970s and 1980s the ANC, hesitantly at first, but then with greater conviction, challenged its own racial exclusions, no doubt spurred by developments inside South Africa in which anti-apartheid resistance raised the banner of non-racialism. As Anthony Marx put it, the UDF

> preferred to err on the side of inclusion and tried to avoid alienating potential white supporters by referring to its enemy as an impersonal 'system' of oppression ... The Front also rejected ties based on ethnic nationalism, reinforced by the state, as well as Africanist conceptions of 'orthodox' nationalism that included only indigenous people with a historical claim to the land. Consistent with more general theories of nationalism, such as that formulated by Benedict Anderson, the UDF conceived of the South African nation as a self-defined 'imagined community,' united by the experience of 'simultaneous existence,' shared ideas, and a sense of historical destiny. In a sense, this concept of nation was a catchall form of identity, claiming to represent common interests, rather than the interests of more exclusive identities.[12]

As the NIC discussion document on the future of the organisation underscored, the ANC had yet to confront the challenge of reconciling non-racialism with other identities:

> At one level the ANC is utterly remarkable for its non-racialism. It will be very difficult to find a parallel for the ANC anywhere in the world. At another level, sitting somewhat uneasily with this

non-racialism are ethnic, regional, racial, gender, and other identities. These identities do not find easy or open expression within the ANC. The ANC will, however, at some appropriate time have to confront these identities and reconcile them with its non-racialism. The ANC's present non-racialism is somewhat abstract; and coming to terms with these other identities will provide a more materialistic foundation for its non-racialism ... Struggles over the meaning and content of non-racialism will continue. There needs to be much more open debate within the ANC about ethnicity, race, non-racialism, and nation-building, and there is a need for appropriate strategies to be developed in this regard.[13]

A cameo of these challenges played out when Mac Maharaj wanted to appoint Ketso Gordhan as director general of transport. He informed Nelson Mandela of his intentions, as Mandela 'was conscious that I'm of Indian origin and I was appointing a person of Indian origin, although one with an impeccable record in the ANC'.[14] Mandela supported him, but Maharaj recounted:

> Months later I got wind of murmurings among many of the ANC comrades. I think it was in ... a black magazine ... that ministers were appointing people from similar race groups, and in particular they made a remark about me ... and then – surprise, surprise – I learned from Madiba one day during a casual chat that one of the veterans of the ANC who was in parliament and on the Transport Committee had gone to Madiba to complain about the appointment of Ketso. So the matter stayed on the public agenda.[15]

It is revealing that in spite of all the talk of non-racialism, Maharaj had to walk on eggshells. Of course, he could rely on Mandela's social and political capital. Those without access to those resources felt the sting of marginalisation because of race and, unlike Maharaj, had nowhere to turn. The NIC might have collapsed into the ANC, but the wheel still bore the imprint of its racial spokes.

Marked by increasing economic disparities, poor service delivery, unemployment and corruption, the political terrain has shifted dramatically since Maharaj's exchange with Mandela and the NIC's discussion document. But the changing reality only serves to reinforce and make more urgent the issues that were raised. Such disparities provide fertile ground for authoritarian populists to stoke the racial fires of hate. Yunus Carrim, for example, spoke of the situation in KwaZulu-Natal in the context of:

> the emerging hostility of African people, partly because of the EFF, partly because of the failure to reduce inequalities and create more spaces where we all interact ... So we have this social explosion remaining in this province. Nobody is doing enough to bridge the gap and as we fail to deliver on economic growth, job creation, reducing inequality ... if you don't reduce the gap between Indians and Africans, we are in big trouble here ... All over the world you are getting the same sense of belonging, of identity, of who belongs and who doesn't, our country is not escaping it.[16]

In many contexts, middleman minorities have become scapegoats par excellence and a lightning rod for violence as they are placed in the role of 'economic villain'. For 'victims of adversity it is at least some comfort to explain their misfortune by attributing it to evil machinations of villains rather than as a consequence of remote, complex and hardly comprehensible forces'.[17]

Over the past decade the EFF has emerged as a strong voice in South African politics. The party's muscular, aggressive African nationalism is increasingly prone to using the language of indigenous Africans as 'the people', the antithesis of the 'broad nationalism' that Albert Luthuli preached and more like the 'extreme nationalism' he warned against.[18] The ANC position, which 'recognises indigenous Africans as the most oppressed and exploited members of society, and places special emphasis on African leadership, as well as prioritising the conditions of African people',[19] lends itself to being tugged towards the orientation of the EFF.

In an environment where the ANC government has failed to live up to expectations in terms of delivery to the poorest, this African chauvinism has struck a chord. A language of anger is becoming normalised in the body politic. Indians have come under particular attack as exploiters and anti-African racists. Alongside this, at a time of failed promises and economic stagnation as well as mounting exposés of corruption, the big man as saviour, coupled with an authoritarian populism, is on the rise globally. As Francis Fukuyama explains, in the search for better lives many are 'seduced by leaders who tell them that they have been betrayed and disrespected by the existing power structures ... New parties are firmly rooted in identity issues.'[20]

Julius Malema is a leader in this vein, despite allegations of prominent EFF members living corrupt lifestyles and siphoning money from the poor into their own pockets. His power will likely grow if he is able to tap into a strong Africanist lobby that is increasingly becoming mainstream in the ANC as well. Jesse Duarte, lifelong ANC member and its deputy secretary general at the time of writing, delivered the 2019 Albertina Sisulu Memorial Lecture in Soweto, where she levelled severe criticism at the ANC, her party, the governing party:

> We have almost become tribalists in the way we present ourselves. We are racist in the ANC because we marginalise people who are not black African people; keep them out of the ANC at all costs. We won't accept the fact that non-racialism is a core value of the ANC. We don't want to accept that.[21]

Duarte accused ANC members of speaking without first-hand information about poorer coloureds (and Indians). African members of the ANC did not even visit coloured communities, but on ANC WhatsApp groups, young Africans 'talk about amak*** and amab****** (racial slurs for Indian and Coloured people)'.[22]

The Jacob Zuma presidency, from 2009 to 2018, was to prove the most debilitating of the ANC years in power, as Zuma allegedly joined with the Gupta family in looting state resources. Ironically, despite the Guptas' hailing from India, the racist rhetoric of the Africanist lobby in the ANC intensified as they found a champion in Zuma. The removal of the corrupt Zuma in 2018 engendered new optimism in the body politic as a whole. President Cyril Ramaphosa promised to return the ANC to its path of redressing the legacy of the past while keeping the flame of non-racialism burning.

Ramaphosa's 2019 national election victory allowed him to consolidate his dominance in the ANC, but this has been under constant counter-attack from still influential remnants of Zuma's people, who seek to undermine him by fighting rearguard battles inside the party.

The announcement of the State Capture Commission of Inquiry forced those who acted with impunity during the Zuma presidency to account before it and face the possibility of prosecution. The National Prosecuting Authority (NPA) and the South African Revenue Service (SARS) have had some capacity restored. Investigative journalism, so critical during the Zuma years, has continued to expose corruption.

What is less clear is whether Ramaphosa's holding pattern while pushing back the proponents of state capture signals a deeper and more fundamental shift, especially at the level of the economy. In this context it is difficult to discern what the impact of Covid-19 will have on contending social forces, as the harsh lockdown imposed in March 2020 has had a devastating effect on the economy and exposed the graft that lies at the heart of the ANC.

Given the ANC's seeming inability – some might say unwillingness – to move beyond celebrating liberation as a 'fancy dress parade and the blare of trumpets' accompanied by a few 'reforms from the top',[23] the promise of a 'better life for all' and an abiding non-racialism appears a pipe dream.

Some would argue that there is little likelihood of 'creating identities that are broader and more integrative'.[24] But so it appeared in the early 1970s, when the apartheid state was at its height of draconian authoritarianism and a small group of men and women at the Phoenix Settlement revived the NIC. Rather than letting the course of history determine their futures, they chose to make their own history, as part of a struggle to free all the peoples of South Africa.

The NIC was an anti-apartheid voice that not only fought and won significant battles against the co-option attempts of the apartheid regime but also kept the ideals of the ANC alive in the public domain. The NIC's endorsement of the Freedom Charter and a non-racial inclusive nationalism spoke to people beyond the confines of its own ethnic base as it made a fundamental contribution to the UDF and the ANC underground and armed struggle. At a time when racial discrimination was ripping South Africa apart, and violence and repression were stalking the land, people were asked to step up to fight. The cadres of the NIC, whatever their shortcomings, enlisted and fought with courage and tenacity. Thus the NIC rightly takes its place in the pantheon of anti-apartheid fighters.

History will not be as kind to the present generation if they turn their backs on the ideals that powered the imagination and actions of people who came before them. While today's activists must find new ways of organising, new languages and new targets of dissent, and be critical of roads travelled, the memories and lessons of what went before are vital in formulating strategies and maintaining resolve.

It is hoped that, in laying bare this history, this book will contribute to that process.

Introduction

1 Gregory Houston et al., *The Other Side of Freedom: Stories of Hope and Loss in the South African Liberation Struggle 1950–1994* (Cape Town: HSRC Press, 2017), 45.

2 Kesaveloo Goonam interviewed by Goolam Vahed, 31 May 1989.

3 See Mamphele Ramphele, *A Life* (Cape Town: David Philip, 1995); Daniel R. Magaziner, *Law and the Prophets: Consciousness in South Africa, 1968–1977* (Athens: Ohio University Press, 2010); and Ian MacQueen, *Consciousness and Progressive Movements under Apartheid* (Pietermaritzburg: University of KwaZulu-Natal Press, 2018).

4 Denis MacShane, Martin Plaut and David Ward, *Power! Black Workers, Their Unions and the Struggle for Freedom in South Africa* (Boston: South End Press, 1984).

5 Tony Morphet, 'Brushing History against the Grain: Oppositional Discourse in South Africa', *Theoria* 76 (October 1990): 89–99.

6 Ramphele, *A Life*, 43.

7 Houston et al., *Other Side of Freedom*, 42.

8 Houston et al., *Other Side of Freedom*, 42.

9 Hoosen (Jerry) Coovadia interviewed by Goolam Vahed, 5 December 2019.

10 Julie Frederikse, *The Unbreakable Thread: Non-racialism in South Africa* (Johannesburg: Ravan Press, 1990).

11 Quoted in David Everatt, *The Origins of Non-racialism: White Opposition to Apartheid in the 1950s* (Johannesburg: Wits University Press, 2009), 2.

12 Ahmed Kathrada, *Memoirs* (Cape Town: Zebra Press, 2004), 292.

13 Tom Lodge, *Black Politics in South Africa since 1945* (Longman: London, 1983), 301.

14 Nhlanhla Ndebele and Noor Nieftagodien, 'The Morogoro Conference: A Moment of Self-reflection', in *The Road to Democracy in South Africa: Volume 1, 1960–1970*, edited by B. Magubane, 573–599 (Cape Town: Zebra Press, 2004), 599.

15 The ANC had adopted the 'four nations' thesis, which resonates into the present with debates over the unresolved national question.

16 Pippa Green, *Choice, Not Fate: The Life and Times of Trevor Manuel* (Johannesburg: Penguin Books, 2008), 138.

17 Daniel Friedman, 'Malema Says He's Not Racist, Brings Up Gordhan's "Indian Cabal"', *Citizen*, 16 July 2018, https://citizen.co.za/news/south-africa/1979906/malema-says-hes-not-racist-brings-up-gordhans-indian-cabal/ (accessed 20 August 2019).

18 See, in particular, Ashwin Desai and Goolam Vahed, 'The Natal Indian Congress, the Mass Democratic Movement and the Struggle to Defeat Apartheid: 1980–1994', *Politikon* 42(1) (2015): 1–22; Goolam Vahed and Ashwin Desai, 'An Instance of "Strategic Ethnicity"? The Natal Indian Congress in the 1970s', *African Historical Review* 46(1) (2014): 22–47; Ashwin Desai, 'Indian South Africans and the Black Consciousness Movement under Apartheid', *Diaspora Studies* 8(1) (2015): 37–50; and Goolam Vahed, 'Chota Motala: The Making of a South African Political Biography', *Politikon* 4(2) (2019): 175–191.

19 See Ashwin Desai and Goolam Vahed, *Monty Naicker: Between Reason and Treason* (Pietermaritzburg: Shuter and Shooter, 2010); Goolam Vahed, *Muslim Portraits: The Anti-apartheid Struggle* (Durban: Madiba Publishers, 2012); and Goolam Vahed, *Chota Motala: A Biography of Political Activism in the KwaZulu-Natal Midlands* (Pietermaritzburg: University of KwaZulu-Natal Press, 2018).

20 Uma Dhupelia-Mesthrie, 'The Revival of the Natal Indian Congress', in *The Road to Democracy in South Africa: Volume 2, 1970–1980*, South African Democracy Education Trust, 883–904 (Pretoria: UNISA Press, 2006).

21 Notable here are Mewa Ramgobin's papers in Iain Edwards, *Faith and Courage: The Political Papers of Mewa Ramgobin* (Johannesburg: Iain Edwards (digitally published), 2015), and the compilation of Fatima Meer's key writings in Shireen Hassim, *Fatima Meer: A Free Mind* (Cape Town: HSRC Press, 2019). Given the value of the Ramgobin papers, we hope that other activists of the time will also place their collections in the public domain.

22 E.P. Thompson, *The Poverty of Theory* (London: Merlin Press, 1995), 38.

23 Alessandro Portelli, 'What Makes Oral History Different?', in *The Oral History Reader*, edited by Robert Perks and Alistair Thomson, 63–74 (London: Routledge, 1998), 69 (emphasis in original).

Chapter 1   Repression, Revelation and Resurrection

1 'Voices of Resistance' Collection, Gandhi-Luthuli Documentation Centre, University of KwaZulu-Natal, Westville (hereafter VOR), Eli Gandhi interviewed by Vino Reddy, 18 May 2002.

2 Elinor Sisulu, *Walter and Albertina Sisulu: In Our Lifetime* (Cape Town: David Philip, 2006), 120–121.

3 Nelson Mandela, *The Long Walk to Freedom* (Randburg: Macdonald Purnell, 1994), 115.

4 Mandela, *Long Walk*, 115.

5 Saul Dubow, *Apartheid, 1948–1994* (Oxford: Oxford University Press, 2014), 76–77.

6 *Natal Witness*, 1 April 1960.

7 *Natal Witness*, 7 March 1961.

8 Dubow, *Apartheid*, 87–89.

9 David Welsh, *The Rise and Fall of Apartheid* (Charlottesville: University of Virginia Press, 2010), 127.

10 Houston et al., *Other Side of Freedom*, 92.

11 For the Transvaal, see Rashid Seedat and Razia Saleh, eds, *Men of Dynamite: Pen Portraits of MK Pioneers* (Johannesburg: Shereno Printers, 2009); for Natal, see Desai and Vahed, *Monty Naicker*.

12 Mandela, *Long Walk*, 285.

13 Dubow, *Apartheid*, 131.

14 Duncan Innes, *Anglo American and the Rise of Modern South Africa* (New York: Monthly Review Press, 1984), 173.

15 Robert Davies, *Capital, State and White Labour in South Africa, 1900–1960: An Historical Materialist Analysis of Class Formation and Class Relations* (Atlantic Highlands, NJ: Humanities Press, 1979), 350.

16 Anne Kelk Mager and Maanda Mulaudzi, 'Popular Responses to Apartheid', in *The Cambridge History of South Africa: Volume 2, 1885–1994,* edited by Robert Ross, Anne Kelk Mager and Bill Nasson, 389–395 (Cambridge: Cambridge University Press, 2011).

17 Vahed and Desai, 'An Instance of "Strategic Ethnicity"?', 26.

18 J.J.C. Greyling, 'Employment Opportunities for University Trained Indians', Institute for Social and Economic Research 4, University of Durban-Westville, Durban, 1977, 36.

19 Department of Indian Affairs (DIA), Report, 3 August 1961.

20 H.A. Prinsloo, 'Road to Self-development: A Survey of the Function of the Department of Indian Affairs', *Fiat Lux* 1(1) (May 1966): 22–23.

21 *Daily News* 3 August 1961.

22 Prinsloo, 'Road to Self-development', 23.

23 Muriel Horrell, ed., *A Survey of Race Relations in South Africa: 1962* (Johannesburg: South African Institute of Race Relations, 1963), 202.

24 Surendra Bhana and Bridglal Pachai, eds, *A Documentary History of Indian South Africans* (Cape Town: David Philip, 1984), 252.

25 Goolam Vahed and Thembisa Waetjen, *Schooling Muslims in Natal: State, Identity and the Orient Islamic Educational Institute* (Pietermaritzburg: University of KwaZulu-Natal Press, 2015), 267.

26 *Fiat Lux*, August 1966, 71.

27 South African Indian Council (SAIC), Minutes, 1963–1983: 4/15 October 1971. A copy of the Minutes was provided to Ashwin Desai by Amichand Rajbansi when Desai was doing his doctoral research *c.* 1990.

28 *Leader*, 26 September 1969.

29 VOR, Mewa Ramgobin interviewed by Christian de Vos, 19 May 2002.

30 Edwards, *Faith and Courage*, 65.

31 *Leader*, 3 October 1969.

32 *Daily News*, 3 October 1969.

33 *Leader*, 3 October 1969.

34 VOR, Mewa Ramgobin interviewed by Christian de Vos, 19 May 2002.

35 VOR, Mewa Ramgobin interviewed by Christian de Vos, 19 May 2002.

36 *Graphic*, 26 March 1971.

37 VOR, Mewa Ramgobin interviewed by Christian de Vos, 19 May 2002.

38 They included George Sewpersadh, Dilly Naidoo, Ela Gandhi, S.P. Pachy, B.D. Maharaj, Ramlall Ramesar, D. Bundoo, M.R. Moodley, N.N. Naicker and Billy Reddy.

39 Dhupelia-Mesthrie, 'Revival of the Natal Indian Congress', 887.

40 Quoted in Edwards, *Faith and Courage*, 206.

41 VOR, Dilly Naidoo interviewed by D. Shongwe, 23 July 2002.

42 Hoosen (Jerry) Coovadia, e-mail correspondence with Goolam Vahed, 21 January 2013.

43 Surendra Bhana, *Gandhi's Legacy: The Natal Indian Congress 1894–1994* (Pietermaritzburg: University of KwaZulu-Natal Press, 1997), 34.

44 Dhupelia-Mesthrie, 'Revival of the Natal Indian Congress', 886.

45 Dhupelia-Mesthrie, 'Revival of the Natal Indian Congress', 887.

46 Bhana, *Gandhi's Legacy*, 117.

47 Thumba Pillay, e-mail correspondence with Goolam Vahed, 23 January 2013.

48 Yunus Carrim interviewed by Goolam Vahed, 5 October 2019.

49 Hoosen (Jerry) Coovadia interviewed by Goolam Vahed, 5 December 2019.

50 *Graphic*, 30 July 1971.

Chapter 2 Black Consciousness and the Challenge to the 'I' in the NIC

1 See Gail M. Gerhart, *Black Power in South Africa: The Evolution of an Ideology* (Berkeley: University of California Press, 1978), 45–83 for a discussion of Lembede and 173–204 for Sobukwe.

2 Steve Biko, *I Write What I Like*, 40th anniversary edition (Johannesburg: Picador Africa, 2017), 52.

3 VOR, Saths Cooper interviewed by Musa Ntsodi, 14 April 2003.

4 VOR, Strini Moodley interviewed by D. Shongwe, 24 July 2002.

5 Biko, *I Write What I Like*, 40.

6 VOR, Strini Moodley interviewed by D. Shongwe, 24 July 2002.

7 Ramphele, *A Life*, 60.

8 Hoosen (Jerry) Coovadia, e-mail correspondence with Goolam Vahed, 22 January 2013.

9 Julie Frederikse Collection, AL246, South African History Archives (hereafter JF), Mewa Ramgobin, interview, 1986, A18.4.

10 Gail Gerhart Collection, Historical Papers Research Archive, University of the Witwatersrand (hereafter GG), Mewa Ramgobin interviewed by Gail Gerhart, 12 July 1989.

11 GG, Mewa Ramgobin interviewed by Gail Gerhart, 12 July 1989.

12 Ratnamala Singh and Shahid Vawda, 'What's in a Name? Some Reflections on the NIC', *Transformation* 6 (1987): 1–21.

13 JF, Pravin Gordhan, interview, 1986, A07.07.

14 Jason Hickel, *Democracy as Death: The Moral Order of Anti-liberal Politics in South Africa* (Oakland: University of California Press, 2015), 209.

15 African National Congress (ANC), 'Strategy and Tactics of the ANC', document adopted by the Morogoro Conference of the ANC, Morogoro, Tanzania,

25 April – 1 May 1969, https://www.marxists.org/subject/africa/anc/1969/strategy-tactics.htm (accessed 26 September 2019).

16 Zarina Maharaj, *Dancing to a Different Rhythm* (Cape Town: Zebra Press, 2006), 150.

17 Paul David interviewed by Goolam Vahed, 20 January 2017.

18 C. Sewpersadh, 'Natal Indian Congress – The Significance of Its Revival', *Reality* (May 1972): 12–13, 13.

19 JF, Mewa Ramgobin, interview, 1986, A18.4.

20 JF, M.D. Naidoo, interview, 1986, A14.02.

21 VOR, Daya Pillay interviewed by Musa Ntsodi, 16 October 2002.

22 Hoosen (Jerry) Coovadia, e-mail correspondence with Goolam Vahed, 22 January 2013.

23 Houston et al., *Other Side of Freedom*, 75.

24 Houston et al., *Other Side of Freedom*, 74.

25 Biko, *I Write What I Like*, 94.

26 *Graphic*, 4 February 1972.

27 Ben A. Khoape, ed., *Black Review 1972* (Durban: Black Community Programmes, 1973), 7.

28 Davinder S. Dhillon, 'The Indians of Natal: Resistance to Apartheid, 1970–1985', BA (Hons.) thesis, National University of Singapore, 1999, 45.

29 Khoape, *Black Review 1972*, 7.

30 *Graphic*, 14 January 1972.

31 Houston et al., *Other Side of Freedom*, 74–75.

32 Dhupelia-Mesthrie, 'Revival of the Natal Indian Congress', 888.

33 Khoape, *Black Review 1972*, 4.

34 *Natal Mercury*, 23 July 1973.

35 *Natal Mercury*, 23 July 1973.

36 Bhana, *Gandhi's Legacy*, 119.

37 *Daily News*, 21 July 1973.

38 *Daily News*, 23 September 1974.

39 Thabo Mbanjwa, ed., *Black Review 1974/75* (Durban: Black Community Programmes, 1975), 116.

40 Mbanjwa, *Black Review 1974/75*, 116.

41 *Graphic*, 24 November 1978.

42 Ela Gandhi, e-mail correspondence with Goolam Vahed, 24 January 2013.

43 *Graphic*, 19 January 1979.

44 Houston et al., *Other Side of Freedom*, 75.

Chapter 3 Between Principle and Pragmatism

1 *Leader*, 6 August 1971.

2 Nigel Gibson, 'Why Is Participation a Dirty Word in South African Politics?', *Africa Today* 37(2) (1990): 23–52, 41.

3 Gibson, 'Why Is Participation a Dirty Word', 47.

4 Neville Alexander, 'Aspects of Non-collaboration in the Western Cape, 1943–1963', *Social Dynamics* 12(1) (1986): 1–14, 4.

5   Nelson Mandela, 'Our Struggle Needs Many Tactics', *Liberation: A Journal of Democratic Discussion* (February 1958): 14–17, 15–16. https://www.sahistory. org.za/sites/default/files/DC/Lin2958.1729.455X.000.029.Feb1958.5/ Lin2958.1729.455X.000.029.Feb1958.5.pdf (accessed 26 October 2019).

6   Nelson Mandela, 'Clear the Obstacles and Confront the Enemy: Whither the Black Consciousness Movement? An assessment', in *Reflections in Prison*, edited by Mac Maharaj, 7–21 (Cape Town: Zebra Press, 2001), 13.

7   Ahmed Kathrada, 'Indian South Africans – A Future Bound with the Cause of the African Majority', in *Reflections in Prison*, edited by Mac Maharaj, 97–124 (Cape Town: Zebra Press, 2001), 123.

8   Walter Sisulu, 'We Shall Overcome!', in *Reflections in Prison*, edited by Mac Maharaj, 71–90 (Cape Town: Zebra Press, 2001), 89.

9   Govan Mbeki, 'The Anatomy of the Problems of the National Liberation Struggle in South Africa', in *Reflections in Prison*, edited by Mac Maharaj, 131–146 (Cape Town: Zebra Press, 2001), 142.

10 Mbeki, 'Anatomy of the Problems', 145–146.

11 ANC, 'Strategy and Tactics'.

12 *Leader*, 5 May 1972.

13 Khoape, *Black Review 1972*, 7.

14 *Daily News*, 21 July 1973.

15 *Daily News*, 14 September 1974.

16 *Post*, 31 July 1974.

17 M.J. Naidoo, Presidential Address, NIC Conference, 20–22 September 1974. Document in possession of authors.

18 Padraig O'Malley Collection, Nelson Mandela Foundation (hereafter POM), Mahmoud Rajab, 25 July 1990. (This date appears to be an error, as Rajab quotes Mandela's biography in the interview, which was published in 1994.)

19 *Graphic*, 27 September 1974.

20 *Daily News*, 23 September 1974.

21 *Daily News*, 23 September 1974.

22 Hoosen (Jerry) Coovadia interviewed by Goolam Vahed, 5 December 2019.

23 *Leader*, 27 June 1975.

24 SAIC, Minutes of meeting, 26–28 November 1974.

25 SAIC, Minutes of meeting, 26–28 November 1974.

26 SAIC, Minutes of meeting, 26–28 November 1974.

27 SAIC, Minutes of meeting, 26–28 November 1974.

28 *Graphic*, 11 February 1972.

29 SAIC, Minutes of meeting, 26–28 November 1974.

30 SAIC, Minutes of meeting, 17–20 February 1976.

31 Cindy Postlethwayt, 'What If They Gave a Puppet Show and Nobody Came? The SAIC 1964–82', Honours thesis, Department of Economic History, University of Cape Town, 1982, 64.

32 Bhana and Pachai, *Documentary History*, 254–255.

33 Muriel Horrell, *A Survey of Race Relations in South Africa: 1977* (Johannesburg: South African Institute of Race Relations, 1978), 7.

34   *Leader*, 27 June 1975.
35   *Leader*, 12 March 1976.
36   *Leader*, 19 March 1976.
37   *Leader*, 19 March 1976.
38   *Leader*, 19 March 1976.
39   *Sunday Times Extra*, 28 March 1976.
40   *Leader*, 19 March 1976.
41   *Leader*, 26 August 1977.
42   *Leader*, 11 November 1977.
43   *Leader*, 2 December 1977.
44   M.J. Naidoo, 'My Case against SAIC Participation', NIC Collection, Gandhi-Luthuli Documentation Centre, University of KwaZulu-Natal, 1977/78.
45   M.J. Naidoo, 'My Case against SAIC Participation'.

Chapter 4   Changing Geographies and New Terrains of Struggle

1   *Graphic*, 8 September 1972.
2   *Graphic*, 15 September 1972.
3   *Graphic*, 15 September 1972.
4   *Daily News*, 22 September 1972.
5   *Graphic*, 29 September 1972.
6   *Leader*, 29 September 1972.
7   Yunus Carrim interviewed by Goolam Vahed, 5 October 2019.
8   *Post*, 22 October 1972.
9   *Natal Mercury*, 19 October 1972.
10   *Post*, 29 October 1972.
11   *Graphic*, 27 October 1972.
12   *Leader*, 2 February 1973.
13   *Leader*, 28 September 1973.
14   VOR, Yousuf Vawda interviewed by Musa Ntsodi, 8 October 2002.
15   VOR, Yousuf Vawda interviewed by Musa Ntsodi, 8 October 2002.
16   *Fiat Lux*, July 1976, 12–13.
17   *Fiat Lux*, July 1976, 12–13.
18   Filipe E. Maglaya's *Organizing People for Power: A Manual for Organizers*, first published in 1974, is based on the author's experiences in community organising in the Philippines. This text has been used widely as a manual for organising people and communities in many parts of the world. Drawing inspiration from Paolo Freire's *The Pedagogy of the Oppressed* and Saul Alinksy's *Rules for Radicals*, Maglaya emphasises people's empowerment at local levels. Various sections focus on the concept of oppressed and oppressor, characteristics of strong organisers, organisational structure, and the importance of organising people for power.
19   Paul David interviewed by Goolam Vahed, 20 January 2017.
20   Hoosen (Jerry) Coovadia interviewed by Goolam Vahed, 5 December 2019.
21   Detainees Oral History Project, South African History Archives, Collection No. AL293, SAHA (hereafter DOHP), Pravin Gordhan, 22 October 2002.

22 POM, Pravin Gordhan, 30 January 2003.
23 VOR, Yunus Mahomed [Mohamed] interviewed by Musa Ntsodi, 22 September 2002.
24 Daryl Glaser, 'South Africa and the Limits of Civil Society', *Journal of Southern African Studies* 23(1) (1997): 5–25, 7. See also Jeremy Seekings, 'Civic Organisations in South African Townships', *South African Review* 6 (1992): 216–238.
25 VOR, Yousuf Vawda interviewed by Musa Ntsodi, 8 October 2002.
26 Phoenix Working Committee (PWC) brochure, 2003, http://phoenixcommunitycentre.com/?page_id=17 (accessed 14 September 2019).
27 *Sunday Tribune*, 27 April 1980.
28 *Natal Mercury*, 18 May 1982.
29 VOR, Sharm Maharaj interviewed by Musa Ntsodi, 9 October 2002.
30 Roykumar (Roy) Sukuram interviewed by Goolam Vahed, 23 June 2018.
31 Roykumar (Roy) Sukuram interviewed by Goolam Vahed, 23 June 2018.
32 *Daily News*, 2 August 1976.
33 Roykumar (Roy) Sukuram interviewed by Goolam Vahed, 23 June 2018.
34 Houston et al., *Other Side of Freedom*, 57.
35 VOR, Charm Govender interviewed by D. Shongwe, 20 September 2002.
36 *Post*, 7 November 1979.
37 *Post*, 13 February 1980.
38 VOR, Charm Govender interviewed by D. Shongwe, 20 September 2002.
39 VOR, Maggie Govender interviewed by D. Shongwe, 13 September 2002.
40 *Natal Mercury*, 1 April 1980.
41 *Post*, 30 August 1980.
42 *Leader*, 26 December 1980.
43 JF, Pravin Gordhan, interview, 1986, A07.07.
44 Jeremy Seekings Collection, Alan Paton Centre, University of KwaZulu-Natal, Pietermaritzburg (hereafter JS), Khetso Gordhan, interview, 9 July 1992.
45 JF, Pravin Gordhan, interview, 1986, A07.07.
46 JF, Pravin Gordhan, interview, 1986, A07.07.
47 Jeremy Seekings, *The UDF: A History of the United Democratic Front in South Africa, 1983–1991* (Cape Town: David Philip, 2000), 77.
48 GG, Jerry Coovadia interviewed by Gail Gerhart and Steve Mufson, 2 June 1988.

Chapter 5 Class(rooms) of Dissent

1 Quoted in Hassim, *Fatima Meer*, 300.
2 GG, Mewa Ramgobin interviewed by Gail Gerhart, 12 July 1989.
3 Ismail (I.C.) Meer, *A Fortunate Man* (Cape Town: Zebra Press, 2002), 230.
4 Fatima Meer, *Prison Diary: One Hundred and Thirteen Days, 1976* (Cape Town: Kwela Books, 2001).
5 Vahed, 'Chota Motala', 175.
6 Vahed, 'Chota Motala', 175–178.
7 GG, Mewa Ramgobin interviewed by Gail Gerhart, 12 July 1989.

8 Desai and Vahed, 'Natal Indian Congress', 3.
9 JF, Alf Karrim, interview, 1986, A11.01.1.
10 Pregs Govender, *Love and Courage: A Story of Insubordination* (Johannesburg: Jacana, 2007), 56.
11 *Leader*, 26 December 1980.
12 VOR, George Sewpersadh interviewed by Mwelela Cele, 11 August 2002.
13 VOR, Yunus [Yunis] Shaik interviewed by D. Shongwe, 18 August 2002.
14 VOR, Sharm Maharaj interviewed by M. Ntsodi, 9 October 2002.
15 VOR, Charm Govender interviewed by D. Shongwe, 20 September 2002.
16 JF, Alf Karrim, interview, 1986, A11.01.1.
17 Martin Plaut, 'Changing Perspectives on South African Trade Unions', *Review of African Political Economy* 11(30) (1984): 116–123, 116.
18 Jerome T. Barrett and Anne Finbarr Mullins, 'South African Trade Unions: A Historical Account, 1970–90', *Monthly Labor Review* (October 1990): 25–31, 25.
19 Welsh, *Rise and Fall of Apartheid*, 318.
20 Barrett and Mullins, 'South African Trade Unions', 26.
21 Anthony Marx, *Lessons of Struggle: South African Internal Opposition, 1960–1990* (Oxford: Oxford University Press, 1992), 198.
22 VOR, Yunus [Yunis] Shaik interviewed by D. Shongwe, 18 August 2002.
23 Johnny Copelyn, *Maverick Insider: A Struggle for Union Independence in Time of National Liberation* (Johannesburg: Picador Africa, 2016), 187.
24 Copelyn, *Maverick Insider*, 187.
25 R.T. Bell, 'Growth and Structure of Manufacturing Employment in Natal', Report No. 7, Institute for Social and Economic Research, University of Durban-Westville, 1983, 54.
26 Bill Freund, *Insiders and Outsiders: The Indian Working Class of Durban 1910–1990* (London: James Currey, 1995), 90.
27 VOR, Kovin Naidoo interviewed by D. Shongwe, 5 September 2002.
28 Quoted in Raymond Suttner, *The ANC Underground in South Africa* (Johannesburg: Jacana, 2008), 67.

Chapter 6 Lenin and the Duma Come to Durban

1 Craig Charney, 'The Right to be Different', *Work in Progress* (July 1991): 24–27.
2 *Rand Daily Mail*, 2 June 1978.
3 SAIC, Minutes of meeting, 2–3 November 1978.
4 SAIC, Minutes of meeting, 2–3 November 1978.
5 SAIC, Minutes of meeting, 26–29 March 1979.
6 *Natal Mercury*, 28 March 1979.
7 *Natal Mercury*, 28 March 1979.
8 *Leader*, 4 May 1979.
9 *Graphic*, 8 June 1979.
10 *Leader*, 4 May 1979.
11 POM, Pravin Gordhan, 30 January 2003.
12 POM, Pravin Gordhan, 30 January 2003.

13 JS, Yunus Mahomed [Mohamed], interview, 9 July 1992.
14 Yunus Carrim interviewed by Goolam Vahed, 5 October 2019.
15 Thula Simpson, *Umkhonto we Sizwe: The ANC's Armed Struggle* (Cape Town: Penguin Random House, 2016), 33.
16 Pregs Govender, *Love and Courage.*
17 *Sunday Tribune*, 6 May 1979.
18 *Graphic*, 18 May 1979.
19 *Post*, 9–13 May 1979.
20 *Leader*, 11 May 1979.
21 *Sunday Times*, 20 May 1979.
22 *Leader*, 11 May 1979.
23 Padraig O'Malley, *Shades of Difference: Mac Maharaj and the Struggle for South Africa* (London: Penguin, 2007), 156.
24 African National Congress (ANC), 'The Green Book: Report of the Politico-Military Strategy Commission to the ANC National Executive Committee', August 1979, https://www.marxists.org/subject/africa/anc/1979/green-book.htm (accessed 20 September 2019).
25 ANC, 'The Green Book'.
26 POM, Mac Maharaj, 16 September 2003.
27 POM, Mac Maharaj, 16 September 2003.
28 POM, Mac Maharaj interviewed by Howard Barrell, 30 November 1990.
29 Yousuf Vawda, e-mail correspondence with Goolam Vahed, 22 January 2013.
30 Copy of letter from Yusuf Dadoo to Fatima Meer, 12 June 1979, in possession of Goolam Vahed.
31 Edwards, *Faith and Courage*, 86.
32 *Natal Mercury*, 3 September 1979.
33 *Graphic*, 14 September 1979.
34 *Natal Mercury*, 3 September 1979.
35 Houston et al., *Other Side of Freedom*, 76.
36 *Graphic*, October 1979.

Chapter 7 The Anti-SAIC Campaign of 1981

1 *Graphic*, 29 June 1979.
2 *Daily News*, 26 July 1979.
3 *Daily News*, 26 July 1979.
4 VOR, Kovin Naidoo interviewed by D. Shongwe, 5 September 2002.
5 VOR, Charm Govender interviewed by D. Shongwe, 20 September 2002.
6 Suttner, *ANC Underground*, 152–153.
7 DOHP, Pravin Gordhan, 22 October 2002.
8 *Natal Mercury*, 20 February 1981.
9 *Daily News*, 9 October 1981.
10 SAIC, Minutes, Vol. 5, 1981.
11 SAIC, Minutes, Vol. 5, 1981.

12 *Daily News*, 17 March 1980.

13 *Natal Witness*, 27 August 1981.

14 Quoted in Bhana and Pachai, *Documentary History*, 255.

15 *Natal Mercury*, 22 October 1981.

16 DOHP, Pravin Gordhan, 22 October 2002.

17 DOHP, Pravin Gordhan, 22 October 2002.

18 *Natal Witness*, 26 February 1982.

19 Ashwin Desai, 'The Origins, Development and Demise of the South African Indian Council 1964–1983: A Sociological Interpretation', MA dissertation, Rhodes University, 1987, 204.

20 Desai, 'Origins, Development and Demise', 207.

21 Quoted in Desai, 'Origins, Development and Demise', 215.

22 Desai, 'Origins, Development and Demise', 222.

23 *Post*, 16 June 1982.

24 Anthony Lemon, 'Issues and Campaigns in the South African General Election of 1981', *African Affairs* 81(325) (1982): 511–526, 519.

25 Loraine Gordon, ed., *A Survey of Race Relations in South Africa 1980* (Johannesburg: South African Institute of Race Relations, 1981), 77.

26 Newell M. Stultz, 'Interpreting Constitutional Change in South Africa', *Journal of Modern African Studies* 22(3) (1984): 353–379, 361.

27 Tony Weaver, 'The President's Council', in *South African Review 1*, edited and compiled by South African Research Service (Johannesburg: Ravan Press, 1983), 116.

28 Natal Indian Congress (NIC), 'The Congress Position on the New Constitutional Proposals', Bhana Collection, Gandhi-Luthuli Documentation Centre, University of KwaZulu-Natal, Accession No. 1256/49, 1983.

29 NIC, 'The Congress Position'.

30 NIC, 'The Congress Position'.

31 Quoted in Hassim, *Fatima Meer*, 301–303.

32 Phillip Selznik, *TVA and Grassroots: A Study in the Sociology of Formal Organisations*, second edition (Trieste: Trieste Publishing, 2018), 23.

33 SAIC, Minutes, 1983.

34 SAIC, Minutes, 1983.

35 SAIC, Minutes, 1983.

36 SAIC, Minutes, 1983.

37 Stultz, 'Interpreting Constitutional Change', 366.

38 It is not our intention here to discuss the differences between the NF and the UDF. Suffice to say that while the UDF sought a conciliation of classes through emphasising the Freedom Charter, the NF emphasised the need for working-class leadership of the liberation struggle and openly called for a socialist Azania.

39 Kagila Moodley, 'South African Indians: The Wavering Minority', in *Change in Contemporary South Africa*, edited by Leonard Thompson and Jeffrey Butler, 250–279 (Berkeley: University of California Press, 1975), 279.

Chapter 8 Botha's 1984 and the Rise of the UDF

1 Green, *Choice, Not Fate*, 175.
2 Green, *Choice, Not Fate*, 175.
3 POM, Pravin Gordhan, 30 January 2003.
4 GG, Jerry Coovadia interviewed by Gail Gerhart and Steve Mufson, 2 June 1988.
5 Hoosen (Jerry) Coovadia, e-mail correspondence with Goolam Vahed, 21 January 2013.
6 Liliesfield Trust (Johannesburg), M. Naidoo, 20 October 2016. Interview quote provided by Ismail Vadi.
7 Quoted in Anthony Sampson, *Mandela: The Authorised Biography* (London: Harper Collins, 1999), 330.
8 Zak Yacoob, 'The National Question in South Africa', speech presented at the General Meeting of the Transvaal Indian Congress, Ramakrishna Hall, 1 May 1983. Copy provided by Ismail Vadi.
9 *Sunday Tribune*, 3 July 1983.
10 GG, Mewa Ramgobin interviewed by Gail Gerhart, 12 July 1989.
11 VOR, Daya Pillay interviewed by Musa Ntsodi, 16 October 2002.
12 VOR, Sharm Maharaj interviewed by Musa Ntsodi, 9 October 2002.
13 *Leader*, 26 August 1983.
14 *Leader*, 26 August 1983.
15 GG, Mewa Ramgobin interviewed by Gail Gerhart, 12 July 1989.
16 VOR, Yunus Mahomed [Mohamed] interviewed by Musa Ntsodi, 22 September 2002.
17 VOR, Ela Gandhi interviewed by Vino Reddy, 18 May 2002.
18 VOR, Sharm Maharaj interviewed by Musa Ntsodi, 9 October 2002.
19 Jerry Coovadia, 'Change through Organisations of the People', in *Strategies for Change*, edited by Stephen Fourie, 43–50 (Cape Town: Institute for a Democratic Alternative for South Africa, 1989), 46–47.
20 POM, Pravin Gordhan, 30 January 2003.
21 GG, Mewa Ramgobin interviewed by Gail Gerhart, 12 July 1989.
22 GG, Mewa Ramgobin interviewed by Gail Gerhart, 12 July 1989.
23 Seekings, *The UDF*, 77–78.
24 GG, Jerry Coovadia interviewed by Gail Gerhart and Steve Mufson, 2 June 1988.
25 GG, Mewa Ramgobin interviewed by Gail Gerhart, 12 July 1989.
26 GG, Jerry Coovadia interviewed by Gail Gerhart and Steve Mufson, 2 June 1988.
27 VOR, Charm Govender interviewed by D. Shongwe, 20 September 2002.
28 Yunus Carrim interviewed by Goolam Vahed, 5 October 2019.
29 *Daily News*, 14 November 1983.
30 *Daily News*, 14 November 1983.
31 *City Press*, 20 November 1983.
32 *Daily Dispatch*, 15 November 1983.
33 Charles Nqakula, *The People's War: Reflections of an ANC Cadre* (Johannesburg: Mutloatse Heritage Trust, 2017), 118–119.
34 Seekings, *The UDF*, 97.

35 JS, Yunus Mahomed [Mohamed], interview, 9 July 1992.
36 JS, Yunus Mahomed [Mohamed], interview, 9 July 1992.
37 JS, Yunus Mahomed [Mohamed], interview, 9 July 1992.
38 GG, Mewa Ramgobin interviewed by Gail Gerhart, 12 July 1989.
39 M.J. Naidoo, speech presented at Krish Rabilal Memorial Meeting, 5 February 1984. Copy in possession of authors.
40 Seekings, *The UDF*, 98.
41 Vahed, *Chota Motala*, 234.
42 Roykumar (Roy) Sukuram interviewed by Goolam Vahed, 23 June 2018.
43 JF, Kumi Naidoo, interview, 1987, A14.04.1.
44 JF, Pravin Gordhan, interview, 1986, A07.07.
45 *South Coast Herald*, 10 August 1984.
46 JF, Fatima Meer, interview, 1986, A13.23.
47 Quoted in Edwards, *Faith and Courage*, 92.
48 JF, Fatima Meer, interview, 1986, A13.23.
49 Quoted in Edwards, *Faith and Courage*, 275.
50 Quoted in Desai and Vahed, *Monty Naicker*, 307.
51 GG, Mewa Ramgobin interviewed by Gail Gerhart, 12 July 1989.
52 Dennis Austin, 'The Trinitarians: The 1983 South African Constitution', *Government and Opposition*, 20(2) (1985): 185–195, 193.
53 Chris Alden, *Apartheid's Last Stand: The Rise and Fall of the South African Security State* (London: Macmillan Press, 1996), 141.
54 *Rand Daily Mail*, 30 August 1984.
55 *Rand Daily Mail*, 30 August 1984.
56 Austin, 'The Trinitarians', 194.
57 Welsh, *The Rise and Fall of Apartheid*, 209.
58 Lodge, *Black Politics in South Africa*, 341.
59 Hoosen (Jerry) Coovadia interviewed by Goolam Vahed, 5 December 2019.
60 Marx, *Lessons of Struggle*, 16.
61 Copelyn, *Maverick Insider*, 207.
62 Copelyn, *Maverick Insider*, 209.

Chapter 9 Letters from Near and Afar

1 *Citizen*, 1 November 1984.
2 Edwards, *Faith and Courage*, 18.
3 Paul David interviewed by Goolam Vahed, 20 January 2017.
4 Paul David interviewed by Goolam Vahed, 20 January 2017.
5 GG, Mewa Ramgobin interviewed by Gail Gerhart, 12 July 1989.
6 Paul David interviewed by Goolam Vahed, 20 January 2017.
7 VOR, Farouk Meer interviewed by Musa Ntsodi, 9 October 2002.
8 Edwards, *Faith and Courage*.
9 Iain Edwards, e-mail correspondence to Goolam Vahed, 4 November 2019.
10 Edwards, *Faith and Courage*, 110.
11 Edwards, *Faith and Courage*, 110.

12 Edwards, *Faith and Courage*, 111.
13 Edwards, *Faith and Courage*, 111–112.
14 Edwards, *Faith and Courage*, 112–113.
15 Edwards, *Faith and Courage*, 113–114.
16 Farouk Meer interviewed by Goolam Vahed, 12 May 2012.
17 Edwards, *Faith and Courage*, 117.
18 Edwards, *Faith and Courage*, 114–115.
19 Edwards, *Faith and Courage*, 141.
20 Edwards, *Faith and Courage*, 154.
21 Edwards, *Faith and Courage*, 116.
22 Edwards, *Faith and Courage*, 116.
23 Edwards, *Faith and Courage*, 169–170.
24 *Citizen*, 1 November 1984.
25 *Post*, 6 November 1984.
26 *Citizen*, 12 November 1984.
27 Edwards, *Faith and Courage*, 23.
28 Iain Edwards, e-mail correspondence to Goolam Vahed, 4 November 2019.
29 Margaret Thatcher, Letter from Margaret Thatcher to Robert Hughes, 29 October 1984, AAM Archive, Bodleian Library, MSS AAM 779, https://www.aamarchives.org/archive/campaigns/government/gov29-letter-from-margaret-thatcher-to-robert-hughes.html.
30 *Pretoria News*, 15 November 1984
31 *Natal Mercury*, 17 November 1984.
32 *Leader*, 21 December 1984.
33 Edwards, *Faith and Courage*, 18.
34 The 16 accused were Mewa Ramgobin, George Sewpersadh, M.J. Naidoo, Essop Jassat, Aubrey Mokoena, Curtis Nkondo, Archie Gumede, Paul David, Albertina Sisulu, Frank Chikane, Ebrahim Saloojee, Ismail Mohamed, Thozamile Richard Gqweta, Sisa Njikelana, Samuel Kikine and Isaac Ngcobo. The latter four were members of the South African Allied Workers' Union (SAAWU); the others were members of the UDF/NIC/TIC.
35 Patrick MacEntee, 'The "Treason" Trials at Pietermaritzburg and Delmas', United Nations Centre Against Apartheid, 1986, 4.
36 MacEntee, 'The "Treason" Trials', 5.
37 MacEntee, 'The "Treason" Trials'.

Chapter 10 Inanda, Inkatha and Insurrection

1 Dubow, *Apartheid*, 212.
2 Robert M. Price, *The Apartheid State in Crisis: Political Transformation of South Africa, 1975–1990* (Oxford: Oxford University Press, 1991), 191.
3 Fatima Meer, 'South Africa's Tomorrow', *Third World Quarterly* 9(2) (1987): 396–407, 402–403.
4 Christopher Merrett, 'Detention without Trial in South Africa: The Abuse of Human Rights as State Strategy in the Late 1980s', *Africa Today* 37(2) (1990): 53–66, 54.

5   VOR, Maggie Govender interviewed by D. Shongwe, 13 September 2002.

6   VOR, Maggie Govender interviewed by D. Shongwe, 13 September 2002.

7   A.S. Chetty, 'Memoirs', Alan Paton Centre and Struggle Archives, University of KwaZulu-Natal, Pietermaritzburg, PC 161/2/1/1/4.

8   Heather Hughes, 'Violence in Inanda, August 1985', *Journal of Southern African Studies* 13(3) (1987): 331–354.

9   *Daily News*, 14 August 1985.

10 Black Sash, 'The Durban Unrest', Paper presented at the Black Sash National Conference, March 1986, https://www.jstor.org/stable/10.2307/al.sff.document. cnf19860314.026.001.000 (accessed 22 October 2019), 2.

11 *Daily News*, 14 August 1985.

12 *Sunday Tribune*, 18 August 1985.

13 *Daily News*, 14 August 1985

14 *Fiat Lux*, September 1985, 2.

15 *Daily News*, 12 August 1985.

16 VOR, Sharm Maharaj interviewed by Musa Ntsodi, 9 October 2002.

17 Black Sash, 'Durban Unrest', 3.

18 VOR, Mewa Ramgobin interviewed by Christian de Vos, 19 May 2002.

19 C.K. Hill, 'Who Burnt the Mahatma Gandhi's Settlement at Inanda? A Final Report', Durban, 24 January 1986; available at the Gandhi-Luthuli Documentation Centre, University of KwaZulu-Natal, Accession No. 887/1.

20 Black Sash, 'Analysis of Conflict in Inanda', Paper presented at the Black Sash National Conference, March 1989, https://www.jstor.org/stable/10.2307/al.sff. document.cnf19890303.026.001.000b (accessed 22 October 2019), 6.

21 Hughes, 'Violence in Inanda', 331–332; see also Black Sash, 'Durban Unrest' and 'Analysis of Conflict'.

22 Fatima Meer, *Resistance in the Townships* (Durban: Madiba Publishers, 1989), 154.

23 Kumi Naidoo, 'Class, Consciousness and Organisation: Indian Political Resistance in Durban, South Africa, 1979–1996', PhD dissertation, Oxford University, 1997, chapter 4, https://www.sahistory.org.za/sites/default/files/archive_files/Class% 2C%20Consciousness%20and%20Organisation%20Indian%20Political %20Resistance%20in%20Durban%20South%20Africa%201979-1996%20by %20Kumi%20Naidoo.pdf (accessed 3 February 2021).

24 *Daily News*, 7 January 1988.

25 Richard Levin, 'Class Struggle, Popular Democratic Struggle and the South African State', *Review of African Political Economy* 14(40) (1987): 7–31, 28.

26 Ari Sitas, 'The Making of the "Comrades" Movement in Natal, 1985–91', *Journal of Southern African Studies* 18(3) (1992): 629–641, 631.

27 Fatima Meer, 'South Africa's Tomorrow', 403.

28 Douglas Booth, 'A Strange Divide: Townships on Contested Terrain', in *Political Conflict in South Africa: Data Trends 1984–1988*, edited by Mark Bennett and Deborah Quin, 73–80 (Cape Town: Indicator SA Focus, 1988), 74.

29 David Welsh, *The Buthelezi Commission* (Durban: H & H Publications, 1982).

30 *Natal Mercury*, 12 March 1982.

31 *Natal Mercury*, 12 March 1982.
32 Mewa Ramgobin, 'On Geopolitical Manoeuvres', in *New Frontiers: The KwaZulu/ Natal Debates*, edited by Karin Roberts and Graham Howe, 50–53 (Durban: Indicator Project, University of Natal, 1987), 53.
33 *Sunday Times*, 27 January 1980.
34 *Daily News*, 7 April 1988.
35 JF, Pravin Gordhan, interview, 1986, A0707.
36 Houston et al., *Other Side of Freedom*, 77.
37 Quoted in Welsh, *Rise and Fall of Apartheid*, 334.
38 Seekings, *The UDF*, 78.
39 Hickel, *Democracy as Death.*
40 Ari Sitas, 'Class Ethnicity Nation', in *The Flight of the Gwala-Gwala Bird* (Cape Town: South African History Online, 2016), 197–230, 221.
41 JS, Yunus Mahomed [Mohamed], interview, 9 July 1992.
42 JS, Khetso Gordhan, interview, 9 July 1992.
43 Govender, *Love and Courage*, 59.
44 Kumi Naidoo, 'The Politics of Youth Resistance in the 1980s: The Dilemmas of a Differentiated Durban', *Journal of Southern African Studies* 18(1) (1992): 143–165, 146.
45 Kumi Naidoo, 'Politics of Youth Resistance', 152.
46 Kumi Naidoo, 'Politics of Youth Resistance', 165.
47 Ari Sitas, 'Durban's Carnage: Where Wealth and Power and Blood Reign Worshipped', in *The Flight of the Gwala-Gwala Bird* (Cape Town: South African History Online, 2016), 98–131, 124.

Chapter 11 Building Up Steam

1 Hoosen (Jerry) Coovadia interviewed by Goolam Vahed, 5 December 2019.
2 Yusuf Dadoo, 'The Role of the Indian People in the South African Revolution: An Interview in 1968', South African History Organisation, https://www.sahistory.org.za/archive/role-indian-people-south-african-revolution-interview-1968 (accessed 10 October 2019).
3 VOR, George Sewpersadh interviewed by Mwelela Cele, 11 August 2002.
4 Simpson, *Umkhonto we Sizwe*, 422.
5 VOR, Neela Naidu interviewed by Vino Reddy, 31 May 2002.
6 Truth and Reconciliation Commission (TRC), 'Amnesty Hearings: Eugene de Kock', Special Report, 26 July 1999, sabctrc.saha.org.za/hearing.php?id=53564&t=piet+retief+ambushes+de+kock&tab=hearings (accessed 3 February 2021).
7 VOR, Yunus [Yunis] Shaik interviewed by D. Shongwe, 18 August 2002.
8 POM, Ivan Pillay, 11 December 2002.
9 POM, Pravin Gordhan, 30 January 2003.
10 This chapter looks specifically at the NIC role within the armed struggle. Broader ANC strategies during this period, including the years in Lusaka, the armed struggle and the influence of communists within the ANC, are covered in

depth by Stephen Ellis, *External Mission: The ANC in Exile, 1960–1990* (London: C. Hurst and Co., 2012); Hugh Macmillan, *The Lusaka Years: The ANC in Exile in Zambia, 1963 to 1994* (Cape Town: Jacana, 2013); Simpson, *Umkhonto we Sizwe*; Stephen R. Davis, *The ANC's War against Apartheid: Umkhonto we Sizwe and the Liberation of South Africa* (Bloomington: Indiana University Press, 2018); and Dale T. McKinley, 'Umkhonto we Sizwe: A Critical Analysis of the Armed Struggle of the African National Congress', *South African Historical Journal* 70(1) (2018): 27–41.

11   POM, Moe Shaik, 7 May 2004.

12   POM, Moe Shaik, 7 May 2004. Some of this heroic work was undone when the director of public prosecutions in post-apartheid South Africa, Bulelani Ngcuka, was named as a 'probable collaborator' by Moe Shaik, an allegation backed up by Mac Maharaj. A commission of inquiry found no substance to the claim. See Moe Shaik, *The ANC Spy Bible: Surviving across Enemy Lines* (Cape Town: Tafelberg, 2020), 212.

13   See Connie Braam, *Operation Vula* (Johannesburg: Jacana, 2004).

14   Nqakula, *The People's War*, 282.

15   McKinley, 'Umkhonto we Sizwe: A Critical Analysis', 35.

16   Raymond Suttner, *The ANC Underground in South Africa, 1950–1976* (Boulder, CO and London: First Forum Press, 2008), 17.

17   McKinley, 'Umkhonto we Sizwe: A Critical Analysis', 36.

18   McKinley, 'Umkhonto we Sizwe: A Critical Analysis', 39.

19   Janet Cherry, 'Book Review: Umkhonto we Sizwe: The ANC's Armed Struggle', *South African Historical Journal* 70(1) (2018): 291–294, 292.

20   POM, Pravin Gordhan, 30 January 2003.

21   POM, Pravin Gordhan, 30 January 2003.

22   POM, Pravin Gordhan, 30 January 2003.

23   O'Malley, *Shades of Difference*, 258.

24   POM, Pravin Gordhan, 30 January 2003.

25   POM, Ivan Pillay, 11 December 2002.

26   Shaik, *ANC Spy Bible*, 144.

27   POM, Pravin Gordhan, 30 January 2003.

28   O'Malley Archives, 'Vula Eight: Charge Sheet', Nelson Mandela Foundation, https://omalley.nelsonmandela.org/omalley/index.php/site/q/031v03445/041v03996/051v04000.htm (accessed 3 February 2021).

29   O'Malley, *Shades of Difference*, 383–385.

30   O'Malley, *Shades of Difference*, 386.

31   POM, Pravin Gordhan, 30 January 2003.

32   POM, Ivan Pillay, 11 December 2002.

33   Cherry, 'Book Review', 294.

34   Suttner, *The ANC Underground* (2008), 163–164.

35   Vahed, *Muslim Portraits*, 350–353.

36   VOR, Billy Nair interviewed by D. Shongwe, 12 July 2002.

37   DOHP, Pravin Gordhan, 22 October 2002.

38 Nqakula, *The People's War*, 203.
39 Quoted in O'Malley, *Shades of Difference*, 286–287.
40 Quoted in O'Malley, *Shades of Difference*, 286–287.
41 Govender, *Love and Courage*, 101.
42 Quoted in O'Malley, *Shades of Difference*, 274.
43 Shaik, *ANC Spy Bible*, 128–129.
44 Quoted in O'Malley, *Shades of Difference*, 270. O'Malley writes: 'On occasion Mac displayed his displeasure at what he considered the excessive sums Schabir Shaik levied on transactions as his fee ... On one occasion he wrote to Slovo: "Although the sums we received were more than we estimated while we were working on a budget, I still think Pits [Schabir Shaik] is making a killing from the deals. He is giving us 10% and I doubt his claim of the rate having been 4.08 on the date the deposit was made"' (*Shades of Difference*, 563).
45 Shaik, *ANC Spy Bible*, 144.
46 Quoted in Nqakula, *The People's War*, 202.

Chapter 12   Between Fact and Factions

1 Yunus Carrim interviewed by Goolam Vahed, 5 October 2019.
2 Ismail (I.C.) Meer, *A Fortunate Man*.
3 Iain Edwards, e-mail correspondence to Goolam Vahed, 4 November 2019.
4 Iain Edwards, e-mail correspondence to Goolam Vahed, 4 November 2019.
5 Thumba Pillay, e-mail correspondence with Goolam Vahed, 23 January 2013.
6 Ashwin Desai and Goolam Vahed, *A History of the Present: A Biography of Indian South Africans, 1990–2019* (New Delhi: Oxford University Press, 2019), 40.
7 Desai and Vahed, *A History of the Present*, 40.
8 GG, Jerry Coovadia interviewed by Gail Gerhart and Steve Mufson, 2 June 1988.
9 GG, Yunus Mahomed [Mohamed] interviewed by D.R. Chetty, 22 November 1990.
10 *Daily News*, 7 January 1988.
11 *Daily News*, 14 January 1988.
12 Edwards, *Faith and Courage*, 151.
13 Edwards, *Faith and Courage*, 150.
14 *Post*, 12 December 1987.
15 VOR, Charm Govender interviewed by D. Shongwe, 20 September 2002.
16 Quoted in Edwards, *Faith and Courage*, 215.
17 *Daily News*, 14 January 1988.
18 *Weekly Mail*, 29 January 1988.
19 Yunus Carrim interviewed by Goolam Vahed, 5 October 2019.
20 GG, Jerry Coovadia interviewed by Gail Gerhart and Steve Mufson, 2 June 1988.
21 Edwards, *Faith and Courage*, 216.
22 Edwards, *Faith and Courage*, 217.
23 Edwards, *Faith and Courage*, 218.
24 Seekings, *The UDF*, 75.

25 VOR, Charm Govender interviewed by D. Shongwe, 20 September 2002.
26 Roykumar (Roy) Sukuram interviewed by Goolam Vahed, 23 June 2018.
27 Hoosen (Jerry) Coovadia interviewed by Goolam Vahed, 5 December 2019.
28 Paul David interviewed by Goolam Vahed, 20 January 2017.
29 VOR, Charm Govender interviewed by D. Shongwe, 20 September 2002.
30 VOR, Charm Govender interviewed by D. Shongwe, 20 September 2002.
31 Kumi Naidoo, 'Class, Consciousness and Organisation'.
32 Yunus Carrim interviewed by Goolam Vahed, 5 October 2019.
33 Yunus Carrim interviewed by Goolam Vahed, 5 October 2019.
34 Govender, *Love and Courage*, 60.
35 JF, Pravin Gordhan, interview, 1986, A07.07.
36 GG, Mewa Ramgobin interviewed by Gail Gerhart, 12 July 1989.
37 *Natal Mercury*, 7 March 1983.
38 Roykumar (Roy) Sukuram interviewed by Goolam Vahed, 23 June 2018.
39 Copelyn, *Maverick Insider*, 186–188.
40 Govender, *Love and Courage*, 60.
41 Bhana, *Gandhi's Legacy*, 148.
42 Hoosen (Jerry) Coovadia interviewed by Goolam Vahed, 30 November 2015.
43 Shaik, *ANC Spy Bible*, 48.
44 Yunus Carrim interviewed by Goolam Vahed, 5 October 2019.
45 Govender, *Love and Courage*, 100.
46 *Daily News*, 7 January 1988.
47 *Weekly Mail*, 29 January 1988.
48 *Weekly Mail*, 5 February 1988.
49 *Natal Mercury*, 10 February 1988.
50 GG, Jerry Coovadia interviewed by Gail Gerhart and Steve Mufson, 2 June 1988.
51 *Leader*, 14 October 1988.
52 Gibson, 'Why Is Participation a Dirty Word', 49.
53 Gibson, 'Why Is Participation a Dirty Word', 49.
54 Edwards, *Faith and Courage*, 219.
55 Quoted in Edwards, *Faith and Courage*, 221.
56 Shaik, *ANC Spy Bible*.

Chapter 13 'Caught With Our Pants Down'

1 Farouk Meer, 'The Freedom Charter and the Future: The Position of the Natal Indian Congress', in *The Freedom Charter and the Future*, edited by James A. Polley, 26–37 (Cape Town: Institute for a Democratic Alternative for South Africa, 1989), 27.
2 Niël Barnard, *Secret Revolution: Memoirs of a Spy Boss* (Cape Town: Tafelberg, 2015), 151–152.
3 Fatima Meer, 'South Africa's Tomorrow', 399–400.
4 Fatima Meer, in Hassim, *Fatima Meer*, 423.
5 Quoted in McKinley, 'Umkhonto we Sizwe: A Critical Analysis', 40.

6   Anthony Sampson, *Black and Gold: Tycoons, Revolutionaries and Apartheid* (London: Hodder & Stoughton, 1987), 244.

7   Quoted in Sampson, *Black and Gold*, 246.

8   Edwards, *Faith and Courage*, 20.

9   John Saul and Patrick Bond, *South Africa – The Present as History: From Mrs Ples to Mandela and Marikana* (Johannesburg: Jacana, 2014), 114.

10   *Leader*, 14 October 1988.

11   *Leader*, 14 October 1988.

12   VOR, Charm Govender interviewed by D. Shongwe, 20 September 2002.

13   *Daily News*, 17 February 1989.

14   Edwards, *Faith and Courage*, 223.

15   *Sunday Tribune*, 1 May 1989.

16   *Post*, 24 May 1989.

17   *Post*, 24 May 1989.

18   *Post*, 24 May 1989.

19   VOR, Charm Govender interviewed by D. Shongwe, 20 September 2002.

20   Dubow, *Apartheid*, 254.

21   Barnard, *Secret Revolution*, 200.

22   See Vishnu Padayachee and Robert van Niekerk, *Shadow Liberation: Contestation and Compromise in the Economic and Social Policy of the African National Congress, 1943–1996* (Johannesburg: Wits University Press, 2019).

23   GG, Mewa Ramgobin interviewed by Gail Gerhart, 12 July 1989.

24   In Hassim, *Fatima Meer*, 431.

25   Mandela, *Long Walk*, 540.

26   F.W. de Klerk, *The Last Trek – A New Beginning: The Autobiography* (New York: St. Martin's Press, 1999), 162.

27   Vahed, *Chota Motala*, 287.

28   Ismail (I.C.) Meer, *A Fortunate Man*, 260.

29   In Hassim, *Fatima Meer*, 433.

30   In Edwards, *Faith and Courage*, 227.

31   VOR, Mewa Ramgobin interviewed by Christian de Vos, 19 May 2002.

32   Dubow, *Apartheid*, 264.

33   Alexander Johnston, 'South Africa: The Election and the Transition Process: Five Contradictions in Search of a Resolution', *Third World Quarterly* 15(2) (1994): 187–204, 188. Although the ANC had suspended the armed struggle in August 1991, there was conflict between the IFP/ANC-UDF in KwaZulu-Natal; between the Black Consciousness Azanian People's Organisation (AZAPO) and the ANC-UDF in the Eastern Cape and the Witwatersrand; and between IFP hostel dwellers and other hostel dwellers in the Witwatersrand. There were also uprisings and coup attempts in Ciskei and Venda. In November 1991 white right-wingers led by Eugene Terreblanche's paramilitary group, the Afrikaner Weerstandsbeweging (AWB), got involved in a confrontation with police in Ventersdorp when F.W. de Klerk was speaking in the town. These are just some of the incidents of confrontation and violence in the transition period; see T.R.H. Davenport, *The Transfer of Power in South*

Africa (Cape Town: David Philip, 1997), 9–16. According to Johnston, 'although the Goldstone Commission has pinpointed rivalry between black political movements (notably the ANC and the Inkatha Freedom Party – IFP) and acts of commission and omission by the security forces, political violence has no clear-cut axis of conflict and is overlaid with many exacerbating factors. These range from generational conflict between radical youth and traditional elders, disputes over chiefship succession, crime, economic rivalry (as in the so-called "taxi" wars) and cycles of vendetta-like clan conflict. Central to many of these conflicts is the legacy of apartheid policies which have created two marginalised classes of person – the migrant worker who lives in a hostel, and the squatter' ('South Africa: The Election', 188).

34 Padraig O'Malley, 'From Buthelezi IFP to Third Force Theory', n.d., https://omalley.nelsonmandela.org/omalley/index.php/site/q/03lv02424/04lv03275/05lv03294/06lv03299.htm (accessed 20 October 2019).

35 Johnston, 'South Africa: The Election', 188.

36 VOR, Ela Gandhi interviewed by Vino Reddy, 18 May 2002.

Chapter 14 Snapping the Strings of the UDF

1 GG, Yunus Mahomed [Mohamed] interviewed by D.R. Chetty, 22 November 2002.

2 VOR, Yunus Mahomed [Mohamed] interviewed by Musa Ntsodi, 22 September 2002.

3 Howard Barrell, 'The Turn to the Masses: The African National Congress's Strategic Review of 1978–79', *Journal of Southern African Studies* 18(1) (1992): 64–92.

4 Seekings, *The UDF*, 268–269.

5 Coovadia, 'Change through Organisations', 46.

6 Marx, *Lessons of Struggle*, 176–177.

7 Edwards, *Faith and Courage*, 386.

8 Edwards, *Faith and Courage*, 386.

9 Seekings, *The UDF*, 308.

10 Reproduced in Edwards, *Faith and Courage*, 302–306.

11 Mark Gevisser, *Thabo Mbeki: The Dream Deferred* (Cape Town: Jonathan Ball Publishers, 2007), 633.

12 Edwards, *Faith and Courage*, 302–303.

13 O'Malley, *Shades of Difference*, 287.

14 O'Malley, *Shades of Difference*, 287.

15 Ineke van Kessel, *'Beyond Our Wildest Dreams': The United Democratic Front and the Transformation of South Africa* (Charlottesville and London: University Press of Virginia, 2000); Greg Houston, *The National Liberation Struggle in South Africa: A Case Study of the United Democratic Front, 1983–1987* (Brookfield, VT: Ashgate, 1999).

16 Quoted from the report: 'Transvaal: Ismail Momoniat, Laloo Chiba, Cassim Salojee. Part of the Cabal in the Transvaal is seen as Eric Molobi and Amos Masondo. Western Cape: Persons identified as members of the Cabal in the Western Cape since the early eighties are amongst others Jonathan de Vries, Hadley King, Cathy Macrae, and Ebrahim Patel. Dullah Omar is also currently exceeding his vested

authority and seems to be part and parcel of the Cabal. Black comrades in Natal who suffered at the hands of the Cabal as far back as 1985 were amongst others Ian Mkhize, Samson Nkozi, Kwenza Mlaba, Nozizwe Madlala, Russel Mapanga, and Pius Langa. The Cabal also slandered and diminished the role of stalwarts in the Transvaal. Amongst others Essop Jassat, Ismail Mohammed, Aubrey Mokoena, Curtis Nkondo, Thozamile Gqweta and Sam Kikine were isolated and diminished as leaders in the struggle.' African National Congress (ANC), 'Report and Recommendations of Commission on the Cabal', 14 March 1990, https://omalley. nelsonmandela.org/omalley/index.php/site/q/03lv03445/04lv04015/05lv04154/ 06lv0181.htm (accessed 15 September 2019).

17 ANC, 'Report and Recommendations'.
18 ANC, 'Report and Recommendations'.
19 Raymond Suttner, 'Review Article: The UDF Period and Its Meaning for Contemporary South Africa', *Journal of Southern African Studies* 30(3) (2004): 691–701, 693.
20 *Mail & Guardian*, 29 October 2019.
21 Edwards, *Faith and Courage*, 233.
22 Edwards, *Faith and Courage*, 233.
23 O'Malley Archives, 'African/Indian Relationship', Nelson Mandela Foundation, https://omalley.nelsonmandela.org/omalley/index.php/site/q/03lv03445/04lv0 4206/05lv04254/06lv04255.htm (accessed 3 February 2021).
24 Simpson, *Umkhonto we Sizwe*, 486–487.
25 Quoted in Edwards, *Faith and Courage*, 299.
26 O'Malley, *Shades of Difference*, 479.
27 Govender, *Love and Courage*.
28 *Sunday Times*, 25 November 1990, quoted in Iain Edwards, e-mail correspondence to Goolam Vahed, 4 November 2019.
29 Quoted in Booth, 'A Strange Divide', 78.
30 Hoosen (Jerry) Coovadia interviewed by Goolam Vahed, 5 December 2019.
31 O'Malley, *Shades of Difference*, 345.
32 VOR, Charm Govender interviewed by D. Shongwe, 20 September 2002.
33 Gevisser, *Thabo Mbeki*, 604.
34 Aziz Pahad, *Insurgent Diplomat: Civil Talks or Civil War* (Johannesburg: Penguin Books, 2014), 243–244.
35 O'Malley, *Shades of Difference*, 388.
36 Gevisser, *Thabo Mbeki*, 604.
37 O'Malley, *Shades of Difference*, 433.
38 Gevisser, *Thabo Mbeki*, 607.
39 Gevisser, *Thabo Mbeki*, 607.
40 O'Malley, *Shades of Difference*, 392.
41 Fred Khumalo, *Sunday Times*, 24 October 2010.
42 O'Malley, *Shades of Difference*, 479.
43 Eric Louw, 'Rejoinder to "Opposing Apartheid": Building a South African Democracy through a Popular Alliance which Includes Leninists', *Theoria: A Journal of Social and Political Theory* 73 (May 1989): 49–62, 55.

44 Suttner, 'Review Article', 699.
45 VOR, Billy Nair interviewed by D. Shongwe, 12 July 2002.
46 Seekings, *The UDF*, 283.

Chapter 15 Digging Their Own Grave

1   Mewa Ramgobin, 'Interview', *Sechaba* (April 1990): 7–8, 8.
2   Quoted in Edwards, *Faith and Courage*, 229.
3   *Daily News*, 11 May 1990.
4   *Daily News*, 11 May 1990.
5   *Natal Witness*, 12 May 1990.
6   *Natal Witness*, 22 May 1990.
7   *Financial Mail*, 11 June 1990.
8   *Maritzburg Sun*, 9 December 2013.
9   Vahed, *Chota Motala*, 242.
10 The ANC was represented by Walter Sisulu, Joe Slovo, Alfred Nzo, Mac Maharaj, Aziz Pahad, Steve Tshwete, Mosie Moola, Jessie Duarte, Essop Pahad and Valli Moosa. There were ANC apologies from Jacob Zuma, Harry Gwala, S'bu Ndebele, Pallo Jordan, Joe Nhlanhla and 'Terror' Lekota. The NIC was represented by George Sewpersadh, Farouk Meer, Mewa Ramgobin, Thumba Pillay, Zak Yacoob, Pravin Gordhan, Yunus Mohamed, Hassim Seedat, Alf Karrim, Roy Padayachie, Ismail Meer, Yusuf Bhamjee and Kamal Vishwas. The TIC was represented by Cassim Saloojee, Ismail Momoniat, Laloo Chiba, Prema Naidoo, Fuad Cassim, Rashid Seedat, Reggie Vandeyar, Firoz Cachalia, Kadir Saloojee, Ismail Vadi, Rehana Adam, Firoze Cassim, Azhar Cachalia and Ramlall Bhoolia. Ismail Vadi, e-mail correspondence to Goolam Vahed, 3 September 2020.
11 Ismail Vadi, e-mail correspondence to Goolam Vahed, 3 September 2020.
12 Edwards, *Faith and Courage*, 235.
13 Seekings, *The UDF*, 268.
14 Edwards, *Faith and Courage*, 237.
15 Edwards, *Faith and Courage*, 237.
16 Edwards, *Faith and Courage*, 236.
17 Edwards, *Faith and Courage*, 236.
18 Edwards, *Faith and Courage*, 236.
19 Edwards, *Faith and Courage*, 236.
20 Edwards, *Faith and Courage*, 236.
21 Edwards, *Faith and Courage*, 237.
22 O'Malley, *Shades of Difference*, 588.
23 O'Malley, *Shades of Difference*, 588.
24 Edwards, *Faith and Courage*, 237.
25 Edwards, *Faith and Courage*, 237.
26 Edwards, *Faith and Courage*, 237.
27 Edwards, *Faith and Courage*, 238.
28 Edwards, *Faith and Courage*, 238.

29 Ismail Vadi, e-mail correspondence to Goolam Vahed, 3 September 2020.
30 *Daily News*, 18 March 1991.
31 *Natal Mercury*, 21 March 1991.
32 *Natal Mercury*, 21 March 1991.
33 *Natal Mercury*, 28 March 1991.
34 Edwards, *Faith and Courage*, 242.
35 The 19 parties and organisations were the NP; ANC; South African government; SACP; IFP; Labour Party; the Inyandza National Movement; the Transvaal and Natal Indian Congresses; the Venda government; the Bophuthatswana government; the Transkei government; United People's Front; Solidarity Party; Democratic Party (DP); National People's Party (NPP); Ciskei government; Dikwankwetla Party; Intando Yesizwe Party and Ximoko Progressive Party. The first plenary session was chaired by Chief Justice Michael Corbett and Justices Ismail Mohamed and Petrus (Piet) Schabort.
36 Welsh, *Rise and Fall of Apartheid*, 435.
37 *Leader*, 20 December 1991.
38 In addition to Gordhan, the other members were Zach De Beer (DP), Peter Hendrickse (Labour Party), Frank Mdladlose (IFP), Selby Rapinga (Inyandza), Roelf Meyer (NP), Zamindlela Titus (Transkei) and Jacob Zuma (ANC).
39 Welsh, *Rise and Fall of Apartheid*, 441.

Chapter 16 The Ballot Box, 1994

1   Edwards, *Faith and Courage*, 232.
2   Edwards, *Faith and Courage*, 232.
3   *Natal Witness*, 19 February 1990.
4   *Sunday Tribune*, 11 February 1990.
5   *Sunday Tribune*, 11 February 1990.
6   *Sunday Tribune*, 11 February 1990.
7   *Sunday Tribune*, 11 February 1990.
8   *Natal Mercury*, 16 February 1990.
9   Edwards, *Faith and Courage*, 232.
10 JF, Frene Ginwala, interview, 1986, A07.01.3.
11 JF, Frene Ginwala, interview, 1986, A07.01.3.
12 Vahed, *Chota Motala*, 262.
13 Yunus Carrim, 'Why Indians Should Vote ANC', March 1994, document provided to authors by Y. Carrim.
14 Vahed, *Chota Motala*, 262.
15 VOR, Charm Govender interviewed by D. Shongwe, 20 September 2002.
16 Paul David interviewed by Goolam Vahed, 20 January 2017.
17 Shaik, *ANC Spy Bible*, 194.
18 Tom Lodge, 'The South African General Election, April 1994: Results, Analysis and Implications', *African Affairs* 94(377) (1994): 471–500, 476.
19 Lodge, 'South African General Election', 473.

20 Ashwin Desai, *Arise Ye Coolies: Apartheid and the Indian, 1960–1995* (Johannesburg: Impact Africa Publishing, 1996), 87.

21 Yunus Carrim interviewed by Goolam Vahed, 13 February 2016.

22 Natal Indian Congress (NIC), 'Revisiting the National Question: What Future the NIC?', Discussion document presented to a meeting of the ANC Natal PEC and NIC Executive, 26 March 1995, document provided to authors by Ismail Vadi.

23 Adam Habib and Sanusha Naidu, 'Race, Class and Voting Patterns in South Africa's Electoral System: Ten Years of Democracy', *Africa Development* 31(3) (2006): 81–92, 91.

24 Lodge, 'South African General Election', 478.

25 VOR, Ela Gandhi interviewed by Vino Reddy, 18 May 2002.

26 Thomas Blom Hansen, *Melancholia of Freedom: Social Life in an Indian Township in South Africa* (Princeton, NJ: Princeton University Press, 2012), 136–137.

27 Alexander Johnston and R.W. Johnson, 'The Local Elections in KwaZulu-Natal: 26 June 1996', *African Affairs* 96(384) (1997): 377–398, 388.

28 Johnston and Johnson, 'Local Elections', 389.

29 *Die Burger*, 1 February 1994, in Lodge, 'South African General Election', 483.

30 Lodge, 'South African General Election', 485.

31 Lodge, 'South African General Election', 499.

32 NIC, 'Revisiting the National Question'.

33 NIC, 'Revisiting the National Question'.

34 *Leader*, 26 August 1994.

35 *Leader*, 26 August 1994.

36 *Post*, 7–10 December 1994.

37 *Post*, 7–10 December 1994.

38 *Post*, 7–10 December 1994.

39 NIC, 'Revisiting the National Question'.

Chapter 17 Between Rajbansi's 'Ethnic Guitar' and the String of the ANC Party List

1 Hoosen (Jerry) Coovadia interviewed by Goolam Vahed, 5 December 2019.

2 Yusuf Bhamjee interviewed by Goolam Vahed, 14 June 2016.

3 Yusuf Bhamjee interviewed by Goolam Vahed, 14 June 2016.

4 Yunus Carrim interviewed by Goolam Vahed, 13 February 2016.

5 Yusuf Bhamjee interviewed by Goolam Vahed, 14 June 2016.

6 JF, Fatima Meer, interview, 1986, A13.23.

7 Hassim, *Fatima Meer*, 70.

8 Ismail (I.C.) Meer, *A Fortunate Man*, 261.

9 Houston et al., *Other Side of Freedom*, 49.

10 Thumba Pillay, e-mail correspondence to Goolam Vahed, 23 January 2013.

11 Anand Singh, 'Cultural Entrepreneurship and the Culturalisation of Politics among Indians in South Africa', *Alternation* 4(1) (1997): 93–115, 107.

12   Singh, 'Cultural Entrepreneurship', 108.
13   Singh, 'Cultural Entrepreneurship', 110.
14   Singh, 'Cultural Entrepreneurship', 100–111.
15   Kumi Naidoo, 'Class, Consciousness and Organisation', chapter 8.
16   Christi van der Westhuizen, *White Power and the Rise and Fall of the National Party* (Cape Town: Zebra Press, 2007).
17   VOR, Charm Govender interviewed by D. Shongwe, 20 September 2002.
18   Farouk Meer interviewed by Goolam Vahed, 12 May 2012.
19   VOR, Yunus Mahomed [Mohamed] interviewed by Musa Ntsodi, 22 September 2002.
20   VOR, Sharm Maharaj interviewed by Musa Ntsodi, 9 October 2002.
21   Copy of letter to Nelson Mandela dated 2 December 1993 provided to authors by Yunus Carrim.
22   Yunus Carrim interviewed by Goolam Vahed, 5 October 2019.
23   Yunus Carrim interviewed by Goolam Vahed, 5 October 2019.
24   Hoosen (Jerry) Coovadia interviewed by Goolam Vahed, 5 December 2019.
25   Yunus Carrim interviewed by Goolam Vahed, 5 October 2019.

Conclusion: A Spoke in the Wheel

1   DOHP, Pravin Gordhan, 22 October 2002.
2   Govender, *Love and Courage*, 58.
3   Copelyn, *Maverick Insider*, 207–208.
4   Farouk Meer, 'The Freedom Charter', 31–32.
5   Govender, *Love and Courage*, 58.
6   Govender, *Love and Courage*, 59.
7   Suttner, *The ANC Underground* (2008), 156.
8   POM, Fatima Meer, 22 July 1992.
9   O'Malley, *Shades of Difference*, 247.
10   Hoosen (Jerry) Coovadia interviewed by Goolam Vahed, 5 December 2019.
11   NIC, 'Revisiting the National Question'.
12   Marx, *Lessons of Struggle*, 15.
13   NIC, 'Revisiting the National Question', 3.
14   O'Malley, *Shades of Difference*, 412.
15   O'Malley, *Shades of Difference*, 412.
16   Yunus Carrim interviewed by Goolam Vahed, 5 October 2019.
17   Irwin D. Rinder, 'Strangers in the Land: Social Relations in the Status Gap', *Social Problems* 6(3) (1958): 253–260, 257.
18   Quoted in Everatt, *The Origins of Non-racialism*, 177.
19   Eddie Webster and John Mawbey, 'Revisiting the National Question', in *The Unresolved National Question: Left Thought under Apartheid*, edited by Eddie Webster and Karin Pampallis, 1–18 (Johannesburg: Wits University Press, 2017), 2.
20   Francis Fukuyama, *Identity: Contemporary Identity Politics and the Struggle for Recognition* (London: Profile Books, 2019), 165.

21 Loyiso Sidimba, 'The ANC Is Racist and Tribalistic, Says Gatvol Jessie Duarte', *IOL*, 23 November 2019, https://www.iol.co.za/news/politics/the-anc-is-racist-and-tribalistic-says-gatvol-jessie-duarte-37806623 (accessed 30 November 2019).
22 Sidimba, 'The ANC Is Racist'.
23 Frantz Fanon, *The Wretched of the Earth* (London: Penguin, 2001), 118.
24 Fukuyama, *Identity*, 166.

Oral Interviews
1. Detainees Oral History Project (DOHP), 1981

South African History Archives, Collection No: AL2933. SAHA
Gordhan, Pravin, 22 October 2002.

2. Gail Gerhart Collection (GG)

Historical Papers Research Archive, University of the Witwatersrand
Coovadia, Jerry, 2 June 1988. Interviewed by Gail Gerhart and Steve Mufson.
Mahomed [Mohamed], Yunus, 22 November 1990. Interviewed by D.R. Chetty.
Ramgobin, Mewa, 12 July 1989. Interviewed by Gail Gerhart.

3. Goolam Vahed

Bhamjee, Yusuf, 14 June 2016.
Carrim, Yunus, 5 October 2019; 13 February 2016.
Coovadia, Hoosen (Jerry), 30 November 2015; 5 December 2019; e-mail correspondence, 21 and 22 January 2013.
David, Paul, 20 January 2017.
Gandhi, Ela, e-mail correspondence, 24 January 2013.
Goonam, Kesaveloo, 31 May 1989.
Meer, Farouk, 12 May 2012.
Meer, Fatima, 28 February 2008.
Pillay, Devan, 19 September 2012.
Pillay, Thumba, e-mail correspondence, 23 January 2013.
Sukuram, Roykumar (Roy), 23 June 2018.
Vadi, Ismail, email correspondence, 3 September 2020.
Vawda, Yousuf, e-mail correspondence, 22 January 2013.

4. Jeremy Seekings Collection (JS)

Alan Paton Centre and Struggle Archives, University of KwaZulu-Natal, Pietermaritzburg
Gordhan, Khetso, 9 July 1992.
Mahomed [Mohamed], Yunus, 9 July 1992.

5. Julie Frederikse Collection (JF)

Collection (AL246), deposited at South African History Archives (SAHA)
Ginwala, Frene. 1986. A07.01.3.
Gordhan, Pravin. 1986. A07.07.
Karrim, Alf. 1986. A11.01.1.
Meer, Fatima. 1986. A13.23.
Naidoo, Kumi. 1987. A14.04.1.
Naidoo, M.D. 1986. A14.02.
Ramgobin, Mewa. 1986. A18.4.

6. Padraig O'Malley Collection (POM)

Nelson Mandela Foundation
Gordhan, Pravin, 30 January 2003.
Maharaj, Mac, 16 September 2003.
Maharaj, Mac, 30 November 1990. Interviewed by Howard Barrell.
Meer, Fatima, 22 July 1992.
Pillay, Ivan, 11 December 2002.
Rajab, Mahmoud, 25 July 1990. [This date appears to be an error, as Rajab quotes
     Nelson Mandela's biography in the interview, which was published in 1994.]
Shaik, Moe, 7 May 2004.

7. 'Voices of Resistance' Collection (VOR)

Gandhi-Luthuli Documentation Centre, University of KwaZulu-Natal, Westville
Cooper, Saths (Musa Ntsodi), 14 April 2003.
Gandhi, Ela (Vino Reddy), 18 May 2002.
Govender, Charm (D. Shongwe), 20 September 2002.
Govender, Maggie (D. Shongwe), 13 September 2002.
Maharaj, Sharm (Musa Ntsodi), 9 October 2002.
Mahomed [Mohamed], Yunus (Musa Ntsodi), 22 September 2002.
Meer, Farouk (Musa Ntsodi), 9 October 2002.
Moodley, Strini (D. Shongwe), 24 July 2002.
Naidoo, Dilly (D. Shongwe), 23 July 2002.
Naidoo, Kovin (D. Shongwe), 5 September 2002.
Naidu, Neela (Vino Reddy), 31 May 2002.

Nair, Billy (D. Shongwe), 12 July 2002.
Pillay, Daya (Musa Ntsodi), 16 October 2002.
Ramgobin, Mewa (Christian de Vos), 19 May 2002.
Sewpersadh, George (Mwelela Cele), 11 August 2002.
Shaik, Yunus [Yunis] (D. Shongwe), 18 August 2002.
Vawda, Yousuf (Musa Ntsodi), 8 October 2002.

8. Liliesfield Trust, Johannesburg

Naidoo, M., 20 October 2016. Interview quote provided by Ismail Vadi.

Periodicals

Citizen
City Press
Daily Dispatch
Daily News
Fiat Lux
Financial Mail
Graphic
Leader
Mail & Guardian
Maritzburg Sun
Natal Mercury
Natal Witness
Post
Pretoria News
Rand Daily Mail
South Coast Herald
Sunday Times
Sunday Tribune
Weekly Mail

Primary and secondary sources

African National Congress (ANC). 'The Green Book: Report of the Politico-Military Strategy Commission to the ANC National Executive Committee'. August 1979. https://www.marxists.org/subject/africa/anc/1979/green-book.htm (accessed 20 September 2019).

African National Congress (ANC). 'Report and Recommendations of Commission on the Cabal'. 14 March 1990. https://omalley.nelsonmandela.org/omalley/index.php/site/q/03lv03445/04lv04015/05lv04154/06lv0181.htm (accessed 15 September 2019).

African National Congress (ANC). 'Strategy and Tactics of the ANC'. Document adopted by the Morogoro Conference of the ANC, Morogoro, Tanzania, 25 April – 1 May 1969. https://www.marxists.org/subject/africa/anc/1969/strategy-tactics.htm (accessed 26 September 2019).

Alden, Chris. *Apartheid's Last Stand: The Rise and Fall of the South African Security State.* London: Macmillan Press, 1996.

Alexander, Neville. 'Aspects of Non-collaboration in the Western Cape, 1943–1963'. *Social Dynamics* 12(1) (1986): 1–14.

Austin, Dennis. 'The Trinitarians: The 1983 South African Constitution'. *Government and Opposition* 20(2) (1985): 185–195.

Barnard, Niël. *Secret Revolution: Memoirs of a Spy Boss.* Cape Town: Tafelberg, 2015.

Barrell, Howard. 'The Turn to the Masses: The African National Congress's Strategic Review of 1978–79'. *Journal of Southern African Studies* 18(1) (1992): 64–92.

Barrett, Jerome T. and Anne Finbarr Mullins. 'South African Trade Unions: A Historical Account, 1970–90'. *Monthly Labor Review* (October 1990): 25–31.

Bell, R.T. 'Growth and Structure of Manufacturing Employment in Natal'. Report No. 7. Institute for Social and Economic Research, University of Durban-Westville, 1983.

Bhana, Surendra. *Gandhi's Legacy: The Natal Indian Congress 1894–1994.* Pietermaritzburg: University of Natal Press, 1997.

Bhana, Surendra and Bridglal Pachai, eds. *A Documentary History of Indian South Africans.* Cape Town: David Philip, 1984.

Biko, Steve. *I Write What I Like*, 40th anniversary edition. Johannesburg: Picador Africa, 2017.

Black Sash. 'Analysis of Conflict in Inanda'. Paper presented at the Black Sash National Conference, March 1989. https://www.jstor.org/stable/10.2307/al.sff.document.cnf19890303.026.001.000b (accessed 22 October 2019).

Black Sash. 'The Durban Unrest'. Paper presented at the Black Sash National Conference, March 1986. https://www.jstor.org/stable/10.2307/al.sff.document.cnf19860314.026.001.000 (accessed 22 October 2019).

Booth, Douglas. 'A Strange Divide: Townships on Contested Terrain'. In *Political Conflict in South Africa: Data Trends 1984–1988*, edited by Mark Bennett and Deborah Quin, 73–80. Cape Town: Indicator SA Focus, 1988.

Braam, Connie. *Operation Vula.* Johannesburg: Jacana, 2004.

Carrim, Yunus. 'Why Indians Should Vote ANC'. March 1994. Document provided to authors by Y. Carrim.

Charney, Craig. 'The Right to be Different'. *Work in Progress* (July 1991): 24–27.

Cherry, Janet. 'Book Review: Umkhonto we Sizwe: The ANC's Armed Struggle'. *South African Historical Journal* 70(1) (2018): 291–294.

Chetty, A.S. 'Memoirs'. Alan Paton Centre and Struggle Archives. University of KwaZulu-Natal, Pietermaritzburg. PC 161/2/1/1/4.

Coovadia, Jerry. 'Change through Organisations of the People'. In *Strategies for Change*, edited by Stephen Fourie, 43–50. Cape Town: Institute for a Democratic Alternative for South Africa, 1989.

Copelyn, Johnny. *Maverick Insider: A Struggle for Union Independence in Time of National Liberation*. Johannesburg: Picador Africa, 2016.

Dadoo, Yusuf. 'The Role of the Indian People in the South African Revolution: An Interview in 1968'. South African History Organisation. https://www.sahistory. org.za/archive/role-indian-people-south-african-revolution-interview-1968 (accessed 10 October 2019).

Davenport, T.R.H. *The Transfer of Power in South Africa*. Cape Town: David Philip, 1997.

Davies, Robert H. *Capital, State and White Labour in South Africa, 1900–1960: An Historical Materialist Analysis of Class Formation and Class Relations*. Atlantic Highlands, NJ: Humanities Press, 1979.

Davis, Stephen R. *The ANC's War against Apartheid: Umkhonto we Sizwe and the Liberation of South Africa*. Bloomington: Indiana University Press, 2018.

De Klerk, F.W. *The Last Trek – A New Beginning: The Autobiography*. New York: St. Martin's Press, 1999.

Department of Indian Affairs (DIA). Reports: 3 August 1961 – December 1970.

Desai, Ashwin. *Arise Ye Coolies: Apartheid and the Indian, 1960–1995*. Johannesburg: Impact Africa Publishing, 1996.

Desai, Ashwin. 'Indian South Africans and the Black Consciousness Movement under Apartheid'. *Diaspora Studies* 8(1) (2015): 37–50.

Desai, Ashwin. 'The Origins, Development and Demise of the South African Indian Council 1964–1983: A Sociological Interpretation'. MA dissertation, Rhodes University, 1987.

Desai, Ashwin and Goolam Vahed. *A History of the Present: A Biography of Indian South Africans, 1990–2019*. New Delhi: Oxford University Press, 2019.

Desai, Ashwin and Goolam Vahed. *Monty Naicker: Between Reason and Treason*. Pietermaritzburg: Shuter and Shooter, 2010.

Desai, Ashwin and Goolam Vahed. 'The Natal Indian Congress, the Mass Democratic Movement and the Struggle to Defeat Apartheid: 1980–1994'. *Politikon* 42(1) (2015): 1–22.

Dhillon, Davinder S. 'The Indians of Natal: Resistance to Apartheid, 1970–1985'. BA (Hons.) thesis, National University of Singapore, 1999.

Dhupelia-Mesthrie, Uma. 'The Revival of the Natal Indian Congress'. In *The Road to Democracy in South Africa: Volume 2, 1970–1980*, South African Democracy Education Trust, 883–904. Pretoria: UNISA Press, 2006.

Dubow, Saul. *Apartheid, 1948–1994*. Oxford: Oxford University Press, 2014.

Edwards, Iain. *Faith and Courage: The Political Papers of Mewa Ramgobin*. Johannesburg: Iain Edwards (digitally published), 2015.

Ellis, Stephen. *External Mission: The ANC in Exile, 1960–1990*. London: C. Hurst and Co, 2012.

Everatt, David. *The Origins of Non-racialism: White Opposition to Apartheid in the 1950s.* Johannesburg: Wits University Press, 2009.

Fanon, Frantz. *The Wretched of the Earth*. London: Penguin, 2001.

Frederikse, Julie. *The Unbreakable Thread: Non-racialism in South Africa*. Johannesburg: Ravan Press, 1990.

Freund, Bill. *Insiders and Outsiders: The Indian Working Class of Durban 1910–1990*. London: James Currey, 1995.

Friedman, Daniel. 'Malema Says He's Not Racist, Brings Up Gordhan's "Indian Cabal"'. *The Citizen*, 16 July 2018. https://citizen.co.za/news/south-africa/1979906/malema-says-hes-not-racist-brings-up-gordhans-indian-cabal/ (accessed 20 August 2019).

Fukuyama, Francis. *Identity: Contemporary Identity Politics and the Struggle for Recognition*. London: Profile Books, 2019.

Gerhart, Gail M. *Black Power in South Africa: The Evolution of an Ideology*. Berkeley: University of California Press, 1978.

Gevisser, Mark. *Thabo Mbeki: The Dream Deferred*. Cape Town: Jonathan Ball Publishers, 2007.

Gibson, Nigel. 'Why Is Participation a Dirty Word in South African Politics?' *Africa Today* 37(2) (1990): 23–52.

Glaser, Daryl. 'South Africa and the Limits of Civil Society'. *Journal of Southern African Studies* 23(1) (1997): 5–25.

Gordon, Loraine, ed. *A Survey of Race Relations in South Africa 1980*. Johannesburg: South African Institute of Race Relations, 1981.

Govender, Pregs. *Love and Courage: A Story of Insubordination*. Johannesburg: Jacana, 2007.

Green, Pippa. *Choice, Not Fate: The Life and Times of Trevor Manuel*. Johannesburg: Penguin Books, 2008.

Greyling, J.J.C. 'Employment Opportunities for University Trained Indians'. *Institute of Social and Economic Research 4*. University of Durban-Westville, Durban, 1977.

Habib, Adam and Sanusha Naidu. 'Race, Class and Voting Patterns in South Africa's Electoral System: Ten Years of Democracy'. *Africa Development* 31(3) (2006): 81–92.

Hansen, Thomas Blom. *Melancholia of Freedom: Social Life in an Indian Township in South Africa*. Princeton, NJ: Princeton University Press, 2012.

Hassim, Shireen. *Fatima Meer: A Free Mind*. Cape Town: HSRC Press, 2019.

Hickel, Jason. *Democracy as Death: The Moral Order of Anti-liberal Politics in South Africa*. Oakland: University of California Press, 2015.

Hill, C.K. 'Who Burnt the Mahatma Gandhi's Settlement at Inanda? A Final Report'. Durban, 24 January 1986. Available at the Gandhi-Luthuli Documentation Centre, University of KwaZulu-Natal, Accession No. 887/1.

Horrell, Muriel, ed. *A Survey of Race Relations in South Africa: 1977*. Johannesburg: South African Institute of Race Relations, 1978.

Horrell, Muriel, ed. *A Survey of Race Relations in South Africa: 1962*. Johannesburg: South African Institute of Race Relations, 1963.

Houston, Gregory. *The National Liberation Struggle in South Africa: A Case Study of the United Democratic Front, 1983–1987*. Brookfield, VT: Ashgate, 1999.

Houston, Gregory, Shepi Mati, Hangwelani Magidimisha, Elme Vivier and Mojaleta Dipholo. *The Other Side of Freedom: Stories of Hope and Loss in the South African Liberation Struggle 1950–1994*. Cape Town: HSRC Press, 2017.

Hughes, Heather. 'Violence in Inanda, August 1985'. *Journal of Southern African Studies* 13(3) (1987): 331–354.

Innes, Duncan. *Anglo American and the Rise of Modern South Africa*. New York: Monthly Review Press, 1984.

Johnston, Alexander. 'South Africa: The Election and the Transition Process: Five Contradictions in Search of a Resolution'. *Third World Quarterly* 15(2) (1994): 187–204.

Johnston, Alexander and R.W. Johnson. 'The Local Elections in KwaZulu-Natal: 26 June 1996'. *African Affairs* 96(384) (1997): 377–398.

Kathrada, Ahmed. 'Indian South Africans – A Future Bound with the Cause of the African Majority'. In *Reflections in Prison*, edited by Mac Maharaj, 97–124. Cape Town: Zebra Press, 2001.

Kathrada, Ahmed. *Memoirs*. Cape Town: Zebra Press, 2004.

Khoape, Ben A., ed. *Black Review 1972*. Durban: Black Community Programmes, 1973.

Lemon, Anthony. 'Issues and Campaigns in the South African General Election of 1981'. *African Affairs* 81(325) (1982): 511–526.

Levin, Richard. 'Class Struggle, Popular Democratic Struggle and the South African State'. *Review of African Political Economy* 14(40) (1987): 7–31.

Lodge, Tom. *Black Politics in South Africa since 1945*. Longman: London, 1983.

Lodge, Tom. 'The South African General Election, April 1994: Results, Analysis and Implications'. *African Affairs* 94(377) (1994): 471–500.

Louw, Eric. 'Rejoinder to "Opposing Apartheid": Building a South African Democracy through a Popular Alliance which Includes Leninists'. *Theoria: A Journal of Social and Political Theory* 73 (May 1989): 49–62.

MacEntee, Patrick. 'The "Treason" Trials at Pietermaritzburg and Delmas'. United Nations Centre Against Apartheid, 1986. https://www.jstor.org/stable/10.2307/al.sff.document.nuun1986_23 (accessed 23 October 2019).

Macmillan, Hugh. *The Lusaka Years: The ANC in Exile in Zambia, 1963 to 1994*. Cape Town: Jacana, 2013.

MacQueen, Ian. *Black Consciousness and Progressive Movements under Apartheid*. Pietermaritzburg: University of KwaZulu-Natal Press, 2018.

MacShane, Denis, Martin Plaut and David Ward. *Power! Black Workers, Their Unions and the Struggle for Freedom in South Africa*. Boston: South End Press, 1984.

Magaziner, Daniel R. *Law and the Prophets: Black Consciousness in South Africa, 1968–1977*. Athens: Ohio University Press, 2010.

Mager, Anne Kelk and Maanda Mulaudzi. 'Popular Responses to Apartheid'. In *The Cambridge History of South Africa: Volume 2, 1885–1994*, edited by Robert Ross, Anne Kelk Mager and Bill Nasson, 369–408. Cambridge: Cambridge University Press, 2011.

Maglaya, Filipe E. *Organizing People for Power: A Manual for Organizers*. N.p.: Asian Committee for People's Organization, 1974.

Maharaj, Zarina. *Dancing to a Different Rhythm*. Cape Town: Zebra Press, 2006.

Mandela, Nelson. 'Clear the Obstacles and Confront the Enemy: Whither the Black Consciousness Movement? An assessment'. In *Reflections in Prison*, edited by Mac Maharaj, 7–21. Cape Town: Zebra Press, 2001.

Mandela, Nelson. *The Long Walk to Freedom*. Randburg: Macdonald Purnell, 1994.

Mandela, Nelson. 'Our Struggle Needs Many Tactics'. *Liberation: A Journal of Democratic Discussion* (February 1958): 14–17. https://www.sahistory.org.za/sites/default/files/DC/Lin2958.1729.455X.000.029.Feb1958.5/Lin2958.1729.455X.000.029.Feb1958.5.pdf (accessed 26 October 2019).

Marx, Anthony. *Lessons of Struggle: South African Internal Opposition, 1960–1990*. Oxford: Oxford University Press, 1992.

Marx, Anthony. 'South African Black Trade Unions as an Emerging Working-Class Movement'. *Journal of Modern African Studies* 27(3) (September 1989): 383–400.

Mbanjwa, Thabo, ed. *Black Review 1974/75*. Durban: Black Community Programmes, 1975.

Mbeki, Govan. 'The Anatomy of the Problems of the National Liberation Struggle in South Africa'. In *Reflections in Prison*, edited by Mac Maharaj, 131–146. Cape Town: Zebra Press, 2001.

McKinley, Dale T. 'Umkhonto we Sizwe: A Critical Analysis of the Armed Struggle of the African National Congress'. *South African Historical Journal* 70(1) (2018): 27–41.

Meer, Farouk. 'The Freedom Charter and the Future: The Position of the Natal Indian Congress'. In *The Freedom Charter and the Future*, edited by James A. Polley, 26–37. Cape Town: Institute for a Democratic Alternative for South Africa, 1989.

Meer, Fatima. *Prison Diary: One Hundred and Thirteen Days, 1976*. Cape Town: Kwela Books, 2001.

Meer, Fatima. *Resistance in the Townships*. Durban: Madiba Publishers, 1989.

Meer, Fatima. 'South Africa's Tomorrow'. *Third World Quarterly* 9(2) (1987): 396–407.

Meer, Ismail (I.C.). *A Fortunate Man*. Cape Town: Zebra Press, 2002.

Merrett, Christopher. 'Detention without Trial in South Africa: The Abuse of Human Rights as State Strategy in the Late 1980s'. *Africa Today* 37(2) (1990): 53–66.

Moodley, Kagila. 'South African Indians: The Wavering Minority'. In *Change in Contemporary South Africa*, edited by Leonard Butler and Jeffrey Thompson, 250–279. Berkeley: University of California Press, 1975.

Morphet, Tony. 'Brushing History against the Grain: Oppositional Discourse in South Africa'. *Theoria* 76 (October 1990): 89–99.

Naidoo, Kumi. 'Class, Consciousness and Organisation: Indian Political Resistance in Durban, South Africa, 1979–1996'. PhD dissertation, Oxford University, 1997. https://www.sahistory.org.za/sites/default/files/archive_files/Class%2C%20 Consciousness%20and%20Organisation%20Indian%20Political%20 Resistance%20in%20Durban%20South%20Africa%201979-1996%20by%20 Kumi%20Naidoo.pdf (accessed 3 February 2021).

Naidoo, Kumi. 'The Politics of Youth Resistance in the 1980s: The Dilemmas of a Differentiated Durban'. *Journal of Southern African Studies* 18(1) (1992): 143–165.

Naidoo, M.J. 'My Case against SAIC Participation'. NIC Collection, Gandhi-Luthuli Documentation Centre, University of KwaZulu-Natal, 1977/78.

Naidoo, M.J. Presidential Address, NIC Conference, 20–22 September 1974. Document in possession of authors.

Naidoo, M.J. Speech presented at Krish Rabilal Memorial Meeting, 5 February 1984. Copy in possession of authors.

Natal Indian Congress (NIC). 'The Congress Position on the New Constitutional Proposals'. Bhana Collection, Gandhi Luthuli Documentation Centre, University of KwaZulu-Natal, Accession No. 1256/49, 1983.

Natal Indian Congress (NIC). 'Revisiting the National Question: What Future the NIC?' Discussion document presented to a meeting of the ANC Natal PEC and NIC Executive, 26 March 1995. Document provided to authors by Ismail Vadi.

Ndebele, Nhlanhla and Noor Nieftagodien. 'The Morogoro Conference: A Moment of Self-reflection'. In *The Road to Democracy in South Africa: Volume 1, 1960–1970*, edited by B. Magubane, 573–599. Cape Town: Zebra Press, 2004.

Nqakula, Charles. *The People's War: Reflections of an ANC Cadre.* Johannesburg: Mutloatse Heritage Trust, 2017.

O'Malley, Padraig. 'From Buthelezi IFP to Third Force Theory'. N.d. https://omalley. nelsonmandela.org/omalley/index.php/site/q/03lv02424/04lv03275/05lv0329 4/06lv03299.htm (accessed 20 October 2019).

O'Malley, Padraig. *Shades of Difference: Mac Maharaj and the Struggle for South Africa.* London: Penguin, 2007.

O'Malley Archives. 'African/Indian Relationship'. Nelson Mandela Foundation. https://omalley.nelsonmandela.org/omalley/index.php/site/q/03lv03445/04lv0 4206/05lv04254/06lv04255.htm (accessed 3 February 2021).

O'Malley Archives. 'Vula Eight: Charge Sheet'. Nelson Mandela Foundation. https://omalley.nelsonmandela.org/omalley/index.php/site/q/031v03445/ 041v03996/051v04000.htm (accessed 3 February 2021).

Padayachee, Vishnu and Robert van Niekerk. *Shadow Liberation: Contestation and Compromise in the Economic and Social Policy of the African National Congress, 1943–1996.* Johannesburg: Wits University Press, 2019.

Pahad, Aziz. *Insurgent Diplomat: Civil Talks or Civil War.* Johannesburg: Penguin Books, 2014.

Phoenix Working Committee (PWC). Brochure. 2003. http://phoenixcommunitycentre.com/?page_id=17 (accessed 14 September 2019).

Plaut, Martin. 'Changing Perspectives on South African Trade Unions'. *Review of African Political Economy* 11(30) (1984): 116–123.

Portelli, Alessandro. 'What Makes Oral History Different?' In *The Oral History Reader*, edited by Robert Perks and Alistair Thomson, 63–74. London: Routledge, 1998.

Postlethwayt, Cindy. 'What If They Gave a Puppet Show and Nobody Came? The SAIC 1964–82'. Honours thesis, Department of Economic History, University of Cape Town, 1982.

Price, Robert M. *The Apartheid State in Crisis: Political Transformation of South Africa, 1975–1990.* Oxford: Oxford University Press, 1991.

Prinsloo, H.A. 'Road to Self-development: A Survey of the Function of the Department of Indian Affairs'. *Fiat Lux* 1(1) (May 1966): 22–26.

Ramgobin, Mewa. 'Interview'. In *New Frontiers: The KwaZulu/Natal Debates*, edited by Karin Roberts and Graham Howe, 50–53. Durban: Indicator Project, University of Natal, 1987.

Ramgobin, Mewa. 'On Geopolitical Manoeuvres'. *Sechaba* (April 1990): 7–8.

Ramphele, Mamphele. *A Life.* Cape Town: David Philip, 1995.

Rinder, Irwin D. 'Strangers in the Land: Social Relations in the Status Gap'. *Social Problems* 6(3) (1958): 253–260.

Sampson, Anthony. *Black and Gold: Tycoons, Revolutionaries and Apartheid.* London: Hodder & Stoughton, 1987.

Sampson, Anthony. *Mandela: The Authorised Biography.* London: Harper Collins, 1999.

Saul, John and Patrick Bond. *South Africa – The Present as History: From Mrs Ples to Mandela and Marikana.* Johannesburg: Jacana, 2014.

Seedat, Rashid and Razia Saleh, eds. *Men of Dynamite: Pen Portraits of MK Pioneers.* Johannesburg: Shereno Printers, 2009.

Seekings, Jeremy. 'Civic Organisations in South African Townships'. *South African Review* 6 (1992): 216–238.

Seekings, Jeremy. *The UDF: A History of the United Democratic Front in South Africa, 1983–1991.* Cape Town: David Philip, 2000.

Selznik, Phillip. *TVA and Grassroots: A Study in the Sociology of Formal Organisations*, second edition. Trieste: Trieste Publishing, 2018.

Sewpersadh, C. 'Natal Indian Congress – The Significance of Its Revival'. *Reality* (May 1972): 12–13.

Shaik, Moe. *The ANC Spy Bible: Surviving across Enemy Lines*. Cape Town: Tafelberg, 2020.

Sidimba, Loyiso. 'The ANC Is Racist and Tribalistic, Says Gatvol Jessie Duarte'. *IOL*, 23 November 2019. https://www.iol.co.za/news/politics/the-anc-is-racist-and-tribalistic-says-gatvol-jessie-duarte-37806623 (accessed 30 November 2019).

Simpson, Thula. *Umkhonto we Sizwe: The ANC's Armed Struggle*. Cape Town: Penguin Random House, 2016.

Singh, Anand. 'Cultural Entrepreneurship and the Culturalisation of Politics among Indians in South Africa'. *Alternation* 4(1) (1997): 93–115.

Singh, Ratnamala and Shahid Vawda. 'What's in a Name? Some Reflections on the NIC'. *Transformation* 6 (1987): 1–21.

Sisulu, Elinor. *Walter and Albertina Sisulu: In Our Lifetime*. Cape Town: David Philip, 2006.

Sisulu, Walter. 'We Shall Overcome!' In *Reflections in Prison*, edited by Mac Maharaj, 71–90. Cape Town: Zebra Press, 2001.

Sitas, Ari. 'Class Ethnicity Nation'. In *The Flight of the Gwala-Gwala Bird*. Cape Town: South African History Online, 2016, 197–230.

Sitas, Ari. 'Durban's Carnage: Where Wealth and Power and Blood Reign Worshipped'. In *The Flight of the Gwala-Gwala Bird*. Cape Town: South African History Online, 2016, 98–131.

Sitas, Ari. 'The Making of the "Comrades" Movement in Natal, 1985–91'. *Journal of Southern African Studies* 18(3) (1992): 629–641.

South African Indian Council (SAIC). Minutes, 1963–1983. Copy in possession of Ashwin Desai.

Stultz, Newell M. 'Interpreting Constitutional Change in South Africa'. *Journal of Modern African Studies* 22(3) (1984): 353–379.

Suttner, Raymond. *The ANC Underground in South Africa*. Johannesburg: Jacana, 2008.

Suttner, Raymond. *The ANC Underground in South Africa, 1950–1976*. Boulder, CO and London: First Forum Press, 2009.

Suttner, Raymond. 'Review Article: The UDF Period and Its Meaning for Contemporary South Africa'. *Journal of Southern African Studies* 30(3) (2004): 691–701.

Thatcher, Margaret. Letter from Margaret Thatcher to Robert Hughes, 29 October 1984. AAM Archive, Bodleian Library. MSS AAM 779. https://www.aamarchives.org/archive/campaigns/government/gov29-letter-from-margaret-thatcher-to-robert-hughes.html (accessed 3 February 2021).

Thompson, E.P. *The Poverty of Theory*. London: Merlin Press, 1995.

Truth and Reconciliation Commission (TRC). 'Amnesty Hearings: Eugene de Kock'. Special Report, 26 July 1999. sabctrc.saha.org.za/hearing.php?id=53564&t=piet+retief+ambushes+de+kock&tab=hearings (accessed 3 February 2021).

Vahed, Goolam. *Chota Motala: A Biography of Political Activism in the KwaZulu-Natal Midlands*. Pietermaritzburg: University of KwaZulu-Natal Press, 2018.

Vahed, Goolam. 'Chota Motala: The Making of a South African Political Biography'. *Politikon* 4(2) (2019): 175–191.

Vahed, Goolam. *Muslim Portraits: The Anti-apartheid Struggle.* Durban: Madiba Publishers, 2012.

Vahed, Goolam and Ashwin Desai. 'An Instance of "Strategic Ethnicity"? The Natal Indian Congress in the 1970s'. *African Historical Review* 46(1) (2014): 22–47.

Vahed, Goolam and Thembisa Waetjen. *Schooling Muslims in Natal: State, Identity and the Orient Islamic Educational Institute.* Pietermaritzburg: University of KwaZulu-Natal Press, 2015.

Van der Westhuizen, Christi. *White Power and the Rise and Fall of the National Party.* Cape Town: Zebra Press, 2007.

Van Kessel, Ineke. *'Beyond Our Wildest Dreams': The United Democratic Front and the Transformation of South Africa.* Charlottesville and London: University Press of Virginia, 2000.

Weaver, Tony. 'The President's Council'. In *South African Review 1*, edited and compiled by South African Research Service. Johannesburg: Ravan Press, 1983.

Webster, Eddie and John Mawbey. 'Revisiting the National Question'. In *The Unresolved National Question: Left Thought under Apartheid*, edited by Eddie Webster and Karin Pampallis, 1–18. Johannesburg: Wits University Press, 2017.

Welsh, David. *The Buthelezi Commission.* Durban: H & H Publications, 1982.

Welsh, David. *The Rise and Fall of Apartheid.* Charlottesville: University of Virginia Press, 2010.

Yacoob, Zak. 'The National Question in South Africa'. Speech presented at the General Meeting of the Transvaal Indian Congress, Ramakrishna Hall, 1 May 1983. Copy provided by Ismail Vadi.

Index

Printed and bound by CPI Group (UK) Ltd, Croydon, CR0 4YY

09/06/2025